# The Culture
# of Western Europe

Third Edition

# The Culture
# of Western Europe.

## The Nineteenth and
## Twentieth Centuries

George L. Mosse

**Westview Press**

BOULDER & LONDON

# For Hilde L. Mosse

Copyright © 1988 by Westview Press, Inc. A Member of the Perseus Books Group

Published in 1988 in the United States of America by Westview Press, Inc., 5500 Central Avenue, Boulder, Colorado 80301

First edition published in 1961 by Rand McNally & Company; second edition published in 1974 by Rand McNally College Publishing Company

Library of Congress Cataloging-in-Publication Data
Mosse, George L. (George Lachmann), 1918–
    The culture of Western Europe.
    Includes index.
    1. Europe—Civilization—19th century.  2. Europe—
Civilization—20th century.  I. Title.
CB415.M62  1988      940.2'8      88-5529
ISBN 0-8133-0736-8
ISBN 0-8133-0623-X (pbk.)

Printed and bound in the United States of America

⊗  The paper used in this publication meets the requirements of the American National Standard for Permanence of Paper for Printed Library Materials Z39.48-1984.

20 19 18 17 16 15 14 13

*PERSEUS*
**POD**
*ON DEMAND*

# Contents

## Contents

# Acknowledgments

I wish to express my gratitude to several generations of graduate students who joined in the discussion of the problems raised in this book during seminars in cultural history at the University of Wisconsin. In particular the following provided many new insights: Richard Soloway of the University of North Carolina; George Kren of Kansas State University; John Thayer of the University of Minnesota; Seymour Drescher of the University of Pittsburgh; Sterling Fishman of the University of Wisconsin; Paul Breines of Boston College; and Anson Rabinbach of Cooper Union. Several friends and colleagues read parts of the manuscript: Henry B. Hill of the University of Wisconsin; George T. Romani of Northwestern University; and Harry J. Marks of the University of Connecticut. Their criticisms were stimulating and important in helping me formulate my ideas. Here I must single out for special mention my former colleague William Appleman Williams of Oregon State University and Jost Hermand of the University of Wisconsin. The late George Lichtheim gave the manuscript the criticism of one of the best and most learned minds it has been my privilege to know. Without the devoted assistance of Beth Irwin Lewis, Paula Quirk, and Carl Weiner of Carleton College the making of this book would have been a less enjoyable task. The editorial work of Jennifer Knerr, Constance Clark, and Libby Barstow was much appreciated. The Graduate College of the University of Wisconsin as well as the College of Letters and Science have provided generous assistance which made the completion of the book possible.

Much of the writing of this book was originally done at the American Academy in Rome and the rewriting for this edition in London and Jerusalem. Librarians and friends in these three cities added much to the rethinking involved in making a new edition, while my students at the Hebrew University in Jerusalem provided new viewpoints and new challenges. This has become an over-long catalogue of names and places which to anyone but the author will make dreary reading. But for the author it not only puts some of his gratitude on record but, in addition, serves to remind him of many worthwhile intellectual experiences. That none of

*Acknowledgments*

these friends and colleagues can be held responsible for the many interpretations or even the general thesis of the book should be taken for
granted. Many of them would question all of these, which makes their
contribution not less valuable but more so.

*George L. Mosse*
Madison and Jerusalem
January 1988

# *Statement and Definitions* ·

THIS BOOK IS A CULTURAL HISTORY OF MODERN EUROPE, AND THE word "culture" in its title must be defined. This would not be the case for political, economic, or social histories of Europe, as their frames of reference are well understood, designating approaches to the writing of history which are traditional and allow for objective analysis. But the word "culture" seems both vague and fraught with preconceptions. Is cultural history identical with the history of ideas which examines mainly patterns of human thought, or is it part of the history of folkways as investigated by anthropologists? Or is the word "culture" to be used, as in the past, to designate a specific attitude towards life and ways of perceiving the world which would preclude any dispassionate analysis? For German Romantics, culture was the outward expression of history's hidden qualities. Their concept of culture centered upon an inward feeling rather than emphasizing those social and economic realities which to many are a prerequisite for orderly progress in the world. Oswald Spengler's distinction between culture and civilization brings this out in stark relief: A culture possesses a soul while civilization is the "most external and artificial state of which . . . humanity . . . is capable."

*1*

## The Culture of Western Europe

The hidden qualities of history express themselves through the soul of a civilization. To try to probe the "soul" of European civilization might be tempting—provided one believed that such a soul did indeed exist. We cannot conduct such a search, one which has usually resulted in the discovery of mythical racial or national roots. For any sustained historical analysis, this concept of culture is much too imprecise. Yet one of the pioneers in the analysis of cultural history, Jakob Burckhardt, did seem to believe in something of that sort when in 1860 he described the task of cultural history as that of seeking for the "spiritual essence" of an epoch. When he coined this term he was himself reacting against the growing industrialism, urbanism, and materialism of his time. Such a search for the "spiritual essence" or the "soul" of Western history is apt to produce a philosophy of history rather than a work of historical analysis. To be sure, every work of history has certain underlying preconceptions (some will be stated in this book), but it should attempt to see events from within the historical framework itself. It must try as much as possible to penetrate the minds of historical figures; it should not attempt to read history backward. The hazard of this procedure is that no clear pattern may emerge, at least no pattern that can be reduced to a formula like that of culture against civilization. It will, however, be closer to historical reality.

A glance at the pages of this book must make it clear that in the West many conflicting ideologies attempted to meet the dilemmas of human existence and that they cannot be explained by a formula. Communism was a western movement and so was the Christian revival of the twentieth century and the nihilism after the First World War. Who is to say which was more basic to our culture, a culture that has included a multitude of alternatives? We should not search for common denominators of thought but rather pride ourselves upon that diversity of ideologies which our culture has produced. That is what makes cultural history exciting and, perhaps, our civilization great.

*The Culture of Western Europe* will attempt to encompass the principal trends of modern times; it will not search for the "soul" or for the "spiritual essence" of modern Europe. *In this study, culture is defined as a state or habit of mind which is apt to become a way of life intimately linked to the challenges and dilemmas of contemporary society.* What the West has in common is not a soul but certain historical movements which have formed it. These are not solely social or economic in nature; often they are movements of thought which have developed out of certain historical situations. Romanticism would be unimaginable without the thought of the eighteenth century and the political events of the age of the French Revolution; Marxism could not be envisaged apart from the Industrial Revolution, and existentialism aside from the First World War and the crisis of European thought which followed it. Though all of this may seem obvious, it needs restatement; and cultural history has so often been discussed outside of a proper historical framework.

This approach to history requires a still more precise definition, however. True, a state or habit of mind is the product of historical development, but whose mind are we talking about? It is the people themselves who provide their culture's texture, then a historian must also assess their frame of mind. Thus he must deal with popular ideas and practices, with folklore and community sentiment. Stuart Hughes cites with approval the term "retrospective cultural anthropology," which describes such efforts, and historians have engaged in such studies, sometimes with outstanding success. In the modern period there are ample artifacts, from the shilling shocker to Sicilian banditry, upon which to base such "anthropological" efforts. But do the people themselves create patterns of thought or do these patterns filter down from above? Stuart Hughes's approach stresses the ". . . history of the enunciation and development of the ideas that eventually will inspire such governing elites." What counts are ideologies which inspire those men and women who stand at the center of historical development. There is much in this point of view that is reasonable. After all, movements like Marxism were not evolved by the people but by an intellectual who built upon ideas of other intellectuals. The same could be said for all the cultural movements discussed in this book. What these intellectuals created was a fund of ideas upon which men could and did draw as suited their purposes.

Yet it would be mistaken to center this study entirely upon an analysis of the thought of certain important and creative men and women whose ideas, at one period of history, influenced the rulers of men. We have defined cultural history as a habit of mind, and such a habit draws upon a much greater variety of influences. For cultural development does involve an interaction of ideas between intellectuals conscious of what they are about and the general mood of their times. Liberalism is a good illustration of this. Though the ideology was elaborated by certain thinkers, liberal thought in general reflected a mood on the part of the bourgeoisie; the moral part of liberalism was inspired by a European middle-class morality. Similarly, what we call the change in the public spirit of Europe at the turn of the century reflected not only consciously-stated and elaborated ideas but a general mood which was not confined to or created by intellectuals. This interaction seems to us at the root of European cultural development.

3

But what do we mean by a "general mood"? It consists of reactions to the complexities of daily life as well as of images of a better future. Such hopes and reactions can be expressed by political or social action, at the ballot box or in the factory. But the more urbanized and industrialized society became, the more people tended to solidify their world through familiar myths and symbols. Christianity had fulfilled the function of providing such myths and symbols for many centuries, but since the eighteenth century, at least, they began to be secularized—transposed upon a society which was becoming a mass society and upon politics which was becoming mass politics. Thus symbols like the sacred flame, the flag, and national monuments became the self-representation of the nation, the means by which the people represented and indeed worshipped themselves.

Nationalism provided shelter from personal isolation and so did the labor movement which had its own red flag and silent May Day parades. Clearly, the more rationalized life in industrial society became, the more people fled into an irrationalism which gave them security and made sense out of the threatening world of modernity. This is one part of the content of a "mood" and one which contains, as we shall see, a longing for a healthy and happy world in terms of traditional myth and symbols as well as a sense of beauty which took the classics, newly rediscovered in the eighteenth century, as its norm. For the whole world should worship the order and symmetry which they represented: the clarity of form which contrasted with that chaos which men have always feared. That is why during some of the nineteenth and most of the twentieth century we can no longer talk of formal political theory (though it continues to exist). Instead we must deal with attitudes toward life which deny the validity of such constructs as the social contract against secular and political religions.

To be sure, there were many who rejected this kind of reaction to modernity and instead stressed rational responses and political action based upon the limitation of government and the greatest possible individual freedom. The religion of liberty confronted romantic political thought which considered itself as an attitude towards life as a whole. But this liberalism was accompanied by a middle-class morality which did set limits to freedom and gave shelter. Moreover, eventually liberalism adopted certain scientific ideas which pushed it towards an environmentalism and a positivism well suited to the age of acquisitiveness and imperialism, seeming to deny human creativity and man's soul. The generation which grew up in the last decades of the nineteenth century started a revolt against this liberalism which was to dominate much of the twentieth century and eventually merged with the secular religions we have discussed.

But how could the search for individuality merge with a world of myth and symbol which typified a "healthy" world standing above and determining individual fate? The answer lies in the longing for a true community which would at one and the same time allow the individual to unfold his creativity and to be sheltered within its confines. Since the end of the nineteenth century such a community was believed to be based upon a voluntary affinity of the like-minded or those of the same stock, and as such it was contrasted with society which imposed its method of organization. This concept of community (or *Bund* as the Germans called it) is basic to the fascist regimes of the twentieth century but also to other authoritarian ideals forming part of mass politics. Here individuality and community seem fused, able to counter a world of loneliness and disorder.

These, then, are some of the themes which make up the mood of the population which interacts with the ideas built up by intellectuals. How does this interaction take place? The intelectual can be a barometer of ideas, voicing them clearly and formulating a mood, making it articulate in his own time and for the future. But even if the intellectual creates a fund of ideas for society, these depend for their effectiveness upon his analysis of the mood, hopes and needs of the times, or indeed of some future time. Schopenhauer, Kierkegaard, and even Marx were fringe figures during much of their own lifetime and were only "discovered" when their ideas seemed to fit a mood or hope at a particular time in history. But intellectuals did not have to be effective or influential in creating or helping to create a political, social, or literary movement. Instead they could regard themselves as the "conscience" of society and hold up before it eternal values which must not be sullied through compromise. We shall come across such intellectuals in the socialist movement and in nationalism. At times they could stand outside any movement as social and cultural critics, holding aloft the banner of purity. Like Karl Kraus (1874–1936) in Vienna or so many intellectuals in the Weimar Republic, such men tended to become embittered and increasingly more ineffectual. From the purity they held up for all to see, and their attacks upon anyone who failed to give it homage, they became destructive forces in a society which was at the brink of dissolution into fasicism or authoritarianism. As with Karl Kraus, self-hate became a hate which failed to differentiate the political forces making for fascism from all others within society.

It is worthwhile to dwell on the intellectuals for they are apt to stand in the forefront of an analysis of cultural history as articulators of a mood, as systematizers of influential ideas, or as critics. The workers, and indeed the bulk of the population, are apt to be mute, making it difficult to capture their thought. This is, of course, a matter of degree for the masses do act in a mass age, sometimes on the street, sometimes through the ballot box, and increasingly as members of mass movements, as participants in the mass rites of the secular religion of politics. But of necessity we shall watch their moods and attitudes of life through the eyes of intellectuals.

The geographical limits of this book are confined to western Europe, including Germany and Austria. There were important cultural developments in eastern Europe but it seems that their texture was different from that of the West. It would be fair to say that all the movements discussed traveled to eastern Europe, but, in adjusting to the different conditions of eastern Europe, they underwent many changes. Moreover, it might seem as if there was undue concentration within the book upon certain nations in the West itself. France, Germany, England, and Italy dominate—Germany perhaps more than any of the others. These are, of course, the strongest and most populous nations of western Europe; their preponderance arises naturally out of the subject matter and is not imposed upon it. For we do not in this book proceed by nations but by attitudes of mind, though some are more firmly based upon a particular nation than others. Throughout European history one nation or another has been the chief laboratory of thought: Germany in the age of the Reformation; France and England in the seventeenth century; France itself in the first part of the eighteenth; in the nineteenth and twentieth centuries the European nations mentioned fulfilled this function.

The particular stress upon Germany relates to the fact that this book has a point of view about the direction of modern culture. Since we discussed our definition of cultural history and the limits within which we shall proceed, something must now be said about the preconceptions of the writer of these pages. This would not have been necessary during most of the nineteenth century. Then history, as so many other disciplines, was firmly trying to establish itself as a science. With the reaction against such positivism at the turn of the century, the nature of the writing of history was reexamined, for many believed that the historian could not be just a recorder of facts. Benedetto Croce neatly summarized this view when he said that all historical facts has to pass through the mind of the historian and that therefore his mind was central to any historical analysis. Since the thought processes of the individual historian were of prime importance, Croce believed that only a vivid interest in the present could move a man to investigate the past. History must be relevant to the present situation of the historian. With that we must agree. All the cultural movements we discuss have direct bearing on our present dilemmas.

The shadow of totalitarian society has darkened much of the thinking of those of us who passed through the decades after the First World War. The years between the First and Second World wars witnessed the triumph of totalitarianism in many western European nations, a triumph opposed only by men who were both confused and unorganized. Looking at it from this vantage point, one feels impelled to ask how the cultural history of Europe could have led to such a development.

The abasement of individualism in fascism and national socialism, the small value these movements put on life itself, and the mass exterminations which eventually resulted made a deep imprint upon the generation to which the writer of this book belongs. The Second World War did not stop this trend and the problem of totalitarian society remains a general problem not confined to eastern Europe. This theme dominates this book. The emphasis upon Germany is due to the fact that eventually, in this century, that unhappy nation came to typify the totalitarian state at its most extreme.

Looking over the span of cultural history with which we are concerned, it would seem that men have constantly longed for an authority to which they could relate themselves. Moreover, they saw this authority in terms of hope for a better life and a happier future. These longings took the form of a rejection of present reality, leading to the contention that the future could not be constructed from the existing human situation. Throughout history there have been men who, like the Puritans, wanted to "build Jerusalem without tarrying." In the modern age too, this desire seemed to provide much of the general mood of the times. There is a reason for this. These last centuries were periods of rapid change as Europe was becoming both urban and industrialized. In this period many people felt pushed to the wall, while others saw changes they could not understand and problems which defied solution. More men were alienated from their society than ever before in human history. No wonder that they longed for a more hopeful future, and it is not astonishing that they conceived of this future as outside the present reality of European life.

This escape from reality took many forms, but perhaps the most important was the search for a reality beyond the one which appeared on the surface to govern the lives of men. Both the nineteenth and twentieth centuries were to witness a search for the "genuine" or the "true" which was also a search for roots, for a sense of "belonging" in the age of the Industrial Revolution. Some, like Hegel and Marx, eventually saw this in the "secret" workings of history which would inevitably lead to an emancipation from the present. Others craved for such roots and sense of belonging through an integration with a higher ideal such as the race or

7

that "soul" of Western civilization which was mentioned at the beginning of this introduction. However they did it, they sought for a "deeper" reality—a search which would lead to totalitarianism because it was always the search for some sort of authority with which one could identify and which would liquidate the present situation of man.

Such habits of mind consistently criticized that rationalism which had dominated much of the eighteenth century. The Enlightenment had planted its feet firmly on the ground, working within the context of present reality. French *philosophes* believed that the application of reason was superior to authority, tradition, or human intuition. As Voltaire put it, whatever is not accessible to human reason is chimerical. The *philosophes* repudiated a search for the "genuine" and the "true" divorced from those phenomena which reason could grasp. Thus they had faith in experimentation and, in the last half of the eighteenth century, tended to become increasingly utilitarian in their world outlook. This world view implied an optimistic analysis of human nature—man was capable of unlimited progress; the Christian concept of original sin was denied. The Enlightenment believed in a happier future for humanity, but this would not come about through a rejection of the present; instead it would be ushered in by man's reason and by experimenting within existing society.

Nineteenth-century men were apt to criticize this ideology as naively rationalist. As a matter of fact, this was far from the truth. Most of the *philosophes* acknowledged the limitations of human reason but they still felt that in building their earthly city a faith in rationalism promised the best results. Those who opposed them in their own century did not so much deny reason as emphasize those forces beyond its ken. Jean-Jacques Rousseau, for example, accused the *philosophes* of rationalizing rather than reasoning, for they were unconscious of those super-rational forces, like man's instincts, which sharply limited man's reason. A very similar point was made a century later by the French philosopher Henri Bergson. Indeed, it is the French culture of modern times which retained most of the Enlightenment's heritage. Nineteenth- and twentieth-century critics of the Enlightenment with their emphasis upon the irrational rather than upon the super-rational rejected reason in the name of an emotional integration with some higher authority.

The Enlightenment was not sufficiently aware of man's need of a faith, of a belief in a stable and eternal force impervious to ever-changing external realities, a force which would lead man toward a better and fuller life. Christianity had fulfilled this need and one could not simply pronounce it dead, as some of the *philosophes* did, without allowing for the need which it had filled. The increasing alienation of so many men, the feeling

8

of helplessness in the industrial age, could not be resolved successfully solely by a faith in reason as a method of human improvement. To be sure, there were movements, especially liberalism, which forwarded the Enlightenment's impetus, forming it in its own image. The eventual decline of liberalism, however, provides one of the themes of this book. Moreover, some did see a hope for the future in the application of reason to society and attempted under the inspiration of achievements in science to construct a science of society. But they, too, were eclipsed by the twentieth century, as having supported a shallow positivism.

Yet the nineteenth century was the age of the greatest advances in science. It is striking to what extent an unbridgeable gulf existed between work in the laboratory and the realization of the implications of such work for human social and political attitudes. We know the reluctance of Charles Darwin to extend his ideas on evolution from the life of plants and animals to the life of man. It is also significant that the greatest popularizer of Darwin's thought in Europe, Ernst Haeckel, for all his materialism, surrounded the doctrine of evolution with a mystical and sentimental appeal. Alfred North Whitehead inadvertently divined the cause of men's reluctance to connect science and the modern world in the close relationship which Whitehead thought did, in fact, exist between them: "Modern Science has imposed upon humanity the necessity of wandering. Its progressive thought and its progressive technology make the transition through time, from generation to generation, a true migration into unchartered seas of adventure."

From what has been said, it must be clear that men did not wish to wander; they sought for safety and roots rather than adventure. Those who welcomed adventure did so either with an eye to a romantic past or because of a belief in power for its own sake, itself a kind of quest for security. That adventurous voyaging of which Whitehead speaks was never a dominant habit of mind, not even for many scientists once they left the laboratory. The fact that by the end of the nineteenth century most ideologies called themselves scientific must not disguise this. Thus systems of thought like racism had the best of both worlds. The impressive progress of the sciences could be enlisted as a slogan to denote truth, and at the same time the application of the scientific method of society could be rejected. At times science was utilized—Spengler constructed his cultural history partly upon biology—but it was misused from a scientific point of view to bolster theories which appealed to those longings closer to the European habit of mind.

Throughout this book the battle lines are drawn between ideologies like liberalism and Marxism which based themselves on the Enlightenment and advances in science and technology, in order to transform society, and others, like modern nationalism, which emphasised rootedness and whose adherents thought that truth could only be found beneath the appearance of things. Some systems of ideas like racism wanted to combine both approaches but in reality were captive of one or the other, if to a greater or lesser degree. After we have discussed "the changing pace of life" (Chapter 1) which informed all states of mind during our epoch, we will pass to romanticism as a search for the "genuine" and the "true" which will never end and which will fascinate all those who put a premium on rootedness and security. Then we shall deal with "the challenge of liberty" in Chapter 6, considering liberalism as the reaffirmation of progress and the heritage of the Enlightenment.

# THE NINETEENTH CENTURY:
## 1815-1870

CHAPTER ONE

# The Changing
# Pace of Life

THE IDEAS AND IDEALS discussed in this book played a large part during the nineteenth and twentieth centuries in determining the outlook of articulate men and women upon their world, for how we perceive our world—our state or habit of mind—influences our actions. The ideas and ideals which fill this book served as a vehicle through which men and women confronted the times in which they lived, their own situation, and the kind of society they desired. During the last two centuries the innumerable ideas and notions which moved people and fired their enthusiasm became more easily accessible: new inventions in printing, such as the rotary press, facilitated cheaper production of books and journals. Moreover, while censorship did exist at times in many western nations, it tended to be sporadic and ineffective at best. Europe during much of the nineteenth and and twentieth centuries enjoyed a freedom of thought and expression which did not foreshadow the brutal oppression of opinion in many nations between and after the two world wars. We have had to select for this book those ideas which seemed dominant at the time as well as portentous for the future.

All these ideas and ideals were shaped by the rapid changes brought by the Industrial Revolution. European men and women were conscious of the transformation wrought by industrializing and urbanizing Europe, even in the more backward regions, and from the beginning of the nineteenth century onwards many had the sensation of riding a roller coaster to the edge of chaos. Sir Walter Scott, for example, looking at the rapidly changing countryside of once backward Scotland, wrote as a postscript to his Waverly novels in 1828 that the gradual influx of wealth and the extension of commerce had rendered the people of Scotland a class of beings as different from their grandfathers as contemporary English were from those of Queen Elizabeth's time. At roughly the same time the results of such a confusing change were described by the German novelist W. H. Hacklaender in his *Wandel und Handel* (Trade and change), in which a merchant was driven insane because he traveled too much. At the close of the nineteenth century Max Nordau in his famed *Degeneration* (1892) ascribed what he saw as the deformation of modern arts and letters to nerves shattered by railway travel.

Starting in the nineteenth century the sense of living in a world at risk and at sea was widespread. The ideas discussed in subsequent chapters will try to confront this perception in different ways: for example, romanticism provided historical and emotional roots not touched by modernity, while liberalism accepted the results of the Industrial Revolution and attempted to keep control by the imposition of a strict code of public and personal morality.

The threat of class conflict, of riots and revolutions, was present in the minds of many people during the second half of the nineteenth century when the laboring classes began to organize themselves, forming their own political movements, and attempted to create their own culture as well. At the same time the tenor of politics seemed to undergo fundamental change: the age of mass politics was dawning. Its dress rehearsal was the movement led by General Boulanger (1886–89), directed against the weak French Third Republic. Here Socialists, Liberals, and Conservatives joined in mass meetings, demonstrations, and speeches calling for responses from the crowd, in order to support the charismatic general. Politics became a drama in which the people themselves were the actors, marching, chanting, gesturing, and shouting slogans, fired by charismatic leadership. This was a new kind of politics which did not depend upon the obedience to a hereditary ruler or upon representative government but was instead regarded by many people as a means through which they could participate directly in the political process. Such a mobilization of the masses had first been encouraged by the French Revolution. Through its festivals, mass meetings, demonstrations, and ceremonies it transformed a rioting mass into a disciplined crowd and provided a political structure which functioned as an alternative to hereditary kingship or representative government. After the French Revolution the mobilization of the masses was used sporadically by both nationalism and nineteenth-century revolutions as a weapon against established governments. The masses were transformed into a crowd which had a definite political aim, such as national unity or the attainment of political power.

France, with its strong tradition of popular movements—for or against the revolution—was the laboratory for such a mobilization of the masses regardless of social class or traditional political parties: the use made of them by General Boulanger in his effort to overthrow the Republic, and subsequently by those who supported or opposed the trial of Captain Dreyfus for espionage, set the pace and further transformed the masses into a crowd with a set political purpose and program, however vague. Gustav Le Bon's *The Crowd* (1890) summed up the lessons gained from the Boulanger crisis and its mobilization of the masses and passed them on to the political leaders after the First World War. Le Bon believed that the substitution of the unconscious action of crowds for the conscious activities of individuals was the principal characteristic of his age. He went on to use his skill as a psychologist to analyze this unconscious activity, emphasizing the effect upon crowds of the theatrical imagination, of appeals to glory, honor, and patriotism, and above all, of its need for leaders whose intensity of faith gave power to their words—leaders who must not be innovative but share the sentiments of the crowd and express its prejudice and feelings. This advice was heeded by leaders like Hitler and Mussolini who knew of Le Bon: his book heralded a new kind of politics which came into its own after the First World War when the old order had collapsed or was in danger of collapsing, and millions of men had actually experienced mass action through their participation in battle.

Before the First World War the masses were only latently present, mobilized at intervals by nationalist or socialist parties. In immediate terms, the changes brought by industrialism pervaded individuals' daily lives in a continuous manner and forced confrontation with a new reality as the traditional way of life was being transformed. This kind of confrontation had a special importance for cultural history because it meant an adjustment of human consciousness—an adjustment not just to the new and episodic but to changes which seemed here to stay and which could not be supported or opposed as one could take up sides for or against the labor movement or the new mass politics. Certainly, the labor movement or the new politics, however important, did not pervade all aspects of life and were ignored by many important thinkers, while changes in daily life had to be confronted and dealt with—the new speed of time, the problems of urban living, the destruction of nature—everything that was once immutable and fixed for all time now seemed in motion.

The new means of communications symbolized the adjustments required by the accelerated process of industrialization. They penetrated daily life as the immediate and tangible heralds of a new age, a product, it seemed, of the newly expanded cities. The railroad which conquered Europe in the 1830s and 1840s seemed to tear nature itself from its moorings: looking out of the window of a train, to cite Victor Hugo, writing in 1837, trees seemed to perform wild dances and blend crazily with the horizon. The flowers which grew along the rails were no longer flowers, but mere dots of color. New technology towards the end of the century promised to abolish space and to accelerate time. The invention of the telephone in 1867 made it possible, so it seemed at the time, for people to be in two places at one and the same moment, while the motor car and the bicycle encouraged the rapid passage of individuals from one place to another. During the 1890s the City of Berlin finally let bicycles use its streets; previously they were thought too dangerous because of their speed. At the same time, the mass manufacturers of bicycles lowered their price so that after 1900 they became the preferred means of transportation of the German working classes. Many other inventions, like the incandescent lamp, the wireless, and the cinema could be added to the list of new technologies which changed the tenor of daily life. Such technologies demanded a new awareness of change which seemed fraught with immediate or potential danger to the cohesion of society.

The newspaper became one of the most powerful symbols of the threat posed by modernity. Newspapers had made their impact from the end of the eighteenth century onwards, even then regarded with suspicion as enemies of a steady life and devotion to "higher things." Thus in 1790 Goethe, Germany's cultural pope, had asked how true and lasting poetry, indeed the human imagination, could survive when an audience came into the theatre fresh from reading the news. This condemnation of the press as the enemy of true culture increased rather than diminished among the more conservative and nationalistically inclined men and women with the rise in the 1880s of the so-called yellow press. For example, the English novelist, George Gissing, described one of his characters living in 1887 has having read no book since boyhood, for much diet of newspapers had rendered him all but incapable of sustained attention.

But it was the modern city which became the all-encompassing symbol and metaphor of modernity. The growth of cities had indeed been startling, especially in the last three decades of the nineteenth century. The increase of population in some of the chief cities of Europe tells the tale: in the course of the nineteenth century London (which was already considered large in 1800) increased 340 percent, Paris 345 percent, Vienna 490 percent, and Berlin 872 percent. The growth of population in Berlin and Vienna took place almost entirely in the short span of the last three decades of the century, and this bears directly upon the special hostility with which these particular cities were viewed by many Germans and Austrians desirous of order and stability.

The cities were regarded as the breeding ground for vice, providing a home for those excluded by the norms of society. Already by mid-century Balzac had pictured the inhabitants of Paris as "dreadful to behold," while London was often referred to as a new Gomorrah. We will see the thrust of many ideologies turned against urban life, praising the settled life of the small town or village. It was no coincidence that European nations represented themselves through pre-industrial symbols: the native landscape, medieval cathedrals, Greek or Roman temples. National symbols like Marianne or Germanis wore medieval or ancient dress and were set in landscapes unblemished by modern industrial life. Even England, which had led the Industrial Revolution, made sure after the First World War that the cemeteries for her fallen soldiers resembled country churchyards.

This rejection of the city was by no means unanimous; not only many Liberals and Socialists accepted the urbanization of life but most of those who thought of themselves as progressive and forward looking. Ben Jonson's saying that ". . . when a man is tired of London he is tired of life" was apt to be repeated in modern times—for example, Victor Hugo wrote about the Paris he loved that the smoke which rose from its roofs provided the ideas which fueled the universe. German working-class youth, in accordance with the socialist tradition, rejected the flight into nature and pointed with pride to what human labor had accomplished in cities. Cities may have symbolized the evils of modernity, but there was hardly any emigration from the city to the countryside, aside from artists or writers who settled in villages in order to found their own communities or the wealthier middle class which sometimes moved into the surrounding country.

To be sure, German middle-class youth began exploring the countryside in order to discover their national roots, as we will see when discussing the youth movement. These were not migrations but instead attempts to escape city life for a time; it was no coincidence that the English coming from the most industrialized nation led the rush to the Alps during the second half of the nineteenth century, making Switzerland a modern tourist paradise. At the same time, an attempt was made to import the countryside into the city, not only with the founding and extension of city parks (most of which date back to the mid-nineteenth century) but also with the building of so-called garden cities in England and Germany. Here there were no tenements or barren streets, but houses with gardens and streets sheltered by trees. Originally, in the city itself, there had been no proper distance between factory and home, but now, as in Berlin at the end of the century, the distance which divided the villa of the owner from the factory became a status symbol.

The more effectively the private lives of the wealthier middle class were shielded from the factory and the street, the higher their status. The tangible presence of industrialism had to be masked by the very industrialists and merchants responsible for its triumph. The villas built by the newly rich in Germany (and not in Germany only) from the last decades of the nineteenth century onwards imitated the Italian villas of the Renaissance. These villas, which still stand in many European cities, gave shelter from the winds of change and a sense of participating in a historical tradition, important for the newly rich. Thus they sometimes had themselves and their families painted in Renaissance costume. This was a tradition of culture and cosmopolitanism, and these rich and usually liberal magnates or successful professionals, as forward-looking men, could not be expected to imitate their Germanic or Celtic forefathers with a much narrower vision.

Civic buildings also imitated the past. Town halls were built as Gothic cathedrals or Renaissance palaces. Love for Italy played its part, especially in Germany; after all, in 1810 Munich had been rebuilt as an imitation of Renaissance Florence. At the *fin de siècle* the need to tame the rapid pace of urbanization through anchoring it within a historical tradition seemed pressing and was partially solved by building Tuscan villas which dominated the wealthier suburbs and by commissioning civic architecture which adopted Renaissance as well as medieval and ancient models. History and nature mediating the changes of industrialism will meet us at every turn—giving the appearance of immutability to that which in reality was new and insecure.

The city both repulsed and fascinated as a symbol of all that was frightening and exciting in the world which the Industrial Revolution had made. Like the newspapers or the new methods of transportation it exemplified haste, the superficial, the awesome kaleidoscope of experiences which assaulted the mind. We shall see how all the ideas which concern us had to confront this challenge of modernity: it shaped European culture in the last two centuries.

## The Changing Pace of Life

Culture in order to be effective and lasting has to address the needs of men and women, serving to make the world intelligible to their understanding. The change in manners and morals—in lifestyle—which accompanied Europe's entry into the modern age was important, helping to determine the perceptions of men and women about themselves and about their world. The various ideologies discussed in this book encompass this change as an unspoken assumption, and yet it must be made explicit in order that we can understand the mode of life which they addressed. We have discussed the transformation of society through industrialization, and it was equally true that the new pattern of manners and morals during the course of the nineteenth century transformed the attitudes of men and women towards themselves. We are apt to take what is considered respectable as a God-given and immutable force, when in reality the modes of behavior and moral attitudes which modern respectability advocated became firmly rooted only during the last part of the eighteenth and the first part of the nineteenth century.

The concept of respectability began as a system of manners and morals congenial to the middle classes and eventually spread to all segments of the European population. The new moral tone demanded control over one's passions, restraint, and self-reliance—it drew clear and unambiguous distinctions between what was allowed and what was forbidden, what was to be considered normal and what abnormal in a decent and respectable society. Respectability depended upon conformity in manners and morals, private and public behavior. Through respectability the middle classes had, at first, sought to maintain their status against the aristocracy and the lower classes. The new moral tone enabled the middle classes to define themselves sharply against the other classes, though in a relatively short time they succeeded in forcing their standards of behavior upon the aristocracy and the lower classes. Nevertheless the latter were always regarded with suspicion by the respectable as having to be forced into conformity. Those who accepted the consequences of the Industrial Revolution—who were, for the most part, Liberals—used such conformity in manners and morals in order to keep control in the midst of change and to preserve the fabric of society.

Sexuality and modesty became potent metaphors for that control over the passions which respectability demanded as essential to the coherence of society. To feel ashamed of the nude human body had a long history, although the feeling was never universally accepted, especially by the aristocracy. The nineteenth century set the seal of shame upon all nudity as evoking sexual appetites, and any loss of control over one's sexuality, so it was thought, led to nervousness and exhaustion. Such personal decline had social consequences as well. Nervousness became a dreaded disease during the century, attacking the very presuppositions of society: control and moderation, personal energy used for the purposes of individual advancement and social progress. Just as it was believed that railway travel shattered one's nerves, so in 1760 Simon-August André Tissot in *L'Onanisme* had seen masturbation and undue sexual passion in marriage as leading to exhaustion and finally to death. For others following Tissot such lack of control was dangerous to society as a whole; the diseased body of those given to sexual excess could never muster the kind of energy needed for social progress. A famous sexologist, Richard von Krafft-Ebing, summed up the priorities of respectability in 1886 when he wrote that under all circumstances man must be able to master his sexual urge as soon as it comes into conflict with the demands of society.

Respectability required the acceptance of the "gospel of work." Laboring in one's trade or profession was proclaimed the supreme duty, and idleness or the quest for pleasure was supposed to lead to bad habits and bad thoughts. Such a doctrine was congenial to the ambitious, for during the early stages of the Industrial Revolution it did bring tangible rewards, and even later such an attitude towards work was crucial to the founding of the great European fortunes. Respectability, then, defined the middle classes and provided an avenue of upward mobility; above all, through the conformity it required, respectability provided society with the cohesion it needed at a time of rapid change.

The evolution of modern morals and manners took place over a long period of time, however sudden the onslaught of respectability at the turn of the eighteenth and nineteenth centuries. What has been called the "civilizing process" evolved as feudal society changed to court society. This change was not abrupt but gradual and at first affected manners, the polite behavior required in company, rather than morals. A feeling of sensibility towards others and a growing respect for hygiene was part of *politesse:* it became distasteful to be seen in society with dirty hands or to perform so-called private bodily functions in public. To be sure, this new emphasis upon manners did at times involve new attitudes towards the body, towards what was considered proper and decent.

The Protestant religious revivals of the eighteenth century were instrumental in making the ideal of respectability an all-encompassing way of life which determined both manners and morals. The religious revivals led by pietists in Germany and evangelicals in England had their roots in a revolt against the rigid structures of the traditional churches. The so-called loose living of the court and upper-class society served pietists and evangelicals as the foil to the pure and chaste behavior which they advocated.

Personal behavior was to be an expression of inward piety leading to acceptance of the sacredness of all human relations and the common duties of life. Sexual relations between men and women were stripped of their sensuousness; marriage was to be based upon the joint practice of piety. Sins real or imagined had to be atoned through a single-minded concentration upon one's vocation in life.

The French Revolution reenforced this religious revival, for it was seen by many of its opponents as a judgment of God upon the profligate nobility. The Napoleonic Wars encouraged the condemnation of "immoral France." Purity crusades accompanied those wars in England, and in Germany the rising national self-consciousness during the Wars of Liberation against Napoleon linked national defense to proper moral behavior. The nation and its citizens must be chaste and pure in heart, devoting their energies to the national cause. The example supposedly set by France led to a renewed dedication to control one's passions and the rejection of any personal excess (that of nationalism was considered a different matter).

The reality of the French Revolution was quite different, and so was the morality of Catholicism, regarded with suspicion by Protestants. Both made their contribution to the rooting of respectability. At the same time that Robespierre condemned all quest for pleasure and enjoyment, the attempt during the revolution to legitimize children born out of wedlock failed. Here not inner piety but devotion to the revolutionary cause and to the nation meant proper private and public behavior. Catholicism did not fare well in its battle with the Enlightenment during the eighteenth century, though here also a religious revival was in the making. The worship of the Virgin Mary encouraged since the seventeenth century by the church provided a continuous example of purity and chastity for church and people. The Catholic revival emerged strongly at the beginning of the nineteenth century with its nostalgia for the Middle Ages and its senti-mentalization of monastic life. A group of German artists who settled in Rome in an abandoned monastery in 1810 was to have a disproportionate influence upon popular art and upon the image of woman as well. They were called the Nazarenes by Romans because of their Christian religious paintings, sometimes done in the medieval mode and other times imitating the Renaissance. Their Raphael-like Madonnas showered with roses idealized woman as passive and chaste, a kind and beautiful mother.

The Nazarenes were romantics, and romanticism while at times encouraging a revolt against the growing pattern of decency also made its contribution towards the rooting of respectability. For example, romanticism projected not only the Nazarene ideal of woman but also—through its preoccupation with medieval chivalry—an ideal of manliness in all its purity. Romanticism coincided with the wars of the French Revolution and Napoleon in which, for the first time in modern history, large citizen armies rather than mercenaries fought for national greatness or independence. Poets and writers during those wars exhorted citizen soldiers to prove their manliness through sacrificing themselves for a noble ideal in battle. This concept of manliness symbolized energy and at the same time a spirituality dear to the age—that purity, quiet strength, and self-control thought necessary for progress. Woman's functions were clearly separate from those of man—mother and spouse confined to the household, preserving the family, a living link with tradition.

The division of function between the sexes was basic to the concept of respectability and through it to bourgeois society. Hegel at the start of the nineteenth century, and Marx at mid-century, held that a division of labor characterized capitalist society. Individual work processes were narrowed down until the individual lost sight of the unity of all labor as an expression of the creativity of mankind. They advocated modification or abolishment of this division of labor, which was not separated into equal parts and thus created and reenforced social inequality. But neither Hegel nor Marx objected to the sexual division of labor; indeed they took it for granted. Neither man lived to see it challenged by rebellious youth or by the Woman Rights Movement, challenges which began to make their mark only at the end of the nineteenth century, during the period which we have called in Chapter 13 "the change in the public spirit of Europe." Those thought to threaten respectability were often accused of confusing genders, as some examples in Chapter 5 on racism will demonstrate.

The division of labor between the sexes was deemed necessary in order to reenforce the family, the institution which formed the heart of respectability and which functioned as the policeman of manners and morals without which—so it was thought—respectability would surely disintegrate. The triumph of the nuclear family as a separate and self-contained unit within which each member was assigned his or her function took place at roughly the same time as the rise of respectability. No longer, for example, as in the past, were business and home under one roof where the mistress of the house also kept the accounts, dealt with apprentices, or sold wares. We saw earlier that the distance of the factory or business from the home had become a sign of prestige or status. Now the mistress only supervised the domestic staff and devoted herself to the education of her children. This ideal of self-contained middle-class family life, however, proved less true for the upper middle class. Many upper-middle-class families engaged wet nurses and nursemaids who looked after young children in the mother's stead. The number of the nannies in nineteenth-century London alone was impressive (in 1871 there were nearly 104,000 of them), but this was true for Berlin and Paris as well. The ideal of middle-class family life was dependent, in any case, upon the availability of servants who constituted a class separate from the working classes, a subordinate part of the family circle. The working-class family was different again inasmuch as the wife often worked in a factory or labored for an employer, while the middle-class wife was kept separate from the male world of work and public affairs. Yet here, among the working class, the family also meant shelter and self-help, bound together by the demands of respectability which in this case did not necessarily mean subordination to the middle classes but often a sense of one's own worth and dignity.

The immediate family of mother, father, and children was the basic institution to which almost everyone belonged, though the extended family still played a role in determining close social relationships. Marriage was no longer seen mainly as a commercial transaction (though it kept this function as well) but was based upon the mutual affection of husband and wife. The ideals which were a part of the concept of respectability, such as manliness, chastity, self-control and restraint in all things, were supposedly anchored in family life.

Hand in hand with the sexual division of labor and belief in family life, society proceeded to strengthen the protective walls around respectability in order to guard itself better against the onslaught of modernity. Here it is important to note that during the nineteenth century in the cities the influence of the Catholic priest or Protestant minister declined and the physician tended to take his place as the guardian of morality. The admiration for scientific accomplishments played its role here, the wish to act according to the most up-to-date information. Medicine proved itself hardly more "objective" or scientific than religion when it came to making moral judgments. Staying within the social norms, so-called normal behavior, was considered healthy, and all that stood outside these norms, or attempted to challenge them, was branded as sick. Thus respectability annexed scientific judgment in order to strengthen its cause.

We have already mentioned how in 1760 Dr. Tissot saw sexual excess as the reason for abnormal behavior leading to nervousness and even death. Nervousness was viewed as an onslaught upon social values, the very opposite of manliness; nervous habits were projected upon real and potential outsiders. For example, in 1880 Jean-Martin Charcot, lecturing at Paris's famous insane asylum, the *Salpetière,* stressed that nervous illnesses were more frequent among Jews than among other groups. Indeed the kind of "moveable physiognomy" which was said to characterize the insane was at times projected upon the Jews as well. The fidgety behavior of such outsiders, those thought to be sick, contrasted with the calm comportment of manliness. Women were thought to be subject to hysteria, tender creatures guided by their emotions who must be sheltered from the harsh world of men.

Forensic medicine, that medical opinion used by courts of law, contributed its share to the stereotyping of the outsider, for it was forced to describe those who possessed so-called abnormal sexual drives in order that the courts could enforce the sodomy laws. Thus Johann Ludwig Casper in Germany and Ambroise Tarduieu in France at mid-nineteenth century described those whose sexual drives seemed abnormal or excessive as pale, red-eyed, effeminate, and exhausted. Outsiderdom was accompanied by medical judgments of health and sickness which informed the manly as well as the stereotype of the Jew, the homosexual, or of the so-called lower races which we will analyze in Chapter 5 on racism.

Such outsiderdom was intimately linked to the effort of respectability to hold its own, and those thought to threaten society's norms were stereotyped as diseased as one vice led to another. For our argument, not only these definitions of outsiderdom are important but also the kind of conformity which respectability demanded. It provided the background which an overwhelming number of thinkers took for granted, and typically enough, those wo embraced the "challenge of liberty," confined themselves to political and economic freedom and enthusiastically embraced the new morality in order to help society maintain cohesion and avoid chaos.

The concept of respectability was not without its challengers. The generation which grew up in the *fin de siècle* found a new joy in their bodies and seemed to oppose the respectability of their elders. Some of those challenges we shall analyze in Chapter 13 on the change in the public spirit of Europe; for example, the German Youth Movement proclaimed youth to be autonomous, and avant garde writers attempted to change the bourgeois ethos of Europe. Freeing sexuality from the constraints imposed by society was part of their quest. Thus Frank Wedekind in his play *Springs Awakening* (1891) let his schoolboys experiment with all sorts of sexual experiences upon the stage: masturbation, heterosexuality, and a fleeting homosexual scene. The play could not be performed in Germany until fifteen years after it was written, and even then the more explicit scenes were cut. The Youth Movement and the avant garde were accompanied by other movements which also called for a certain freedom from convention: nudist movements which advocated a return to the genuine forces of nature as well as movements to reform women's fashions, getting rid of the corset in favor of a healthier and more spacious dress.

What we have called the change in the public spirit of Europe in the last decades of the nineteenth century was a watershed. The new movements that were taking shape were not limited to youth or the avant garde; political movements like socialism and the allied movement for women's rights were also making their mark. The traditional order sought to keep its hold upon society, and its quest was made easier by the irrationalism which informed some of the rebellion against it—an irrationalism which was easily co-opted by nationalism and respectability.

None of these movements which challenged respectability wanted to bring about social change—as distinct from manners and morals—except perhaps for some avant garde writers. Men and women were interested in finding the "genuine" in nature and in themselves. Their newly found joy in their bodies was chaste, nudity made transparent by the rays of the sun. However, those physicians who dealt with human sexuality at the turn of the century, known as the sexologists, did call for greater understanding of the so-called abnormal. They believed that a variant from the norm like homosexuality was partly congenital and thus must be treated with compassion, but they did not believe that the so-called abnormal could ever be integrated into society. For example, Richard von Krafft-Ebing held that every person must wage a constant war against the instincts. Sexual excess led to nervous tensions and consequently to the decline of society and the state. Sigmund Freud was one of a number of sexologists when he first wrote, at the turn of the century, and his war of the ego against the id, reason against instinct, was a rather commonplace theory at the time, though what he made of this was to be unique. Freud, as we shall see, wanted the limits of the permissible extended in order to ease the pressures of society which caused so much psychological strain. The parameters of respectability must be expanded for the sake of mental health; for example, he approved of pre-marital sex and had compassion for so-called sexual perversions. However, sex roles must not be confused, and while it was normal at childhood to feel attracted to both male and female, maturity meant a clearly defined male or female sexuality. Freud did not want to abolish respectability but to extend its limits. He thought that greater tolerance would strengthen the fabric of society by making it easier to adjust to its norms. Yet Freud's frank and open discussion of sexuality helped make what had been hidden in shame part of the human discourse.

Thus there was change as the twentieth century opened: sexuality was more openly discussed, the so-called abnormal pushed closer to the surface. Yet respectability held and if deviance was allowed a greater scope, this was because it was seen as exotic and not because the clear division between the normal and the abnormal had been weakened. The controls and restraints of respectability, the cohesion of society, were not in danger, reenforced as they were by educators, the police, physicians, and clergy. The travails of industrialism seemed unending, and so did the need to keep control in a nervous age. The First World War and its aftermath only reenforced the felt need for order and cohesion.

Throughout this book we will find men and women reaching out to make contact with nature or religious belief in order to stabilize their lives. Here they could claim a share in the eternal as over against the "vibrations of modernity." The historical origins of modern manners and morals which we have tried to sketch were ignored; instead, manners and morals were sanctified, lifted into immutability, and removed from current controversy and debate. Many of the ideas we are about to discuss must be seen against this background: attempts to claim immutability through annexing a piece of eternity or to expand the limits while not destroying the clearly defined bounds of social acceptability. But there were others, as we have mentioned, who wanted to revolt against such constraints for the sake of their own personal freedom. Friedrich Nietzsche's influence in the twentieth century was so great in part because he distinguished between a real and an apparent world—that created by the individual personality for itself and that which was only apparent because it was created by others seeking to restrict individual expression for the sake of some ideology or social requirement. Nietzsche stood for and inspired a heightened awareness of individuality and a more violent rebellion in the first decade of this century.

The Italian Futurists, who were in the vanguard of those who seemed to follow Nietzsche's example, in their Manifesto of 1909 saw in modern technology and the new speed of time an analogy to their own revolt against the bourgeois order. But the Futurists always praised self-discipline and a voluntary commitment to patriotism. When the First World War broke out the Futurists saw it as an opportunity to reap military glory for Italy and to destroy the existing order. Side by side with Benito Mussolini, Futurists advocated Italy's entry into that war. After the war they were one of the groups which formed the Fascist Party: their individualism was tamed, though never with complete success. They were artists for the most part, and the relative artistic freedom in Fascist Italy gave them room to express themselves as painters or poets, though they had sacrificed most other individual expression to a disciplined mass movement.

German Expressionist artists and writers, at the same time, were individualists eager to express themselves, men for whom the outside world existed only as it was reflected within the poet or writer himself. They

24

sought to challenge all accepted social values; for example, they wrote plays picturing the murder of fathers by sons, incest, and homosexuality. Theirs was a shriek of protest against the bourgeois world, the result of boredom and disgust with a society whose long period of prosperity had dulled perceptions and numbed sensitivity. Thus George Heym, one of the founders of German Expressionism, wrote in 1910 that the world was too boring, one day was like another, and if only war broke out he might recover his health. Expressionists had always contained a streak of cruelty directed against bourgeois society, and they welcomed the First World War as had the Futurists. And like the Futurists the war tamed their shriek: many became Socialists through the wartime experience of camaraderie; others ended up on the German far right. Both movements were co-opted by ideals of community, just as Nietzsche himself was annexed by German nationalists as the philosopher of the superman; his hatred of Germans and what he called their slave morality were conveniently forgotten.

These were middle-class youths, most of them under thirty years of age, in rebellion against their elders. Their revolution was directed against social conventions rather than economic problems, and it produced an avant garde which determined literary and artistic expression for much of the twentieth century; it was tamed into social and political but not literary or artistic conformity. The separation between art and life which resulted concerned not only Expressionists or Futurists; it became a general feature of artistic and middle-class life. Middle-class audiences flocked to plays or read books which condemned their society, from the Expressionist attack on manners and morals to the social and political persiflage of Bertolt Brecht's *Three Penny Opera* (1932). Such audiences did not merely reflect a desire to be titillated, to taste of forbidden fruit, but demonstrated the extent to which liberalism had penetrated a part of the middle class with its ideal of the continued process of self-education.

The ideal of a never-ending self-education, through which the inherent abilities of the individual were supposedly realized, was a heritage of the eighteenth-century Enlightenment which liberalism had made its own. For that bourgeoisie among whom commitment to liberalism remained strong it meant a certain openness to the avant garde, as well as the cultivation of a critical faculty which could be turned upon existing society provided that it did not threaten its survival. But it was precisely that survival which artists and writers wanted to question. Confronted with such attitudes on the part of their audience or their readership, the relationship between art and life became a prime concern for many writers and artists, from the *fin de siècle* onwards; we will see the concern reflected in many of the later chapters of this book.

Most of those who wanted to escape the demands of society were not avant garde but sought regeneration through the supposedly genuine forces of nature. Nature as an instrument of personal regeneration fed the stream of later romanticism which was to have a vital effect specifically upon German culture. Through romanticism and its close association with nationalism, back-to-nature movements became enmeshed in right-wing politics emphasizing emotion and intuition, as we shall see later in our discussion of "romaniticism and idealism transmitted" (Chapter 14).

Romanticism made a deep impact upon Germany, and to a lesser extent upon England, while in France any worship of nature was regarded with some skepticism and irony. For example, Madame de Staël, puzzled by the German worship of nature, wrote in 1813 that Germany with its enormous woods gave the impression of an only recently civilized country. The French gardens and parks, with Versailles as their model, attempted to control and dominate nature, while the so-called English gardens in the nineteenth century, popular in Germany as well, touched nature as little as possible. Romanticism was important in France as well, as we shall see, but here countervailing forces made themselves felt, above all a certain rationalist tradition absent in Germany. Regeneration through nature as part of the romantic mood was easily co-opted by the society against which it was supposedly directed. For example, German nationalism became the instrument through which youth and life reform movements were controlled, making untamed nature symbolic of national roots. Here men and women sought inspiration through a historical continuity symbolized by the unchanging landscape, where they encountered their ancestors, whose healthy and vigorous lives were passed in intimate contact with nature, an eternal fountain of purity as over against the vice-ridden city. The native landscape thus provided a firm center for attempts at personal and national regeneration.

While nature performed the double function of inspiring the escape from the existing order, and at the same time exercising control over it, one of its principal functions in the age of industrialism was to restrain the onslaught of modernity. Nature fulfilled this function through masking the progress of industrialization, surrounding rapid change with the ideals and symbols of a pre-industrial utopia. John Ruskin at mid-nineteenth century claimed that the basic pleasures of life—to watch corn grow and the blossoms set—had never changed even while England had sold its soul to iron and steam. The garden cities, city parks, and the discovery of the Alps belong to this pattern of thought as well. As Germany caught up with England in industrial might at the end of the nineteenth century, nature was used in a similar manner: emphasizing the values of a nation rooted in nature and those of the medieval craftsman living close to his natural and national roots which must inspire the modern working class.

Romanticism and industrialism had to be reconciled: there were only a very few who in practice wasnted to retreat into a more primitive and pre-industrial age. As a result, technology and the factory were accepted as necessary but superficial, while the moving power behind events was supposedly human beings themselves regenerated through nature and the nation. This ideology informed much of the political right and eventually Fascism and National Socialism, both fascinated by modern technology. Those who paid allegiance to the Marxist tradition differed, rejecting both nation and nature, which Karl Marx called the "idiocy of the countryside." Nevertheless, the metaphor Marx used to describe his own ideal society, in which the division of labor was abolished, was one which permitted people to hunt in the morning and fish in the afternoon—itself a tribute to nature as providing a powerful utopia which not even those fully accepting industrialism as the new reality could avoid. Socialism continued to use metaphors derived from nature in order to express hope for the future and to symbolize the workers' emancipation. Nature played an important role in the changing pace of life which industrialism created.

The perceptions of life, the fear and hopes we have discussed, will be reflected throughout the book. The culture of western Europe was set within social and national conflict. There is no room here to describe the crucial social, economic, and political events. That is why we have tried to analyze the changing pace of life by way of the perceptions of men and women, for how individuals see their world and how they attempt to live their lives have a direct impact upon culture—indeed upon all of history.

Romanticism, which we have mentioned so often, was the great survivor of modern cultural history. It will accompany us throughout this book as one way of meeting the challenges of modernity. Any movement which attempted to ignore its force did so only at its peril.

# CHAPTER TWO

# Romanticism:
# The Poetry of Life

*T*HE ROMANTICISM which became all pervasive in modern European culture was a "mood" which escaped any rigid scheme of classification. That was part of the strength of the movement, for it could change from person to person and combine with various political and social ideals. Romanticism did have one explicit ideological base, however—it accorded the greatest importance to the emotions and to the imagination. The feelings of the heart, however irrational, were considered more valid than the thoughts of the head. The enemy was that cold reason which Charles Dickens had symbolized in Scrooge and which had provided the essence of the Enlightenment's hope for a better world. The rationalism of the eighteenth century had not been cold or selfish, but the Romantics made no distinction between a Scrooge and those who believed that progress was possible only because of the rational nature of people. For Romantics, human nature was best described through the "soul" which contained emotions and which furthered imagination. All else was abstract "intellectualizing," typical of people who lacked true emotion and therefore a true soul.

Because human feelings became all-important in this romantic mood, the Romantics concentrated upon the intensity of the emotions. If feeling was the test of true virtue, of the possession of a soul, the story of a person who exemplified feeling was especially interesting, but of still greater importance was that moment when an emotion was at its height. To the Romantic the true nature of the world and life was more clearly revealed by emotion and vision than by the dry and comprehensive power of analysis. As Margaret Dalziel has shown, this emotionalism could be easily caricatured. Louisa of Mrs. March's *Tales of Woods and Fields* (1842) "faints when the horses run away with the carriage, falls into a decline when crossed in love ... news of an even mildly exciting event had to be broken gently to the heroine if perfect prostration was to be avoided."

Yet such a heroine should not disguise the lasting impact of the movement. It formed a habit of mind which was hostile to rationalism—and which thought of people in terms of soul rather than reason. Focusing on the inner workings of human nature, it claimed that they alone were "genuine" and "true." Not only reason but also reality was held to be superficial, merely an "outward" thing not directly related to the individual's soul. The romantic mood thus capitalized on the dissatisfactions engendered by rationalism's disavowal of the emotions, particularly the need for security which discounted external reality by escaping into a contemplation of the inner person. No doubt the change of Europe from a rural to an industrial and urban civilization enhanced the attractiveness of this habit of mind. It gave people a feeling of importance, of stability in terms of their own souls amid rapid and incomprehensible changes.

The origins of romanticism lie within the age of reason itself. Jean-Jacques Rousseau (1712–78) foreshadowed many aspects of this mood. The ideal of the "natural man" which he popularized but which also existed in many other thinkers of the period emphasized that the individual was good and virtuous when removed from the fetters of civilization. In such an ideal state heart and head were unspoiled and therefore functioned properly. For Rousseau and other eighteenth-century thinkers this meant that humans were both reasonable and virtuous. However, the element of human reason in the state of nature played, for Rousseau, a lesser part than the goodness of the heart. This foreshadowed the romantic belief in the essential rightness and virtue of mankind's proper emotions when they are left to develop freely. The concept of natural man became a widespread fad in the eighteenth century; Louis XVI and his queen had a rural village built for themselves behind their palace of the Trianon where they could play at "natural" man and wife. Moreover, this image was associated with rural life, the kind of Arcadia which writers had idealized for centuries. It should be kept in mind that the ideal of natural man associated with rural life was not only a background for the romantic movement, but also went into the making of one

30

of the most important preconceptions of the nineteenth century, indeed of modern times: namely, that the peasant represents the greatest virtues in a society which is growing ever more industrial and urban.

The concept of "natural man" was not the only element which went into the making of the romantic atmosphere. Evangelicalism in England and pietism in Germany provided important stimuli for romanticism, just as they were to be important in the making of the new middle-class morality. Both stressed "piety of the heart"—religion as an emotional experience. Pietism was more temperate than the evangelical movement; nevertheless, the emotional appeal was present. Evangelicalism with its outright appeal to emotional conversion, "coming to Christ," implanted an emotionalism in all classes of the English population. The emphasis upon hymn singing together with preaching as the chief outward appeals of faith played an important part. Nor can the increasing stream of oratory and moral exhortations which marked both movements be neglected. Many other causes, like the Temperance League and the Society Against Vice, depended on similar methods. All over Europe the reading public was increasing and what they read, above all, were books of edification or moral exhortation to lead a good life. Education by exhortation was prominent in the making of middle-class morality, as Dr. Thomas Arnold of Rugby can show, but it also created an atmosphere congenial to life viewed as an emotional experience.

Though Rousseau foreshadowd the romantic mood in France and evangelicalism did much to encourage it in England, Germany seemed at the head of the movement during the eighteenth century. Not only German pietism, but particularly a literary movement known as the storm and stress (*Sturm und Drang,* 1765–85) set the romantic tone. Making its home in Weimar, the movement's importance for the cultural revival in Germany was equal to its contribution to romanticism. Friedrich Schiller (1759–1805), in particular, portrayed his heroes in terms of their inner responses to life, abstracting people from their environment. In depicting the *Robbers,* for example, he made their inner conflicts and the resulting tragedy take precedence over the morality or the effects of their actions. Johann Wolfgang von Goethe (1749–1832), the greatest German man of letters of that century, passed through the Enlightenment and classicism to a romantic mood. The narrative of his journeys to Italy did much to stimulate a new emphasis upon nature as emotional and sentient rather than as imprisoned within rational laws of nature.

It was to Weimar that a remarkable French intellectual went in search of the modern in the arts. Madame de Staël first coined the word "romanticism" in her book on Germany (1813). It is significant that she used this term in connection with literature, for this became for the Romantics symbolic of their view of life. Her definition occurred in the section on poetry in which she contrasted classical and romantic poetry. Such a contrast was telling; not only had classical thought been a living reality in France for several centuries but it was also associated with rationalism. Madame de Staël found the basic difference to be in the artificiality of the classical and the naturalness of the romantic poetry. Ancient epics made their characters appear artificial, for all their actions were caused by "external events" outside the actual character and nature of the actors in the drama. Such persons were captives of their destiny and of the inexorable workings of necessity.

"Action was all in antiquity and character played not the same role as in modern times." The greatness of the Romantics came from elevating character above action. These moderns avoided artificiality of action. Placing character in the foreground, they centered their attention upon honor, love, and bravery—in short, upon the internal condition of individuals rather than upon those external forces the ancients thought guided human destiny. This meant the primacy of "emotion" and "sentiment," since the human character must be detached from the environment and analyzed in terms of the individual's own emotions. External events were mere superficialities when compared with the true self. Reality was rejected as a determinant of human action or of human nature. The distinction between outward phenomena and the real essence of things was thus present from the very beginning of romanticism, a part of its original definition. The tone was set for German idealism, indeed for a mood widely spread throughout Europe during the last century and a half. This distinction will be one of the principal themes running throughout this analysis of modern European culture.

Madame de Staël's praise for the moderns and hostility toward the ancients epitomized a feeling quite prevalent at the beginning of the century. The theatre can well serve to illustrate this. Plays tended to become mere vehicles for violent emotions displayed upon the stage. Thus the period was marked by a low point in playwriting and a high point in acting. An English play from the first decades of the century can scarcely be remembered, but great actors like Edmund Kean are still living legends. Oratory and emotion were prized far above well-constructed action. Not the construction of his plays but the ideal of character portrayal which contemporaries saw in Shakespeare led to a renewed international popularity of his works. When Shakespeare was first revealed to France in 1827 by Kemble and his troupe of actors, the audience was struck by the "sentiment" and "emotion" which they contrasted favorably with the great French classical writers like Racine and Corneille. In Germany Schlegel and Tieck, whose genius lay precisely in an empathy with the internal conflicts of the characters, made their famous Shakespeare translation. The romantic enthusiasm for Shakespeare was so great in Germany that by the end of the century one writer wrote a whole book entitled *Shakesperomania* (1873) in order to save German literature from such contaminating English influence.

Romantics saw in Shakespeare an anticipation of the modern in the arts. He seemed to have put into practice that concentration upon the internal condition of man which Madame de Stael had praised. This "inner man" seemed to be subsumed under a series of words which the Romantics used constantly: character, emotion, sentiment, and soul. Such terms are distressingly vague even if they imply a definite world outlook which distinguished between outward appearance and such "genuine" and "true" concepts. These words did come to have a more clearly-defined content within the romantic mood, however. Romantics used them to oppose rational systematizing: "He who believes in systems expells love from his heart." Yet, when the consequences which flowed from its view of life are analyzed, it is apparent that romanticism tended to become a system itself.

Romantics themselves summarized their attitude in the phrase "the poetry of life." Not only did this term imply the primacy of poetry as an expression of the human soul, but it also contained a view of an individual's feelings which was central to romanticism. These feelings were thought "private" and "secret," something which only that person who was actually swayed by them could understand. Wilhelm Heinrich Wackenroder in *The Hartfelt Outpourings of an Art Loving Monk* (1797) defined this emphasis on feeling and what it meant: "...his inner self he valued over all things, and kept it hidden from others. Thus one keeps hidden a treasure whose keys one gives into no one's hands." Translated into the everyday realm, Harold Nicolson tells of the disappointment felt by his German landlady at the end of the century because he lacked a secret sorrow: "The Frau Baumeister would sigh wistfully when she thought how delightful a large secret sorrow would have been." This is one of the many romantic elements which was to flow beneath the complacency of German middle-class morality.

On the surface, the secrecy of the soul was not well maintained by the Romantics. Undoubtedly Rousseau's *Confessions* (1783), which were widely read and admired, stimulated the outpouring of their feelings to one another. Rousseau had set out in the very beginning of his book maxims which the Romantics were to imitate: "I desire to set before my fellows the likeness of a man in all the truth of nature, and that man myself." The Romantics still lived in the great age of letter writing and it was through this medium that they analyzed each other's feelings at great length. To Henriette Herz, Schleiermacher wrote "one more word about your sentimentality" and continued for ten pages to praise the "noble, tender, and perceptive" qualities in his friend. This pathology of souls, which was popular in early roman-

*33*

ticism, not only in letters written among friends but also in novels dissecting minutely the feeling of the characters, became a necessary prerequisite of the modern in the arts. The exhibitionism which often went hand in hand with this seemed to remove the secret sorrow still further from its hidden cell in the heart. Heroines fainted, soul mates greeted each other with exaggerated gestures. But all this display, in reality, stood outside the real essence of the soul. The fainting heroine gave outward testimony of her feelings, but only she knew what was going on in her soul. The pathology of souls was widespread. There were exceptions because, in the last resort, the real secretness of inner feelings was revealed in stark relief only when the person hurled himself against a world which did not understand him. The art-loving monk, a pseudonym for Wackenroder who was not a monk at all, was constantly misunderstood by his father and friends. In consequence he retreated from the battle of life into his "secret" inner life removed from the philistines. Wackenroder died, worn out by life in his twenties; Goethe's young *Werther* was driven to suicide. The image of the misunderstood genius was set for the century.

These concepts of human feelings, of their souls, were central to the poetry of life and they came to involve not only people but nature as well. Madame de Staël had written about the naturalness of the moderns and she meant by this a concept of nature which was closely related to the romantic view of people. As Rousseau had done, it stressed the innate correspondence between the individual and nature. This was not a correspondence in the sense of the eighteenth century's laws of nature. The individual and nature were not bound together by general laws but by an inner, emotional correspondence. Human feelings were stimulated by nature which was itself emotional and sentient. It was a unity of the passions, a correspondence between the turbulent emotions of the individual and nature. Madame de Staël expressed it succinctly in her famous analysis of romantic poetry. She felt that Goethe's ballad, "The Fisherman," admirably expressed the increasing pleasure which could be derived from contemplating the pure waters of a flowing stream; the measure of the poem's rhythm and its harmony imitated the motion of the waves and produced an analogous effect upon the imagination.

The romantic poet translated nature's emotions into those to which humanity was susceptible, a task in which music and painting were equally important expressions. Artists concentrated on the wild landscapes which symbolized emotional experiences and sought for inspiration in nature. When Berlioz had reached a dead end in his musical composition he took a walk in the Tivoli gardens outside Rome. The intoxication of his senses by nature led him back to his true self—nature's emotions had found a correspondence in his own.

34

At times this stress on nature was apt to lead toward a realism which tried to present nature as it actually was. This "romantic realism" was also connected with a defiance of conventions in the name of naturalness. Berlioz, for example, created a sensation when, in his opera *Benvenuto Cellini* (1838), he put a live and crowing rooster on the stage. Though Paris hissed the rooster, this defiant realism was here to stay. In the end these spectacular elements became an integral part of showmanship. Richard Wagner provided a good example of this, not only in the rushing brook and forest in which Tristan and Isolde sang of their love to each other, but also in the real fire which surrounded the sleeping Bruenhilde.

Romantic realism, however, could go beyond emphasis on nature toward social realism, as it did in the writing of one of the greatest literary geniuses of the century, Alessandro Manzoni. His *The Betrothed* (1827), which had vivid descriptions of landscapes, revolved around the fate of two lovers at the time of the plague in Milan in the seventeenth century. The Christian element was present in the saintly Capuchin who worked among the victims of the plague and in the nun who inwardly was not a nun at all. The flavor of the novel, however, lay in its realism. The descriptions of Milan during the plague were written as if they had been observed at first hand and reported without regard to beauty or ugliness. This account of horror was motivated not by an obsession with the bizarre but by a revulsion induced by forceful realism. Believing in the oneness of man and his surrounding nature, Manzoni felt that the deserted streets and the dying of Milan were as much a part of this environment as the landscape which he described in detail at the beginning of the book.

By mid-century, the unity between the individual and nature was being challenged. As nature seemed more and more to become the domain of scientific investigation, the esential romantic unity was in danger of being rent asunder and the stimulus which it had offered to the poetry of life seemed threatened. At that point melancholy set in among many intellectuals. The Italian poet Giacomo Leopardi (1798–1837) lamented that the loss of a world explainable by myth was causing imagination to shrivel. Nature was no longer animate and sentient but mechanical and necessary.

The wheel seemed to have gone full circle from the nature of the eighteenth century which Romantics regarded as mechanistic to the sciences of the nineteenth century which were also to a great extent mechanistic and schematical. Goethe's shock at the earthquake of Lisbon foreshadowed the later pessimism. Its impact caused him to question the correspondence between humanity and nature. Perhaps nature had nothing to do with humanity? Was nature a hostile force? Goethe recoiled from these thoughts in horror. Later Leopardi believed that science had wrenched nature away and that this would

35

mean an irreparable loss to the human imagination. The poetry of life was endangered. Matthew Arnold (1822–84), contemplating this fate, wrote that "to tunes we did not call, our beings must keep time." Nevertheless, he, along with other Romantics, was saved from complete despair by his belief in the power of nature over the emotion. Arnold concluded that nature was neither a hostile power which seeks to destroy humanity nor a neutral power which humanity has to follow; instead it was a power which stimulated the individual to the highest pitch of the imagination. Which student cannot remember Wordsworth's undespairing lines, "sweet is the lore that nature brings"?

In the same poem Wordsworth accused the intellect of misshaping the beauteous forms of things. This hostility to the intellect always accompanied the basic revolt against reason. Chateaubriand (1768–1848) echoed Wordsworth when, attempting to prove the superiority of poetry over science, he wrote that the poet was alive to remotest posterity by means of a few verses while a scientist was forgotten the day after his death. The person who could bequeath to the world "one single moral precept, one single affecting sentiment" rendered a greater service to the world than any other. It was the poetry of life alone which counted. As the century wore on, an ever more militant tone in opposition to science can be distinguished; science became the "meddling intellect" which threatened to destroy the unity of humanity and nature, just as the Lisbon earthquake had threatened to do in the previous age. In the long run poetry and nature were saved, because the application of science to art and society brought about a reaction against science and because the mechanical aspect of nineteenth-century science was transformed in the twentieth century.

The harmony of humanity and nature was the bedrock of personal feeling, of the soul. Christianity could and did, at times, become involved in this emotional unity. Nature and people could be emotionally linked in an appreciation of the Divine. Chateaubriand, in particular, integrated the Christian element into the romantic ideal of this unity. In his *Genius of Christianity* (1802) he does just this when he describes an ocean voyage: "God of Christians! It is on the waters of the abyss, and on the expanded sky, that thou hast particularly engraven the characters of thy omnipotence!" Chateaubriand himself was in tune with his surroundings. "Religious tears" flowed from his eyes when the sailors prayed amidst the ocean and the setting sun. One more example from Chateaubriand will bring out this unity of people, nature, and God, combined with the vivid imagery which was typical of much romantic writing. Moreover, the love for the bizarre was here joined with the praise of nature in the raw, for Chateaubriand asks: ". . . what is there happier than the Eskimo in his wonderful fatherland?" This primitive creature, which is reminiscent of Montesquieu's savages in the woods of Hanover, shows emotional unity at its best:

> The iceberg balances on the waves, its peaks shining, its hollows ordered with snow, the sea wolves give themselves to the passion of love in its valleys. The whales follow its footsteps over the ocean. The hardy savage, in the shelter of his floating iceberg presses to his heart the woman whom God has given him and with her finds undreamt joys in this mixture of danger and passion.

The iceberg so populated and surrounded is for Chateaubriand the "throne of God and the tempests."

Madame de Staël was particularly impressed by this Christian element in some of the Romantics and she thought that Europe had now emerged into the "Christian era" of the fine arts. This was an emotional Christianity, a part of the emotional correspondence between people and the environment and on this basis romanticism did spark a Christian renaissance. Madame de Staël felt that this new interest in Christianity was combined with what she called "chivalry," a renewed interest in the medieval past. For if nature and Christianity served to stimulate emotions, a vision of history seemed to express the ideal society in which the romantic view of people could have free play.

The inspiration for the cult of the Middle Ages was a literary one. It was to be found in the rediscovery of folk tales and ballads of that bygone age. When Percy first published some of them in his *Reliques* (1765), these ballads seemed to speak of strange and thrilling times. In Germany, Ludwig Achim von Arnim and Clemens Brentano published their collection of folk songs as the *Boys' Magic Horn* (1806). A sense of history, which had been secondary in the rationalism of the eighteenth century, was reawakened and, like the new interest in Christianity, it took an emotional and idealized form. The Middle Ages were a time when human activities had been permeated by transcendent concerns: the knight fighting for justice for the weak, the great and mysterious cathedrals which dominated the countryside, and the ballads which sang of the great deeds of individual men. An emphasis on individual feeling, on the individual soul, could escape, through this historical vision, the growing mass and industrial society of Europe. The historical novel began its vogue of popularity.

Significantly, the most famous practitioner of this genre, Sir Walter Scott (1771–1832), contrasted the rapidly changing England of his day with the England of the medieval past. Everywhere new cities, new factories were springing up; by comparison, the England of old represented an era of stability. Thus, Romantics sought to realize their ideal in history, just as they sought it by concentrating upon their own inner self rather than upon the realities of their society. This new sense of history had important political and social consequences. From the beginning of the century, many people felt stability in Europe could be achieved through the adoption of what they thought was a medieval model for the organization of society: the hierarchical and corporate state, which will be discussed later.

Of more immediate importance were the literary and artistic consequences of this trend. In architecture the longing for this lost age expressed itself in a revival of the medieval style. Castles were built in imitation of what an idealized medieval castle should have looked like. In Germany, the Gothic cathedral of Cologne was, at last, completed amidst the great enthusiasm of the population (1842–80). In England the Houses of Parliament by Barry and Pugin (1840–57) were to be a lasting monument to the Gothic revival. In France this medievalism was expressed not so much in architecture as in painting. The exhibition of 1819 in Paris abounded in Merovingians, troubadours, and the great kings of France. The most important of the early romantic painters, Eugène Delacroix, utilized themes in this period of his development which were almost entirely historical.

This trend in romanticism might be thought to have transformed the movement into an explicit conservatism. Such a generalization would be wrong. From the very beginning, the poetry of life contained a certain revolutionary element. But this urge to revolt was directed not toward transforming society but toward giving each individual the freedom to express and develop his own emotions corresponding to those stimuli which nature, Christianity, or the vision of the medieval past would provide. In the course of their revolt, the Romantics were bound to hurl themselves against the conventions of their age—conventions which the moderns felt were artificial products of tradition to be overcome in the search for the genuine. They rebelled against convention not in the name of equality or economic change but in the name of an individualism seen in terms of the freedom of the "inner man." They condemned artificial conventions as bourgeois and began to hold themselves opposed to the middle-class ethos. This is important because romanticism would, in the end, condemn both the bourgeoisie and the radicals. It became a habit of mind which envisioned a middle way between these two: opposed to bourgeois conventions as shallow and artificial but also to social and economic radicalism as stifling the soul through an emphasis upon the masses. It must already be clear that terms like "emotion," "feeling," and "soul" had within them some definite presuppositions and these became still more explicit through romantic opposition to middle-class conventions. This revolt against conventions took on concrete forms which were both a conscious and a rather naive protest against the traditional. This was well illustrated by the premiere of Victor Hugo's play *Hernani* in 1830. The play itself was of no particular significance; however, since Hugo made use of certain new techniques in the play, the young Romantics chose it as an apt forum for a demonstration of defiance. Though the young men who attended the premiere and returned for many successive nights made the mediocre play a success, their primary aim was the "affirmation of freedom for all the arts." They asserted this freedom by their applause, by the red and pink waistcoats which they wore, and by the long uncut hair which they flaunted in an ostentatious manner. All this was done to annoy the academicians who were dressed in respectable cutaways and top hats.

Amusing though all this may be, the deeper purpose behind it was to show defiance in the name of the modern arts. This show of defiance in terms of dress and manners can also be seen in Germany. Friedrich Ludwig Jahn (1778–1852) and his Gymnasts flaunted their beards and boorishness just as the young Frenchmen flaunted their beards and waistcoats. Behind this German revolt against middle-class mores and ethics, however, there was much more than just a call for the freedom of the arts. Father Jahn was interested in the arts only insofar as they revitalized the German past and recalled Germans to their common nationality. In this the greater national overtones of German romanticism can already be seen. The defiance of these young men reached its climax at the Wartburg castle as they proclaimed national freedom and artistic freedom. In contrast, the artists and writers who made *Hernani* a *scandale de théâtre* were concerned mainly with the arts. But France was a national state and Germany was still politically disunited. Once again such protests foreshadowed the future. At the end of the century dress and beards were once more to be important for the Bohemians as a revolt against the morality of the predominant middle-class society.

These naive protests were not the only way in which the Romantics manifested their opposition to contemporary modes of thought. They also had programs and manifestoes which they spread throughout the land. Breathing defiance, Hugo's preface to his *Cromwell* in 1827 proclaimed that only the romantic which was the product of the sublime and the grotesque was real. Furthermore, drama had to be a combination of comedy and tragedy. These contrasts which Hugo put in the center of his program corresponded with the emotional storms within the individual. Hugo opposed these to the cold formality of the classical French stage, the same coldness and abstraction which Madame de Staël had also contrasted to the modern in the arts.

The German manifesto was a novel which was accepted as formulating a program for romanticism. This was a much earlier work than Hugo's. It was no coincidence that Madame de Staël talked about romanticism in her book on Germany, for that country had clearly formulated the movement before France did so.

Friedrich Schlegel's *Lucinde* (1789) caused the kind of sensation which manifestoes should cause if they fulfill their purpose. The subtitle "An Apology for Nature and Innocence" set the romantic tone. The theme in which Lucinde's nature and her innocence flouted all accepted morality was carried out as a protest against convention. She revealed her feeling in an orgy of sentimentality and sensuality. This natural and innocent girl advocated such diverse matters as free love, the evil of work, and the inconstancy of the emotions because all these come from within and are in praise of nature. We can see a definite link with Rousseau's views of nature—Lucinde was "innocent" because she was following the dictates of her heart. If such freedom transgressed artificial, man-made conventions, these conventions had to give way. Lucinde was, in Schlegel's words, "the resistance to the positive law and conventional rights." The romantic psychology of souls which predominated in the book was combined with an attempt to classify the emotions and to analyze them in their minutest detail until they could all be brought down to a common denominator. This pedantry was quite common in German romanticism. One critic has said about Schlegel and his book that there is nothing worse than the pedant who wants to play the lover.

Neither Goethe, when he wrote his *Sorrows of the Young Werther* (1774), nor Wilhelm Heinrich Wackenroder meant to write a manifesto or program; nevertheless, the themes which they presented in their novels were treated as such by the Romantics. Wackenroder wrote of a hero who was ruined by his defiance of convention. More important as a model for the Romantics was Goethe's Werther. Here was the absorbing story of a young man who greatly wanted freedom in order to fulfill himself, yet one whom society constantly misunderstood. Werther was indeed a futile and pathetic figure in society's eyes, but he knew his own greatness through his inner feelings and emotions. He was ruined not only by conventional society but also by the very strength of his passions which were expressed in pure love for a girl who rejected him. Society and his emotions drove him to suicide—a suicide which moved generations of readers. Though this was a protest against convention, it was not as explicitly defiant as Hugo's. Instead, the Romantics learned from Werther that the romantic hero must inevitably expect to be misunderstood by society.

A further lesson in the book which had general romantic acceptance was that only through suffering could a person really deepen his sensibility, his emotional experience. It was no coincidence that romantic heroines usually suffered greatly. This could lead to excess, as when Charlotte Stieglitz stabbed herself in order that her husband might become a better poet through this sad experience. Unfortunately, his poetry did not improve. The emphasis on suffering led to the Romantics' preference for fragile heroines who suffered illness, usually consumption. One is at once reminded of Mimi and Violetta,

Puccini's and Verdi's heroines whose death through tuberculosis has preoccupied many an opera-goer. Tuberculosis enabled the dramatist to show the emotional greatness of his heroine through long drawn-out suffering, but it must not be forgotten that tuberculosis was, in fact, a widespread disease of which everyone had knowledge and which was usually fatal. Its literary attraction lasted until Thomas Mann's *Magic Mountain* (1924). An analysis of English literature in the first part of the nineteenth century has shown that a heroine who lived beyond twenty-three was a rarity; past thirty, an impossibility. This kind of protest introduced a macabre note into romanticism far from the gay defiance of the men at *Hernani*. The revolt against convention took these various paths and each added something to the movement as a whole.

The emphasis on feeling implicit in the poetry of life can then be dissected into these various parts: a correspondence between humanity and nature into which an emotional view of Christianity could be integrated, a vision of the Middle Ages as part of a renewed consciousness of history, and the urge to rebel against conventions. All of these elements functioned apart from one another or in any variety of combinations. Thus Sarah Flower Adams was the author of both a long ballad about the medieval King Edward I and of the famous hymn "Nearer my God to Thee." Romantics had in common a more general habit of mind which stressed the inner man at the expense of the outward realities of the world and which condemned both bourgeois ways of life and the new industrial society which threatened to drown the soul.

To these facets of the romantic mood must be added the worship of originality and genius. This was a logical consequence of that individualism which we know was inherent in the whole of the romantic mood. The essence of this worship was a concept of the heroic which had been stressed in a special manner by the storm and stress writers at Weimar. Both Schiller and Goethe shared a concept of the heroic which is important in an understanding of the romantic worship of genius. The kind of self-satisfied optimism and confidence the Enlightenment displayed was alien to the romantic concept of genius as an inherent quality in the individual. Genius could no longer proudly and confidently assert that "our century has left no problems unsolved."

Originality and genius could not be bound by human conventions; at the very least such conventions could not stand in the way of the self-fulfillment of a man who had these qualities. Goethe's Goetz von Berlichingen, who was such a genius, died against the law and not with it; he defied all the world. Neither he nor Schiller was interested in the effect of social class or environment upon their characters. The storm and stress school believed that genius developed out of the inner nature of the individual and was not related to external circumstances. Goetz was in tune with nature, but nature in romanticism after all stood for more than mere environment. In his dying words, "Almighty God, how good do I feel under your sky, how free!" Goetz gave full testimony that his genius was in tune with nature and that, at the same time, society had to be defied.

The romantic stress on the development of personality meant that the genius was he who had attained the free development of his personality and had developed his emotional capacity to the fullest extent. Goethe's Faust (1808) was driven forward by his insatiable passions, by his "love for life." What a contrast between him and the pedant Wagner who lived by a system of knowledge. The devil, Mephistopheles, used Wagner's own system to demonstrate that by a system one could prove anything; that is, that all systems were nonsense. Faust was also a warning—until he met pure love and pure feeling in Margaret his own feelings were inconstant, fickle, and ephemeral. Mephistopheles was not a medieval devil but a cynical and superficial man of the world. Faust delivered himself to shallowness of feeling by fighting nature rather than working in correspondence with it. Margaret saved him from the devil by her deep and genuine passion which entailed not shallow enjoyment but silent suffering. This was the way that personality had to be developed, not through the easy temptations of a Wagner or a Mephistopheles.

Goetz was a man of deep passion. He was also a man of action. Side by side with the man of action was the poetic genius who was passive toward the outside world. The *Sorrows of the Young Werther* was a monument to this type of romantic hero. Both Goetz and Werther represented one extreme of the contrast which Goethe made in his *Torquato Tasso* between poetry and the world, between man's nature as cultivated by poetry and man's nature made "cold" and directed by politics. Goetz von Berlichingen and Schiller's robbers were active in the world, but they were poets in the sense that the development of their personalities sprang from an emotional impulse opposed to rational systems and to society. Because they were not shallow but were firm in their passions, they were the prototype of the romantic genius. Success was not the hallmark of this genius, for he was usually a romantic failure, a marked contrast to the heroes of Samuel Smiles's *Self Help* (1859) or Thomas Hughes's *Tom Brown* (1857), which symbolized the kind of practical bourgeois morality of the century.

It was in England, and not in Germany or France, that these romantic features combined with realism in order to form an image of the genius which might lead not to romantic failure but to a program for the future. Thomas Carlyle (1795–1881) popularized a hero who strove to develop his personality and whose impetus came forth from within himself alone. But this hero did not destroy himself by ineffectual protests against society; he changed society instead. In *Past and Present* (1843) contemporary society was rejected. The aristocracy was idle and worthless, the middle classes worshipped the god of mammon, and the working classes were merely a "swarmery"—a gathering of people in swarms. Carlyle's vision of the Middle Ages was not a nostalgia for the past but a program for the future. His rejection of all these segments of society was not an acceptance of defeat, because Carlyle, unlike the Continental Romantics, accepted the Industrial Revolution which had progressed much further in England than elsewhere.

This acceptance of the new industrial age turned the image of the romantic genius toward the emphasis on power. The industrial landscape became as impotrant in Carlyle's thought as unspoilt nature. People had to be in harmony with both. To him the sound of Manchester waking up at five in the morning was as "sublime as Niagara" with "the rushing off of its thousands of mills, like the boom of an Atlantic tide, ten thousand times ten thousand spindles all set humming there." The images of industrial society were likened to the romantic images of nature, but what was stressed was the element of power, not only the wild natural power of the Niagara but the tamed industrial power of Manchester. That latter power brought with it social and economic problems of which Carlyle, unlike most of his contemporary Romantics, was well aware. The solution to these problems was, according to Carlyle, not social and economic, but possible only through the building of men's characters. Here he seemed to be at one with the Liberals; however, his concept of the character needed to control human power was not a liberal one. It was both romantic and centered upon the genius or hero.

Thinking that the romantic ideal of medieval chivalry could help, he wrote about the noble chivalry of labor in which mill owners, united with their workers, would sally forth and subdue nature. He was not alone in this thought. At the same time a Bavarian deputy put forth the same solution for the economic problems of his native land. The vision of the Middle Ages, they thought, could be successfully applied to industrial ills. If the poetry of life expressed the essential nature of man, then surely it could be applied to all problems. To do this, Carlyle thought the genius as leader must solve the dilemmas of the times. This genius with a strong romantic component was scornful of logic or intellectual pursuits and was determined solely to follow nature's laws. Carlyle enjoined upon the leader a part of the liberal morality of his time by declaring that he had to be active and share the gospel of work. The reason for this was linked to the predominant place that power held in Carlyle's view of the hero.

Not only did he admire the romantic power of Manchester, he also felt that the laborer and employer should, together, conquer nature as well as society by force. Herein lay the fulfillment of Carlyle's hero. The drive for success and the ruthlessness of Carlyle's hero contrasted with the poetry of Werther and the passionate strength of Goetz. Carlyle's emphasis on power became a worship of force. He thought in 1842 that if the Chinese refused to trade, England should argue in "cannon shot" and convince them that they ought to trade. The trade which in this instance the Chinese refused to carry on was the opium trade. The hero as a conqueror had to rid himself of emotional uncertainties, since he must not possess a tortured romantic soul. Carlyle was much impressed with Goethe's thought, put forth in his *Wilhelm Meister,* that work could overcome doubt and insecurity. His heroes were strong, silent men who had no doubts as they set out to lead others in fighting dragons, as Carlyle put it, be they mystical, industrial, or human.

The British age in which Carlyle lived was not only the age of industrialism but of imperialism as well. His geniuses accepted the responsibility for leadership in both. The same conditions hardly obtained on the Continent where the romantic worship of genius did not end up as the worship of John Bull—an image first used by Carlyle himself. To be sure, Stendhal in the *Red and the Black* also pointed to a hero who placed his coldness, egotism, and rationality in the service of his passions. In the end, however, Sorel, through his passions, overcame his selfish nature and made a personal sacrifice. John Bull did not make sacrifices for any personal reason, let alone for women; instead he unselfishly served the nation as a whole. Serving the nation, he had disciplined his passions, or rather channeled them, toward the gospel of work and worship of force. Nevertheless, it was still from his channeled emotions that he derived his strength, and it was still the genius who was admired. Thus, through the romantic ideal of genius, the poetry of life became, with Carlyle, transformed into a doctrine of industrial and imperial progress.

The dissection of the romantic poetry of life has made it possible to see some of the implications of the romantic mood and to gauge something of the cultural atmosphere which romanticism introduced into European thought. The ideal of genius emphasized once more some of the common ingredients of romanticism. To be sure, one could be romantic without worshipping genius, without turning to Christianity or even to the Middle Ages, yet most Romantics partook of some of these ingredients. Moreover, romanticism itself began to stress the need for unity which comprised all of life and art. After all, the individual could not artificially divide his emotions; as we have seen, nature itself was thought to be an inextricable part of these emotions. Romantic unity became a phrase associated with the poetry of life. Chateaubriand, for example, believed in a unified, divine, and emotionally-conceived cosmos, an ideal which will be dealt with in a later chapter. This belief in unity was important for the creation of new art forms—art forms which, in turn, illuminate the concept of romantic unity.

The urge to unity led to the combination of poetry with music—two art forms Romantics thought especially valuable for their outlook upon life. Witness the popularity of the "Lied" which represented such a combination. There were people in the eighteenth century who wanted to go beyond the Italian aria form, which they regarded as artificial to nature. In this context nature meant emphasis upon the actual words of the poem, a naturalness which contrasted with the artificiality of the Italian style. From his first "Lied" (1814) Franz Schubert gave this art form its character. Music and poetry were embraced in one unity of mood and emotion. At the same time the ballad set to music began a trend which led to the folk music of modern times.

The importance of music was further underlined by the growth of the symphonic poem. Berlioz felt that a program was unnecessary for his symphonies since the music itself would tell its tale through playing on the emotions of the listener; indeed, music would serve as a unifying device for the emotions just as Hugo thought that drama would do the same thing. In order to strengthen this view of symphonic music Berlioz organized the musical subject in his *Romeo and Juliet Symphony* (1847) around a single theme, at once musical and dramatic, which he called an *idée fixe*. In Germany Karl Maria von Weber had already adopted such an idea as the *leitmotif*. This basic concept was retained in the making of the new operatic form, the music drama.

The music drama was the climax of the romantic idea of unity. It united the text, the music, and the visual element. No longer, as in the *opera buffa*, did the spoken word stand side by side with arias. They were now one, accompanied by leitmotifs to characterize a personality or to give unity to a whole emotional experience. It is significant that such operas, especially early in the century, tended to stress the bizarre as well as the usual romantic images. Marschner called one of his operas the *Vampire*. Karl Maria von Weber loved themes which induced wonder and stupefaction. Wagner was not the first to combine all this with a romantic realism. In Weber's *Freischuetz* (1821) the baying of wolves was heard, thus making the wolf's glen as realistic as possible. For the theoretical formulation of the new music drama it is well, however, to cite its most famous practitioner. Wagner's *Drama of the Future* (1849) stressed the unity of content which such drama must have. Unity of content was obtained through the unity of the emotions, through the totality of the poetry of life. Wagner felt that separately the poet and the musician could not accomplish much. "Both [in that case] had to turn from feeling to reason; the poet to make clear an incompletely aroused emotion, the musician to apologise for an emotion aroused in vain." Genius was a prerequisite for the poet and the musician who would work together, for only a genius could, out of the fullness of the personality, make such a drama meaningful. Wagner rejected frivolity since the action had to be worthy of the poetry as well as of the music. To write music for ballets, fireworks, and intrigues of love he considered unworthy; what was needed was complete, heartfelt, and passionate action.

Most of the romantic operatic composers of the century would have agreed with this, though the ballet maintained itself on the operatic stage, especially in Paris. Such men contrasted their aims with that of the Italian school. For Berlioz, Rossini was the "devil," geared to sensory effect and external form, "perpetually laughing." He broke off his studies in Rome because he felt Italian music had nothing to give him, and it was typical that the Roman landscape was much more important to him than Roman opera. The modern poet Franz Werfel cites Verdi and Wagner as the two giants of the two different operatic traditions of the nineteenth century; however, in Verdi the old Italian tradition was already greatly modified in favor of the new operatic concept of the century. It was from a new impressionistic school, represented by Debussy, that the challenge to Wagner was to come. Despite all its seriousness of purpose, the very romantic unity of the new music drama tended, by Wagner's time, to make it good entertainment rather than an instrument of serious emotional regeneration. The visual realities of the floating Rhine maidens and of Bruenhilde surrounded by fire certainly furthered the tendency toward the spectacular. Sight had to be integrated with poetry and with music; thus, all the senses could join in a complete emotional experience.

Romanticism stimulated new art forms produced by the idea of unity inherent in the poetry of life. Yet the Romantics, in spite of their concentration on their inner self, lived in society. There was no escape from reality into the shelter of one's soul. Every cultural movement, however much it thinks of itself as separated from the troubled world, *affects it and is affected by it*. Romanticism had an immediate effect upon religious and political ideas, and its long-range effect was to touch social thought as well. The social implications were not to occur until the end of the century, however, when romanticism was to become dominant once again. Out of this movement, with its antirational and anti-industrial components, was to come a revolutionary impetus directed against existing conditions: a doctrine of hope for those who saw themselves disenfranchised or who saw their power slipping from their hands. The "new romanticism" of the twentieth century was the romantic ideal transmitted from one age to another. But this effect of romanticism was to come at the end of the century, not at the beginning. Yet the mention of it here can serve to show the continued importance of the romantic impetus. At the beginning of the nineteenth century, however, it was chiefly religion and politics that felt the impact of romanticism.

46

# CHAPTER THREE

# *Romanticism:*
# *Religion and Politics*

T HE FIRST part of the nineteenth century was an age of several religious revivals. Evangelical religion was conceived as both practical (applied to this world and its problems) and emotional (through its conversion experience which led to a piety of the heart). The "Christian Revival Association" of William Booth (1859) and his "conversion shop" in the slums of London's East End symbolized the double aspect of this evangelical impetus. The Salvation Army was militantly Protestant in that it cared nothing for church tradition or liturgy and it concentrated instead on the "coming to Christ" of individuals who would in this way contribute to the solution of the social problems of their time. The other kind of religious revival was quite different. It, too, stressed the "emotion of the heart," but it did not attempt to connect this with social concerns in the age of industrialization. Instead, this revival which stressed the "beauty of Christianity" and the vision of historic truth which Christianity represented concentrated upon liturgy and church tradition. The results were neither "conversion shops" in the East End of London nor a Salvation Army, but the refounding of monastic orders within the Anglican communion and the religious art of the pre-Raphaelites like J. E. Millais (1829–96) or Dante Gabriel Rosetti (1828–82).

The relation of this second religious revival with romanticism was obvious and close. For some Romantics, nature, which stimulated human sentiment, was inexorably linked to the Christian and divine. For others, the religious, Christian sentiment came to dominate and even to partially eclipse the primacy of nature. Wackenroder's *Heartfelt Outpourings of an Art Loving Monk* (1797) derived the love of art from the stimulus of religion. Wackenroder felt that theorists and systematizers could never understand an artist like Raphael whose art worked in secret ways. Raphael could not paint his Madonnas until they came to him in a vision, though he had adored the Virgin Mary since his youth. Art, detached from the physical and rational being of the artist, came to the artist as an expression of a higher religious force. The artist had to be detached from the world in order to be receptive to art. Here the revolt against convention appeared strongly once more. A musician who had overcome parental opposition to his art found that very art growing sour and shallow as he became a success in the world. Genius had to be misunderstood otherwise it would falter and die. Art had to be related not to the world around it but to divine inspiration.

Wackenroder, typically enough, preferred church music. Before the music began he was full of earthly trivialities, but then it seemed to him that heaven had come down to earth as "he envisaged clearly during many of the songs in praise of God, King David dancing around the ark." His feelings were inspired by music rather than nature—religious music which was a transmission of the divine. This was similar to what Chateaubriand had to say about church bells: "It is on the face of it a rather marvellous thing to have found a way, by a single stroke of the hammer, to cause a thousand hearts to feel the same sentiment in a given minute."

The most famous book which, on the Continent, came to typify this religious revival was Chateaubriand's *Genius of Christianity* (1802). An apologia for Christianity against a background of Christianity's partial rejection by both the Enlightenment and the French Revolution, it was a defense based upon neither logic, reason, nor practicality. Chateaubriand wanted to get away from the "babble of science and reason" in order to explain those eternal mysteries of life which science had not been able to analyze. Most important were the mysterious things, those matters like love and friendship which agitate the human soul in a confused manner. Chateaubriand thought these emotional manifestations were so divine that he went to the then-new science of anthropology to establish their divinity. The first people of Asia, he proclaimed, talked about the mysteries of love and friendship only in symbols, so awesome was the reality of love to these primitives. But why was Christianity supreme? Because it alone could explain the essence of humanity; redemption could give an explanation for this as science never could. The human aptitude

48

for pain and anguish was clarified by the doctrine of original sin. For Chateaubriand, Christ was the harmonizing agent between the human and the divine. Now this was nothing unusual, for it was a common theological doctrine, but Chateaubriand related this doctrine in a special way to the concept of romantic unity. Christianity not only explained the emotional aspect of people, it also drew the whole cosmos into an emotional whole.

For Chateaubriand all things were interrelated, just as in the new music drama all arts had to cooperate in order to produce a unity of feeling. Christ reflected a harmony between God and humanity which was also reflected in nature. When he wrote about the church bells he went on to link the effect they produced with the effect produced by winds, seas, volcanoes, and the voice of a whole people. All these caused a thousand hearts to feel the sentiment, the same unity of the emotions. This was what Chateaubriand called the sublime and the beautiful. "There is one God, the grasses of the valleys and the trees of the mountains bless him, the elephant salutes him at the dawn of day, the birds sing in the foliage, the ocean declares his immensity." Though romantic religion had a strong element of pantheism in it, Chateaubriand was not a pantheist. He believed that Christianity was reflected in a divine institution which operated on earth, the Catholic church.

Catholicism was defended not on historical or even theological grounds, but because it reflected the harmony of all things. From the center at Rome branched out, in an orderly manner, missions, bishops, and the other services of the church which extended over the whole earth. Moreover, its liturgy contained the divine mysteries which, together with its centralized organization, reflected the cosmos which was Christian. Protestantism in contrast was chaos. It must be clear why Chateaubriand subtitled the book the *Beauty of Christianity,* for its truth was sublime by the standards of romanticism. From this vantage point Chateaubriand criticized classical tragedy. The grief felt by Gluck's Iphegenia was not true grief, since she grieved only for herself and not for all the world. Here the individualism, the inner development of character which Madame de Staël praised, was not enough. It had to be extended to the larger concern of a unified, a divine, and an emotionally-conceived cosmos. One's own emotional life had to be directly related to the emotional content of all of Christianity. Such a view became popular since it fitted in with the idea, already discussed, that only serious matters are worth treating in art. Generations of young men and women thought that they were suffering from the *Weltschmerz* or *mal du monde,* which gave to a suffering genius an importance that made the suffering more worthwhile and probably more enjoyable.

Chateaubriand's justification of Catholicism was not an isolated phenomenon. Romanticism had a preference for this form of Christianity. It fitted in not only with the kind of ideology which Chateaubriand put forward, but

*suffering ... happy about it.*

also with the Romantics' Gothic vision of history. On the Continent the revival of Catholicism was also stimulated by conservative thought. As an outward sign of this, the Jesuits were reestablished by the Papacy in 1814. In England the Catholic revival brought about a deep crisis in the Anglican State Church. Not only had Anglicanism suffered from the fact that its high offices were distributed on political rather than a religious basis, but also from the fact that when a revival did come about it was led by the sober Evangelicals. To many, the Church seemed committed, therefore, to a religious approach which the Romantics and their followers strongly condemned.

The movement which started at Oxford tried to right this emphasis in the Church and to push Anglicanism in a more Catholic direction. In a series of tracts Hurrell Froude (1803–36) attempted to stress the liturgy of the Church, its tie with the age of the apostles through history, and the mysteries which such a vision of history implied. Historically, the Anglican Church had both a Catholic and a Protestant tradition. It was the preponderance of the latter which Froude wanted to destroy; but to most Anglicans, especially those in authority, the call for a restoration of holy water, of crucifixes, and the emphasis on the apostolic succession of bishops smacked of pseudo-Catholicism. John Henry Newman (1801–90), who soon began to collaborate with Froude, caused the greatest stir with his Tract 90, for in it he attempted to interpret the Elizabethan Thirty-nine Articles in a Catholic direction. He denied that the Lutheran concept of the justification of man by faith alone was the cardinal doctrine of Christianity. He called for a vision of the history of the church in his statement, "the church of the twelfth century must be the church of the nineteenth." Once this was said, there had to be a revival of medieval theology and, beyond that, an emphasis on the primitive church as interpreted by this theology. For Newman the church so defined implied an interplay of authority and private judgment, though in the last resort the human condition was a profound mystery absolutely beyond human solution. The true explanation of this mystery lay in the Catholic Church. Newman attempted to unify Anglicanism and Catholicism, because he, too, was attracted to the ideal of unity, but the attempt was bound to fail since the Anglican Church was at that very time on the defensive against a newly-emancipated Catholicism.

Newman left the Church and became a Catholic, but others remained. The Oxford movement or the Tractarian movement, as it is sometimes called, was led by Edward Pusey (1800–1882) and John Keble (1792–1866). In the end, they did achieve some measure of success. A high Church wing from then on was a part of Anglicanism, opposing the Evangelical low Church. The Oxford movement was more than just romantic religion. Those involved in it came to their views through a thorough study of the primitive and medieval church. Newman especially made an attempt in his famous *Apologia* (1865) to present his point of view logically and rationally rather than emotionally. Yet they shared an atmosphere with the Romantics—the recognition and validity of mysteries which were divine, the strong vision of history (especially medieval history) and the expression of their religious passions in emotional poetry. However much the movement founded its emphasis on liturgy, on Christian harmony, and on logical argument, it still fitted in with the religious urges of the Romantics. It was quite true that Newman based religion on intellectual rather than emotional premises, but it was equally true that the result of his religion approximated the goals of the romantic religious revival everywhere. They, too, were reacting against the Enlightenment as well as against evangelicalism. Newman thought theological training better for the mind than scientific training. While he did not discount science, as Chateaubriand did, he believed that in contrast to religion its results were so uncertain that the Christian should wait for further developments before committing himself to science.

The religious revival did not have a unifying influence on politics. The common saying that Catholicism and reaction went hand in hand in the early part of the century cannot be maintained. Chateaubriand supported the French revolution of 1830 and John Henry Newman, inasmuch as he cared at all for politics, was conservative only in his theological views. Conservatives like Joseph de Maistre (1753–1821) did use these religious ideas to support their opposition to everything liberal, but on the other hand, Lamennais (1782–1854) used them in an attempt to tie Catholicism to progress. If the Church came to support conservative movements and suppressed Lamennais's attempts at a Catholic liberalism, this was due to the policy of the papacy, not to the religious revival which the Italian popes scarcely understood. It was significant that the Church did not know what to do with Newman once he had been converted. He had to wait until the very end of his life for a cardinal's hat and for recognition of his contribution to the Catholic awakening.

Though the religious revival was strongest in Catholicism, Protestantism was also affected. It is difficult, however, to disentangle the romantic impetus from the eighteenth-century pietism which carried over into the nineteenth century. The Prussian Friedrich Schleiermacher combined both elements. His important *Speeches on Religion* (1799), a synthesis of romantic idealist philosophy and German pietism, posited religion as a matter of inward sentiment whose nature was not determined by action or by human thought but solely through feeling. The decisive element in this feeling was the mystical religious experience. Like Chateaubriand, he tied such religious experience to the contemplation of the whole universe. Again, the concept of unity was stressed, but unlike Chateaubriand's, Schleiermacher's unity was typified not by a centralized church but by individual piety sunk in the majesty of the cosmos to which it corresponded. Every man was a priest; dogmas and confessions of faith were purely secondary. In his speeches Schleiermacher did not put Christ into the center of things. Though Christianity was the most sublime of religions, it was possible that another religion might replace it. His pietism and romanticism had a pantheistic flavor at this stage.

He did not escape, in the end, the general Christ-centeredness of this revival. It was, after all, a revival of Christianity after the challenge of the Enlightenment. In his later work he accented Christ the Savior in opposition to rationalism, but he did this in tune with his general concept of piety. Christ's role as a Savior was not bound to his resurrection or to any dogma; instead, He exemplified the lifting of humanity into a consciousness of God. This consciousness of God was necessary for any religious experience, for any correspondence between the individual and the cosmos, for true feeling could only come through Christ; therefore, the only true religious sentiment could be Christian sentiment.

Looking at both this Protestant and the Catholic religious impetus, it must be clear that feeling and sentiment, the very essence of the romantic mood, became firmly linked with Christianity. No non-Christian could have real feeling. There were many Romantics who disagreed and substituted artistic appreciation or the love of nature for outward signs of inward sentiment, but the Christian emphasis had two consequences of some importance. Conversion to Christianity became the rule among those of the now emancipated Jewish middle classes who did much to further romanticism in Germany. Both Rachel Levin (1771–1833) and Henriette Herz (1764–1847), whose salons dominated the movement in Berlin, were converted, as was Felix Mendelssohn, the composer. Secondly, the concept, so important in later racial thought, of the non-Christian, especially the Jew, as devoid of true feeling got its impetus here. In an increasing volume of literature, both novels and plays, the image of the Jew as materialistic was presented to the public. The growing stream of German nationalism made good use of this image. A telling contrast could be drawn between the German with true feeling and the Jew with none. In the course of time the Christian rationale for this was dropped and a nationalist ideology substituted, but once true feeling was linked to one kind of ideological supposition, it was easy to link it to another and to make the contrast accordingly.

This substitution of Germanism for Christianity or art or nature as the only basis for true sentiment was already beginning when Chateaubriand and Schleiermacher wrote their works. It led to the link between romanticism and politics, a connection which existed on this more subtle level rather than to the association of Romantics with one or the other political movements of the times. Romantics were found in all political parties.

*52*

Some patterns do emerge, however, from the relationship between romanticism and politics. In France after the Revolution and during the first years of the Bourbon restoration, romanticism was closely tied to monarchism and the Catholic church. This was hardly surprising, for the Revolution stood for that rationalism and scepticism which Romantics abhorred, while king and pope fitted in with the romantic vision of the Middle Ages. Chateaubriand was at first an enthusiastic supporter of the Restoration, and Conservatives like De Maistre built their theories upon medieval foundations closely related to romanticism. Victor Hugo wrote, in 1824, that the new literature was an expression of a monarchical and religious society. But this society spurned the Romantics. Louis XVIII (1815–24) furthered the classicism which he remembered from pre-Revolutionary days, and the French Academy issued a proclamation against the "romantic sect." Moreover, the regime of Charles X (1824–30) seemed to further a schematic and sterile monarchism in the name of order. Both Lamennais and Chateaubriand suffered persecution—the romantic mood had too many revolutionary implications. To be sure, such implications were directed primarily against literary styles and social conventions, but they might branch out from this and endanger order.

The result of the restored monarchy's opposition to romanticism was the development of precisely those revolutionary implications it had feared—revolutionary inasmuch as they came to be directed against the existing political as well as literary order. French Romantics continued to repudiate the French Revolution but they now also repudiated the *ancien régime.* Chateaubriand worked for a revolution which came about in 1830 and Lamennais began to write about the necessity of disentangling Catholicism from the restored monarchy. Hugo, who had praised the Catholic and monarchical regime in 1824, now wrote in his preface to *Hernani:* "Romanticism is Liberalism in Literature. Literary Liberalism is not less popular than political Liberalism. Liberty in Art and freedom in society are identical goals. ... " By 1827 the Romantics had broken their ties with the Bourbons and allied themselves with the liberal camp. The Greek war of liberation from the Turks (1832) stirred the Romantics in France as it did those of England. For Chateaubriand a defense of the Greeks meant at the same time a defense of freedom and Christianity, though unlike Lord Byron he did not rush into a personal involvement with the cause. What happened in France is a good example of romanticism pushing in a liberal direction. Men like Hugo and Lamennais remained consistent voices for liberalism in the Europe of their age.

But the conservative impetus also continued. In England it was to lead a conversatism which was less rigid than that of De Maistre or De Bonald (1754–1840). The "Tory Democracy" of Benjamin Disraeli (1804–81) and his revitalized Conservative party showed a real concern for the social welfare of the people. Here also a vision of the Middle Ages predominated—a romanticized picture of the relationship of rulers and ruled. The nobility must once more take upon itself the role of leadership in order to improve the lot of the common people. The paternalism of the Lord of the Manor toward his tenants was to be generalized into a social consciousness for political leadership. Social reform, however, should never blur class lines or the necessary aristocratic leadership principle. "The people are not strong, the people can never be strong," Disraeli wrote at a time when the Chartist movement seemed to have failed.

This view of the people, however, was based not so much on any immediate cause as upon a nostalgic vision of the past—the medieval Arcadia of the Romantics. Tory democracy did not stand still in the new age; it tried to apply the vision of the past to the problems of industrial England. Social reform, within definite limits, and the knights of Sir Walter Scott transformed into an active aristocracy—these were Disraeli's goals. After all, the knights of old had not only been charitable toward the weak; they had protected them as well, and Tory leadership must imitate their example in modern politics. It is no wonder that Disraeli's attitudes toward representative government were ambivalent. Romanticism, in so far as it was linked to conservatism, tended to further ideas of government which stood outside the tradition of parliaments. It pointed backwards to what was considered the "harmonious" state of the Middle Ages where no shoddy politics and venial political parties divided the people. Thus Conservatives on the Continent took up the example of the medieval guilds where both masters and journeymen as well as apprentices had been a part of a harmonious whole. From this they envisaged a nation made up of professional and industrial guilds, all regulating themselves and all based on the cooperation of the people within them, whether employers or employees. This ideal will be discussed at greater length in the chapter on conservatism, but no account of romanticism would be complete without mentioning this phenomenon. It is one of the most important contributions of romanticism to politics, for it provided an alternative, neither parliamentarian nor Marxist, to the problem of the state's organization.

If this concept of corporatism was one of the most important contributions of romanticism to politics, there was another. Romanticism gave great impetus to nationalism. In this guise it could penetrate the politics of many divergent political parties. The connection between romanticism and nationalism is best illustrated in Germany where it was to dominate both politics and thought. It produced a type of romantic thought quite different from that which came about in France at the same time. The Frenchman Lamennais, who called himself an anti-materialist, placed the soul above the body of the individual and the soul of peoples above their material organization. With that, the Germans would have agreed. But from these premises Lamennais pleaded not for an exclusive national "soul" nor for return to the vistas of a bygone age; instead, the superiority of the soul of a people meant to him the freedom of the individual spirit, the equality of the rights of each person, and the general fraternity of all peoples. Lamennais wrote in the tradition of Rousseau and of the Jacobins; there was no tradition which could lead to such thought in Germany. The stress in individual freedom which was inherent in romantic expression found an outlet in France and England which were both territorially united nations. But neither German Liberals nor German Romantics could ignore the national problem which their people faced. Germany had to be concerned with her own unity and independence, and those interested in German politics had little time to fight for the independence of others.

Any discussion of the impact of romanticism on German politics must begin with a literary movement. The *Boys' Magic Horn* (1806–8), a collection of folk ballads similar to Percy's *Reliques* in England, expressed in poetic form the feeling of a whole people. These ballads could be a means of historic self-identification in a nation which was divided and living under the shadow of French predominance. Like a similar collection made by Johann Gottfried von Herder (1744–1803), these songs contained no judgment of the superiority of one people's emotional make-up over another; however, the German element was coming to the fore.

Grimm's *Fairy Tales* (1812–14) provided a good example of this new feeling. The brothers Grimm thought at first of their fairy tales as mere extensions of the kind of work which Arnim and Brentano had tried to do in the *Boys' Magic Horn*. Nevertheless, by 1812 they began to invest their tales with a definite national purpose. The Grimm brothers now saw in these simple tales a continuation of the old and glorious German epics, especially the *Niebelungenlied*. Their work began to symbolize the continuity of German history and became a reminder of a more glorious past rather than the present Napoleonic occupation. Snow White and the Seven Dwarfs, an old Hessian folk tale, symbolized in the Grimm brothers' eyes the goddess Snaefried over whose coffin Haraldur had held his vigil. The hunter who appeared in several of the fairy tales was nothing but a reincarnation of the ancient German hero Siegfried. The deeper significance of their interpretation lay in the fact that the Grimm brothers saw the symbolism which they had created as proof that these folk tales were a genuine and spontaneous tradition which was uniquely German. It was only a step to hold that such folk memories were the most typical, because they were an uninterrupted flow of the national genius and that those who did not share them were foreigners who must be excluded.

It was Friedrich von Schlegel (1772–1829) who gave clear expression to the national implications of such ideas. He claimed that national memories, which he equated with the spirit or poetry of a people, were the key to historic survival. Only those peoples who have "great national memories" have survived in history. "History is the self-consciousness of a nation." Self-consciousness in Germany was defined as the folk spirit, as shared national memories, and as poetry. What a different outlook from Lamennais's cry, "make your choice between the Middle Ages and the nineteenth century"! For Germans the choice was made. When young students clamored for the tyrant's blood, it was not the rulers of the German states which they were attacking, but Charlemagne who had defeated and slaughtered the ancient Saxons. Lamennais continued, "recognize the revolution as your mother." But unlike the Frenchman, the Germans had no revolution to recognize. When the student associations staged a rally for freedom, they chose the Wartburg castle of Luther because of its historic and German association.

As part of the romantic mood, the French Revolution appealed to those who wanted freedom. The question arose in many of the best minds at the beginning of the century of how national self-consciousness, defined in romantic terms, could be combined with the longing for freedom. How could the individual retain individualism and yet be integrated with the historic *Volk?* Johann Gottlieb Fichte (1762–1814) illustrated what was happening to this plagued generation. Though the idea of freedom never left him throughout his life, he also desired to see in people a perfect unity of thought and action, for it seemed to him that the eighteenth century had created a gap between thought and action which had to be closed. He saw a dichotomy between what people wanted and what they achieved, not only in the eighteenth-century philosophies but also in the French Revolution. He had welcomed the Revolution with high hopes and had defended the manifestoes of the Revolutionaries, only to see that Revolution turn into oppression in his native land. Analyzing his ideal and looking at the actuality around him, he came to the conclusion that self-realization was possible only through unity and integration.

Fichte then began to call for "culture toward freedom" which could unite in a complete fashion human will and reason, human action and thought. In making this call, however, he found that he had to redefine the idea of freedom itself. His famous Speeches to the German Nation of 1807–8 gave that redefinition even while Berlin, where he was speaking, was under French domination. He stated that unity of thought and action could be achieved only within that nation which was a valid historic community, defined in terms of the literary movement discussed. Within the unity of this community, the highest individual freedom could be found, not the individualized freedom of sentiment and emotion but the freedom found through group integration. This group was defined in the terms of the *Volk*. People had to be integrated with the national memories and the poetry of the *Volk*. Since he defined freedom as integration into the *Volk* memories, Fichte had to deny that other nations could form a valid group as a basis for freedom because he claimed that only the Germans had true national memories, "only the German has character." Fichte came to the conclusion that individuals must be cemented into the national group through education which would obliterate the individual will of the student and integrate it into a higher loyalty and freedom. No class of the population could stand apart from this process of integration. He rejected the whole idea of a class structure and even praised the simple medieval economic system.

Fichte's insistence upon the integration of all classes was strengthened by his concern about the German middle class. This concern was to preoccupy many other German Nationalists, for the German middle classes, like the middle and industrial classes throughout Europe, had connections beyond the boundaries of the nation. Ambitious and restless, they searched for self-fulfillment through economic and social power. This was reflected in the bourgeois liberal ideology of self-advancement. Fichte saw this class as a disruptive element in the nation which was defined as the organic, creative unit of self-fulfillment. His concern for the "integration of the burgher and nation" was accentuated in all his later writings. In this he was not alone. One of the first bourgeoisie-centered novels, Hacklaender's *Wandel und Handel* (1850), painted the frightening picture of a merchant who was driven to insanity through the confusions of foreign travel. Much later than Fichte, Gustav Freytag in his *Debit and Credit* (1855) warned the middle classes to live a steady and nationally-rooted life.

The sociological ideas of Wilhelm Heinrich Riehl (1823–97) were also preoccupied with this problem. He thought that the material and moral power of the middle classes posed a danger for the nation because, unlike the peasant and the nobility, they were in constant motion and lived by competition, while stability and harmony were of the essence in the preservation of a nation. Riehl extolled the settled peasantry and saw in the aristocracy a "peasantry on a higher level." Both were close to the roots of the *Volk* through their unchanging customs. The romantic worship of nature became a romantic worship of those who lived closest to it, and this attitude fused with a longing for security in an age of rapid change. What a contrast there is in Riehl's sociology and the sober voice of the economist Nassau William Senior from across the Channel! Senior proposed that agriculture be treated

like industry, that large nationally-run units take the place of what is now
called the family farm. The economist spoke from the vantage point of a
nation which was already the foremost industrial nation of the world; the
German sociologist, from a fear of this industrialization, combined with
romanticism. The debate continues to the present, but oddly enough it was
the worship of the peasant which penetrated deeper into the present civilization. The idea that there was something morally good about the small holding
(however uneconomical) spread to the United States as well, reinforcing the
traditions of Jeffersonian democracy. Perhaps it represented an uneasiness
about industrial civilization that is always present. In Germany the security
of the nation necessitated a clinging to the ancient customs which exemplified
the historic memories so important to all these men.

Though writers in England and France were concerned with harmony
and unity, they did not pursue the ideal of national integration. In England
liberal morality had the reverse effect. The gospel of work in the Industrial
Revolution made the great Exhibitions of Industry and Trade a mark of
national pride. Samuel Smiles's *Self Help* was the criterion of individualism
rather than works like those of Fichte and Freytag. In France the idea of
freedom never underwent a redefinition as it had in Germany, though ideas
like De Maistre's, which completely denied freedom, did have a very limited
appeal. In Germany even a devoted Liberal like Wilhelm von Humboldt
(1767–1835) came, in the end, to the conclusion that "there are only two
realities, God and the nation." At first he tried to combine individualism
with a confrontation of the national problem as Fichte had done, but he,
too, came to the realization that "man is nothing by himself except through
the force of the whole with which he tries to fuse himself." Such romanticism
swept before it the older cosmopolitan and humanitarian ideas of the last
century. The old Goethe, who still proclaimed such sentiments and who
derided the new nationalism, was as isolated a figure in Weimar as, a century
later, the old Benedetto Croce was to be an isolated figure in the new Italy.
His concept of liberal freedom was as outdated then, so it seemed, as Goethe's
was after the German wars of liberation against the French. Friedrich Ludwig
Jahn was the wave of the future. His book *Volkstum* (1810) glorified the
German *Volk* who represented the whole of humanity and whose task it was
to civilize the world by force. But the *Volk* must keep itself pure and undefiled as a race; Rome had fallen because races had mixed. Here already we
can see the learnings of this glorification of the *Volk* toward an explicit
racism. The state formed by the *Volk* would be democratic—Jahn as yet kept
representative institutions and did not push the mystical unity of the *Volk*
to the point where it superseded all representative forms of government.

The "force of the whole" was the German nation singled out by God as

58

the only valid *Volk*. Jahn organized the *Turnerschaft* to keep the people fit for the war that was coming. Significantly, the word *turnen* came from the medieval tournaments, but gymnastics were practical tasks to enable young men to be the soldiers of tomorrow. From their founding (1811) these *Turnerschaften* became centers of German nationalism; so did the *Burschenschaften* which Jahn was also instrumental in founding (1815). Students were united in them irrespective of their province or social class. Non-Germans, like the Jews, were excluded from the fraternities. These became instruments for German unity, meeting at the Wartburg in Thuringia, the constant symbol of a glorious German past. Here Luther had worked and here the old Minnesaenger had held their festivals of song. Wagner was to put this spirit on the stage in his *Die Meistersinger von Nuernberg* and in *Tannhaeuser* as well. This romantic nationalism was directed, above all, against France which had so recently occupied the country. Jahn's diatribes against that nation were violent, just as Wagner later castigated French perfidy in the last lines of the Meistersinger. This nationalism, then, was inspired by the romantic movement. It was "total" in the sense that it was not concerned with boundaries or even with blueprints for a government, but with "culture" as a whole. Jahn dressed his *Turners* in uniforms representing an age long past, symbolizing the organic *Volk* which has its own and superior way of life.

This nationalism is often described by the term of "cultural nationalism." There is much truth in that description, for it did hold that a nation was great if it was culturally supreme. But the word culture was, in this particular instance, infused with romantic meaning. It was the "German spirit" with which integration was demanded, and that spirit transcended any kind of political and economic reality. In France and England this was unnecessary because both had a very tangible and glorious immediate past but disunited Germany had experienced nothing but political disappointments: the Thirty Years' War, the French domination, the rejection of national aspirations at the Congress of Vienna, and their suppression by the reaction. In political terms, Germany had a history of failure of which the German Romantics were conscious. Furthermore, Germany was also industrially backward. By mid-century the city of London used more coal than the whole of Germany combined. This impotence was reflected in the German romantic stress upon the spirit and in Wagner's statement at the end of the century that the "German" is more interested in conserving than in gaining—"the newly acquired has only value for him when it embellishes the old." Wagner also put Siegfried on the stage to herald a new day for his people, but typically enough, a new day linked to the old.

This has been worth elucidating in some detail, for through this romantic impetus German nationalism got its particular coloring. The irrationalism

*Wagner is back and cooler than ever.*

which was to accompany its most important modern expression in National Socialism had deep roots. In the crisis after the First World War people in all nations were not averse to journeys into the wild blue yonder to escape present misery. In Germany, however, that journey was accompanied by careful appeals to German historical memories, to German rootedness, and to the German "spirit" within which the only true freedom could be found. In German fascism there was none of the ideological pragmatism of the Italian movement. On the other hand this romantic impetus in modern nationalism was not confined to Germany. In eastern Europe, where disunited peoples were also striving for unity, the Pan-Slav movement formed the ingredients of romanticism into a combination of nationalism which was similar to Germany's.

It must be pointed out that this same impetus which played into cultural nationalism had other facets which were important. A whole school of historical jurisprudence grew up typified by Friedrich Karl von Savigny (1779–1861). This school presupposed that the substance of the law was created by the whole of the nation's past, emerging from the innermost being of the nation and its history. Thus, not only the history of law was revived but also the customary law of the past. This had its nationalistic aspect in Father Jahn and the manners and dress which his disciples affected; with Savigny, the same ideology led to important scholarly accomplishments. Similarly, under the impact of the romantic-nationalist vision of history the Middle Ages were freed from the stigma of darkness and superstition and opened to serious scholarly investigation. There was, therefore, a direct connection between cultural nationalism and the rise of nineteenth-century German historical scholarship whose accomplishments held the rest of Europe in awe.

The ideal of integration with the *Volk* put forward a view of the state which was to have fateful consequences for the future. Romantic writers like Novalis (1772–1801) had defined the sublime by picturing a man sitting on a rock by the sea in tune with the immense universe which spread about him on all sides. Now the nation increasingly took the place of that universe. Here there was no place for the foreigner or for any class of the population which might disturb the rootedness of the *Volk*. Ironically, despite the concern over the disturbing element of the middle classes, it was precisely these classes which provided the setting for the ideology of integration. The romantic impetus in Germany was accompanied by an important regrouping of the social framework in which cultural activity had its setting.

In the eighteenth century cultural activity was, as it had been for centuries, centered at royal or princely courts. England was an exception to this as, after two revolutions and with greater economic prosperity, the self-conscious middle classes provided the setting and the impetus for much of the cultural activity of the country. Moreover, a foreign and increasingly unpopular dynasty could not penetrate English cultural activity. Beyond this, the interrelationship between middle class and nobility, so strong in England, made the country house together with the city of London the setting for literary and artistic work. Patrons could be found outside the circles of the royal court. In France, on the other hand, the court still tended to be the center of culture for it was here that both royal and noble patronage could be obtained. During the eighteenth century, however, with the growth of literacy among the middle classes, this was becoming increasingly untrue even there. In any case, the Revolution destroyed such patronage even though Napoleon revived it once more.

Germany, disunited as it was, presented a different kind of problem. In the eighteenth century princely patronage was almost indispensable for cultural activity. The strongest of the states, Prussia, dispensed patronage which was hardly in tune with the awakening national aspiration, for Frederick the Great furthered French culture and made French the language of his court. In another principality, however, there arose a literary renaissance which was German. Weimar became Germany's cultural capital in the midst of political disunion and dissension. Karl August, Duke of Saxe-Weimar (1775–1828), furthered the renaissance for reasons which were similar to those which had made the small principalities in Renaissance Italy stress cultural patronage. Politically, his dukedom was too weak to play any kind of role in Germany, but culturally it might be glorious. It has been said that the small dukedom was not a court with a theatre but a theatre with a court. Madame de Staël, who went to Weimar to find out about the modern in the arts, found to her astonishment that Germany had, for the first time, a cultural capital.

Weimar did not maintain its eminence, even though Schiller and Goethe gave luster to its court long after the foci of cultural activity had shifted to Berlin. After the death of Frederick the Great, French culture relaxed its hold on the Prussian capital. His successor, Frederick William II, something of a mystic, found the romantic movement much to his liking. In Berlin, cultural activity soon slipped out of the hands of the weak and defeated monarch into a middle-class setting. Berlin society, now largely non-noble and removed from the Prussian aristocracy, took over the modern in the arts because the aristocracy was hardly fitted to take upon itself a cultural role. Trained for state service only, the aristocracy's interest was not at court in Berlin but on its East Prussian estates. With few exceptions the Prussian nobility lacked the cultural interest and sophistication which made both the French and English nobility patrons of art in partnership with the middle classes.

In Berlin society all distinctions of birth seemed to vanish before literary talent and sensibility. Influential in this change were ideas of both the Enlightenment and romanticism that people were to be judged not by their heritage but by their allegiance to certain principles, whether it be the moral law of nature or depth of sentiment and feeling. Concretely, this meant that the salon replaced the court as the center of cultural activity. The salon was presided over by a talented and charming woman who had the gift of maintaining debate on an intellectual level. The salon became a pathology of souls through conversation. At the beginning of the century in Berlin, the principal salons were presided over by two Jewish women, Henriette Herz and Rachel Levin. Both, because of a deeply felt need for integration, eventually became Christians.

In a salon like that of Henriette Herz, society mixed as it had never done before. Fichte, Schleiermacher, Gentz (the secretary to the Congress of Vienna), and Schlegel all frequented her gatherings. Her salon first began when she founded a circle of friends for the practice of "sentimentality" which she called the "circle of virtue." This was to be achieved through reading and appreciating emotionally the modern in the arts. They defied convention, though in a genteel manner, by reading books like Schlegel's *Lucinde*. When discussion took the place of readings, the salon had taken on its final form. Some of the nobility joined in. When Henriette had to close her salon for lack of money, the Duchess of Kurland stepped into the breach only to be succeeded by Rachel Levin. Rachel's salon was much more informal than the earlier ones. She had simple gatherings at her mother's house on a special day of the week. The custom of the "jour" or the "at home" had been followed by many hostesses up to the present generation.

The rebuilding of the Prussian state, which fell increasingly under the shadow of cultural nationalism, put an end to salons for a while. Their cosmopolitan, equalitarian base was obviously in conflict with the alliance between the romantic impetus and nationalism. Salons continued, however, through the whole century on a more exclusive social base. In the twentieth century Adolf Hitler met, in the salon of Frau Bechstein, the intellectual elite of the racially-oriented nationalist movement.

The salon did not remain confined to Germany. In France such salons extended from the nobility to the bourgeoisie. Here, too, they served to further romantic sentiment, and the salons of Madame Recamier as well as of Charles Nodier, to mention the most famous, were based upon the reading of romantic poetry. In his salon at L'Arsenal, Nodier (1780–1844) became the guardian of a romantic literary group, and it was this patron, librarian by profession, who wrote the preface for the works of Dumas (1834). Nodier aided playwrights by introducing them to wealthy patrons like Baron Taylor, and it was upon the latter's suggestion that Victor Hugo wrote his *Cromwell*. Taylor, as *Commissaire Royal* of the Comédie Française produced plays by

Hugo, Vigny, and Dumas, whom he met at the salons. Thus, in France salons were important as institutions for the encouragement and dissemination of the "modern," romantic literature.

In France the salon had a longer period of importance than in Germany. Under the Second Empire they continued to encourage literary and artistic talent, while in Germany, at that period, salons tended to concentrate increasingly upon national concerns. Both French and German salons tended to become increasingly informal institutions, the host or hostess receiving on a given day of the week. In this form it continued to fertilize literary endeavors into the twentieth century. For example, the Thursdays of Émile Zola in the 1870s became the nucleus around which the naturalist writers grouped themselves, and in the late nineteenth century the Paris salon of Stéphane Mallarmé (1842–98) became important for a younger group of writers. Not only in Germany and France, but also in other European countries, the salon, the "jours," became the center of intellectual life during the first part of the nineteenth century. The cultural monopoly of court society was broken once and for all, not merely in favor of bourgeois society but in the name of a society open to talent. In spite of the fact that the salon and the jours remained cultural institutions of some importance even after the romantic movement had run its course, there is little doubt that it was romanticism which provided the impetus for this development.

In England the place of the salon was taken by the club and the coffee house (out of which the clubs had developed). Here the court had, since the Revolution, never played a central part in the dissemination of cultural fashions. For example, in the latter part of the seventeenth century Will's was the famous coffee house where Dryden ruled supreme. By the nineteenth century the clubs had taken over, and though some tended to be linked to a political party, others continued to be associated with literary and artistic endeavors.

Whatever the actual setting for intellectual activity, the romantic impetus coincided with the general broadening of the social context within which such activity took place. The framework was everywhere becoming nonaristocratic and centered upon the middle classes. Even Napoleon III found that in France he could no longer organize culture from the court down. His attempts to introduce German idealism and Wagner in this manner were complete failures. Since cultural activity became more diffused throughout society, the romantic impetus touched a much wider variety of people than had been affected by the Enlightenment. This was also due to the greater appeal of an emotionally-centered doctrine over one based on an understanding of science, but it affected not only romanticism but also all other ideological movements of the age. Cultural nationalism could spread with equal effect.

The egalitarianism which was involved in the romantic movement and was concretely reflected in the salons was, in the end, defeated by religion and nationalism. All those who shared the historical memories, and the creativity implied in them, were equal; but only those—here was the limitation which many early Romantics would have denied. Jew, Gentile, aristocrat, and merchant all met on equal footing in the salons of Henriette Herz and Rachel Levin. The German linkage of romanticism and politics was soon to make this impossible, for the Jew became a foreigner who did not share the national memories and thus had no feeling. The merchant with his pushiness might upset the kind of emotional unity necessary for national salvation.

Both the Christian and the national facets of the romantic movement stressed the element of integration or romantic unity. In doing so they restricted the romantic ideal of freedom and the romantic revolt against conventions. The movement was tamed into either a Christian or a national respectability. Nevertheless, a romantic protest did continue throughout the century and into the next. A movement which expressed a mood rather than a fully worked-out and systematized ideology could influence a wide and disparate audience. The facets of romanticism which have been described in these chapters were only part of the movement; however, they were the aspects which were most tangible and which had a lasting and determinable influence on the course of European culture.

CHAPTER FOUR

# Nationalism

$\mathcal{T}$HE DISCUSSION of the relationship between romanticism and
politics has raised the problem of modern nationalism. It has
often been said that modern nationalism was a product of the
French Revolution and of romanticism, but this is an over-
simplification. National consciousness existed in most European nations
during the Middle Ages. In many cases it was attached to a person who
symbolized the nation rather than to an abstract concept of nationalism.
National consciousness centered on the personal allegiance to a king or
dynasty carried over into the nineteenth century. Especially in the smaller
states it was still the prince, *pater patriae*, who symbolized in his person
the national ideal. This dynastic allegiance meant by the seventeenth century, at least, the creation of a common national consciousness even though
it might be focused upon the monarch ruling by divine right. In France,
Richelieu's Academy took it upon itself to create a common language with
common rules for all Frenchmen. Throughout Europe the mercantilist system emphasized the primacy of national interests over those of other
countries.

At the same time, the religious conflicts growing out of the Reformation fostered a type of nationalism which was not directly connected to

the ruling monarchy. The adoption of the "right" faith also meant that the nation was especially chosen by God for a glorious destiny. This impetus was especially strong in England where it was not confined to the Puritans. Elizabeth's Lord Chancellor Ellesmere wrote eloquently about England, the "second Israel"; much later the poet Blake created his famous hymn about the building of Jerusalem in "England's green and pleasant land." The French Revolution gave weight to trends already present. It viewed the nation as the totality of its inhabitants who were not linked to any particular ruling power. The symbolism of a national flag made this clear, for the tricolor was not a dynastic emblem as the fleur-de-lis had been. It was Rousseau's general will transformed into reality. This again fitted in with the romantic drive to comprehend the totality of life. What happened was that national consciousness came to be detached from one particular manifestation of the nation, like the king, and instead comprised the nation as a totality, even as an abstract idea. Since men need symbols, national consciousness was represented by the flag and the national anthem. Significantly some of these anthems antedated the famed "Marseillaise" of 1792; thus "Deutschland über Alles" appeared in 1745.

No doubt the appearance and popularity of these secularized hymns exemplified a heightened national mood, for they all came within a relatively short historical period. Hymns and flags were joined by other symbols: the sacred flame or pillar of fire as well as national monuments which no longer represented a single figure but instead provided national symbols of beauty and grandeur. Such monuments tended to be classical in design, exemplifying a harmony and proportion whose satisfying beauty had been rediscovered in the eighteenth century. J. J. Winckelmann in his *History of Ancient Art* (1776) had praised antiquity for its "quiet restfulness." Beauty was defined as free from passion or, at best, tranquil like the ocean's surface beneath which the turbulence takes place. These ideas were representative of the nations' self-image, a symbol of eternity—a world of order and harmony. It was on this concept of beauty that the national "ideal type" was based all over Europe: the German Aryan had Greek proportions, and the "clean cut Englishman" represented a similar type of beauty. Racial thought based many of its judgments upon a concept of beauty which had become part of the self-representation of the nation: in stone and mortar through national monuments or through the outward appearance of the ideal citizen. Nationalism presented itself through a world of myth and symbol in which the people could participate: singing, folk dancing, forming processions, or strengthening their body through gymnastics.

Public festivals which accompanied the rise of nationalism used the symbols we have discussed and encouraged popular participation. All over Europe nationalism captured masses of people, the more so as the beginning of nationalism coincided with the beginning of mass politics. People longed for a beautiful and healthy world where order reigned and which exemplified the continuity of history among the chaotic change of industrializing Europe. The myths and symbols of nationalism fulfilled this longing.

The enthusiasm and the festivals of the French Revolution had shown the way, but the events of the Revolutionary and Napoleonic wars together with the actual conditions inside each nation were probably of greater importance for the increasing nationalism than the example of the Revolution itself. These wars and the French occupation gave a great stimulus to German national consciousness. In England the war against France had the same effect even though England was never occupied. Occasionally she did, however, fight alone for a long span of time. No wonder that patriotism came to the fore. In 1792 Arthur Young formed the Loyal Associations whose purpose was to "prove their content with the constitution of this kingdom as established at present and to secure the blessings we derive from its influence." In Italy, occupied but for the first time united, Vittorio Alfieri (1749–1803) used his dramas to preach the ideal of a free and united Italy. National sentiment had existed in Italy even before Machiavelli made his famous plea in the Renaissance, but it was now deepened and put into the foreground of the intellectuals' thought. In this way the age of the French Revolution and Napoleon did affect the emergence of a modern nationalism.

This nationalism was not static and it took on many different forms as it fused with other systems of thought current at the beginning of the century. The linkage between nationalism and romanticism has already been discussed. The nation was conceived as a historic and emotional entity with which all men should integrate themselves. Similarly, conservatism came to have a strongly-developed national feeling centered upon the historic tradition of the nation. But here there could be a variety of nationalisms even within one ideology. Edmund Burke (1729–97) stressed national consciousness as developing out of a historical tradition which allowed for the gradual unfolding of liberty within the nation, while most Continental Conservatives thought of the nation in terms of monarchical authoritarianism. Not only Romantics and Conservatives were concerned with strengthening national consciousness, Liberals were also involved in this task. They believed that free individual and economic development would ultimately produce a strong nation.

Nationalism thus took on different forms as it penetrated various ways of looking at the world and at the nation. There is no one "nationalism"; there are instead a variety of "nationalisms." Moreover, these nationalisms evolved within the framework of the diverse European nations. Yet, in this evolution we can discern some common landmarks. The French Revolution accelerated the feeling of national consciousness and the revolutions of 1848 turned it in a different direction. R. R. Palmer has written about the new "tough minded-ness" which permeated nationalism after the failure of these revolutions. This is especially true of those nations which were not territorially united but whose urge toward such unity was spurred on by the very failures of 1848, when both Germany and Italy had made unsuccessful bids for unification. Now the idealists who had formerly been in the forefront were superseded in the leadership of the national cause by statesmen acutely aware of the realities of the European political situation. In Germany Otto von Bismarck (1815–98), the real-politician, came to the front, while in Italy the idealistic Giuseppe Mazzini (1805–72) was superseded by the practical Camillo Cavour (1810–61), whose favorite philosopher was the Utilitarian, Jeremy Bentham. National ambitions were directed toward practical achievements through diplomacy or military aggression. This was only one change in nationalism after 1848; however, there was another.

In central Europe, and in France as well, the bourgeoisie had been frightened by the Revolution and the specter of radicalism which it had raised. They now bolstered nationalism as a bulwark against radicalism. It became bound up with a search for order—thus the support in France for the Second Empire and in Germany and Austria for a strong, nationally-oriented monarchy. Liberty was rejected together with radicalism, and the state was conceived to be an instrument of power both for national glory and for internal order. The liberal idea of nationalism was vanishing and conservative and romantic elements came consistently into the foreground. It is no coincidence that in these years the Tory party was revived in England on the basis of the conservatism and romanticism of Benjamin Disraeli. Practicality and *Realpolitik* were not enough to sustain this ideology; the idea of the nation came to be infused with romantic and racial ideas. This was not the case everywhere, as will be seen in the discussion of France and Italy, but it was certainly a current of thought which gathered strength after 1848. It meant a view of the nation as the exclusive claimant to citizen loyalties, as well as an assertion of its superiority over all other nations.

These trends had always been present; their development was seen in the discussion of romanticism and politics, but they now came to dominate the scene. The nation was the intermediary between the individual and a personal scheme of values and ethics; outside the nation no life or creativity was possible. National glory and the love for order expressed themselves through the symbols and myths mentioned earlier. They acted as a bridge between the people and government, for many taking the place of representative government itself.

The superiority of one nation over all others was not a necessary concomitant of growing national consciousness. Liberals always believed in the peaceful coexistence of a number of nations, and they saw the relations between states as determined by the same principles which govern the relations between free and self-conscious individuals. Even early romantic nationalism was not necessarily aggressive; the Napoleonic wars made it so in Germany. The older territorial view of the nation was still in the forefront during the first half of the century. National ambitions were directed toward certain territories to which there was some sort of historic claim rather than asserting absolute claims to dominance as the only "true" nation, or attempting to unite all of the *Volk*.

Wars, within this context, were limited wars, and once the object was achieved they ended in a peace treaty. It would never have occurred to Frederick the Great in the eighteenth century, once he had taken Silesia, to push on toward Vienna in order to unite all Germans within one nation. But the development of nationalism seemed to lead toward such an end in the name of the dominance of one state over all others and this because its nationalism alone was genuine. It has been pointed out that German cultural nationalism did lead to such an end, and Frenchmen, too, began to talk about the mission of France, even if eventually they saw this exemplified by the French spirit rather than by French military and political domination. If such nationalism was muted in Europe, it must not be forgotten that the second half of the century saw the great expansion of the French and British empires. Here was an outlet for feelings of national superiority and aggressiveness which a nation like Germany lacked. The natives were fair game for a paternally-oriented policy of national dominance which, because of their political or economic situation, these nations could not advocate in Europe. In the discussion of the evolution of nationalism in England and France in specific terms it will be well to remember this.

In Europe the climax of this cultural nationalism came only with the totalitarian movements of the twentieth century. Bismarck thought in strictly territorial terms and not in terms of German domination, as his peace with Austria and his settlement with France show. Similarly, even the more extreme French nationalists after 1870 oriented their ambitions on the reconquest of Alsace-Lorraine rather than upon establishing France's total dominance over Germany. Yet to some, Napoleon III after 1852 seemed already out of date, for the Emperor had no feeling for French minorities outside France or hostility toward other minorities inside it. The territory determined the allegiance and not vague ideas about the "national soul" or a shared, but distant, national past. The fact was that Napoleon and even Bismarck were wedded to an old-fashioned national concept which was not shared by all of their followers.

After the revolutions of 1848 nationalism came under the guidance of realistic manipulators of power, but at the same time national consciousness became both more romantic and exclusive as well as more aggressive in the name of a solitary, absolute dominance. Toward the end of the century, both racial ideas and a romantic revival were to strengthen this trend. These have been general remarks about the nature of nineteenth-century nationalism, but perhaps the most important point remains to be made.

The development of nationalism was not identical within each of the European states; rather, its nature was determined partly by the actual problems which the nation faced and partly by its past history. Every ideology of national consciousness based itself upon history. From the very beginnings of the formation of nation states the idea of historical precedent had been important. Arguments of national pride were often derived from the antiquity of the nation. Had not Geoffrey of Monmouth as well as the Elizabethans thought that Englishmen were descended from Brutus? It was not only the Italians who derived pride from a Roman heritage. In the nineteenth century, the English, the French, and the Germans saw their ancestors in a far distant and mythical past—in Rome, in the tribes of the northern forests, and in the Celts. The historical past was always either mythical or a warping of national history which had little connection with the actual historical process; but then, history used to bolster or to explain an ideology is seldom firmly rooted in the realities of the past. Ideologies fulfill a need, and nationalism certainly did this; therefore, the content of that ideology was related to the need it fulfilled rather than to the verification of actual historical development.

This point can best be illustrated through a discussion of the major English ideology of nationalism in the nineteenth century. The Loyal Associations stressed the constitution of England as it was establishd at the time. Its patriotism was not linked to medieval chivalry or to ancient kings but to the support of the ancient constitution. This constitution had survived two revolutions, the one associated with civil war, commonwealth, and protectorate, and the other associated with peaceful change in 1688. It was this second revolution which formed the immediate basis of the English national consciousness. Here parliamentary government had been preserved against the threat of monarchical absolutism without violence. The Revolution of 1688 was, in G. M. Trevelyan's phrase, the "sensible revolution" under which Englishmen lived peaceably together. Its glory had burned brightly for one hundred and fifty years in contrast to the short, destructive *gloire* of the French Revolution. The successful avoidance of violence in the struggle for the Reform Bill of 1832 seemed to prove the point (the French had had another revolution two years before).

This was a possible interpretation of history, but hardly an accurate one.

In the seventeenth century the British had a universal reputation for unruliness, and it was the violent, bloody Civil War which laid the foundations for the Glorious Revolution. But the Civil War was widely held to be an aberration in the long and peaceful development of representative government in England, a development which favorably distinguished England from the unpredictable French. This was an extension of the ideology of the Whigs who, as the "Revolutionaries" of 1688, were wedded to the concept of peaceful evolution but who also rejected the radicalism which was disturbingly obvious in the great English Revolution. Built on this view of history, English nationalism became centered on an image of a sensible, pragmatic people preferring peaceful change, if change there had to be, and rejecting the ideological splurge of a French Revolution. Liberal morality, discussed in a subsequent chapter, was closely linked to this kind of national image.

The will for peaceful change was a part of this image. An emphasis was constantly placed upon a steadiness of growth or evolution of representative government. The Stuarts were seen as an evil interruption in this process. It was universally held against James I that he, unlike Queen Elizabeth, was too much of a theoretician, while Catholic Mary Tudor suffered from an overdose of principle. Parliament was at the center of this English nationalism. This was not surprising considering the unpopularity of the English monarchs at the beginning of the nineteenth century when even England saw the rise of a strong republican movement. The ideal of the gradual evolution of English government led to claims illustrated by an example from a textbook written at the beginning of this century, not in England but in the American Midwest: "English history is world history for through it, and it alone, can be known the advent of political democracy."

The isolationism of this kind of national consciousness is clear. England had pointed the way to representative institutions; that was her glory, and she had done it without going through a turbulent revolution. That was why she had succeeded where others failed. Edmund Burke's attacks upon the French Revolution must be seen in this context. His emphasis on tradition, on "prescription," was meant to establish a link not with despotism but with the slow evolution of freedom. His warning against violent change, like his opposition to fundamental parliamentary reforms, would prevent a break in this national consciousness. The antiquity of Parliament was also assumed; its origins lay not in the Middle Ages but in the supposedly free institutions of the Germanic tribes. Thus the argument of antiquity assumed great importance. This was furnished, interestingly enough, not by English but by German scholars. Belief in the Germanic origins of free institutions was shared by both the German and the English national consciousness, so different in other respects from one another. In the end, such common origins did provide a basis for that relationship between "Anglo-Saxon" peoples so important to racial thought.

This kind of English nationalism was not markedly influenced by romanticism. It tended to be pragmatic, rejecting an explicit ideological base in favor of experience based upon tradition. No doubt liberalism, with its stress upon the practical approach to life, was a congenial atmosphere for this national consciousness, while the practical approach of evangelical religion seemed also to be in tune with such an ideology. A book like Charles Kingsley's *Westward Ho!* (1855) combined the advocacy of an honest and practical morality with enmity toward the dishonest and casuistic foreign Spaniard. Elizabethan heroes, dressed in the garb of liberal morality, fought sneaky foreigners. The image of John Bull embodied the national ideal of practical, honest clear-headedness and anti-intellectualism. The vision of history was definitely congenial to liberal morality. John Bull was the product of the slow, pragmatic growth in an orderly and peaceful manner of England and her institutions.

English nationalism allowed for some degree of liberty, for its very core was the representative institution of Parliament. Burke never denied the growth of freedom; he only wanted to retain the primacy of tradition and evolution over revolution which could destroy freedom. The stress upon tradition could be used to idealize not only the inevitable growth of Parliament but also the social and political relationships of a past and happier age. In this manner Burke looked back to the "unbought grace of life" of a preindustrial aristocracy. Romanticism entered not into the Whig but into the Tory view of English national consciousness.

Benjamin Disraeli's touchstone was not 1688 but a mythical medieval England where social justice reigned through the paternalism of the nobility. A recapturing of that age would serve to solve the problems of contemporary England, to unite what he called the "two nations"—that of the rich and that of the poor. It is typical that such a romantic impetus, when applied to national consciousness, was immediately infused with racial ideas. For Disraeli, race was the clue to history. He was contemptuous of the traditional principles of nationality because he feared their equalitarian implications; instead, the idea of race would restore to society the proper tradition of nationality.

Racial thought never assumed the prominence in English nationalism that it did in Germany, for the Whig impetus was dominant and not that of Disraeli. Yet that concept of national consciousness did, at times, blend with racial ideas. The superiority of British stock in pioneering representative government could be explained through racial superiority. The supposedly Germanic foundations for Parliament provided one basis for such an explanation, and Darwinism could provide another. The survival of the fittest implied the survival of the English constitution because of inherent racial characteristics which were the ideals of Victorian morality read back into the Germanic forests. Francis Galton in his *Hereditary Genius* (1869) thought that this was the result of natural selection. Since the idea of inherited genius could be ascribed to a whole people who had proved so adept at governing themselves, it was a mere step to ascribing this to the hereditary genius of a race. Some Englishmen took this step, just as some viewed the growing Empire in racial terms. It is interesting that more did not do so, for racialism was becoming common on the Continent. The very nature of English nationalism made the intrusion of racial ideas more difficult than elsewhere, since it was connected with that pattern of morality associated with liberalism, usually called Victorian. The idea of self-government as an integral part of this national consciousness prevented it from becoming seriously entangled with racism, as the works of the historians Seeley and Froude, advocates of empire, clearly showed. Even in Rudyard Kipling there was a tone different from the racism of the Continent. The Empire was for him, as for so many others, the place where Englishmen could live a life that approximated the Victorian ideal, the life of Tom Brown; at home this was no longer possible.

English nationalism thus fed on a certain view of the English past. It prided itself on the slow growth of liberty through Parliament and it rejected ideologies which led to abrupt change. The "Rights of Man" seemed to Disraeli as abstract and unexciting as they were to Burke. Because of this kind of national consciousness, equality was never a part of English nationalism as it was of the German or the French national tradition. As Burke had said, the development of liberty was traditional, but ideas of equality smacked of a foreign ideology. England had neither the tradition of Jacobin rule nor the problem of achieving unity in a nation which had been disunited since the Middle Ages. Because its nationalism was, quite consciously, less spectacular than that of the Continent, it has sometimes been overlooked as a motivating force in modern English history. Nevertheless, it was important. The denial of ideology can be one of the most powerful of ideologies.

French nationalism was more complex because it fed on several historical traditions. There was that tradition which saw its ideal in Jacobin equality; there were those who combined acceptance of the Revolution with a stress upon *la gloire* as Napoleon had exhibited it; and there were those whose decisive national image was that of the *ancien régime* with its social and political inequality. By and large, Carnot's fiery words about the fatherland encompassing all the objects of a man's affection describe that canvas upon which the diverse images of France's tradition were painted. It is, however, important to note that the French national impetus which was based upon the revolutionary tradition was much less centered upon the distant past than English or German nationalism. It stressed liberty, human dignity, and the Rights of Man. All of these were criticized by Englishmen, precisely because of their nonhistorical nature. Liberty was an integral part of this concept of the nation. As has been seen, this could be combined with the romantic mood—witness Lamennais's equation of the "soul of a people" with individual freedom and social equality.

But this freedom and equality were seen in a patriotic context. The historian Jules Michelet wrote his work *The People* (1846) to resurrect what was to him the real essence of French history. As he said, condemning the salons and the aristocracy, "I come to establish against all mankind the personality of the people." It is they who are good: ". . . at the time of the cholera, who adopted the orphan children? The poor." The history of France was the history of her people. Michelet saw the people not only as good but as the repository of national values. To the peasant a Prussian was still a Prussian and an Englishman still an Englishman. Such a viewpoint was quite similar to that romantic view of the peasant which arose in Germany at the same time. Here it led not to a redefinition of freedom toward rootedness and conservatism; instead, for Michelet, the great Revolution was and is the eternal destiny of France. The Revolution was the climax of history for it exemplified that unity through free association which bound the nation together. In his writings on history Michelet believed that it was the great mission of France to conserve and spread this freedom. As late as 1938 Paul Valéry, speaking for French intellectuals, echoed these thoughts, though he despaired of France's ever fulfilling her mission in a world of rapid social and technological change.

The end of the Revolutionary era and the restoration meant the revival of a national consciousness which centered not on Revolutionary glories but on the idea of monarchy. Through its monarchy France had, in the last centuries, exercised a particular influence upon other nations. De Bonald believed that the Revolution caused France to lose this position; the Revolution was the nation's sin. Now that it was over, however, the old glory could once again be restored. Joseph de Maistre talked about a world which had two centers: Rome with a spiritual pope and Paris with a secular pope, the King of France. Within this context, France also had a mission and that mission was not dissimilar to the one which Michelet proposed; namely, to civilize the world. For while the ideas of freedom of Michelet and men like de Bonald and de Maistre were different, they nevertheless shared one great characteristic of French nationalism; as one historian put it, with some exaggeration, it tended to be a civilizing nationalism rather than a chauvinistic nationalism.

What is meant by this is that France's mission was conceived to be one of the spirit rather than of conquest and force. Joseph Ernest Renan summarized it in 1887, at the end of the century, when he defined a nation as a shared soul but above all a shared spirit and intellect. This nation shared common memories, battles, and fame but it was not a race, for such an idea would rob the concept of spontaneous agreement, forcing man into a mold. Man does not belong to a race; he belongs only to himself. What a difference between this and the German concept of nationality at that time! This difference concerns not only race but also the emphasis upon the intellect. For Germans it was the instinctive soul which counted; the English were suspicious of intellectual brilliance, but the great French tradition of rationalism asserted itself. This, in the last resort, gave a different flavor not only to French nationalism but to French intellectual endeavor as a whole. France, after all, was the nation of Descartes and of Comte.

Guizot (1787–1874) enlarged upon the idea of France as the leader of civilization. In 1822 he defined this concept as "clarity of thought, spirit of community and sympathy." Notice that clarity of thought came first. In returning to Paul Valéry once more it will be found that he voiced the same kind of thought as Guizot at the very moment, 1933, when the "soul" was triumphing in its own peculiar fashion in Germany: If true spirituality and idealism were still to be found anywhere in Europe, then it was thanks to France.

This kind of nationalism could well be linked to the declining power of France throughout the century. The dynamism of the newly-unified Germany thought in terms of conquest and struggle. Yet one facet must be added to this dominant mode of national consciousness. France was a Catholic nation and a part of her past was bound up with Saint Louis and Saint Joan of Arc. The Catholic revival after the Revolution was bound to affect national thought. Lamennais's attempt to forge a link between the unity of the Church and the urge toward freedom in the nation has already been mentioned— only Catholicism could lead to true social unity and progress. The first steps were taken along a path which led to a strong Catholic revival among French intellectuals after the First World War. In de Maistre, national consciousness, centered on the monarchy, was intertwined with France's Catholic mission as the eldest daughter of the Church. Romantic visions of the past fused with their Catholic foundations. But again, this nationalism was not aggressive and it also thought in terms of a civilizing mission. Yet it rejected the dominant rationalism, just as Jacques Maritain in the present century called the great sin of France that of Descartes.

After the defeat of 1870 the diffused current of aggression and race entered France. In bitterness, the old Michelet witnessed the force of an aggressive, monarchical and clerical nationalism combined with racism. Men of this ilk aggressively attacked the new Republic, sparking the anti-Semitism of the Dreyfus affair. For it was in France that racial appeals were first used, on a large scale, in order to organize the masses. This has been called "counter revolutionary patriotism" for it opposed the Revolutionary tradition's belief in the primacy of freedom. Yet, until the last decades of the century romantic, monarchical, and Catholic patriotism had seen its mission in the same non-aggressive terms as that of the tradition of the great Revolution.

Defeat by Germany and the quarrels within the new Republic mark a change in French nationalism just as the revolutions of 1848 did for Italy and Germany. In France, however, the change was of a more transitory nature. Chauvinism did come to the forefront for a period of time, culminating in the Dreyfus affair. *Revanchist* feelings against Germany were the core of nationalism. Moreover, such patriotism was not confined to the right but was especially rampant among the left. Here it could feed upon the Jacobin tradition. There is little doubt, however, that this nationalism became, after the Dreyfus affair, a minority movement. Not until about 1906 did French nationalism get a second lease on life. This "Nationalist revival," as Eugen Weber has called it, was based not so much on France's mission in the world, or even upon aggression against neighbors, but instead upon fear. Above all, fear of Germany now dominated the national consciousness. Together with this fear of Germany there was, at the same time, a feeling that the Republic was weak and that it was not able to protect itself against external aggression or internal radicalism. Extremist movements enjoyed some success with those French citizens already disposed toward nationalism. The most important of these was the *Action Française* born of the Dreyfus affair (1899). The *Action* fused clerical and royalist opposition to the Republic into an aggressive nationalism. Not surprisingly, Alsace-Lorraine, lost to Germany in 1870, played a great part in its thought. Charles Maurras (1868–1952) became the official philosopher of the movement. He believed France to be decadent and called for an end to this decadence through an "intuitive" understanding of the French heritage. Foreigners, like the Jews, who swarmed over France usurping high positions could not understand this tradition; it could only be understood by the French people who shared this common heritage. Maurras's approach was a familiar one, close to that romanticism discussed earlier.

What was this common heritage? The French people had acquired unity around its monarchy. This had provided a principle of unity in the nation, and once the Revolution had broken that unity the nation had been set adrift. Instead of unity there were merely party politicians who were interested solely in grasping for power. Here was the root and source of France's decline. The monarchy must be restored, this was clear, but before that restoration French life must be purified. For Maurras this meant a renewed emphasis upon Catholicism as well as the elimination of all foreigners (including Jews) from public life. Democracy must be abolished for it opposed the real needs of social life, needs which only a monarchy could fullfill.

Maurras was an opportunist in politics; all means were good if they led to the desired end. He believed that end to be a monarchical dictatorship. The *Action Française* was never a dominant movement, though eventually, in Vichy France, many of its ideas became popular. But in our period it also touched many who were not members of the movement itself. The monarchical part of its program proved illusionary; men rejected this element and concentrated instead upon the Catholic Church as the best guardian of national unity and the best symbol of a shared past. They stressed the Church as an authoritarian institution opposed to the weaknesses of representative government. Moreover, at the turn of the century, people were groping for some sort of intellectual security, and the Church could easily provide this. The anticlericalism which followed the Dreyfus affair persisted, but now many French people gave an impetus to a Catholic revival, largely for nationalist reasons. In this pattern of thought Charles Péguy (1873–1914) and those who followed him provided an exception. Péguy wanted to combine a passionate attachment to freedom with an equally passionate attachment to Catholicism. For him the Church was not authoritarian; its emphasis on free will gave ideological support to democracy. Péguy will be discussed later, but it is worth noting that in the first decades of the twentieth century some men attempted to reconcile Catholicism and democracy just as had the earlier Lamennais. But now this reconciliation was based on strong national premises, viewing the Church as the cement of national life.

The national revival did not stop with monarchism or clericalism. Indeed, it came to influence all French political parties as the menace from across the Rhine loomed ever larger. Republicans and anticlericals also called for national unity and national discipline. For them democracy came to have a nationalistic function. Georges Clemenceau (1841–1929) held that democracy's function was the reconciliation of individual and group interests so as to produce solidarity. This resolution of differences meant a type of mutual thrust and counterthrust for which representative government was supremely fitted. Clemenceau viewed the nation as an assembly of diverse interest groups, a view other nationalists rejected since it opposed the concept of the organic national state. But this very view meant a nationalism based upon the necessity of representative government, which alone could produce national unity. Clemenceau's views were more typical for the direction of French nationalism before the First World War than those of the *Action Française* or of men like Péguy. What all of these views had in common was a desire for national unity in the face of the German threat and the imperial growth of other nations. Coupled with these considerations were the fears of internal disorganization which might open the door to leftist radicalism.

French nationalism illustrated the dynamic qualities of this ideology. As it evolved through the century, it took different forms according to whatever historical tradition was used and whatever difficulties the nation encountered in foreign and domestic policy. There is an obvious contrast between French and English nationalism, but then France did not have either the Whig tradition or a continuity of representative institutions on which national consciousness could be built. France had undergone two revolutions and a crushing military defeat since 1789, while England's revolution lay far in the past; nor did England suffer any military defeats during the century. There was no one on whom to center *revanchist* feelings, and no close neighbor constituted a continual threat to the nation's security.

Italian nationalism was different again from that of both England and France. The French Revolution had come to Italy not as the disrupter of an ancient pattern of nationhood but as the harbinger of unification. For the first time since Rome, Italy had been united. At Vienna, Italy lost that unity once more to a patchwork of small and arbitrary governments. But the impulse toward a rapidly-developing national consciousness remained. Italian patriots had to fight both for unity and against the illiberal governments which dominated the country. This turned Italian nationalism in this period toward a concern for liberty. Alfieri denounced all monarchical government as tyrannical and eventually envisaged an Italy governed by the principles of constitutionalism. There must be a division of powers, for even elected legislators could become tyrannical. Alfieri's dramas, which expressed such views, introduced a stream of liberalism into Italy's quest for unity. The exiled priest Vincenzo Gioberti (1801–52) envisaged a united Italy built around a liberal papacy. The unsuccessful attempt at unity in 1848 imperilled these liberal dreams.

In Italy, as in Germany, the failure of 1848 had a profound effect upon the direction of the nationalist cause. Gioberti who, before this event, had stressed the idea of the division of powers so central to liberalism and had rejected democracy as a new tyranny, changed his tune. He now turned against the bourgeoisie and toward the people—national unity must have as a consequence the salvation of the masses. Property relationships must be modified. He was still not willing to see a pure democracy but he wanted the people, led by men of reason, to enjoy a greater degree of social justice. Such a new emphasis upon the people can also be seen in Germany after 1848. Nationalist leaders grew increasingly preoccupied with rooting national consciousness in the growing working classes. In Germany this concern deepened a romantic concern with the "whole *Volk*," an equality of all Germans loyal to this great ideal. The social legislation of Bismarck was part of this new nationalist atmosphere after 1848. While in Germany this meant an increasing emphasis upon absolutism, in Italy it did not.

The *risorgimento* retained its concern with freedom. This was due both to the moral inspiration of Mazzini and to the practical liberalism of Cavour. Mazzini stressed both liberty and equality, but these were only valid if they were viewed as moral principles. The minds of people must be freed from oppressive materialism and transformed through the mission of creating a united Italy. Fulfilling this mission meant turning to the "religion" of liberty and equality as the highest moral law. By liberty, Mazzini did not mean individualism but people banding together for the cause: "life is for me a mission: the perfection of the nation and through its instrumentality of all humanity." He condemned socialism as materialistic and liberalism as egoistic, nor did he have any use for the political parties which make up representative government. All problems would be solved if the minds of people were educated to the high moral goals exemplified by a united Italy.

Mazzini was inspirational in his approach and never worked out the practical problems which had to be faced. It is important to note that he was a skillful organizer of conspiracies but a failure when it came to politics. Yet his vague, moral precepts continued to emphasize freedom in Italy when there was no one to play a similar role in Germany. This may have been Mazzini's greatest contribution to Italian unity. He gave to that movement high moral aspirations and, at the same time, stressed liberty combined with a concern for humanity in general. Perhaps this also had its negative side. When Italy was united these high aspirations seemed to get bogged down in the kind of party politics he had deplored. The consequence was that many Italians became disillusioned with a reality so far from this ideal of the *risorgimento*.

Cavour was the real architect of Italian unity. While Bismarck disliked parliaments, Cavour believed in the free interplay of interests and ideas. He enjoyed the game of parliamentary politics and felt that unity could only come about through the reconciliation of interests and not through absolute rule. Each group must be given its fair opportunity and everyone must trust in reason which would produce a consensus without abolishing liberty. This was a thoroughly liberal view of nationalism, and it was to be echoed later in almost the same terms by Clemenceau. In practice Cavour was less liberal than in theory, yet in Italy it was a Liberal who became the architect of unity. Like Mazzini, though in an entirely different fashion, he made it possible for Italian nationalism to combine liberal ideas of freedom with an emphasis of national consciousness.

In Germany no one fulfilled a parallel function. Eighteenth-century pietism vitally influenced German nationalism, and many of the early champions of German unity came from a pietistic background. Here love of God was joined to love of the disunited fatherland. "He who does not love the fatherland which he can see, how can he love the heavenly Jerusalem which he does not see?" Romanticism, the storm and stress movement which existed simultaneously with pietism, contributed its share to the emotional hold of nationalism on Germany. Yet, at the beginning of the century both Ernst Moritz Arndt (1769–1860) and Humboldt had believed that freedom must be an essential ingredient in the construction of the nation. The romantic impulse did not necessarily abrogate the linking of the nation with the slow and historic development of freedom. The influential philosopher Friedrich Hegel (1770–1831) stressed the nation as the all-encompassing entity of human life, but he coupled with that a belief in constitutional liberties. Nevertheless, amidst the disunity of Germany, nationalism was apt to go hand in hand with the exaltation of the power of the state.

Liberalism became national liberalism; the historic state was more important than the historical freedom of Germans. For the sake of the state such Liberals were willing to sacrifice liberal principles, except free trade. This national liberalism will be discussed at greater length when liberalism itself is at issue, but it must be noted here that in Germany, nationalism came to stifle even the fundamental liberal belief in freedom. There were those who opposed this, especially that group of learned men who saw the new German nation in legal terms rather than in terms of power. They tried to carry on liberal ideals centered upon the rule of law which guaranteed freedom to the individual regardless of the state's power. The advocates of the *Rechtstaat* (the state viewed as a legal organism) will be discussed later. But they, too, could not succeed against the growing national impetus.

After 1848 this nationalism took two forms. There was a deepening of a cultural nationalism, to which reference has already been made. Racial ideas suffused this national concept, making the nation the instrument of the race's struggle for dominance. This concept of nationalism required total allegiance; people must be integrated completely with the *Volk;* only in this way could they become truly creative. Liberty was the freedom to carry through such an integration.

After 1848, however, there was also a new realism in the approach to the national question represented not only by Cavour but also by Bismarck. As mentioned above, it was still possible to have a territorial view of the nation instead of a cultural one. Bismarck typified this. He was not interested in the state as an all-encompassing organism. He was most willing to let minorities in Germany, like the Poles in the east, keep their identity and their language. Nor did Bismarck advocate a unitary nation which shared one cultural outlook. The south German states kept control over their cultural affairs. Germany became unified only to the degree that Bismarck thought necessary for its maintenance as a state among other states. He was a federalist, a position quite incompatible with any kind of cultural nationalism.

For Bismarck, the state was an instrument of power. But that power was not aggressive but rather directed toward keeping the nation safe from both internal and external disturbances. He saw the internal danger not in Polish or Jewish minorities but in the revolutionary program of Marxism. Thus, he suppressed the German Social Democratic party. But at the same time he also attempted to link the poorer classes to the state—not through an exaggerated nationalism but through social-welfare legislation. Here he typified the greater concern of nationalism with the people—its democratization—which we saw in Italian thought. If the state needed it he was even willing to advocate universal suffrage, though he had come to power as the man who could bridle the Prussian parliament.

Bismarck was above all a technician of power. That does not mean the absence of ideology or a cynical view of the world. Rather, for Bismarck, this meant a sense of responsibility to God. Such a responsibility was defined in terms of keeping the nation safe once it was established and, before that, to work toward its establishment. To be sure, what are called "Machiavellian" methods could be used; Cavour had believed this also. But such methods had, after all, always been used by statesmen throughout history and they had also always been put into a larger ideological framework. For Cavour this framework was liberalism, the conciliation of interests; for Bismarck it was a feeling of responsibility to God which allowed him to operate on an earth tainted by sin. "Blood and iron" could be used, but only in extreme cases when the existence of the state was in peril. True, after the failure of 1848 he thought Germany was indeed in grave danger of never becoming a state at all.

Bismarck's concept of nationalism was an older one than the cultural nationalism of his age. He thought in terms of the state, of safeguarding its territory and its power, but he rejected cultural unity and aggressiveness for the sake of the *Volk*. Yet his concept of nationalism was not transmitted to his successors. Cultural nationalism became dominant in most German minds, including that of Emperor William II. Though this was primarily due to the strength of cultural nationalism after 1848, it was not the sole reason. The end of the century saw a revival of romanticism which further strengthened the view of the nation in terms of culture and race. Indeed, cultural nationalism in Germany became racial nationalism. Although a nation like France also received an infusion of this kind of national consciousness during the Dreyfus affair, in Germany it was to be more lasting and was to lead directly

*81*

into national socialism. Such considerations must make it clear that Bismarck was not a forerunner of national socialism; indeed, his very nationalism harkened back to an age innocent of that combination of romanticism and nationalism which made up cultural nationalism—the wave of the future in Germany.

It must be clear by now that nationalism in its various forms constituted one of the great intellectual appeals during the century. The old cosmopolitan order of the eighteenth century was not dead; its ideals were shared by many Liberals and by statesmen like Metternich, but it was challenged by nationalism. Which classes of the population provided this challenge? Can any connection be made between the European class structure and the impetus toward cultural nationalism in its various forms?

There seems to be little doubt that it was the bourgeoisie in the various nations which furthered this ideology. In the eighteenth century many writers had accepted the dichotomy between state and society. The young Fichte had written that society in general should not be confused with the empirically necessary form of society which is called the state. The rising bourgeoisie in their quest for equal rights tended to see themselves as a society different from the state of the absolute monarchs. Freedom could only be obtained by revolutionary action against the state. This was undoubtedly one of the motivating factors for looking at the nation as an emotional and historical unit divorced from the current political system. The bourgeoisie did achieve this emancipation at the time when its economic interests were increasingly linked to the nation, while more often than not, in contrast, the political system of the nation was not responsive to its interests.

The link between the economic interests of the bourgeoisie and the interests of the nation dates back to the growth of the mercantilist system. Even when free trade and laissez faire were proclaimed as more beneficial for commerce than the mercantilist system, Adam Smith still called his famous book the *Wealth of Nations* (1776). Free trade was supposed to strengthen national interests. On the Continent, where industrial evolution had not progressed as far as in England, laissez faire was never so popular. In Germany Friedrich List (1789–1846) argued for a national customs union and national tariffs as the necessary prelude to any free trade. Moreover, railroads and canals brought scattered markets together on a national rather than international scale.

This economic argument for the national interests of the bourgeoisie must not be overstressed. It has been held that the great era of European peace after the Congress of Vienna was due in part to the international nature of the economy at this stage of the Industrial Revolution. No doubt there was a great deal of economic interchange as demonstrated by French banking investments in Germany. Yet this seemed to affect principally the *haute finance,* the patriciate of the middle classes, which were never to lose their cosmopolitan orientation. It was, rather, the interests of the lower bourgeoisie which were tied to national interests and who had most to gain by the tangible benefits such national ties might confer upon them. Apart from the economic factor, as such, there may well be another, less tangible, consideration involved. The emancipation of the bourgeoisie was achieved only in part and only at times. By and large during the first part of the century decisions were made by the state without taking the masses into consideration. A feeling of frustration undoubtedly played a part in the national stances which they took. But such psychological analysis of nationalism can also move much beyond any class-centered consideration of this movement. Nationalism could be, and indeed was, an outlet for the frustrations of all elements of the population whose ambitions and wishes were thwarted.

It must never be forgotten that the vision of a better life was a part of all nationalisms. In none of the ideologies discussed was the worship of the nation something in and of itself; it was always the necessary way to a better life, a new freedom. In fact this seems to have played a somewhat similar role in modern times as chiliasm and millenarianism played in an earlier period in which religious thought had been dominant. Germans, French, Greeks, and Turks all believed that once they had been united by a true national spirit greater happiness for everybody would result. Nationalism was a modern road to a better destiny. Part of that destiny was undoubtedly a feeling of belonging. The Industrial Revolution, with its growing urbanism, was in danger of atomizing men, to produce what David Riesman in recent times has called the "lonely crowd."

This, together with the political situation already discussed, spurred on the search for common roots in the national past. In turn this meant an increasing emphasis on the land in much of this nationalism. The peasant novels and the glorification of peasant life were, of course, not written by peasants or holders of large estates. They were an idealized view of rural existence put forward by writers from middle-class backgrounds. It was shown in the last chapter how many German writers were concerned with the danger of the middle class to the nation. It is surely significant that it was middle-class writers who raised this problem. They wanted to avoid the estrangement from the nation which their competitiveness and their outlook seemed to promise. The irrational and exaggerated nationalist outbursts of the mid-twentieth century give evidence that nationalism is a means of self-identification and belonging. Hegel may well have been correct when he called history a stage for men's passions. Two of their strongest passions have been the hope for a better life and the sense of belonging. The dislocations of revolutions and industrial society gave a new spur to these passions. Nationalism seemed to meet these needs. This seemed a better analysis of the appeal of the movement than that based on class alone, for the bourgeoisie were not the only nationalists. Since they contained the writers and the publishers of the age, nationalism seemed at times to be a middle-class movement. Looking at nationalism from the vantage point of the mid-twentieth century, it seems as if ideas of race and racial superiority should somehow be placed within its context. But, as has been seen, this idea played a relatively secondary part in it; sometimes no part at all. Yet racial thought was in the ascendant, though in no way was it necessarily connected with nationalism or any other movement. It was an ideology by itself, and a powerful one.

# CHAPTER FIVE

# *Racism*

T HE WORD "race" has diverse meanings which are not even today fully differentiated one from another. It has been used ever since the Renaissance to denote family traits and the characteristics of nations. In addition, the word race has been used to describe groups not even related by inheritance. "Racism" refers to a world view which relates all of human behavior and character to the so-called race to which the individual or the group is said to belong. The impact of racism in modern times derives from the fact that it became a secular religion based upon science and history: it laid claim to the best of two worlds, that of science, which provided new "truths" from the eighteenth century onward, and that of history, which forged a link to traditions which were fast dissolving in the modern world.

We can trace the evolution of racism through several well-defined historical stages. The theoretical foundations were laid during the eighteenth and the first half of the nineteenth centuries. From the second half of the nineteenth century to the end of the First World War racism increased in intensity and assumed a more clearly defined direction. Between the world wars it became linked to European political mass movements like national socialism and was able to put its theories into practice over much of the continent. Racism provides a total view of the world which besides science and history also encompasses aesthetics and morality. Racism with its claim to tribal exclusiveness was not really operative in European life until the last decades of the nineteenth century.

The romantic revival of history which took place in the eighteenth century was as fundamental for the growth of the racial ideal as it has been for modern nationalism. It posited laws of organic development which were transferred to anthropology and linguistics, both of which were to play key parts in the growth of racist thought. The journey of a people through time was regarded as crucial for its formation. For men like G. L. de Buffon (1707–81) and Charles de Montesquieu (1689–1755), historical development was conditioned by environmental factors such as climate and geography: the differences between peoples were merely chance variations. But the organic approach to history carved a deeper gulf between men and nations which was not man-made but said to reveal a divine plan. Johann Gottfried Herder (1744–1805) had such a vision which influenced western as well as eastern Europe. Nature and history were the creative forces of the universe. Natural instinctive spontaneity was at the root of the shared characteristics of every people as it evolved through time. This expressed itself through the national language and folk poetry as well as the literature which a *Volk* had produced in the past. The individual existed only as a part of such a *Volk*. Herder gave nationality an aesthetic, historical, and linguistic dimension which made it an organism separate from any temporary form of political organization. That the organic *Volk* was supreme over the state became important for all later racist thought. But Herder himself did not believe in national supremacy, for as a man of the eighteenth-century Enlightenment his love for his own *Volk* did not preclude respect for all others.

Herder's emphasis upon language as the expression of a shared past was common to a whole generation of philologists at the end of the eighteenth and the beginning of the nineteenth centuries. However, for the most part this school rejected Herder's humanitarianism and concentrated instead upon the scientific search for linguistic roots. Philologists concluded that Sanskrit had been the basis of all western European languages and that it had been imported into Europe from Asia by the migration of Aryan peoples. It is here that the word "Aryan" first appears. Yet the scientific search for linguistic roots immediately gave way to value judgments and fused with the organic historical approach so popular among the romantics.

Language symbolized the experience of a people through time, therefore, the Aryans who gave Europe its languages were thought to reflect in their past the supposed superiority of contemporary Europe. Romantics found through linguistics a link with the Aryan prehistory of the Germanic peoples and a common bond among the Aryan *Volk*. Philologists pictured the Aryans as strong and virile peasants with a healthy family life. Linguistic science became historical myth. Scientific investigation led to claims of moral superiority, a thought process which will remain constant throughout the development of racist thought. Thus Count Arthur de Gobineau (1816–82) repeated a linguistic commonplace of his time when he claimed that the "pure" language of the Aryans demonstrated their ability to transcend the merely material substance of life.

Language became an index of true spirituality and continuity with an undefiled past. Already during the first decades of the nineteenth century it was claimed that strangers such as the Jews were characterized by an inherent inability to speak the national language. This handicap symbolized different historical origins and a materialism which did not interact with God or nature. When Max Müller lectured to English audiences (1859–61), he presented racial doctrines under the mantle of linguistic investigation. The Aryans had been driven into northwest Europe (England and Germany) by an irresistible impulse. This migration had strengthened that independence and self-reliance which were hallmarks of Aryan superiority. We must notice that ideas of racial superiority were not necessarily attached to nationalism but could also be used to support liberal qualities of self-reliance and private initiative.

Indeed both linguistics and historical myth led some Englishmen to feel that the Anglo-Saxons were predestined for the exercise of liberty through free institutions. Thus the historian Edward August Freeman (1823–92) was only one of many who believed that England owed her parliamentary institutions to her Anglo-Saxon roots. The organization of the Germanic tribes (*Comitatus*) was thought to exemplify democratic practices. It followed that those races which did not share this past lacked the quality of mind necessary for self-government. Such an appropriation of self-government resulting from the proper racial traditions forged a connection between representative government and racial exclusiveness. Not only Englishmen but Germans as well could annex the *Comitatus* and, in addition, cite Tacitus's *Germania* as proof that the ancient Germans had already combined love of freedom and independence with sterling moral qualities.

Liberty and freedom were not denied at the beginning of racism, instead they were given racial roots. The French followed suit. Here it was not the *Comitatus* which mattered but instead a Celtic and Roman heritage which supposedly made the French predestined custodians of liberty. Here also love of freedom was associated with moral qualities, for whether German or Celt the virtues which the ancestors exemplified were precisely those cherished by the middle classes in nineteenth-century Europe: manliness, honesty, hard work, and family life.

The concept of "race" itself came from anthropology rather than the history of linguistics. The word received a more precise meaning and contributed to racism at exactly the same time as the developments of history and linguistics took place. Eighteenth-century anthropology began the classification of races. Karl von Liné (1707–78) and G. L. de Buffon divided peoples according to their color, size, and form of body. The similarities discovered in this manner were said to constitute a race. But here also this purely scientific approach led to judgments of human temperament and character. The outward appearance and measurements of men were supposed to symbolize their quality of mind as well.

The Dutch anatomist Peter Camper (1722–89) explored racial typology by comparing the facial and skull measurements of Negroes and monkeys. These measurements defined an ordered progression: from Greek statuary as the ideal form through European races to the Negro as the lowest human species. The standard of beauty was provided by the ancients, another reflection of the importance attached to their rediscovery in the eighteenth century. J. J. Winckelmann in his *History of Ancient Art* (1776) had praised the Greek profile and the Greek nose as archetypal beauty. The association of anthropology with such aesthetic criteria proved basic to the development of racism. The "ideal type" which it advocated always combined outward and inward form: the shape of the body bore witness to man's soul. An eighteenth-century pseudo-science influenced the direction racism was to take. Franz Joseph Gall (1758–1828) founded phrenology on the principle that the moral and intellectual predispositions of men could be determined through the configuration of their heads. Skull measurements became essential to so-called "racial biology" in order to determine the "ideal type" and the Nazis were to make much use of it.

Though anthropological observation was intertwined with aesthetic and moral judgments, environmental factors stood in the forefront during the eighteenth century. However, those thinkers concerned with exalting the organic growth of a people had already denied the importance of environmental factors. They now received powerful support from Immanuel Kant (1724–1804), who used the anthropological concept of race only to detach it from the influence of climate or geography. The purity of a race is essential and must be maintained despite outward circumstances. For Kant Negroes and whites were separate races because throughout history they had never mixed. Here race tended to become a categorical imperative, a "thing in itself." However, Kant never posited the superiority of one race over all others. Like Herder he still belonged to the Enlightenment.

Now that environmentalism had been shown not to affect the purity of race, anthropologists became increasingly concerned with the origins of races.

Some believed in a common origin of all races as it was described in Genesis (Monogenists), but others believed that physical differences among races were too great to be encompassed within a single species. God must have created other species of man besides Adam (polygenism). This concept was first embraced in the eighteenth century by those who wanted to get away from religious and biblical thought, but by the nineteenth century it became one more method by which a pure race could be distinguished from all others. Anthropologists, like historians and linguists, assumed the presence of an hereditary essence which expressed itself in the visible peculiarities of the race.

Such ideas were propagated by a number of learned societies, like the Societé Éthnologique of Paris (1839), which proclaimed that races were to be distinguished by "physical organization, intellectual and moral character, and historical traditions." The supposed identity of race and culture was also central to the program of the Ethnological Society of London (1843). Racism was not yet fully accepted, for the English society with its concern for the native races of the Empire believed that primitive people could be "improved" and consequently condemned slavery. However, anthropologists and linguists had already prepared the way for an attitude which regarded all foreign races as falling somewhere between men and apes. From mid-nineteenth century onward many scientific societies like the Anthropological Society of London (1863) adopted clear-cut racial attitudes toward the black peoples whom they were studying. One of its leaders, James Hunt (1833–69), put forward arguments that the cranial sutures of the Negro closed earlier than that of the white man, thus limiting their potential mental growth. Racism leaped ahead, becoming firmly rooted in a segment of the educated and literate population.

Count Arthur de Gobineau's *Essay on the Inequality of Races* (1853–55) built upon anthropology and linguistics as they had evolved by mid-century. He added an explicit political and cultural thrust: his racial theories were designed to explain the bewildering world in which he lived. In his hands racism became an explanation for the decadence of modernity. Gobineau feared the growth of centralized government on the one hand, and the mob on the other. Between them they were destroying true nobility and freedom. The key to this development lay in a world made up of superior and inferior races.

Gobineau classified the black, yellow, and white races according to their social structure and the societies which they had produced. The yellow races had proved themselves competent at commerce and industry but incapable of looking beyond such material pursuits. The black races were not able to produce stable societies and were always in need of outside control. Clearly Gobineau projected upon these races the modern characteristics which he despised: the yellow races were the bourgeoisie while the black races were *Sans Culottes*. The white race alone embodied all that he thought noble: a higher spirituality, love of freedom, and a personal code built upon honor. Gobineau used the scientific foundation for the classification of races in order to fashion a tract for the times. The white or Aryan race symbolized a utopia in contrast to the reality of the mid-nineteenth century.

This was indeed a utopia, for Gobineau believed that miscegenation was inevitable. The Aryan had not remained pure and, therefore, that formerly superior race was degenerating to the level of other inferior races. The dominance of the bourgeoisie, the modern state, and the rise of democracy supported this observation. Gobineau's pessimistic conclusions were omitted from many later reprints of his work. The *Essay* itself attained only limited popularity and influence, but it is significant in indicating the direction which racism was to take. Nonscientific judgments increasingly came to the fore. Thus his contemporary Gustav Klem (1802–67) divided humanity into active and passive races. The former were virile and masculine while the latter were feminine and passive. The theme was popularized later in Otto Weiniger's *Sex and Character* (1903), where the Jews were said to be a passive and feminine race while the Aryan was masculine and creative. Weininger's book became a staple of subsequent racial literature.

Another contemporary of Gobineau, Carl Gustav Carus (1789–1869) took racial thought one step further toward the creation of a racial mystique. Carus, like Peter Camper before him, concentrated upon finding ideal racial types. These were determined by the mystical force of the sun. The ideal Aryan type was light in pigmentation, and endowed with blond hair and blue eyes reflecting the life-giving strength which the sun symbolized. This ideal type stressed aesthetic elements in racism which had developed hand-in-hand with scientific observation. Contemporary philosophers believed that unchanging aesthetic principles manifested themselves in reality. Racists continued to advocate this theory. The concept of Aryan beauty, based partly on Greek models and partly on sun symbolism, was of special importance.

These concepts were used against those races that did not look like the ideal type. By the second half of the nineteenth century such racism was applied within Europe by Germans to the French and by the French to Germans, but it was the Jews who proved of central importance in providing the dynamic for European racial ideas. The reason for this was simple: the Jews seemed to represent a foreign culture in the midst of Europe. As long as Jews had been forced to live in ghettos few writers had shown a special interest in them, but with Jewish emancipation at the beginning of the nineteenth century this attitude changed. Emancipation had been granted on the assumption that Jews would shed what the Enlightenment had regarded as their bad qualities: the preference for commercial activity and the superstitions of their religion. They must cast off a Jewishness which was associated in the Gentile mind with ghetto civilization. But as Jews gained citizenship and competed successfully with Gentiles in economic activity and social life, their enemies accused them of continuing their "Jewish" habits despite emancipation.

For those who opposed emancipation and resented Jewish success in the Gentile world, the continued existence of ghettos in eastern Europe provided proof that the differences between Jews and other peoples could never be bridged. The ghetto Jews, urbanized and living at the margin of economic subsistence, seemed to provide a startling contrast to supposed Aryan virtues and ideal types. Jews in the ghetto and those that emigrated into western Europe tended to preserve, at first, their special dress (caftan), beards, and earlocks. To many in western and central Europe the outward appearance of these Jews was strange and mysterious.

Racial thought had already stressed the symbolism of outward appearance and in this context even assimilated Jews were thought to form a fifth column in the Gentile world. The accusation that Jews were a state within a state dates back to the very beginning of emancipation and led, almost inevitably, to the belief that Jews must once again be excluded from European life. Jews were thought to desire domination over Europe through their economic skills supposedly based upon their ingrained materialism. They were successful in finance capitalism which was open to them as a profession because it was new and not bound to older traditional institutions such as the guilds, which excluded Jews. But as men like the Rothschilds and the Pereiras rose to great wealth, all those classes of the population which feared finance capitalism saw such success as proof of a criminal Jewish conspiracy.

The wave of hatred against the Jews found an outlet in the anti-Jewish riots in Germany in 1819 which were joined by those classes which were being hard-pressed by the industrialization of Europe. During the revolution of 1848 craftsmen and artisans, the prime victims of industrialization, once more demanded the exclusion of Jews from European life, though opposition to Jewish emancipation was not confined to these classes alone. Conservatives and liberals, middle class or aristocrat, who longed for economic and social stability tended to blame the Jews for the disruption of European life. Early socialists like F. M. Charles Fourier (1772–1835) and Pierre Joseph Proudhon (1804–65), in turn, saw the Jews as exploiters of the working class.

Such anti-Jewish sentiment did not necessarily lead to racism, for there were those who continued to believe that "good Jews" could shed their "Jewish" qualities. However, those who believed in racial differences and in the reality of a Jewish conspiracy began to advocate race war. Darwinism gave a scientific foundation to ideas of fighting and struggle during the second half of the century, but here, once more, the irrational attitudes which had emerged earlier were more important than the scientific theory which they annexed.

Social Darwinism proclaimed that the survival of the fittest together with the right of the strong provided the principle by which the lives of people and states must be governed. The survival of the fittest pitted race against race.

This race war provided one of the principal themes of Houston Stewart Chamberlain's influential *Foundations of the Nineteenth Century* (1899). The Germans were the saviors of world history and the carriers of western culture; all cultural achievements of modern times must be fired with their spirit, a spirit sharpened through incessant struggle. The Aryan existed amidst a "chaos of races," but there was one race other than the Aryan which had remained pure: the chief antagonist in the never-ending struggle for survival. The Jews symbolized the opposite of all that Aryans held dear; they were incapable of higher thought and culture. The Jews were characterized by an iron will to power which lacked all metaphysical depth. Chamberlain's race war was a total war which could only end in extermination or victory. The Aryans needed a leader in order to triumph over the Jews, and toward the end of his life Chamberlain believed that he had found this leader in Adolf Hitler. *Foundations of the Nineteenth Century* is one of the classics of racial thought; not only was it read widely but it also summed up the development of this thought during the second half of the nineteenth century.

Chamberlain's stress upon cultural and spiritual factors once more catapulted racial thought from science to myth. For him all culture was based upon spiritual concerns, and all true spirituality was Aryan opposed to anything Jewish. Christ himself became an Aryan prophet. Racism in central and eastern Europe increasingly became a mysticism which claimed to be a new religion: Christ was integrated with the force released by the sun, the aesthetic principles of the ideal type and a spirituality which denied any influences from outside itself. Chamberlain typically rejected all environmentalism. Here the science of racial classification and Darwinian evolution were lifted into the realm of myth and symbol.

Julius Langbehn's popular *Rembrandt as Educator* (1890) further illustrates this development. Germans must become truly creative and this meant embracing an Aryan mystique. For Langbehn the life force descended from the cosmos to the *Volk*, a part of the extrasensory world which was the only world of reality. Racism was transformed into a mysticism which built upon the occult movements of the late nineteenth century. Langbehn was not alone, for in Munich after the turn of the century a whole group of "cosmic philosophers" (e.g., Ludwig Klages [1872–1957]) put forth similar ideas. For them Aryan blood had a particular quality which linked it with the extrasensory world: the cosmos was reflected in the blood stream of the superior and metaphysical race.

The war between races was one of spirituality against materialism and such a Manichean view of the world gave impetus to the flight into mysticism. This racism had an easier time in Protestant than in Catholic regions. Catholic theology presented a well-defined view of the world, reinforced by its hierarchy. Protestantism had a less well-defined theology and was tied to the secular state. This, however, was a matter of degree only: eventually, for example, most Catholics and Protestants complied with the dictates of National Socialist Racial Policy, while some leading churchmen of both faiths took a stand against it.

Those who came into contact with this mystical racism before the First World War carried it over into the twentieth century. Certainly Adolf Hitler (1889–1945) was the most important of these men. The creation of the Aryan was no longer discussed in terms of polygenism by these racists, but was thought to be a product of divine gestation, usually an electric shock produced by the cosmic life-force.

There were other racists, however, who attempted to keep in touch with the scientific foundations of racism. Here Social Darwinism led to a concern with eugenics, for the pure race must be properly bred in order to assure its survival in the universal struggle of man and nature. In England Francis Galton (1822–1911) believed that nature assured the survival of the fittest and that interference with it to protect the weak and feeble would lead to the decline of the race. He used the word race to describe inherited characteristics: a race which had managed to survive and produce the carriers of a superior culture must be protected and furthered by the state. Galton was the father of racial eugenics; they were further elaborated by his disciple Karl Pearson (1857–1936). In France Georges Vacher de Lapouge (*L'Aryen son rôle social* [1899]) derived the need for racial eugenics from Darwin's struggle for survival. But, above all, in Germany such racial eugenics became popular. Untold schemes were invented to enable Aryans to breed under ideal conditions. The climax of this development came with the unsuccessful attempt of the SS in Nazi Germany to ensure racial purity through the attempted mating of certified and selected Aryan partners (*Lebensborn*).

Such programs suggested the euthanasia which the Nazis were to practice later. It became a commonplace of racial eugenics that for the sake of racial survival the incurably-ill, insane, or physically deformed must be sterilized. They typified the degeneration of the superior race, a consequence of miscegenation. Racists derived the concept of "degeneration" from psychologists like A. B. Morel (1809–37) and Cesare Lombroso (1836–1909), who believed that certain physical deformities were symptoms of a degenerate personality. Pre-Freudian psychology based itself upon physical characteristics similar to the correspondence between outward appearance and inward personality which characterized racism. Through eugenics the Aryan stereotype became a self-fulfilling prophecy: if the race did not reflect it, then its own ranks must be purged until the ideal type predominated.

Racism as a fully blown theory was associated with the left as well as with the right. For example, in France anti-Semitism was spread by the early socialists from the 1830s onward. The Jew, conceived in racist terms, was symbolic of the exploiter of the working classes. What Proudhon and others emphasized at mid-century, Edouard Drumont carried on during its final years. *La France Juive* (1886) stressed the image of the Jew as the enemy of the working class. Drumont shared this obsession with a right wing of the Socialist party. The collapse of the Panama Company in which Jews were involved reinforced the picture of Jews as the financial exploiters and manipulators of Europe. But Drumont, typically enough, drifted away from any association with socialism into the national camp. The Dreyfus case (1894–99) seemed to confront the French and the Jewish race, as the writer Maurice Barrès (1862–1923) believed. The Jew used Marxist doctrines of the class war in order to destroy the fabric of the nation and with it all of its inhabitants.

Drumont and Barrès became national socialists who believed that a more equal distribution of wealth was essential but that this must come about without destroying the class hierarchy. The Right throughout Europe tended to regard the working classes as the "soul of the nation," but at the same time allowed them only job security and employment insurance but never political power or economic equality. In Germany Eugen Dühring regarded himself as a national socialist and in his *Jewish Question* (1880) pointed to that race as the true enemy. But unlike Drumont who wrote in a Catholic country and in the end even made his peace with the Church, Dühring looked to the ancient Germanic gods to inspire his nation with a sense of national unity and social justice, which would give Germany the courage to eliminate the Jews. Here the Jews became the enemy of all classes, including the workers. Jews were the enemy of the nation and one way in which they undermined it was by advocating the concept of an industrial proletariat which would tear the nation apart through class struggle.

The worker was viewed as a medieval artisan with roots in his race rather than in his class. He was put into the same category as the peasant whom racism always exalted as having preserved ties with the historical roots of the race. Peasants had resisted change and supposedly kept themselves pure, and now the worker must do likewise. This national socialism was strongest in France before the First World War: its time of triumph in Germany and central Europe came after 1918.

Conspiracy theories were bound to play a large part in racism, for the inferior race must fight but obviously lacked the chivalry to do so openly. Names like Rothschild had become symbols of a "secret power" which manipulated the world. The Jewish world conspiracy received its so-called proof in a document forged in the midst of the Dreyfus affair not only for use in France, but as part of a scheme of the czarist secret police to foment pogroms in Russia. *The Protocols of the Elders of Zion* were dressed up as a verbatim report of a secret meeting of the leaders of international Jewry. They were plotting to take over the world by stealth and violence, inciting revolution as well as digging tunnels under cities. That such a document came to be accepted after 1918 as gospel truth by much of the European Right can further attest to the irrational power of racism.

France played an important role in the formulation of racism while Italy was the backwater of racist thought. Catholicism on the one hand, and the humanistic nationalism exemplified by Giuseppe Mazzini, on the other, provided strong barriers to the development of racism. To be sure, Catholic anti-Semitism existed in Italy as in France, but such anti-Semitism which ceased with Baptism did not break through to form a racist tradition.

It was in central and eastern Europe that racism and nationalism made their most effective alliance. In many nations such as Hungary, Rumania, and Poland, Jews constituted the most visible part of the commercial middle class and all the national socialist factors which we have discussed could come into play. Moreover, the presence of an urban ghetto civilization encouraged the belief in race differences. In addition, the industrial revolution had come with a rush to some nations, like Germany, and racist ideas helped to maintain a national cohesion which class warfare seemed about to destroy. Furthermore, all of these nations had irredenta against their neighbors. Nationalism was a fortress besieged from within and without and racism could be used to justify tribal exclusiveness and superiority.

The results of such nationalism were constant attempts to undo Jewish emancipation. In Germany a whole series of anti-Semitic groups and political parties arose during the last two decades of the nineteenth century. Some, like Adolf Stoecker's *Christian Social Party* (1878–90) were conservative, basing their anti-Semitism upon Protestant orthodoxy. But others like Otto Boeckel's *Hessian Peasant Ligue* (1887–94) and the various anti-Semitic leagues founded by men like the indefatigible Theodor Fritsch (1868–1933) were national socialist and racist in orientation. The climax was reached in 1893 when the combined groups of anti-Semites polled some 116,000 votes. After this they declined rapidly and spent their time quarrelling among themselves.

More important was the alliance of the German Conservative party with anti-Semitic forces (Tivoli Programm, 1892). Though conservatives at first believed that Jews should be excluded because Germany was a Christian state, but accepted them if they converted, an influential faction of the party became racist through alliance with the Agrarian Association of Landowners (*Bund der Landwirte*) which had propagated racism for many years. Conservatives did not appeal to violence before the First World War; such an appeal was confined to fringe groups, except in Tsarist Russia where pogroms were part of government policy.

Before 1918 racism also found a home in many small sects which warred with each other. These sects continued the mystical rather than the scientific tradition of racism: they were concerned with the Aryan as a creature of the sun, with his connection with the cosmos, and they drew their ideal type from such inspiration rather than anthropology or linguistics. Lanz von Liebenfels (1874–1954), for example, called his journal *Ostara* (after the Germanic Goddess of Spring), a journal for blond people, and sold it on the streets of Vienna. There the young Adolf Hitler read it, for his racism was drawn from this kind of source. It was based upon the fear of the mysterious and unknown, for as he tells us in *Mein Kampf* he became an anti-Semite upon seeing east European Jews in their peculiar dress on the streets of Vienna. The clash of cultures, which we mentioned earlier, was instrumental in providing a world view to the unlettered and naive boy from the provinces. Hitler's reaction was no different from that of Fritsch or many other men of the second half of the nineteenth century who felt compelled by differences in outward appearance to wage a race war on behalf of the Aryan spirit. Hitler came into contact with this racism before the First World War and it remained basic to his thought until his death.

The end of World War I saw the active implementation of racism in in Europe. Defeated nations sought for a scapegoat, while the preponderance of Jews in the left-wing revolutions all over Europe during 1919 and 1920 seemed to prove the subversive nature of the Jewish conspiracy. Rosa Luxemburg in Berlin, Kurt Eisner in Munich, Belâ Kun in Budapest, and the many Jewish leaders of the Bolsheviks were held up as proof of racist contentions. The shock of those years threw a shadow into the future. Though racism had been applied to native peoples outside Europe and had born fruit in the United States, it was in Europe itself that genocide became history as part of government policy. Racist thought itself would not change; it remained static. When controversy among racists erupted between the world wars it always took place within the framework of past development. Thus Hans F. K. Günther (1891–1968), the chief Nazi racial theorist, stressed, for example, the physical differences between the Aryan and the Jewish race and compiled a list of typical "Jewish" gestures and traits. His adversary L. F. Clauss (*The Nordic Soul* [1932]) held that outward appearance was not as essential as the "inward qualities" of race. Clauss attempted to side-step the fact that not all Aryans were blond or looked like Greek statues. But this never presented a problem for racists as they used the concept of the "ideal type." Thus all

Aryans had some ideal qualities but did not have to present all of them. In contrast every Jew or black was endowed with all of the supposedly ugly physical and mental qualities of his race. These qualities contrasted with the Aryan ideal of beauty, emphasizing a lack of proportion and awkwardness. Moreover, unlike the Greek ideal, Jews and blacks were given ugly noses, kinky hair and a strong smell. They were also endowed with great sexual potency, making them the aggressor and despoiler of the white race. Though some of these qualities can be traced back to the Middle Ages as far as anti-Semitic feelings were concerned, nevertheless within racism Jews and blacks were regarded the same. Just as the Aryan stereotype symbolized the superior race, so the anti-type symbolized inferior races regardless of whether it was Jew or black. Imperialism, when it was a racism directed at blacks, usually went its separate way from anti-Semitism directed against the Jews. Yet one racism could stimulate the other: for example, the Italian fascist anti-Jewish legislation of 1938 was connected to the Italian conquest of Ethiopia and the confrontation of blacks and whites in that territory.

Though racial thought itself did not change significantly, after 1918 several new factors came to play a role in its justification. Psychology began to emphasize racial differences, not the psychology of Sigmund Freud but, for example, that associated with Carl Gustav Jung (1875–1961). Jung's psychology tended to slide off into a mystical symbolism and his emphasis upon unchangeable archetypes which were created by history and religion easily took on racial connotations. It was Jung who assumed the editorship of the most important German psychological journal under Nazi rule. Many scientists were prone to differentiate between the laboratory, where they adhered to a scientific method, and the outside world, where they paid allegiance to all manner of irrational thought. This differentiation would not work, and the irrationalism with which they regarded the social and political order soon led to Aryan physics, Aryan medicine, and Aryan biology.

However, the crucial new aspect of racism after the war was its growth as a mass movement. As a mass movement racism shared a common foundation with earlier national socialism. Within the mystique of the *Volk*, all members presumably were equal and none were exploited. Liberalism was as divisive as Marxism, and parliament an obsolete bourgeois form of government. Racism annexed the ideal of the hero as political leader which had developed throughout the nineteenth century. From Thomas Carlyle (1795–1881) to Richard Wagner (1813–83) such heroes exemplified in their person the virility of their people. For Wagner such leaders were part of the *mythos* of the *Volk* whose life-giving forces which derived from the distant Germanic past still continued. He redefined the concept of myth which had been applied to the legends of the ancients and the customs of primitive peoples. Myth was defined as *mythos:* standing outside historical development, nordic and eternal, it gave man his roots. Wagner popularized this world view by giving his ancient German heroes, fathers of the race, an emotional and spectacular setting which appealed to the neo-romanticism of the German middle classes. Houston Stewart Chamberlain harnessed the *mythos* to the politics of racial war, but the hunger for such a myth was especially widespread in the Germany of the nineteen twenties. Alfred Rosenberg considered several titles before he called his book the *Mythos of the Twentieth Century* (1928). Here *mythos* became central to the religion of race which Rosenberg confronted with Christianity. The *mythos* of an unchangeable past gave German racism a special dimension.

The proper governance of the race was through a leader who symbolized it by uniting in his person all the qualities associated with the vibrant *mythos* of racial superiority. The people themselves were equal to one another in theory, but in practice unequal in the hierarchy of functions which each member of the race performed. Gobineau's nightmare of Caesar and people confronting each other seemed to have become the ideal of racist political thought. In reality, as we found in our discussion of nationalism, the liturgy of politics took the place of representative government as a bridge between governors and governed. Mass participation in Nazi or fascist mass meetings (and those of all similar movements in eastern and central Europe) symbolized this form of government and indeed became the setting for a liturgy which eventually supplanted the institutions of representative government. Massed groups of people performing in unison contrasted with the loneliness of the leader whose contours were illuminated by the sacred flame. Eventually National Socialism introduced a cycle of new national festivals to celebrate the mythical racial past, sun symbolism, and those martyrs who had died for the movement. As a mass movement racism annexed the traditional Christian liturgy for its own purposes: Christian *responsas* became speaking choruses (pioneered by the communists); the racist "Confession of Faith" was solemnly recited. Hitler himself explained his successes in peace and war as a "miracle of Divine Providence."

This created additional belief in the faith. However, social paternalism, such as the *Strength Through Joy* movement which organized the workers' leisure time, supplemented political rites. This satisfied many workers and went hand in hand with equality of status which racism granted, helping to disguise the dictatorial regulation of work. The racist world view had another advantage as well. Racists were flexible in economics, for they believed that economic problems would solve themselves once the race was in power.

This discussion of racism has led us away from the beginning of the century and from definitions of individual freedom as the basis for liberty. Romanticism, nationalism, and racism were not the only forces determining man's attitude toward himself and his society in the first part of the nineteenth century. Liberalism, "the religion of liberty," vitally influenced man's thought. For man living under the shadow of a variety of political and economic dictatorships during the twentieth century such a religion may well seem strange and archaic. Quite wrongly liberalism itself has been blamed for creating twentieth century dictatorships. In reality, while liberalism undoubtedly furthered capitalist developments, it also provided the challenge of human liberty to the European reaction of the nineteenth and twentieth centuries.

# CHAPTER SIX

# The Challenge
# of Liberty

H ISTORIANS STILL call the decades after 1815 the "Age of
Reaction." True, the slogan of the French Revolution,
"Liberty, Fraternity, Equality," had been repudiated by
most European governments. On the surface at least, it
seemed that Napoleon's fall had sounded the death knell of liberty. Yet
the generation of men who had lived through the Napoleonic era felt that
the century was being reborn in his collapse and the central feature of this
rebirth was, to them, a rebirth of liberty.

Was this hope a mere continuation of the great Revolution's inspired
worship of the Goddess of Liberty? Was it a revival of that "natural liberty" of the Enlightenment in which people were governed solely by the
natural laws of the cosmos? Neither of these. It was instead the redefinition of a liberty which this generation believed had been obscured by the
philosophers of the immediate past. Eighteenth-century philosophers based
their concept of liberty on reason and natural law, deriving liberty from
their belief in man's inherent rationality. Such men repudiated the historical past not only because it had failed to contribute to human freedom
but also because it was replete with those superstitions so hostile to the free
use of rationality. History was condemned by the light of reason. "Happiness," said the revolutionary Saint-Just, "is a new word in Europe."

A revival of history underlay the new concept of liberty in the post-Napoleonic generation. This revival had been foreshadowed by the Italian historian, Giambattista Vico, who, in his *Scienza Nuova,* the *New Science* (1725), had confronted the rationalism of his age with a philosophy of history. Vico felt that history also worked according to natural laws, laws which determined its movement which Vico took to be cyclical. Civilizations arose and decayed, descending from the age of the gods to that of the heroic and on to the human age and its subsequent decay. Vico's cyclical theory of history had little impact on his contemporaries. Much later, at the end of the nineteenth century, Benedetto Croce refurbished Vico's status as a historian, and still later Oswald Spengler espoused, in part, his theories. Nevertheless, to this post-Napoleonic generation, Vico displayed a philosophy of history governed by natural laws which moved through the engine of the human spirit. Central to this spirit was a concept of liberty.

What emerged, then, from Vico's thought was a concept of liberty which worked as a natural law in history and through history. "Everything is history," the Neapolitan maintained, a remark Croce was fond of repeating later on. While accepting the primacy of the spirit in the human struggle for liberty, the adherents of the religion of liberty abandoned the cyclical rhythm of history in favor of a concept of progress based, as it was, on the optimistic belief of the Enlightenment in the triumph of reason. Now, however, this concept of progress was combined with an awareness of the importance of historical development. Human progress developed through the laws of history and not through the inevitable triumph of reason alone. A concept of liberty was central to this human progress in the sense of liberty's progress as a part of man's progress through history.

But had liberty not led to the Terror, to Jacobin tyranny and, in the end, to Napoleon's iron grip on Europe? Would liberty, even if conceived in historical terms, not lead to new excesses? The adherents of this new liberty had to face this problem. They believed in liberty but hated what Robespierre and Napoleon had made out of this human longing. The emphasis on history helped here, for such an emphasis precluded sudden innovations. They went one step further and repudiated the revolutionary concept of democracy, a concept they felt led not to liberty but to absolutism. They blamed Rousseau's doctrine of the general will and Robespierre's use of it. Madame de Staël, in her *Considerations upon the French Revolution* (1816), spoke of the Revolution as a crisis in the history of liberty. She contrasted ancient liberty, sanctified by history, to the modernity of despotism. Jacobin popular democracy was, for her, just another form of tyranny; liberty had to be obtained in another way, a way outlined by the French constitution of 1791 and the constitution of England (for Madame de Staël admired the English constitution as did Montesquieu before her). "It is a beautiful sight this constitution, vacillating a little as it sets out from its port, like a vessel launched at sea, yet unfurling its sails, it gives full play to everything great and generous in the human soul." Through such a constitution liberty unfolds within the historical process. Liberty was all-important to this talented and famous woman; she hated the Terror but she did not lay it at the doorstep of the Revolution. The *ancien régime* had so corrupted the morals of the people that despotism, not liberty, had to be the outcome of their justified revolt. She held to the oft-repeated view that the champions of reaction, not the revolutionaries, were the ultimate causes of revolutions.

To avoid the excesses of revolutionary freedom, Madame de Staël believed that the people had to be morally raised before such freedom could be granted. The historical framework of a constitutional development would provide the means to achieve this. Such a tie between morality and freedom was to be typical for much of nineteenth-century liberalism. To these men and women the French Revolution had perverted freedom because the Revolution had been immoral. The new liberty must therefore be linked to a moral base. This important facet of liberalism will be examined in greater detail later; it came to temper the individualism of the liberal faith. Furthermore, Madame de Staël thought this road to liberty could only be traveled by a historical entity like the nation: "Nothing durable can be accomplished except in the nation." The stress on the new liberty also meant a change, not only from rationalism to historicism, but also from the cosmopolitanism of the eighteenth century to the nationalism of the nineteenth.

This liberty was the theme of Benjamin Constant in his Paris lecture of 1819 on ancient and modern liberty. One of the liberal leaders of the French Chamber after 1819, Constant's writings and lectures were much admired by that generation. He, too, felt that liberty was modern and that it must be distinguished from the liberties of the Greeks and Romans. With Constant, concern for the preservation of that individual liberty which had been destroyed by the demagogues of ancient democracy was central. Ancient democracy meant to him the sovereignty of the mob, a collective sovereignty which Rousseau had advocated and which had led directly to the guillotine on the Place de la Concorde. This democracy was, in fact, a tyranny, for it had no constitutional guarantees other than those designed to preserve the liberty of popular participation in government. Such guarantees did not insure freedom; true constitutional guarantees had to be designed to protect individual liberty both from governmental authority and tyrannical democracy. General participation in government was valid only through the constitutional principle of parliamentary representation.

Liberty for Constant meant the right to submit solely to laws and not to

*"new liberty" Constitutional & Moral.*

men, to choose one's own profession and to dispose of and even abuse one's own property. This modern liberty Constant saw as part of a progression within a historical context. The idea of progress was important to him; in fact, he considered that modern progress had made war obsolete. Since in history war predated commerce, commerce was therefore an advanced development which would surely bring universal peace. This high optimism was not confined to Constant. Later in the century the poet Tennyson sang about the bales of commerce which drove away war. Both Madame de Staël and Constant redefined liberty at the beginning of the century, a redefinition based upon a revival of history.

The principle of submission to laws instead of to men and the principle of representative government were central to liberalism, but so was the rejection of democracy. The redefinition of liberty included the idea that there were limits to the law's and to parliament's jurisdiction over the individual. He stood in the center of things. Constant once more expressed this well: "... there is a part of human life which necessarily remains individual and independent, and has the right to stand outside all social control." For Liberals, this part of human life was all important; both absolutism and democracy would erode it. Thus, they turned back to an eighteenth-century idea—the idea of checks and balances which Montesquieu had put forward. Like the French philosopher, they saw this ideal practiced in the English constitution and their admiration of England was based on this view of English government. At the same time that the Frenchman Constant expressed the importance of such guarantees of freedom, Alfieri said that same thing in Italy. In England there was an equilibrium of political forces which prevented oppression. The aristocracy, the people, and the king each had their rights and yet they were united. A little later, de Tocqueville in France was to express much the same ideas and analyze England in a more thorough fashion.

Liberals did not object to interest groups; indeed, they saw, in the balance between them, a guarantee for liberty. The modern historian Guido de Ruggiero has called the essence of political liberalism "an opposition of parties transcending the opposition of classes." This opposition of interests was to eventually result in a balance between them which would make for a true kind of unity. It has already been seen that Cavour held such ideas. This view of politics reinvigorated the trend toward constitutional rule which seemed so apparent in Europe after 1815. This advance toward constitutionalism, in its turn, seemed to confirm liberal ideas of progress.

The idea of progress and the ideal of constitutional government were to remain part of the vision of Liberals throughout the century. The ideal of individual freedom, however, confronted not only the recent revolutionary past but also the present of the Industrial Revolution. How could this stress upon freedom solve the problem of the working classes, of the rapidly changing social structure of society? As long as industrial development meant an expanding economy, liberty could be defined as freedom to move along with this expansion. This led to an increasing emphasis upon economic freedom among those preoccupied with the grave social problems of the age. The religion of liberty had tried to profit from the lessons learned from the French Revolution, but now it faced the grim, inexorable facts of the Industrial Revolution. In order to preserve the religion of liberty was it feasible to tell the poor, "Enrich yourselves and all will be well"? By 1848 the failure of such an appeal was manifest.

Liberalism, however, was capable of adjusting its central concern with human liberty to the realities of society. Here England set the tone, for England was, after all, the chief laboratory of liberal thought during the century. The admiration of the Continental Liberals was based upon the operation of the English constitution, but it was increased through the influence of Britain's dynamic liberal thought. It is therefore English liberalism which must be discussed before that of the Continent, for it tried to meet the challenges of industrialism in the most constructive way. But then, English liberalism, unlike that of the Continent, was working against the backdrop of a most rapid industrial change.

Adam Smith's *Wealth of Nations* began the effort in 1776. In this work of the Enlightenment, liberty was put into the context of laws of nature, of the natural liberty of humanity: "Every man is committed by nature to his own care." The optimism of the Enlightenment dominated Smith's work. Every man, in following his own nature or interests, would be led by an invisible hand to promote an end which was not part of his intention—the good of all. Smith did allow for the state—indeed, he thought it necessary— but only to give men security, to protect them in their lives and possessions. Government had a purely negative function, for Smith hated that "crafty animal," the politician; he thought the natural rules of justice better than human ones. The historical element in his idea of liberty was lacking. Smith wrote before the French Revolution, but the idea of natural liberty had a certain appeal for Liberals even after Napoleon's fall. In mid-century England the industrialist and reformer, Richard Cobden (1804–65), wrote that one might as well regulate the seasons as try to regulate the relationship between employer and laborer. Momentarily at least, the historical element of this liberalism seemed to have lapsed. The reason for this was that in Cobden's time the Conservatives stressed the ameliorative effects of traditionalism as the main plank in their platform. Nevertheless, the attachment to constitutionalism, to representative and parliamentary forms of government remained. These were the forms of political liberty, while popular democracy continued to be rejected as de Staël and Constant had rejected it.

Smith's optimism stood at the beginning of the Industrial Revolution. In 1798 Thomas Robert Malthus's *Essay on Population* had made a further adjustment to economic fact. Believing in natural law also, he posited that when population began to outrun food supply nature checked population by war, pestilence, famine, and disease. The rapidly growing population of England and the resultant problems were reflected in his thesis. There was in the theory of the Anglican clergyman little of the earlier optimism of liberal thought. Experience had shaken the belief that an abundant and just life for all men would arrive through peaceful means. Malthus introduced into liberal thought the concept of struggle. Life was a struggle for survival against war, pestilence, and famine. Governments could not attempt to abolish these scourges since they were part of this same inexorable scheme of nature. Despite what may seem the inhuman aspects of his thesis, Malthus had in mind the welfare of his fellowmen, for he felt that government interference would increase the harsh effects attendant on human life in this world. Under natural liberty population and food supply would find their own level.

While Malthus opposed state interference with the workings of nature, he did believe that the individual could do something about it. People must become virtuous and resist temptations. The answer to hunger and misery was not legislation but the virtue of the individual. Malthus was here at one with the growing emphasis upon morality within the liberal context. The clergyman was not as callous as subsequent writers have pictured him. Freedom from government was necessary but so were the self-restraint and virtuous behavior of the individual. Malthus did, however, see freedom in terms of struggle— this was necessary because individual freedom meant struggling for survival. Such a belief did lead, despite Malthus's intentions, toward a justification of economic acquisitiveness; it gave the competitive spirit of the businessman a moral credence in society. This concept of struggle became an integral part of liberal ideology, a part of the tacit equation between enrichment and freedom.

The benefits of competition also entered David Ricardo's attempt to prove that wages find their own subsistence levels. His *On the Principle of Political Economy and Taxation* (1817) pictured the interests of social classes as vastly divergent. Society was not based upon each man's interest benefiting all, as Smith had thought; instead it was based upon the struggle between diverse elements of that society. Once again life was a struggle for existence. In Ricardo, liberal thought was adjusted to a poverty which was more visible than ever in the new industrial towns of England, a poverty which did not seem to improve with time.

The most fundamental restatement of liberalism, however, came during the years 1776 to 1832 under the inspiration of Jeremy Bentham. Bentham, keenly aware of the condition of England, attempted to cope with these problems by rejecting the eighteenth-century framework of natural law and seeking a more realistic basis for his thought.

The test for liberty in society was not natural freedom but utility—the famous phrase, "the greatest happiness for the greatest number." This happiness was to be determined through what he called the pleasure principle. Since there were two masters over mankind, pleasure and pain, the object of society was to produce the maximum of pleasure and the minimum of pain for the individual. Bentham's individualism was tempered by the fact that he saw people not as individuals but as associating in groups; the happiness of the individual was linked to the happiness of the group, the "greatest number." To preserve this happiness he permitted interference with individual liberty for the sake of social harmony. In the application of coercion, which he equated with pain, a balance had to be maintained in order to preserve happiness. Who was to enforce this balance? Bentham answered this question in a most important way, for it was the legislator who received this function. Bentham raised the tasks of Parliament from the low estate Smith had initially assigned to government in English liberal ideology. He himself was in the forefront of the fight for parliamentary reform.

What was liberal about Bentham's principles? Bentham thought that social harmony must be produced by legislation, while Smith, Malthus, and Ricardo thought that such harmony was produced by an absence of governmental interference. Substituting utility for natural law might seem to lead to an abandonment of that complete individual liberty which the religion of liberty treasured above all else. It must be remembered, however, that the pleasure principle was equated with individual freedom. Bentham fought for a middle-class parliament; he wanted no privileged classes in society. Still more important, the eighteenth-century tradition remained in Bentham's emphasis on rationalism. Reason would arrive at the proper balance between pleasure and pain which would preserve the maximum of freedom. He believed in the possibility of a truly scientific political science which would carefully calculate this balance. Classifying everything according to Benthamite criteria, he and his successors couched their arguments in abstract scientific terms. With the help of this science even Parliament would not be able to rule arbitrarily since the legislator was to be guided by concrete and rational politics, by actual mathematical and statistical calculations between the pleasure and pain principles.

Bentham used the scientific beliefs of the age to counter governmental absolutism. This belief in the existence of a positive science of government and society was substantially similar to that held in France by Auguste Comte and Proudhon. The latter claimed, in fact, that a prime minister needed simply to be an expert on statistics. Through such an approach Bentham tried to combine freedom and legislation. He achieved impressive concrete results: the reform of an antiquated penal code, prison reform, and a significant contribution toward the reform of Parliament itself. To liberalism he gave a thoery of legislation and a theoretical basis for the advocacy of reforms through Parliament. There was also a negative side to his thought. He did not advocate economic reforms; indeed, his theories tended to divide the cause of political reform from that of economic amelioration. He posited, on the one hand, the possibility of an enlightened social coercion, on the other he left complete economic freedom. This led to a schizophrenia in liberal thought which became increasingly evident.

Bentham's weaknesses were analyzed with much perception by John Stuart Mill (1806–73), himself a product of a Benthamite education. Bentham's belief that all could be related to external and measurable circumstances and then codified into absolute principles which would never fail when reasoned on the basis of utility held grave flaws for Mill. Politics, for him, was not a matter of geometry but was more often than not dominated by human feelings. Bentham was too much in the abstract, schematical tradition of the Enlightenment for Mill, and he turned back to history, reintroducing the historical viewpoint into the religion of liberty. Though Bentham had regarded parliamentary democracy as an absolute principle, for Mill such democracy became a form of government linked to certain times, places, and circumstances. Historically oriented, he returned to the old liberal concern with the tyranny of the masses and the problem of the power of numerical majorities. Thus he proposed the leadership of an intellectual elite, advocating a second vote in parliamentary elections for university men.

This concern of Mill's was very similar to that of Madame de Staël, but now it was seen against the backdrop of the Industrial, not the French Revolution. "In politics it is almost trivial to say that public opinion now rules the world. The only power deserving the name is that of the masses ... their thinking is done for them by men much like themselves ... that does not hinder the government of mediocrity from being mediocre." Approaching the problem of liberty with historical depth, he saw an issue which had escaped Bentham, an issue which increasingly plagued the best minds of the century. His solution to the problem of the masses gave liberalism a theory of leadership, for his aristocracy was based not upon inherited privileges but upon intellectual attainments. Significantly, Mill's ideas

108

came on the scene at a time when the wealthier middle classes were founding educational institutions and sending their sons to the better English public schools.

Mill also believed in reform; he was deeply concerned with the fate of the poor. He belonged to the group called "philosophical radicals," who combined a belief in absolute freedom of discussion with an equal belief in social improvements. Opposed to Malthus, they advocated compulsory birth control which would, in their opinion, lead to higher wages. Mill, with his historical approach, came to think that England was standing on the threshold of a new "positive" stage of history, a stage in which the social question would be solved. But how could this be done without touching private property which was sacred to Liberals and an integral part of their definition of individual liberty? Mill's answer came with his realization that personal liberty and the freedom to use or abuse one's property (Constant's formula) could no longer be combined. After 1847 he drifted close to socialism, breaking with the liberal camp. As all social arrangements were provisional, seen within a historical context, perhaps socialism could provide that balance between justice and freedom which the liberal ideology seemed to lack. Not the sacredness of private property but the equitable division of the product of labor had to be the principle of justice.

It was at this stage of his development that he wrote his most famous book, *On Liberty*. Like Constant's earlier work it stressed individual liberty, but it diverged from the older pattern by the lack of emphasis it placed on the sanctity of private property. There had to be free, untrammeled discussion and the maximum of self-development without interfering with others. This development could not be reached through Adam Smith's "enlightened selfishness" but only through the search for equality of opportunity for all. Mill, who had already perceived Bentham's weaknesses, now attacked additional flaws in liberal arguments. How could there be a maximum of freedom when the economic system excluded some men from advancement? By the middle of the century it was becoming clearer that there was neither unlimited access to or room at the top of the social and economic hierarchy. Mill, whose ideas were later taken up at the turn of the century by social reformers, both reintroduced a historical perspective into the religion of liberty and provided it with a theory of the elite acceptable to the "captains of industry."

The concept of the struggle for existence continued as an important element of liberalism. Darwinism gave it a new lease on life when its rigors were translated into the social realm by Herbert Spencer. The unimpeded struggle for existence led to freedom. That the weak perish in the struggle was not regrettable; it was a positive good. So the laws of nature, as inter-

*[handwritten marginal note:] Personal property — ways to exploit others, that's not liberas.*

preted by Darwin, decreed. The religion of liberty became a harsh doctrine which associated individual freedom with the survival of the fittest. In effect, Spencer's liberalism adapted the movement to the rising tide of European imperialism, while to some it became a justification for extreme economic ruthlessness.

The fall of Napoleon had not meant the end to ideas of liberty. Liberalism was increasingly carried on the shoulders of a rapid industrialization of European society. Economic freedom became ever more basic to that individual freedom the Liberals desired. Whatever Mill's ideas on the subject were, liberal political parties opposed restraints on economic life, and many Liberals believed that free trade would solve all international tensions. There were, however, problems which had to be faced. The economy's rate of expansion faltered, and even when expanding it produced widespread social distress. By the decade of the 1840s Benjamin Disraeli talked about two Englands: that of the rich and that of the poor. Liberal ideas, however, did adjust and tried to meet these problems. Bentham gave new status to Parliament and to liberalism as a political reform movement. Mill believed in an elite which could lead the masses. These men represented just one element of liberalism; equally as important was the moral side of the movement. For many, the problems of society were primarily moral, not economic or social.

There had always been a strong tendency in liberalism to view the world in moral terms. In France Alexis de Tocqueville (1805–59) believed that liberal government rested, in the last resort, upon the spirit with which it was infused: "No; it is not the machinery of laws that produces great events in the world: what brings events to pass is the spirit of government." Or, as he put it on another occasion: ". . . man must believe if he does not want to be a slave." But believe what? In the free play of political expression and the vitality of political life, to be sure, but above this, in a kind of vague religion whose moral purpose centered upon such freedom. Continental Liberals were prone to talk about the moral imperative of liberalism in vague terms, but not Englishmen. Here liberalism was supported by those classes who tended toward nonconformity in religion, those who were neither Anglicans nor Catholics. This nonconformity was imbued with a Calvinistic spirit of individual initiative. But we must not build a theory upon this fact, as Ruggiero did in his *History of European Liberalism* (1927). There he implied that the strength of liberalism had to lie in Protestant rather than in Catholic ideology because Protestantism stressed individualism and Catholicism did not. Ruggiero linked Protestantism with this nonconformity in England. Such Protestantism also stressed a community of believers, however, and it was used, it will be seen, as an inspiration for Christian socialism as well as for liberalism.

Moreover, there were a good many men, especially in France, who thought that Catholicism and liberalism could, and indeed should, work together.

Yet, when English Liberals spoke of the moral imperative, and most of them did just that, they meant a specific type of morality which was not at all vague. Indeed, this morality tempered the liberal idea of freedom and liberty to so great an extent that we might well raise the question of how much remained. Historians, by concentrating upon the liberal idea of struggle and economic freedom, have overlooked the strict morality which accompanied these ideas. Here very little freedom was allowed. For Liberals accepted and furthered that change in morality which came about at the turn of the century. It is important, therefore, to discuss this morality in connection with liberalism, even though it became the dominant morality in England generally and in much of Europe as well. Liberal freedom which we have discussed up to this point was severely circumscribed and restricted by this development.

It is difficult to analyze the moral pattern which accompanied liberal thought. There is no doubt that the turn of the century saw a change in the moral tone of society, which is easily illustrated. Sir Walter Scott's aged aunt asked him to procure for her some of the books she had enjoyed in her youth during the previous century. Sir Walter did as he was bid and later when he ventured to hope that she had enjoyed this recapturing of her youth her answer greatly surprised him. His aunt blushed at the mention of the books and allowed that she had destroyed them because they were not fit reading. Similarly, in Germany, a lady sitting next to the writer Brentano told him how much she had enjoyed a play he had written in his youth. How startled she must have been when the author, instead of being pleased, replied that as a woman and mother she should have been ashamed to read such a work. This change is what Harold Nicolson has characterized as the "onslaught of respectability." It was, as these examples show, quite rapid, almost within one generation.

What lay behind this tightening up of morality? Only tentative answers can be given, for as yet little is known about this phenomenon. It seems certain that the evangelical movement in England, the strongest element in nonconformity, and the pietistic movements in Europe had a direct influence on the morality of the age. Both these movements had remained outside the mainstream of the Enlightenment; both were opposed to its main tenets. It is often forgotten that the eighteenth century witnessed a religious revival even while the *philosophes* were writing their enlightened tracts. This revival stressed piety, not the piety of Church attendance but the piety of the heart. Dogma had no great interest for either the Wesley brothers in England or

Count Zinzendorf in Germany; true conversion of the spirit was the center of their religious thought. Such piety required a casting off of worldly frivolities. Especially in England it revived the Puritan idea of life as a struggle between the world and the spirit, between the lusts of the flesh and dedication to one's calling.

Two other factors strengthened this reawakened moral passion. There was a moral reaction against the French Revolution and its antireligious bent. Madame de Staël had seen in the Reign of Terror a moral failing on the part of the people; many Englishmen linked the events of the French Revolution to the prevalence of immorality in that nation. Men and women of the nobility and the middle classes called for moral reform at home in order that Revolutionary immorality might be better withstood in the struggle between the two nations. Pamphlets and diaries give ample evidence of an attempted reform of manners. Frivolity, worldly and sexual excesses were regarded as unworthy of a nation engaged in a life and death struggle with forces which symbolized all that was immoral. The Evangelicals in England benefited by this feeling of distaste. Sunday observances were revived; frivolity was taken as a sign of levity in a time of serious crisis. William Wilberforce persuaded King George III to issue a royal proclamation in 1787 which condemned vice. Considering the immoral tone of his sons, this could not have lacked irony.

The second factor, associated with the expanding economy, was the rapid rise within the social hierarchy of the newly rich. This self-assertive and ambitious bourgeoisie brought with them a dedication to hard work and a sense of the superiority of the values of the self-made man to those of the old aristocracy. These values blended in with the revived Puritan impetus exemplified by the evangelical movement. Never a part of the idle and sophisticated aristocracy, these men, through the increasing fluidity of English class lines, now infiltrated that class. No wonder that Edmund Burke lamented the vanished "unbought grace of life" of a previous age. Now the grace of membership in the upper classes was bought and that, in itself, created a different attitude toward life. Piety, moral revulsion against the French Revolution, and the attitudes of the bourgeoisie all contributed to the new moral tone. This was not confined to England; such conditions were present in all of western Europe, but it was England which best exemplified these moral attitudes, for they fitted in with liberal thought which now took up and furthered this morality as suited to its ideology in the age of the Industrial Revolution. Individualism stood in the forefront combined with the kind of toughness which made for victory in the struggle for existence. What was needed was sobriety, hard work, and an emphasis on action. Such a life exemplified the true Christian spirit and on the basis of the individuality of one's own character led to self-fulfillment.

Two passages from Charles Kingsley's famous novel *Westward Ho!* (1855) demonstrate the conception of this new attitude by a leading Evangelical. The duty of man was to be bold against himself, as one of the book's heroes explained to his young companion: "To conquer our fancies and our own lusts and our ambitions in the sacred name of duty; this is to be truly brave, and truly strong; for he who cannot rule himself, how can he rule his crew or his fortunes?" What the Puritans had designated their "calling" was here named duty. The individualism involved was brought out further in another passage from Kingsley's book. There were two sorts of people: one trying to do good according to certain approved rules he had learned by ear, and the other not knowing whether he was good or not, just doing the right thing because the Spirit of God was within him. It was this sort of piety which became fashionable at the turn of the century. The contemplative side of pietism gave way to a piety of action. This tranformation was in tune with the experiences of the commercial and industrial classes, though seventeenth-century Puritans had already stated repeatedly that "action is all."

This action was exemplified by what the Victorians called the "gospel of work." As Carlyle put it: ". . . not what I have but what I do is my kingdom." It was in work that duty was exemplified. John Henry Newman shared this emphasis on work: "We are not here that we might go to bed at night, and get up in the morning, toil for our bread, eat and drink, laugh and joke, sin when we have a mind and reform when we are tired of sinning, rear a family and die." Work had to be done in the right spirit: the service of God in one's secular calling.

Samuel Smiles's *Self Help* (1859), which propagandized this morality and its application to work, was the most successful book of the century— over a quarter of a million copies were sold by 1905. Its popularity was as great outside England as within the country. Garibaldi was a great admirer of the book, as was the Queen of Italy. In Japan it was the rage under the title *European Decision and Character Book*. The mayor of Buenos Aires compared Smiles, surprisingly, to Jean-Jacques Rousseau. Quite rightly these underdeveloped countries saw in Smiles's book a reflection of attitudes which were making an important contribution to the successful industrialization of England.

The aim of *Self Help* was to aid the working classes in improving themselves so as to reach the top. This path was marked by the improvement of the individual character of those who desired to be a success in life. "The crown and glory of life is character." What this character should be Smiles illustrated through examples of men who had raised themselves to fame and fortune. Character had to be formed by morals, for to Smiles, social and economic problems were really problems of morality. When he talked about thrift and saving it was the moral aspect of self-reliance and restraint which appealed to him and not the economic consequences of such practices. Character was also shaped by the competitive struggle—stop competition and you stop the struggle for individualism. This struggle had to be conducted in a "manly way" if success was to follow. He exhorted the workers to become gentlemen, for this meant the acquisition of a keen sense of honor, scrupulously avoiding mean actions. "His law is rectitude—action in right lines." Here was a rooted belief in a moral code as the sole road to worldly success.

Samuel Smiles was the great popular propagandist of the gospel of work, but this morality was also inculcated and institutionalized through education. Whole generations of Englishmen were brought up in this belief. Thomas Arnold (1759–1842) was the key figure in establishing liberal morality within the schools through his reforms. When Arnold became headmaster of Rugby in 1828 he initiated educational reforms which soon spread to other public schools, schools which educated and still educate the ruling classes of England. Arnold put his educational aims in this order: (1) religious and moral principles, (2) gentlemanly conduct, and (3) intellectual ability. This ordering is of significance; character building came first, intellectual ability last. The headmaster admired the plodder more than the brilliant student, for the plodder exemplified self-discipline in the name of the gospel of hard work. The student of exceptional brilliance was apt to stray outside the mold. Arnold's attitude toward intellectual brilliance linked to the pragmatic ideals of English nationalism had much influence upon the thought of Englishmen who are still apt to look at brilliance as evidence of a moral unreliability.

Arnold wanted to produce gentlemen, and he defined these in the same way as did Smiles: "The gentleman is eminently distinguished by his self respect. He values his character, not so much of it only as can be seen of others, but as he sees it himself, having regard for his inward monitor." This common ideal of Smiles, Kingsley, and Arnold was further elaborated: "The true gentleman has a keen sense of honor, avoiding mean actions. His standard of probity in word and action is high. He does not shuffle or prevaricate, dodge or sulk; but is honest, upright and straight forward."

In order to transform schoolboys into gentlemen Arnold, however, added one element to Smiles's definition—Christianity. He equated boyhood with original sin, a state of natural imperfection out of which men grow to maturity. Such growth could only come from the formation of character and this, in turn, meant the inculcation of the gospel of work and duty through self-discipline. In this way boys were transformed into Christian gentlemen, for Arnold equated these qualities with Christian piety. Arnold's admirer,

Thomas Hughes (1822–96), had done the same thing in a book aptly called the *Manliness of Christ*. The ideal of the gentleman was set in this way upon a nondogmatic theological base; it became a Christian ideal. Boys had to struggle against their sinful selves in order to pass to manhood. Education was geared to aid this struggle, to lead it to a successful conclusion. Instead of punishment by caning, Arnold used moral exhortation—just as he combined his office of headmaster with that of chaplain of the school. He shamed the boys into righteousness; together with exhortation, he used what was to him the great lesson which produced gentlemen, the ability to both command and obey. Putting this into practice was regarded as his greatest innovation. While fagging, the servile use of junior classmen by their seniors, had always been prevalent in public schools, the masters were usually responsible for the conduct of all the boys in the school. Arnold, however, took the highest class, the sixth form, and gave them disciplinary authority over their younger schoolmates. These boys were his lieutenants, responsible directly to him and in return receiving his full confidence and trust. The sixth form became the custodian of the school's ideal, exemplifying altruistic service to the community. This became generalized in the form of applying the concept of the gentleman to public service. Loyalty to the group meant that a gentleman must be upright and honest. This, in turn, meant that he must not "tell" on offenders, for reporting the crimes of another boy to the masters was looked upon as grounds for dismissal from the school.

Harsh punishment for tale-telling rested on Arnold's belief that an offender not only abandoned his upright character as a gentleman, but he also showed disloyalty to the group he was supposed to govern. It is obvious that in such schools generations were trained in leadership. Despising the democratic process of majority rule, Arnold nevertheless believed that among gentlemen as leaders there must be loyalty and equality. There was one more side to this training in leadership which must be mentioned, the emphasis on fair play. While Arnold was not keen on sports, he began to see their value in such training. If being a gentleman was characterized by "action along right lines," then in football and cricket a boy could learn the fair play which must always accompany such actions on the part of a Christian gentleman. Long after Arnold's day one "old boy" could write about Rugby's organized games as constituting the "real religion of the school." So it has remained in many public schools to this day. For them, character was best built upon the football field. Arnold's training, however, was more complex than this simplified version of it. The emphasis on sports can serve to point out one fact which was inherent in all of this morality—it tempered competition through the concept of fair play. Not only one's own side but also that of the adversary was applauded for doing well. This contrasts with college football in the United States where applause is reserved for one's own side. Here the idea is to win at all costs and competition is stimulated without any tempering moral factors, while in sports, as Arnold and the English schools saw them, the education of the gentleman was to be furthered.

Though sensitive souls were soon broken at Rugby, the admirers of Doctor Arnold imitated and popularized his methods. The chief among these was Thomas Hughes, whose *Tom Brown's Schooldays* (1857) glorified the Rugby tradition. Tom was the embodiment of Arnold's ideal. There was no doubt that Tom was a leader; society to him was like a child which had to be guided. As a gentleman Tom defended the weak against cowardly bullies. Cowardice became the chief crime, a shirking of duty both in terms of leadership and physical strength. The physical element stands out in the account of Tom's school days: "Fighting with fists is the natural and English way for English boys to settle a quarrel." Boxing was as important as the virtues learned on the football field. All this was a part, and by now the most important part, of a Christian gentleman. It will be well to quote a passage from Hughes's defense of "muscular Christianity": ". . . the muscular Christian has hold of the old chivalrous and Christian belief, that a man's body is given to him to be trained and brought into subjection, and then used for the protection of the weak, the advancement of all righteous causes and the subduing of the earth which God has given to the children of men." The reflection of a nation in the midst of empire-building can be discerned here. The depreciation of intellectual attainments was similarly mirrored: ". . . for mere power whether of body or intellect, he has, (I hope and believe), no reverence whatever, though caeteris paribus, he would probably himself, as a matter of taste, prefer the man who can lift a hundred-weight round his head with his little finger to the man who can construct a string of perfect sorites, or expound the doctrine of "contradictory inconceivables.""

Hughes was to summarize these ideals in his *Manliness of Christ*, which he addressed to working men in order to help them improve their lot. The qualities of the Christian gentleman were all present, but now they were summed up in the gospel of work. Tom Brown's dedication to his duties of leadership became, when applied to lower classes, the sole dedication to the duty of work. While Arnold was making leaders out of the sons of the middle classes at Rugby, Hughes was training the working classes in the gospel of honest work. Hughes himself was to leave this approach to society and morals behind him. The more militantly Christian he became, the more the social radical in him triumphed. Competition became abhorrent to him and he championed trade unions, but his unquiet spirit found no rest. After 1867 he returned to his earlier ideas. In Tennessee he founded a settlement called "Rugby," where Tom Browns could prove themselves in creating a new society. Since there was no Doctor Arnold to lead them, they failed—in spite of the fact that only public school boys were admitted. Though the ideal failed in Tennessee, it did not fail in England. The gospel of work became the base for Victorian morality, and the Christian gentleman its ideal of leadership.

Education spread this way of life through the schools and working-men's colleges. This education was apt to start in childhood. Martha Butts's *Fairchild Family* (1818) was written for young children. Here this morality was mingled with a streak of brutality that was present even in Tom Brown. As Arnold believed that boys were unregenerate until they mature, so Miss Butts thought that little children had to know that they were sinful. At the age of nine little Lucy Fairchild cried out to her mother: "Oh Mamma. Mamma, you cannot think what a wicked heart I have got." Mrs. Fairchild was pleased: "But happy are those my dear Lucy, who are brought to the knowledge of their own sinful nature while they are young." What brought Lucy to this realization was her pride, jealousy, and uncharitableness. The theme of the book was that ultimate happiness was better than immediate satisfactions; indeed, that being good led to a satisfying life on earth while being bad led to destruction. Thus the vain little Lucy Augusta Noble was burned to death, a warning to the Fairchild children.

What might be called parental cruelty helped children to become moral. Mrs. Fairchild exposed Lucy to blood poisoning in order to teach her that simple shoes were preferable to purple slippers. Henry, aged six, was put on bread and water in a locked room for ten hours after having eaten a forbidden fruit. The two little girls were taken by their father to see a hanged man after they had quarreled. Despite their frightened pleas to go home, they were made to sit under the gibbet while their father explained that quarreling may lead to fratricide. Such cruelty was documented from Scripture. As at Rugby, the Fairchild children learned obedience to a strict moral code, a code which was inculcated and exemplified by their parents. The result was an orgy of self-satisfaction on the part of the elder Fairchilds, who knew that they were virtuous, and the little children, who knew that they were overcoming their sinful hearts. Miss Butts's book exemplified the self-righteousness which accompanied this morality.

This then was the moral pattern which accompanied liberal thought in England. Since there was no laissez-faire here, competitive economic society was tempered by this strict morality. Here also was an idea of leadership which was nonaristocratic and which could appeal to the middle classes. As much as any other single factor, this attitude of life shaped English ideals in its age of European predominance. Liberals held that the foundation of their thought was "the personality of man, which has been more oppressed and flouted than any other social and political value." But liberalism in turn did establish such values. England, in the flush of the Industrial Revolution, produced thinkers who worked out an ideology which stressed free competition as the solution to political and economic problems but at the same time proceeded to put limits on this free competition by encouraging a strict morality. Moreover, this idea of free competition was modified by Bentham's concept of legislation and by the belief that reason would make for a balance of interests in which true freedom could flourish. Liberalism was not mere egoism, as its enemies would have it.

CONSTRUCTIVELY COMPETITIVE:

Fair play,
morality,
rules.

Checks & balances
Don't tear each other apart.
Good Christians.
Build the British Empire.

# CHAPTER SEVEN

# Liberalism on the Continent of Europe

THE RELIGION of liberty took hold on the European continent. In France and Germany as in Italy the fate of liberalism determined to a great degree the course of history in these nations. A liberal regime came to power in France in 1830, and its failure was to leave its impress not only on the revolution of 1848 but also upon subsequent French thought. In Germany the evolution of liberalism has been likened to a tragedy, for there ideas of freedom so important to the movement in other nations were basically modified.

The German modifications of liberalism resulted from the historical position in which Germany found herself. Having suffered the Napoleonic occupation, continued disunity buried German hopes for national regeneration after the Congress of Vienna. No German thinker could ignore the national question or fail to take into account national aspirations. Thus, ideas of freedom had to cope with resurgent national sentiment. The question was whether liberalism could come to terms with it. E. M. Arndt, writing during the wars of liberation, illustrates this problem. His most famous poem was about the God who did not want any man to be subservient. Therefore, He gave into man's right hand sword and musket so that he could defend his freedom. Such sentiments, stressing a defense of liberty, were well attuned to wars of liberation. But Arndt went further: If a ruler acts against human rights he must be disobeyed, even by soldiers. Moral principles of freedom were more important than military obedience; rulers must never use force against the innocent and the just. An English Liberal would have disagreed with none of this. Such ideology could develop into that pacifism based upon moral principles exemplified by John Bright.

But what about the national sentiment? It led Arndt in the end to redefine moral principles and, thus, that freedom which he wanted to protect. Freedom is the right to integrate one's self with the tradition and customs of one's own people. The innocent and just against whom no force must be used are those who desire to live that way. In Arndt's mind these were the Prussians opposed to Napoleon. What is rejected from the "religion" of liberty is its cosmopolitanism based on the view of a natural law which makes the goal of freedom the same all over the world. This emphasis upon freedom as circumscribed by national customs and traditions contrasts with the liberal ideas of men like Cobden and Bright in England. For them liberty was the same in all nations, a moral imperative which transcended nationalism and was indeed hostile to it.

Arndt foreshadowed the future, the rise of what in Germany would be called "national liberalism," the increasing stress upon the historic nation rather than upon the universality of freedom. But at the beginning of the century there seemed to be a chance for Germany to follow the usual liberal pattern. The Prussian reform movement (1807–21) attempted to use liberalism and constitutionalism to strengthen the state, to rebuild Prussia's greatness on liberal foundations. In Germany self-government could not come from below; it had to be initiated from above. One must remember that in the early Middle Ages English representative government had also begun as "self-government through the King's command." This Prussian reform movement was successful in certain particulars. It emancipated the Jews (1812) and initiated military and administrative reforms, but its attempt to introduce liberalism failed. The Prussian state reverted to authoritarianism and militarism. The chance was missed, and it has been held, with some justice, that this failure was as important for the course of German liberalism as the more spectacular failure of the revolution of 1848.

As a result, the German middle classes alone agitated for liberal reforms from below, against the state rather than in cooperation with it. But the German middle classes were weak; unlike England, the Industrial Revolution had not yet infused these classes with enough economic and social strength. They were regarded rather as a problem by their fellow Germans than as a national asset. The middle classes themselves, as was noted in the discussion of nationalism, came to desire unity with the *Volk* rather than freedom and independence. Romantic preoccupation with national roots was in the forefront of all German thought. Here, unlike England, there was no strong drive to push the middle classes into prominence or to raise as many people as possible into that class as Samuel Smiles had desired. Instead the emphasis was always on order; there was a fear that the commercial and industrial classes would destroy the fabric of society.

The revolution of 1848 seemed to give liberalism another chance. But at the high tide of the revolution, the Frankfurt Parliament, the revolution's nationalist impetus became as evident as its liberal framework. From Frankfurt's Church of Saint Paul, where the Parliament sat, came a declaration of the rights of the German people which enumerated all the principles of the religion of liberty: individual freedom under the law, freedom of belief, the abolition of all entrenched privileges, the inviolability of private property and, finally, the call for a constitution. But what was missing from this declaration is equally significant. The principle that "he who governs best governs least" was never apparent. Instead, the declaration insisted that military service was the paramount duty of the citizen; no citizen could be allowed exemption from duty to the state on the grounds of conscience.

The fact that the revolutionaries of 1848 had to resolve the question of nationalism as well as that of freedom produced a change in liberal thought, a change which was foreshadowed in Arndt. The men of 1848 desired liberty—a liberty, however, that rested upon a national base. The revolution failed and a second chance was lost. Its manner of failure further influenced the construction of a national liberalism. The common explanation for this failure has been that the Parliament at Frankfurt talked too much and acted too little. By drawing out their proceedings, the explanation runs, the Parliament gave the territorial rulers ample time to gain back their lost power. But the story involved more than a simple delight in speechifying. There was in this Parliament a minority whose ideas on reform far exceeded those of the majority. They were Republicans, revolutionaries of the left. Encouraged by some local successes, especially in the state of Baden, these men were allied with the Socialists; Karl Marx looked to their successes with hope. In Parliament they filibustered. The Liberals were thus caught between the left and the reaction.

It was the left they feared more than the right even from the beginning of the revolution. Like Liberals all over Europe, they believed that wealth was an open road to be trod by talent and morality in tandem—but they were equally keen to close that road to the challenge of popular democracy. The famous Frankfurt Parliament was not elected by a universal franchise but by restrictive electoral practices which excluded the lower classes from the vote, just as in England parliamentary reform had erected the barrier of a high property qualification for voting. In Germany as in England the lower classes protested. The Chartists and the radical Republicans, as they were called in Germany, tried to establish universal suffrage. Both failed. But where in England the Chartist agitation, though peaceful, accomplished nothing, in Germany the radicals did capture momentary control of some regions. In Baden, for example, their attempted reforms were later called by their adversaries the "red terror."

Though this radicalism was only a small factor in the revolution itself, it was to have a great effect on the future of German liberalism. The middle classes were driven still further into the arms of the state. They now feared a "red terror" and sought, above all, stability, those national roots, which contemporaries had already held up as desirable goals. Within a few years after the event one leading Liberal could characterize 1848 as the "idiotic revolution." German liberalism took on aspects which would have been unthinkable in England or France. A man like the writer Gustav Freytag, regarded as a leading Liberal by both contemporary and future generations of German Liberals, could combine ideas of constitutionalism with racial stereotypes. For him rootedness in the nation was an essential prerequisite for any kind of liberty. Those who preserved any custom or religion alien to the deep roots of the German past were enemies of the German people. Still later Felix Dahn, another Liberal in this tradition, fought Bismarck's antiparliamentary behavior in Prussia. But once such illiberal politics had led to German unification, he was totally converted; later he wrote that his conversations with Bismarck had been the high points of his life. This was not an isolated case. Obviously this national liberalism was unable to fight authoritarian encroachments on individual freedom, as did English and French liberalism. Nationalism swamped the religion of liberty in Germany.

That one National Liberal saw in his conversation with Bismarck the high point of his life does not mean that Bismarck was a part of that movement. As is well known, he was no Liberal; what has not been made so clear is that the National Liberals were more nationalistic than Bismarck himself. As was seen in a preceding chapter, he thought in terms of the state rather than in terms of a nation. After the defeat of France he annexed Alsace-Lorraine, not because it was a supposedly "German" country, but for reasons of military security, in order to guard Germany's territorial sovereignty against France. Hans Rothfels has pointed out that it was the National Liberals who pushed for an annexationist policy in the name of the unity of the *Volk* and who wanted a centralized, unitary Germany—not Bismarck.

While national liberalism was undoubtedly the most important development in German liberalism, there remained in Germany, even after 1848, Liberals of the English school. Men like Heinrich Heine and Ludwig Boerne preached their ideals from exile in France. For them freedom and liberty were essential and more important than the developing nationalism. But much more important were those Germans who advocated a liberalism based upon the primacy of law. They took the ideal of freedom under law as their motto and received their inspiration from what they considered to be the English example. Such men continued a tradition to which we have already referred. Rudolf von Gneist (1816–95) was typical of such an attitude. The state was a juridical association and whatever action it took must be within the forms and limits of law. It was a "sense of right" which must permeate the people, for it was this allegiance to law which reconciled private interests and the state.

Gneist emphasized local government in Germany just as Tocqueville was to emphasize this in France. Popular participation should play a part in local government. Not surprisingly, however, the strength of the state was safe-guarded—it was the state which conferred upon the local government its judicial and administrative functions. Moreover, this idea of self-government did not stress participation at the national, parliamentary level. Gneist feared the excesses of party politics and did not see in them a necessary balancing of interests as did so many other Liberals. The most important thing was that the state must be a *Rechtsstaat* (state as a legal organism), and this would both protect the nation against excesses of party strife and guarantee participation on a local level as well. In addition, the law would also assure a permissible freedom which did not upset order.

A distinguished line of thinkers adhered to these arguments. They began to elaborate the importance of local units of government and some, like Otto von Gierke (1841–1921), constructed a whole political theory on the importance of free, juridical groups which formed the state. These men admired in England the same sort of thing which Tocqueville had stressed: the spirit of government. They saw this spirit in the "sense of right" among the people, in a government of men dominated by the primacy of law. These Germans, then, took an element of liberalism which went back to Montesquieu and sought in it the solution to the problem of orderly government and of freedom within the nation.

They also were defeated, however, by the change in liberalism in Germany, though they had stressed the state much more than Liberals in other nations. Bismarck was less nationalistic than the National Liberals but he was also much more empirical than the advocates of the *Rechtsstaat*. Law was an instrument in the construction and safeguarding of the state and not a limitation upon its exercise of power. The powerful stream of romantic or cultural nationalism would not put the law above the needs of the *Volk*. The "sense of right" gave way either to a sense of the realities of the political situation or to a sense of the necessary dominance of the nation. Gneist criticized the French for not having this "sense of right" and ascribed to this the excessive political fluctuations of that nation. But it can be said, with some justice, that he and his school did not manage to instill this ideal into the bloodstream of German life.

Nevertheless, German Liberals kept one idea basic to the rest of Western liberalism: free trade. But unlike the English Manchester school this ideal was not coupled with a morality which saw free trade's purpose as that of assuring international peace and prosperity. For them it was necessary for German industrial growth; on this issue they broke with Bismarck. One other common bond with Western liberalism assumed importance in Germany—that of the separation of church and state. Men who cared deeply about historic national roots cared nothing at all about enforced religious conformity. The inroads which national liberalism made upon the idea of freedom came in their emphasis upon integration with the state rather than opposition to it. By redefining freedom not as universal but as a liberty to assimilate the customs and traditions of the historic nation, they, in turn, placed limits on the freedom of the individual.

Yet this redefinition of freedom hardly affected the literature which most Germans read. Popular literature reflected a liberal universe which stressed tolerance, was opposed to chauvinism of any kind, and pleaded for compassion for the downtrodden. For example, the extremely popular novels of Karl May (1842–1912) which were set in the Orient or among the Indians of North America condemned violence and cruelty as well as racism (the Indians were as good, if not better than the white people). But typically enough, the dangerous life of trapper and Indian was seen in terms of law and order and of a pietistic universe which deeply penetrated German popular culture. Christian prayer was observed even on the North American prairie, together with the virtues of humility, honesty, and compassion for the weak. Respect for human dignity fills such popular literature but it is combined with sentimentality and opposition to the disturbance of the existing order "where one is at home."

Germans read such novels by the millions, however far they were removed from the reality of their lives. Indeed this liberalism remained a goal but as a utopia which could come about only through that brutality and chauvinism which men like Karl May had despised. The virtues which he had given to all good men, whether white or Indian (and others had conceded them even to Jews in equal measure), were soon thought of as a German racial prerogative. The popular novelists themselves were partly to blame: they had endowed their German characters with liberal virtues and had held them up as examples which others could follow and even surpass. Still, the heroes were proud Germans and it was not a large step to see in such liberalism specifically Germanic virtues which others could never reach. Here the basic plea for tolerance and equality of virtue among all peoples had little political effect contrasted with the exclusiveness which bent this popular literature in a national direction.

In Germany the kind of limiting morality which accompanied English liberalism also took hold. The gospel of work and the ideal of honesty can be found here as well. A question, however, arises. Was the modification of liberal ideology in Germany accompanied by similar changes in this morality?

German reaction against the ancien régime and the preponderance of French culture included a rejection of the "loose" morals associated with pre-revolutionary France. Rousseau's plea that the principles of fashionable society must be destroyed fell on fertile soil in Germany, the more so as it was combined with a stress on "genuineness" rather than sophistication. Such genuineness had been favored by the Weimar poets during the storm and stress period, and it was deepened by the pietistic and romantic emphasis on outward simplicity and inward emotions. All this strengthened the onslaught of respectability. In Germany, however, the romantic element was to remain strong. This is what Heinrich Heine meant when he wrote that beneath the outward *Gemuetlichkeit* of the German there lurked the demoniacal. For all that, middle-class morality became a reality in Germany as it became a reality in England.

In Germany, too, this trend toward a middle-class morality was furthered by a religious movement. Eighteenth-century pietism like evangelicalism was a practical religion. Pietists preached vehemently against luxurious extravagances which Germans imported from France. They emphasized devout and pious feeling combined with devout and pious life-styles. Moreover, Pietists stressed education. Like Thomas Arnold they wanted to build character. No Cicero or Virgil should dominate the education process, one Pietist wrote: Students should be instructed by pious and God-fearing teachers. Such education was training of the will and of the "heart"—"mere understanding not directed by a good heart makes one haughty and leads to danger, perversity and harm." This educational ideal rejected training for leadership of the upper classes; it was to be applied to all classes of the population. There was a parallelism between the role played by the Evangelicals in furthering middle-class morality in England and that of the German Pietists. Both emphasized a practical approach to life, positing a practical morality which disdained luxury and ostentation. Both held character-building to be education's goal, instilling within the student this morality and de-emphasizing the intellectual side of their education. Yet, the absence of the leadership idea among pietism's German supporters is, of itself, significant.

Once again, a reference must be made to the German middle-class preoccupation with rootedness and stability. This preoccupation did not hold within it that concept of leadership already noted in England. The German middle classes had, in fact, no possibility of attaining such a position in their autocratic states. They strove, instead, for a respectability coupled with a sense of being "comfortable"; the tenor of their lives took on what Harold Nicolson has called a "sedative benevolence." It was a rooted, provincial complacency which did not produce, and was not meant to produce, any Cecil Rhodeses or Rudyard Kiplings. This drive for security became the prime ingredient of German middle-class life, especially after the revolution of 1848. The carica-ture of the German bourgeoisie, with their regular habits, comfortable furni-ture, good food, and pipes or cigars, conveys a little of this atmosphere of *Gemuetlichkeit.* Even when some schools on the English model were intro-duced into Germany before the First World War, it was the sons of either the Prussian Junkers or the old south German aristocracies who flocked to them, and not, at first, the scions of the middle class.

These remarks on German middle-class morality must be as tentative as those concerning the English middle class. It is known that such a pattern of behavior came into existence in the nineteenth century, but little is known about why it developed. Nor is much known about the position of the middle classes and their social mobility within the pattern of nineteenth-century Ger-man society. It seems true, however, that in spite of all the ideological reserva-tions that have been noted, business tended to become an ever more respect-able occupation. There were many examples of men giving up positions within the prestigious bureaucracy to go into business. More money could now be made in trade or industry than in any but the very highest governmental of-fices. But here again, in Germany social prestige remained to a large extent a property of the state bureaucracy rather than of business success.

While German liberalism struggled against insuperable odds from the beginning, French liberalism emerged strengthened from the Revolution. It has been shown that Constant, its greatest early theoretician, rejected both democracy and the *ancien régime.* The Charter of 1815 seemed to give hope of a dawn of liberalism, but Bourbon intransigence soon drove the Liberals into opposition. These Liberals were no radicals; they strongly believed in the evolutionary character of freedom. Edmund Burke was influential among them—not his "unbought grace of life" of aristocratic society but his concept of the slow unfolding of liberty. The historically-oriented element of liberal ideology which was mentioned at the beginning of this discussion came to the forefront. Yet, by 1830, these Liberals were instrumental in the making of a revolution which drove out the Bourbons. The bourgeois monarchy of Louis Philippe (1830–48) was to usher in the liberal age.

It did so by enfranchising about 250,000 families, opening more widely

126

the doors of political power—but not widely enough. The vast majority of the people were ignored by the revolution, just as the Liberals who made the English Reform Bill in 1832 permitted only a restricted class of the population to enter into the franchise. In both France and England this liberal initiative marked the beginning not of an era of peace and satisfaction but one of great social and political agitation. This was the result of putting into practice the liberal belief that if the *ancien régime* was bad so was democracy in government. Nevertheless, the accession of Louis Philippe meant, at least for the moment, a liberal victory. The king's chief minister and the theoretician of this liberalism triumphant was François Guizot. Guizot believed strongly in a maximum of individual freedom which permitted the greatest freedom of self-development. What could insure the dominance of the spirit of the religion of liberty? Here Guizot went back beyond Bentham and Mill to a theory of almost complete laissez-faire. He called this the "great tranquility." Government must be harmonious, which in turn meant holding to a "golden mean," a *"juste milieu."*

This "golden mean" implied the deliberate preservation of the status quo. In theory this meant taking no initiative in social or political questions in order to preserve that "great tranquillity" which would allow for the most complete liberty. Guizot's biography of Oliver Cromwell illustrates this rejection of all extreme actions, a rejection which amounted, in theory, to a complete abstinence by the state from decisive action. Cromwell had established liberty in England once he gained power, Guizot said, only through his moderation. But he was not able to maintain this liberty. Why? "God does not grant to these great men, who laid their foundation amidst disorder and revolution, the power of regulating at their pleasure, and for succeeding generations, the government of nations." The same observation might be applied to the regime of which Guizot was the guiding spirit, for were its foundations not laid in revolution? But Guizot believed that 1830 could be overcome by moderation. He may have been correct in this estimate, but the social tensions of the Industrial Revolution were not to be so easily brushed aside.

To the agitation for more social reforms, for an extension of the franchise, Guizot had a reply. He was not the tribune of a class which simply wanted to guard its own power, excluding all others. The usual Marxist interpretation of middle-class ideology is wrong here. For Guizot, as for all Liberals, the "great tranquillity" was not meant to freeze social mobility. The doctrine of laissez-faire would free the individual from artificial restraints furthering his social and economic advancement. Through the right kind of morality—that is, attitude toward life—all could become rich and qualify for the vote. This was implicit in all of English liberalism and Guizot also believed in this kind of individual advancement. His famous admonition to the bankers of France was "enrich yourself," for in this way all classes of the population would benefit. This was not heartless or cynical but can only be understood within the liberal context. To be sure, Guizot feared democracy. But this fear solidified into opposition to those advocates of social and political advancement regardless of moral attitudes; it did not mean opposition to economic and social mobility as such.

Guizot was an enemy of all entrenched privileges, on the one hand, and of the "troublemakers" on the other—men who wanted to use the state in order to enforce what they called social justice, thus destroying individual freedom which Guizot as a Liberal thought the greatest good. Yet the regime of Louis Philippe collapsed in 1848. It must not be forgotten, however, that liberal rule in France lasted for eighteen years; it was no transitory experiment doomed to failure. That it did eventually collapse meant only that Guizot's kind of liberalism was discredited. It had not been able to meet the long-range problems of rising political and social aspirations. The English Liberals, faced at the same time with Chartist agitation, were also unable to meet these demands. French liberalism simply brought out in a more dramatic form the problem inherent in all of liberal ideology.

It was against the background of the failure of the regime of Louis Philippe and the *coup d'état* of Louis Napoleon that Tocqueville wrote his *Ancien Régime.* This greatest of French Liberals saw his ideals swamped by French dependence upon authority, institutional centralization, and blind hatred of inequality. He now saw France oscillating forever between despotisms and revolution. Tocqueville's ideals were different from either of these alternatives. He believed free political activity to be the greatest good for men and governments. This free activity placed no reliance upon the state. Rather its political organization drew upon the vitality of local rather than central units of government. He greatly admired the English pattern of local government through the justice of the peace, just as he came to admire the English aristocracy. Here was an aristocracy which took a crucial part in the free interplay of political expression and was not isolated from politics and government as was the aristocracy in France.

As Tocqueville saw it, free institutions were based not only upon the political vitality of local government but also upon the guarantee of private property. In his earlier writings, he envisaged a society based upon small peasant holdings as the surest guarantee of political life. But when the regime of Louis Philippe had shown that economic arrangements did not necessarily guarantee lasting liberty, he increasingly stressed the spirit of public administration. In France, this administration was oppressive, furthering the reliance of all classes upon the bureaucracy, while in England this did not seem to be the case. Tocqueville saw in England instead an interaction among all classes of society which was the result of a continuing political liberty which, like Burke, he traced back to the Middle Ages. Where before this Tocqueville had stressed the wealth of the English aristocracy, he now emphasized their contacts with the mass of the population due to the vagueness of class lines. His ideal was England, and the United States as an extension of English political habits and English political liberty. Tocqueville's liberalism was much more thoroughly argued than that of Guizot. Strong local government and the stability of property relationships must be its base, but the ultimate cure of all the ills of society lay in the free play of political activity. In the last resort, Tocqueville was more interested in political and social behavior than in building systems of government. He was an acute observer of politics within the limits of his liberalism which ignored the cataclysmic forces of the new working classes. Thus, he analyzed the English scene without even mentioning the Chartist movement. The ideal of free political action would solve all problems: political and economic. Unfortunately the liberalism of Tocqueville, and therefore his analyses of society, proved vulnerable to those forces which were slowly corroding liberalism itself.

Though Guizot's liberalism came to power, it was not the only kind of liberalism in France. The tradition of the great French Revolution stimulated a concept of freedom oriented toward political and social democracy, a liberalism which ignored the prerequisite of liberal morality. It is striking that Lamennais, its chief representative, said nothing about the inviolability of private property, but a great deal about political and social freedom. Like John Stuart Mill in his later development, Lamennais discarded the idea of property as the main political and ethical prop of freedom. His liberalism did not require a middle-class morality, but, instead, the greatest freedom for the "soul of the people." Lamennais was antimaterialist, and his emphasis on the "soul of the people" was connected to a romantic and Catholic regard for the past. But this was not a romantic nationalism; it did not glorify the French people as unique or superior to any other. The government, by guaranteeing a maximum of freedom to its people through social and political as well as economic democracy, would, through this liberty, illuminate the individual souls of all its people.

Lamennais was no Socialist. The methods of gaining his freedom were unimportant to him in comparison to the overriding good this freedom would bring to all. This was a liberalism far removed from Guizot's "enrich yourself." Yet Lamennais also failed in 1848. Nevertheless, his definition of freedom in terms of both social and political democracy was to have some attraction for future Liberals. For the middle classes, however, it was Guizot's liberalism which was to have a stronger appeal, and for the working classes socialism was to provide more concrete techniques of social and political advancement.

In France, too, the morality which was dominating England and Germany took hold. In 1825, one French Liberal ascribed the conditions of the working class to their indolence, apathy, and improvidence. This is certainly identical with the ideas of Smiles or Thomas Hughes. In France the cult of respectability became widespread. England's supreme symbol of respectability, Queen Victoria, had her counterpart in France: Louis Philippe. Nor did Napoleon III ever dare revert to the open promiscuity that characterized Napoleon I. Exceptions to this stodgy middle-class morality were frequent. Thus the can-can, certainly one of the most erotic of dances, delighted audiences during the Second Empire. Again very little is known about either the growth or the extent of the middle-class morality in France. To be sure, in the Second Empire, sexual morality was certainly more permissive than in contemporary England, though England had a problem of prostitution which assumed fantastic dimensions. This may be due, of course, to the very repressive aspects of Victorianism. Middle-class morality may have penetrated less deeply in France, for that nation had not gone through a phase of either evangelicalism or pietism. The French Revolution in its Jacobin stage had advocated a moral puritanism which led Robespierre to proclaim that virtue should be woman's only ornament. Opposition to the *ancien régime* included a distaste for its way of life—yet many rejected the Revolution who accepted this morality.

England, France, and Germany exemplified the evolution of the religion of liberty in Europe. So did Italy. In the discussion of nationalism it has been seen that liberalism and the development of a national consciousness went hand in hand. From Alfieri at the end of the last century to Cavour, the architect of unity, Italy was conceived of as a liberal state. The idea of a society of laws, of checks and balances, and of a rational reconciliation of interests dominated such thought. Italian Liberals also wanted to establish a middle road between absolutism and democracy on this basis; the extension of the franchise was to go no further than the English Reform Bill of 1832 had gone, or the France of Louis Philippe. Cavour like Guizot was a believer in the "golden mean," but unlike Guizot he was a practical politician who could discard liberal principles when it seemed necessary. The art of government was all-important to him and this meant producing national unity through reconciling diverse interests. A liberal statesman had to be a diplomat. In contrast, Bismarck was certainly a great diplomat, but in foreign not domestic affairs, for he believed that interests were not to be adjusted through the free play of ideas. Those who differed from him were enemies of the state.

But Cavour's type of liberalism was not the only kind of liberalism in Italy. It was seen how, after 1848, those driving toward national unity came to be concerned with the working man, with the "people" and their attachment to the state. From this a liberalism arose in Italy which was democratic inasmuch as it rejected checks and balances for freedom seen in terms of a moral purpose which all the people shared equally. This was the kind of nationalism which Mazzini had preached all along and he had linked the quest for national unification with stress upon liberty and equality—not in terms of laws or a division of power but in terms of a moral change in people which would produce a revolution. This revolution was not merely political but would produce a moral impetus toward freedom and equality. In the name of such a view of the coming society, Mazzini modified the individualism of liberal thought and advocated instead a vague ideal of human association. Mazzini's liberalism was very similar to that of Lamennais in France. The Frenchman talked about the "soul of the people" and about a freedom which embraced all in a unity which did not need the checks and balances of constitutionalism. But for Lamennais it did need the Catholic Church, while for Mazzini the religion of freedom, equality, and humanitarianism displaced Catholicism and, in a sense, even Christianity itself.

This liberalism seems utopian when contrasted to the liberalism which was dominant in the century. Yet, where in Germany talk about the "soul of the people" and high moral purpose came to mean the absolutism of the nation, here the same ideas focused on liberty and freedom. For Mazzini, the unification of Italy was to be a step toward the extension of his ideals to all the world. This democratically-oriented liberalism arose in England as well, but in a much more practical manner. Gladstone, for example, believed both in a moderate kind of land distribution and championed the extension of the franchise. "Every man who is not presumably incapacitated by some consideration of personal unfitness or political danger, is morally entitled to come within the pale of constitution." As Gladstone's career progressed he came to look upon the working classes with increasing confidence. What Ruggiero calls the "democratization of liberalism" did come about toward the end of the century, and here the Italians like Mazzini were ahead of their time.

Yet this democratization was never wholly victorious. Many Liberals still believed in those principles of liberalism which have formed the bulk of this and the preceding chapter. The religion of liberty continued to view its definition as the "golden mean" between democracy and authoritarianism.

Changing conditions within each nation modified or enhanced the drive toward this freedom, but it existed everywhere during the first part of the century. The advent of what we have called middle-class morality tempered the scramble for wealth and power toward which liberalism might lead, and this morality profoundly influenced European culture. Respectability became the social goal, together with the gospel of work and the concept of manliness. In Germany the drive for security on the part of the middle classes produced a "sedative benevolence." Everywhere the middle classes strove to replace the aristocracy as the model for the good life.

It must not be thought that the morality which has been discussed meant a life led in comfortable isolation, despite the German warnings against the unsettledness of the middle class. The famous watering places where the aristocracy had formerly gathered were now taken over by the middle classes. Places like Karlsbad in Bohemia and Baden-Baden in south Germany had a phenomenal development during the century. Better roads and, later, the railroad made such travel not only possible but fashionable. At the beginning of the century Gagliani in Paris opened what was to be the first travel agency. Symptomatic of the change in clientele was the change in the character of these resorts. No longer were luxurious dances and other amusements the fashion. Instead, the guests met in the afternoon at the "Kurhaus" where polite music was played for their amusement. Pilgrimages to the monuments of culture and scenic journeys through beautiful landscapes had been popular in the eighteenth century. But the journey to the watering place was made for a different purpose.

New ideas on health played a part, and visitors now diligently took the waters. Fresh air was by this time thought to be good for man, and exercise became popular not only among those of the cult of muscular Christianity. The fashionable afternoon walk provided one of the chief subjects for caricatures of the middle classes. But these watering places also served as marriage markets and here suitable alliances between middle-class families could be arranged. Thus from Bath in England to Vichy in France and to a multitude of German and Bohemian resorts, the middle classes journeyed in search of health and company.

We have witnessed, with liberalism, the emerging patterns of nineteenth-century middle-class Europe. But both the ideology and the morality were, from the first, subject to severe criticism.

# CHAPTER EIGHT

# Conservatism

J F SOME of the Napoleonic generation believed that the new century must bring a rebirth of liberty, others drew a different conclusion from the cataclysmic French Revolution and its aftermath. Not that such men wanted to perpetuate a dictatorship of the Napoleonic kind; on the contrary, they too looked to a rebirh of liberty, but they defined this liberty quite differently from the Liberals. Conservatives believed that maintenance of freedom was only possible within the framework of historical tradition; ideas of natural law and of progress had led to the collapse of order into revolution. Only through an emphasis on history and the hierarchical system which tradition—that is, history—sanctified, could order and therefore liberty be preserved. To Conservatives liberty was at one with a historically derived concept of order and this concept required the preservation of the social and political hierarchy. "Legitimacy," the slogan which dominated the Congress of Vienna, was to be the keystone of this order.

On this ideological basis, several approaches to history, order, and freedom were possible. De Maistre opposed any change: if it is historic it must not be changed. Burke, on the other hand, saw in history itself elements of change—"the past must create the present"—and in this very phrase implied an idea of peaceful evolution. What Burke and De Maistre had in common was the belief that freedom is not an innovation, as Constant had thought, since liberty cannot be "created" by men. Clearly, for the thought these men represented, history displaced the natural laws of the eighteenth century as the all-embracing truth. It has been seen that the Liberals also believed that history justified their faith. But their concept of history, as symbolized by Vico, combined historical progress with natural laws and it was precisely this combination Conservatives rejected.

Edmund Burke rejected the concept of freedom and mass democracy. Universal rights, the rights of man, seemed to have led not toward liberty but toward mobocracy. The Jacobin dictatorship during the French Revolution reinforced this direction of his thought. Individual rights must be preserved upon a different basis. Since for him the past created the present, Burke looked to the feudal derivation of these rights. The medieval *"jus,"* tied to class status and to the development of custom, had guaranteed English freedoms in the past and would develop into a broader freedom in the present. In the Whig view of English history, with which Burke was imbued, feudal liberties had developed, through the Magna Carta and Parliament's supremacy, steadily toward a greater freedom for Englishmen. This was what historical tradition meant to Burke and this was the hope it held out for the future.

Burke's conservatism entailed two other beliefs as well. Everyone must have some basic individual rights, for history, by which he meant the evolution of feudalism, had guaranteed such rights. Thus Burke opposed slavery and supported the American colonists' struggle against what he thought the unhistorical "dictatorship" of Parliament. But no more than in the Middle Ages did such rights imply political or economic freedom, much less social equality. Individual rights and egalitarianism were two entirely different concepts. Egalitarianism meant mobocracy and the eventual destruction of individual rights. Only a hierarchical society could maintain these rights, for they had been maintained in this way throughout history. If the first application of his thought to the present was the necessity of preserving individual rights, the second was that these rights could only be preserved within a hierarchical social and political system. Therefore, it was the aristocracy's task to assume the leadership it had provided in the past. Only such a hereditary leadership could stem the tide of egalitarian revolution. This exaltation of aristocratic leadership led him to say, in his speech to the electorate of Bristol, that once a member of Parliament had been elected he must follow his own conscience and not the wishes of those who elected him. Burke, then, combined ideas of individual rights with a concept of strong leadership.

Burke had at first welcomed the French Revolution as an assertion of the historical rights of man, but the destruction of the nobility, the Jacobin experiment, the Revolution's liquidation of the past, turned him against it. In the process Burke put increasing emphasis upon the necessity of aristocratic leadership, of noble privileges. Let the common man wait, secure in his individual rights, and gradually English history would evolve toward a broader freedom; it had done so before. Man stands still but history evolves and thus the past was tied to the present. The Whig concept of history was at the very root of Burke's thought; it had already become the nationalist version of English history. Burke's conservatism did not deny freedom; it denied the liberal hypothesis of the equality of man. It denied the possibility that man could raise himself in the social and political scale through his own efforts. History to Burke was not the rise and dominance of men through simply their own individual efforts or through their espousal of the right kind of morality. Contrast Burke's emphasis on "prescription"—that is, the importance of tradition defined as custom—to what John Stuart Mill has to say: ". . . though custom be both good as custom and suitable to man, yet to conform to custom, merely as custom, does not educate or develop in man any of the qualities which are distinctive endowments of a human being."

For Mill and many of the Liberals man was an individual in the eighteenth-century sense: under natural law, free to develop those traits which would enable the lowest to rise to importance in all realms of society. Samuel Smiles after all pointed the way to material and moral success through the development of individual character. But for Burke and the Conservatives man was an integral part of history, and Burke spoke, in one of his most famous passages, about the indissoluble union of contemporary man with his ancestors. The link of prescriptive rights and aristocratic privileges was only broken at great peril to all of society, as the events in France had amply demonstrated. Liberals were a product of not only the French but also the Industrial Revolution; Conservatives tended to reject both.

Burke wrote nostalgically about the "unbought grace of life" of the aristocracy in contrast with the *nouveau riche* industrialists and wealthy merchants. Liberal morality was rejected for an idealized aristocratic way of life. Basically, such conservatism was a response to the new fact of a mass society, an attempt to keep this society from disrupting order. A historical elite would guarantee freedom; the mob would only crush it. Here Burke foreshadowed a whole series of elitist theories, theories which proved to be one of the accepted answers to the democratization of the age. But unlike Burke, later theories of the elite were increasingly centered upon an elite based upon actual power rather than on historical rights. Yet Burke's combination of freedom and aristocracy played an important part in the ideology of English Tory democracy.

For this kind of conservatism showed more social awareness of the problems of England's poor than the Liberals ever demonstrated. For them the poor were deficient in character since all could rise in society if they only tried. But conservatism, which did not believe in this kind of progress, viewed the poor as part of the responsibility of leadership. After all, in the past the lord of the manor cared for his peasants, whose rights, like all members of medieval society, had been protected by the feudal *jus*. This protection must be extended to the poor of contemporary England. The Industrial Revolution had broken the nation in two and it was up to the aristocracy to restore the harmony of former times. Though the social ideal of these Tories was the "merrie England" of the feudal past, they did not deny that history evolved. But the same techniques which had been applied to ameliorate the lot of the lower feudal classes could with modification be applied to the industrial worker. Such a social concept was not alive in England alone. In the Bavarian Diet one deputy summed it up well. Love should govern the relationship between labor and employer as it had governed the relationship between lord and peasant in the Middle Ages. Such conservative thought harkened back to an age of social harmony which had vanished with the appearance of industrial mass society.

In restoring this harmony, conservative thought on the Continent increasingly relied upon another historical example from the Middle Ages, that of the guilds. To them, these guilds represented a corporate society in which master, journeyman, and apprentice were part of a harmonious and hierarchial order. Moreover, here each profession regulated itself within the framework of the totality of society, and this regulation was based upon custom. Such a corporate thought was given historical respectability by historians like Gierke for whom the corporate ideal underlay the whole of historical development. This structure of society was cemented not only by tradition but also by the Church. The twin pillars of order, tradition and religion, seemed to be working toward the same end. For Conservatives saw in the evolution of the past not only the influence of tradition but also the might of a revealed Christianity. Indeed, the Catholic Church was to make this corporate theory its own in the nineteenth century, advocating it as the most desirable form of government in the age of the Industrial Revolution. The encyclical of Leo XIII, *Rerum Novarum* (1891), made this official. This transposition of the medieval craft structure onto industrial society implied a view of the modern worker as the successor of the medieval craftsman. Like his medieval predecessor, the modern workingman should possess the dignity which becomes a craftsman and the same pride in his work. A note was struck here which was re-echoed by the Romantics. At the very close of Wagner's *Die Meistersinger* Hans Sachs told the audience, "Do not despise the master craftsmen"—an attempt once more to transpose an older concept of work onto modern industrial society.

Christianity became an integral part of the mainstream of conservative thought on the Continent. Conservatism, in this guise, furthered the religious, Catholic revival, which was an aspect of romanticism. It was a conscious attempt to put the state upon a Christian basis rather than upon a basis of rationalism and natural law, as was attempted in the Enlightenment. With Burke, history was the prime opponent of that rationalism which had led to revolution; Continental thinkers combined this faith in history with the belief that history exemplified the hand of God. Monarchy was for them not only hallowed by custom and tradition but a Christian and Divine phenomenon.

These ideas were exemplified for Europe by the Holy Alliance. This was a treaty eventually signed by Russia, Austria, Prussia, and France (1815), which affirmed that Christian principles should govern the relationship between nations. It allied the monarchs of these countries who thought themselves "delegated by providence" to rule their nations. Monarchical rule as a divine phenomenon was to unite the diverse nations upon the precepts of "justice, Christian charity, and peace." The Holy Alliance was the brainchild of Alexander I who, especially since he saw Moscow burn down during the Napoleonic wars, had become a Christian mystic. Moreover, Alexander was influenced by Chateaubriand's *Genius of Christianity,* as well as by other works proclaiming the identity between politics and religion. Only in this manner could the effects of the French Revolution be overcome.

Metternich (1773–1859), who was possessed of no such Christian mysticism, at first called the Holy Alliance a "loud-sounding nothing." On second thought, however, he found it useful. It strengthened the already formed Quadruple Alliance whose purpose was the enforcement of the peace settlement and the destruction of any future revolutions. To Liberals, the Holy Alliance came to symbolize the forces of reaction, and the mixture of Christianity and monarchical divine right typified a conservatism dedicated to the crushing of progress by force. Such conservatism was also expressed and elaborated by important thinkers, especially in France. Of these Count Joseph de Maistre (1753–1821) was the most important.

For de Maistre, too, "all is history"; only history, not men, can create. But history was a manifestation of the Divine and thus the government of any historical antiquity was Divine. The very word "reform" was blasphemous. As monarchy was a historically ancient form of government, it was Divine, and from this it followed that men must love and obey even an absolutely evil monarch. Monarchy was a hierarchical form of government, and de Maistre stressed hierarchy as much as Burke stressed it, but he gave it a different twist. The whole universe was a hierarchical structure with God at its apex. The authority immediately subordinate to Him, in the world of men, must reflect God's unity. Thus it must combine within it both spiritual and temporal supremacy. The king, however, possessed only temporal supremacy; the Pope must therefore be the real ruler of the world, the true bulwark of all human order. De Maistre resurrected a commonplace medieval argument so that he might remove society and politics from the efforts of "meddling intellectuals" in the name of an absolute authority. It was not astonishing that he defended the Inquisition as a good. Under the pope the king made decisions for the state. But the state was a part of the Catholic, Christian universe, and de Maistre's primacy of history was based upon the complete primacy of the Christian universe. History was important because it reflected this hierarchical system.

Basic to this absolutism was its focus on the necessity of clear-cut decisions and the evils of compromise. De Maistre's absolutism was meant to counter the sapping of the established order and authority by the new forces of the age. The individual must make his uncompromising decision for the truth, as de Maistre saw it. As the Spaniard Donoso-Cortés put it at mid-century: You are either Christ or Barrabas. Cardinal Newman was to write later that there was no mean between Christianity, as he understood it, and atheism. Thus, the reaction to the onslaught of liberalism became intellectually rigid. De Maistre applied this rigidity to the political sphere: "All government is good if it is established. Our concern cannot be whether a problem is decided in this or that manner, but that it be decided without delay and without appeal." In this way conservatism was an ethic of decision directed against the new forces of society—but a process of decision-making from which all were excluded except those at the top of the hierarchy, the pope and then the king. They were, by their very nature, infallible.

This conservatism was ultramontane; it made the pope "at the other side of the mountains (the Alps)" the guarantor of order and harmony. He was, for the Frenchman de Maistre, what custom and tradition had been for the English Whig, Edmund Burke. De Maistre's ideas became influential at the papal court; they provided an image in which the papacy saw its functions reflected. They were popularized in France by Lamennais who actively supported this cause between 1824 and 1826. But Lamennais was to change for he sensed a contradiction between the supreme heads of de Maistre's hierarchical system, the pope and the king. In the end, he was to denounce the papacy for attaching itself to the dying cause of monarchy in Europe. But as he became more liberal in his paper *L'Avenir* (1830–32) he also came into increasing conflict with a papacy vitally influenced by those same ideas he had first sought to popularize.

The papacy seemed enmeshed in the most extreme conservatism. One liberal English historian has written about the war of the Church against modern civilization in the nineteenth century. This is true from a liberal but not from a conservative standpoint. The Church rejected freedom of thought. The encyclical letter against Lamennais by Gregory XVI called freedom of conscience "absurd" and liberty of the press a detestable freedom which misled the common people. The faithful were reminded that even the Apostles burned books. The Church had lost much through the French Revolution and Napoleon's reign; it reacted sharply. Moreover, the papacy made use of the Austrian Hapsburgs to suppress insurrection in the Papal States, and it was thus politically linked to the leading conservative power. Again, the papacy was Italian and Italian Catholicism had long been intellectually sterile.

Perhaps it was a misfortune that at this moment of reaction the Church was governed by an apparatus in the hands of the most intellectually backward section of European Catholicism, for the attitude symbolized by the encyclical *Mirari vos* was to dominate the Church's policy during the century. It rejected Catholic liberalism: not only Lamennais in France, but subsequently Doellinger (1799–1890) and Ketteler (1811–77) in Germany. Rejection of revolution went to the length of accepting the conservative thought of de Maistre. Pius IX, frightened by the revolution of 1848 in Rome, continued such policies, castigating liberalism in all its forms as sinful. This policy of authoritarian conservatism reached its height with the Vatican Council of 1870 and the proclamation of papal infallibility. To Liberals this marked the definite establishment of absolutism within the Church in the name of order and discipline among the faithful.

Nevertheless, this Catholic reaction, as it is sometimes called, was not as sterile as Liberals have made it out to be. For it accepted the corporate theory of the state and society which, as we have already noted, culminated in the encyclical *Rerum Novarum* of Leo XIII. The Church never became liberal but, through this corporate ideal, it did face the social questions of the age. This will be seen in greater detail in a subsequent chapter. Conservatism then was the dominant thought of the papacy during the century just as the papacy was linked politically to Austria while it received intellectual support from France. Such conservatism was not the monopoly of the Vatican or of France; it was found also in Germany.

Adam Mueller (1779–1829) typified it there. But Mueller's conservatism differed from its French model in one important way. De Maistre had seen in Catholic Christianity the guarantor of the historic harmony of the world. Mueller transferred this function to the German state.

The state was not an artificial and transitory creation, a useful convenience of mankind. Instead it encompassed the whole of life itself. For the individual could not be imagined outside the framework of the state; it was a necessary constituent of the human "heart, spirit, and body." As little as man can leave his own self can he leave the state. Mueller summed this up when he wrote:

> Do not all the unhappy errors of the French Revolution coincide in the illusion that individual man could step out of society and from the outside throw over and destroy what does not concern him; that the individual could protest against the work of thousands of years, and instead of the old proven if not perfect constitution give [to the state] a new one, at least perfect for the next fortnight.

These were commonplace conservative sentiments of the beginning of the century, and Mueller combined them with a hierarchical view of society. "Lordship and service" expressed society's basic relationship, a relationship which had not changed in modern times and still was the crux of the desirable balance of interests within the state. For Mueller, both the all-embracing state and the hierarchical relationship within the state were sanctified by God as well as history; both were not subject to change. Not only was the state tied to God and history, but it must be a Christian state by which Mueller, like de Maistre, meant a Catholic state. He himself was closely associated with the clerical reaction in Bavaria, which followed the downfall of Napoleon. One of the guiding spirits behind the founding of the University of Munich (1826), he was in part responsible for its predominantly ultramontane spirit.

Yet it was the state rather than the pope which was the supreme authority and the guarantor of order. Mueller, too, had ties with romanticism, especially in his idea that all must "integrate" with the state. For him, the state was not only a political entity but also one which fulfilled human emotional needs. This state was struggling bitterly against the new political, social, and economic forces. Because of the explicit Christian base which such a state must possess, Mueller thought these new forces part of a conspiracy against Christianity itself. Not surprisingly, he identified the Jews with this conspiracy and thus linked conservatism on a national basis with racial thought. The Jews, "cancers and boils on the body of the state," disrupted its organic nature. Mueller coupled an exaltation of the German state with an emphasis on its Christian foundations and in this manner laid an important foundation for future racist thought. What became of these ideas can be made clear through a quotation from a leading German Conservative of the 1870s, Constantin Frantz: "The Jewish people has rejected Christ the true mediator and messiah and therewith has excluded itself from history, for instead the Germans became God's chosen people."

Thus, this conservatism had connections not only with romanticism but also with the growth of racial thought. Beyond this, the emphasis upon the German state as Christian in this sense foreshadowed that *translatio Christi* from the Jews of the Bible to the Germans of the present and past, espoused by Richard Wagner and Houston Stewart Chamberlain, as well as Constantin Frantz. If de Maistre influenced Catholicism, Mueller influenced the growing German nationalism. Both contrast with Burke who, in his turn, influenced English national consciousness. Neither de Maistre or Mueller had the Whig tradition of history to build upon, a tradition which for Burke meant the certain possibility of society's evolution rather than the unbending conservative authoritarianism of the Continentals.

These diverse variations of conservatism were alien to that man who, for many contemporaries, came to be the symbol of the reaction after the French Revolution—Metternich. The Austrian statesman was not only reactionary as far as Liberals were concerned; even most Conservatives thought him so. For unlike de Maistre he did not base his ideas upon Catholicism or Christianity, and unlike Mueller his turn of mind was foreign to the exaltation of the state. A *grand seigneur* of the eighteenth century, Metternich had no use for either the religious revival or the nationalism of his time. Opposing nationalism, he regarded religious matters skeptically from the vantage point of the Enlightenment; thus he seemed a stranger to these Conservatives. But he was a Conservative nevertheless, as intolerant of liberalism and the heritage of the Revolution as he was of these other forces of his age. His ideas were based upon the necessity of maintaining a balance of forces within the state, just as such a balance of power was important in the relations among states. The way to harness these new forces for the benefit of the state was to erect a balance between the classes in a nation and to guarantee the maintenance of this balance through an absolute monarchy. Again Metternich considered history all-important; it cemented such a social structure. No new, unhistorical creation of states or constitutions could be allowed. Nationalism was such a new force to him, and, unlike Mueller, he thought it chimerical—an adventure without a foreseeable goal—for to his eighteenth-century way of thought it had no historical foundation. Nationalism would upset the historic international balance of power, just as liberalism would upset the internal balance of power within a state.

In Metternich's view it was the middle classes which disturbed this balance through their dynamic. Here the Austrian statesman is at one with most of the conservative thought of his time. It was oriented toward a past in which the middle classes had no part and whose stability was dependent upon throne and aristocracy. The opponent of nationalism and the Nationalists had in common a concern for the middle classes. German Nationalists saw in middle-class "restlessness" a challenge to the rootedness of the *Volk*, while Metternich felt them a challenge to all civic order. The bourgeoisie's attacks on the monarchy, he believed, would inevitably result, in the next stage, in the mob attacking the bourgeoisie. Thus the middle classes were heading straight toward democratic anarchy.

Metternich shared another preconception with other Conservatives—his anti-intellectualism. He was contemptuous of professors and students, believing that though they conspired against order, they were ineffectual conspirators. Opposition to freedom of thought and expression also gave Conservatives like de Maistre and the leaders of the Church an anti-intellectual direction. Nevertheless, in the Carlsbad Decrees (1819) a strict watch was to be put on universities, and student organizations were ordered dissolved.

These decrees were in answer to demonstrations for German unity and attacks upon the Vienna settlement which had involved students and professors at German universities. It extended strict controls to the press and to all political agitation. Metternich pushed the decree through the German Federal Diet and it is said that he never felt so satisfied in his life. For he believed that he had once and for all quashed revolutions and that Carlsbad completed the work begun at Vienna. This may seem false in the light of historical hindsight, but the decrees did keep Germany quiet for a generation. Metternich's confidence was based on an optimism which was part of the make-up of his thought. He believed, as many had believed before him, that God was on the side of order, not revolution, and that therefore he would triumph over disturbances within and among European states. The middle classes would be tamed—and so they were in Germany, though not by Metternich but by the developing nationalism. The great statesman held a dim view of human nature and a dimmer one of the people as a "mob" but he himself had the optimistic feeling that he was carrying out God's work.

In an overall view, Metternich's conservatism was dominated by a desire for order and a belief that such order could only come about on the basis of traditional rule. He invites comparison with the conservatism of Bismarck in the next generation. Both men rejected a nationalism based upon the romantic criterion of the *Volk,* which thought in terms of the dominance of one nation over all others. Both shared a view of Europe in terms of order and both regarded revolutions as the major menace. In Metternich's time that menace came from nationalism, in Bismarck's from Marxism. Thus Bismarck outlawed the Social Democratic party while Metternich authored the Carlsbad Decrees. Moreover, Bismarck also thought order could be based upon a strong monarchical tradition, and both thought more of practicality than intellectual excellence.

If there is a difference between their conservatisms it may lie in the increased stress which Bismarck placed upon the state as an instrument of power. The strong state must rest upon a foundation which was conservative in the sense that it conserved the traditional institutions as a framework for orderly government. Metternich also believed in a strong Austrian state, and he rejected the idea of an imperial parliament as a way of reconciling the interests of the diverse nationalities in the Empire. The Emperor must be supreme. But Metternich, symptomatically, saw the Austrian problem once more as a matter of balancing powers. A supreme emperor would be the umpire above the conflicting nationalities. For Bismarck, the state was supreme and he was not as concerned with balancing interests within Germany as he was with this balance in foreign policy. But then the problems of a multi-national empire and the problems of Germany were different.

In their conservatism both men felt that they were doing the work of God and that this work meant conserving the state rather than making innovations which would lead to basic change. Bismarck was a Protestant, close to certain pietistic sects, and his view of duty was governed by the ideal of a direct responsibility to God. Metternich's religion was without dogma and oriented in a quite similar fashion—for him conservative ideals were expressed in a moral law. Such conservatism was only similar to that of the English Tories in that it was also concerned with the welfare of the people. Metternich attempted to institute mild social reforms in Austria. Bismarck a generation later was more concerned with the masses which might be attracted to socialism. His program of compulsory state health insurance seems to present-day American Conservatives like "creeping socialism." He realized what today's neo-Conservatives forget, that through the state's social action the poorer elements are tied more closely to the state itself and therefore to order. In consequence, they would no longer be interested in changing society for their benefit but rather in helping to preserve it. Both Metternich and Disraeli shared a similar approach to the "masses."

This kind of conservatism was quite different in texture from that of de Maistre or Mueller. It was much more flexible in the sense of being oriented toward practical political action, and there was none of the religious and Catholic content or indeed a romantic one. Beyond this, it showed a greater concern for the immediate welfare of the masses than the evolutionary conservatism of Edmund Burke. To these varieties of nineteenth-century conservatism another type must be added which is more difficult to classify. Like most ideologies conservatism penetrated other ways of thought, even those it deplored. For there was a liberal conservatism by which is meant a liberalism which shared conservative ideals.

Liberalism believed in freedom. It was based to a large extent on the dynamic of the middle classes; how then could it be conservative? In the chapter on liberalism the Moderates were mentioned, among whom Edmund Burke was a dominating influence. It was Burke who introduced Liberals to the England they so much admired. We must also remember the role which history played in liberal thought, a history of freedom of which Burke would have disapproved. It can be argued that the Moderates learned the wrong lessons from Burke. They read of the English aristocracy's reformation, of the franchise's extension accomplished without revolution, and attributed this to the historic spirit of England. But they themselves wanted to imitate these actions at once without waiting for their nations to evolve slowly and peacefully as Burke had advocated. Such a contradiction must not obscure what they did take from Burke: the opposition to violent revolution and the view of freedom as compatible with order. Moderate Liberals wanted to preserve as much history and tradition as possible but wanted to combine these with freedom for the middle class.

Guizot is the outstanding example of a liberal Conservative. He certainly stressed liberty as necessary for man's free development, but having done so he restricted this liberty again in the name of order and opposition to revolution. Guizot restricted liberty precisely where Liberals like Tocqueville saw a need for the extension of liberty: in the realm of political participation in government. Reason alone, Guizot believed, was sovereign and this reason demanded that people live under government. But as liberty was also important, such a government must be constitutional. Not all men could participate in governmental affairs, however. Man was impure. He needed strong rulers, but this strength could only be derived from a class of leaders. Guizot went so far, at one point, as to condone a hereditary aristocracy. Having once been a professor of history, reason for him meant not only strong government but also an emphasis upon historical continuity. When he wrote *"l'histoire, c'est la nation,"* however, he meant not the king and the Church but the development of a constitutional monarchy; for him England and France shared the same historical tradition.

Guizot regarded the democratic French experiments of 1848 with horror because they seemed to open up a prospect of infinite change and encourage promises which no government, if it wanted to rule, could fulfill. Liberalism, as was noted in the last chapter, trod a middle path between democracy and the *ancien régime*. With Guizot this middle path pushed him toward conservatism through the fear of revolution and the desire for strong government. The "great tranquility," which he praised and which was the core of his view of the good society, did not prevent him from interfering in the economic processes of the nation or from advocating the censorship of newspapers. The slogan "enrich yourself" broadened the base of political power, but only for a few and only for those who had the required morality to climb the economic ladder. Such men were presumably no longer impure, and, confident of their custodianship of the nation, the hereditary nobility could be allowed to vanish.

Guizot shared with the Conservatives the desire to preserve as much of the traditional as possible in the name of order; he differed in believing that such a "great tranquility" would automatically lead to a free society where liberty would reign. He, too, did not believe in the new nationalism and saw no future, for example, in the agitation of neighboring Italy. Just as conservatism could fuse with this kind of liberalism, so it could fuse with nationalism and this in an even more decisive way. Conservatives like de Maistre or de Bonald were not Nationalists; in their thought, cast as it was in universal Catholic terms, the papacy played too great a role. But Adam Mueller was a Nationalist. His all-encompassing state, based on a Christian foundation, was combined with conservatism and the kind of nationalism which Metternich and Bismarck abhorred. Similarly, the conservatism of Benjamin Disraeli combined romanticism and a nationalism which refurbished the glory of an empire upon which the sun would never set. Tory democracy wanted to unite the nation around the idealized concept of the English past.

The historical element in conservatism shared the stress upon history of both romanticism and nationalism. All wanted to be at one with the distant past. Moreover, all of these ideologies abhorred revolutions. Furthermore, the social paternalism of conservatism fused with the ideal of the nation uniting all its citizens in a common bond of mutual interest and revered tradition. Liberalism seemed egoistic and divisive in comparison. Nationalists were Conservatives in all these instances. They departed from conservatism in their desire for the overthrow of existing states, both before and after 1870. Moreover, through their nationalism, they were committed to a policy of international disorder. But such men thought of their actions as conservative, for they wanted to recapture the roots of the *Volk* and they saw in modern civilization revolutionary changes which must be undone. They opposed middle-class dynamism; their vision was directed toward a distant, stable, and agricultural past. So complete was the fusion of conservatism and nationalism that nationalist movements are often called conservative movements.

Conservatism was a diffuse ideology. Obviously not all Conservatives were Nationalists or Romantics. Some thought of themselves as Liberals. There were Conservatives who shared the thought of Metternich and of Bismarck and there were those who followed de Maistre and the clerical or Catholic bent of thought. It is not quite clear to which of the conservative traditions the modern neo-Conservatives intend to return; they are handicapped by the very diffuseness of the ideology. In the nineteenth century, however, conservatism had some common features which were outlined at the beginning of the chapter and can be summarized here.

Conservatives sought to cope with the new forces emerging at the beginning of the century by stressing history and order. They believed that the French and Industrial revolutions were menacing the very existence of society, and with it, any freedom which man might possess. While Burke was concerned with liberty, others on the Continent stressed authority rather than freedom. All looked back to the past and sought to apply its criteria to present ills. Burke thought of freedom in feudal and medieval terms; others sought to apply the principles of the corporate state to industrial society. Using history, they revived the Christian view of politics.

It is difficult to make a class analysis of those who came to support conservatism. There were middle- and working-class Conservatives, just as there were liberal aristocrats. Generally, however, conservative ideals appealed to two divergent classes of the population: the aristocracy which wanted to preserve its position and members of the working class who saw in paternalism an amelioration that the liberal ideal of "self help" did not advance. This was especially true in England, and Disraeli built Tory democracy upon both aristocratic and working-class support. It was less true in France where socialist ideas took hold earlier than elsewhere, while in Germany the growing appeal of nationalism engulfed all the classes. This appeal could be combined with the kind of conservatism Mueller had advocated. No doubt the romantic evocation of the past helped the Conservatives all over western Europe. As time went on conservative theories broadened out into a myriad of combinations. They tended to become a "mood" rather than a comprehensive body of political thought, as were both liberalism and romanticism.

These habits of mind were not the only ones whose force made itself felt at the beginning and throughout the century. German idealism had many ties with conservatism and romanticism, less with liberalism. Its consequences were to be equally momentous if still more diffuse, for out of it came not only redefinitions of nationalism, but also the doctrines of Karl Marx.

# CHAPTER NINE

# Idealism Asserted and Rejected

THROUGHOUT THIS book the various ideals men have evolved both for themselves and their society will be discussed again and again. Such ideals are the dynamic of cultural history, indeed of all history in all ages. From the beginning of the nineteenth century the static ideas of conservatism lost ground. Glorifying the status quo proved far less attractive than utopian visions of the future. Conservatism itself began to change; the monarch who murmured "Otranto" (that is, 1780) in a nostalgic wish for the pre-Revolutionary world gave way to the Tory democracy of a Disraeli and the welfare legislation of a Bismarck. Much of the idealistic impulse of the century was connected with romanticism. Later on romanticism was the chief ingredient of a dynamic world view that opposed the positivistic currents of the century. It provided the counterweight to the growing rationalistic and materialistic tendencies of the age epitomized in that definition of progress which stressed material well-being and industrial, as well as scientific, discovery. Above all, romanticism increasingly challenged the individualism of the liberal credo by reminding men of the deeper forces of an irrational destiny which determined the individual's fate. People were encouraged to look beneath the mere appearances of reality into their own soul, for only their intuition could guide men in their search for a principle of existence.

Thus romanticism opposed rationalism, and this strife has been mirrored in previous chapters. Could these two views of man be brought together? Could rational reality be defined in a way which fused it with an idealistic impulse? Friedrich Hegel (1770–1831), attempting such a fusion, became one of the central figures in nineteenth-century thought. His philosophy combined both rationalism and idealism, though in the end his interpreters often emphasized solely his idealistic element. Rationalism was stressed by Hegel himself in his axiom, "whatever is rational is real and whatever is real is rational." Idealism came to the fore in his interpretation of rationalism. For the eighteenth century and for many Liberals, rationalism had been identified with the ability of reason to grasp the reality of the world. But Hegel was the child of another tradition as well. History had played an ever greater role, not only in romantic thought but also in liberal thought. It was this tradition that Hegel used to define reason.

The dynamic might of history provided the basis for reason. With Hegel, history became both the determining factor for and the embodiment of reason. He spoke of the "cunning reason" of history which overrode man to gain its own ends, while, subjectively, man might feel that he was carrying out his own designs. One is reminded of Vico who, in the eighteenth century, had given history a similar content, attempting to integrate it with the Enlightenment. Later, Croce was to say that outside history there can be no reality. Such a view of history seemed to ignore a moral factor: might made right in terms of the necessary justification of whatever history produced. This aspect of Hegel's thought was to be of importance, finding a ready echo among fascist philosophers like Giovanni Gentile (1875–1944). But Hegel did not stop here. How history worked, the principles which moved historical development, were of vital importance to his thought. Hegel was no nihilist, believing that because history is always right therefore what succeeds must be right also and must be accepted unquestionably by man. Hegel and Marx both believed that though history is the reality and the embodiment of reason, its grasp depends upon an understanding of the way history works and the goals toward which history strives.

Here Hegel's idealism asserted itself. Underneath the visible, obvious reality of historical development there must be an ideal, an essence, which constituted the ultimate reality of history. This was reinforced by Hegel's rejection of individualistic varieties of historical development and by his belief in an all-encompassing unity which governed the world. He constantly used the word "fate," something which embraced all mankind. One can see here the urge toward unity which was also reflected in the Romantics and which, with Hegel as well, was stimulated by the revolutionary times in which he lived. The French Revolution and the Napoleonic experience had aroused an

individualism typified by Constant's "lectures on freedom"; it had also produced a growing concern with problems of unity in nations like Hegel's Germany. Unlike Fichte, Hegel sought for unity not in national terms but in
terms of an organizing principle of history. This he found in the spirit of history which progressed toward an ideal. Hegel shared this ideal with many of
his contemporaries—it was the ideal of freedom, the spiritual liberation of
humanity.

With this outlook liberalism could find little quarrel, at least as far as the
end result of historical evolution was concerned. Moreover, Hegel's freedom
was closely tied to his legal ideas, to his belief in the excellence of constitutional government. Influenced by Benjamin Constant, Hegel envisioned this
constitutional government as a monarchy. The end result of Hegelian historical development was closely related to liberal thought which held the great
achievement of the century to be the development of constitutional mon-
archies. However, idealism intrinsic in the way history, according to Hegel,
was to fashion this end, differed sharply with the liberal view of progress. He
characterized history as the world spirit moving up the ladder of historical
evolution. How did this world spirit manifest itself? Not through individuals,
but through a "folk spirit" which, in turn, determined the shape of human
culture and political organization. At the core of this concept was the nation;
it was the direct manifestation of the folk spirit and thus of the world historical spirit. Hegel defined nations not merely as territorial or political units but
as civilizations. At every stage of history one nation had become the particular
vehicle of the world spirit, and thus that nation became a "world historical
people." Superseding all other cultures, it triumphed over its rivals. But that
triumph was limited and transitory, for history progressed through a dialectical process. Hegel envisaged this as a constant conflict of opposing forces, as a
struggle which would produce a lasting synthesis approximating the Hegelian
ideal.

This dialectic consisted of thesis and antithesis. A nation dedicated to
liberty would oppose one which was despotic—whichever one triumphed
would, in time, be defeated by the other which would again find itself confronted by antithesis, the whole process being repeated. The drama of history
was therefore a drama of struggle and of momentary triumphs. In Hegel is
found a vital echo of that concept of struggle prevalent in much of liberal
thought. But here struggle was seen as progressing toward a definite end: the
goal set by the world spirit, thus the emergence of a final synthesis. It cannot
be overemphasized that the nation as the instrumentality of a world historical
people was the key to this struggle. The final synthesis would develop, therefore, within this context. The nation, it must be remembered, was broadly defined as a cultural entity, as, indeed, an all-encompassing force. A world his-

torical people reflected, in the material world, the kind of unity of fate implicit in the spirit of history. The individual was bound by both his fate as a member of the nation and by his larger fate in the process of history.

It has often been said that, for Hegel, the Prussian state was the final synthesis. This is not quite so. Germany, as a nation, was to represent such a synthesis; therefore he exhorted the German people to follow a certain line of action that would enable them to become the final world historical people. At much the same time as Fichte, he asked whether Germany was a nation at all. Hegel felt that Germany needed more discipline and less individualism. Man was a part of the nation through historical reality and the striving for the ideal; therefore Germans must integrate themselves into the national culture and social system. Only in this way would the nation become a cultural whole. The similarity of such ideas with those of the cultural Nationalists is obvious. Moreover, the state must be disciplined in order to win the final struggle. Hegel admired Machiavelli, especially *The Prince's* exhortation to national unification. A new Cesare Borgia would whip Germany into shape. It can be summed up this way: What Germany had to learn and realize was the interdependence of all phases of national life. No individual could stand aside from such an involvement.

But the state could not be static. That would diametrically oppose the historical process, "For what world history reports are the deeds of the spirit of the peoples. . . ." Hegel justified cultural conquest by the nation, but conquest required a unity which he thought could only be achieved in Germany through Machiavellian methods. The practical application of Hegel's ideas to the German situation furthered a nationalism which was not, at this stage, different from Fichte and his like. But there was, nevertheless, an all-important difference. Hegel's final synthesis differed morally from that of the growing German nationalism. Their moral imperative insisted that the real nature of the folk soul must triumph. With Hegel, however, law would triumph, in the end, through the kind of constitutional monarchy that has already been analyzed.

The idea of reason was transformed in Hegel. It became equivalent to historical necessity. The liberal idea of freedom became the end result of national integration. Reality can only be explained through searching for the essence which lies beneath it. It was not concealed in man's soul as the Romantics had believed, but in the world spirit which can be explained and into which man must integrate himself. Finally, Hegel intermingled the static and the dynamic in his world view. History progressed, but the idea within the world spirit remained a constant goal impelling progress itself. This constant core gave German idealism a firm foundation. There must always be a principle, a cosmic idea, to which reality is related. Some saw this in race, others in the folk soul. Many of Hegel's contemporaries held the spirit of the state to be such a cosmic principle. In this guise Hegelianism was preached from professorial chairs, for in the universities it began to gain a general acceptance. Such ideas seemed to fit in with the prevailing patriotism.

Since history played a predominant role in Hegelianism, it is small wonder that he vitally influenced a growing school of historians. They regarded history not as the description of objective reality but as partly spiritual. The historian Wilhelm Dilthey (1833–1911) made the distinction between accessible reality and universally valid truth. This truth was historical consciousness itself: ". . . what man is, only history tells," and man must therefore surrender himself to the great objective forces which history had engendered. This view of history, called "historicism," was to be extremely influential, but it was subject to divergent interpretations. History itself could become the ultimate reality, and the very process of history could be grasped through man's historical consciousness. Such a view meant that the flow of history itself replaced the world historical spirit as the constant factor to which all judgments must be related. The result was a "relativism" which made all of life relative to the march of historical events. Whatever has succeeded in history has to be accepted by the historian, and no moral judgment can be passed upon it. Historicism in general, however, continued to connect history with a cosmic principle which sought expression through events as they occurred.

Leopold von Ranke (1795–1886) became the founder of this school of historians, not only because he wrote a great many works, but principally because he combined a Hegelian approach to history with an emphasis upon the data of historical scholarship. The desire to write "history as it actually happened," in the much quoted phrase, required not only the most rigorous canons of scholarship, but also its meaning implied the relationship of history to a cosmic, moral principle. The way in which Ranke related these two factors was of great significance for the school of "historicism." As Theodore von Laue put it: "Ranke the historian was inspired by the urge to penetrate into the realm of divine knowledge." That knowledge he interpreted in pantheistic terms: God as the idea which stood (in a Hegelian sense) behind historical reality. The events of history were the "externals" of this cosmic and moral reality. God was like a "holy hieroglyphic, understood and preserved through His external nature" and the course of history traced the lineaments of His external nature. Again, Ranke used the symbolism of a tree which shoots up from the earth and sprouts many branches and leaves. At the core of the tree's existence and growth lay the secret seed of life. It was the same with the process of history itself.

History, so understood, must be grasped through historical facts, through its material residues, its documents. They were the stuff of history, and Ranke more than any other man founded the modern science of rigorous historical research in European archives. In this fashion the cosmic force of God behind history could be grasped and understood. Rational historical method was directly related to his definition of the world historical spirit. In the end, however, Ranke defined the dynamic of this relationship differently from Hegel. For Hegel the world historical spirit pointed toward a final synthesis. Hegel believed in progress, but Ranke did not. He thought every historical epoch had a separate and direct relationship to God. The Deity was timeless, viewing the whole historical process in its totality; every epoch, as a part of the whole, had its own peculiar value. The very variety of history had its base in the Divine. Ranke did not believe that permanent laws could be derived from history; thus he also rejected Hegel's schematization of history. Working constantly with documents and thousands of facts, one understands this point of view; one appreciates Ranke's stress on the variety and change inherent in the historical process. Yet there was the cosmic force of the Divine, revealed in and identical with this historical narrative. Here Ranke adopted a strict idealism—the laws of the Divine in history cannot be proved but must, instead, be "intuited."

Ranke's idea of history was not purely empirical, even where the putting together of historical research was concerned. For he saw in history not only change and variety but also balance. There was struggle as well as harmony in human events. The state was Ranke's analytical tool. He saw Europe in terms of competing nation states, a view which was understandable in the nineteenth century but which demonstrates how far we have come from the universalism of the eighteenth. The centrality of the nation state in Ranke's historical framework was directly related to Hegel, for the philosopher also held that the nation had been the instrument of historical change. Ranke's works were histories of nation states and their conflicts; it was in this context that he thought the history of foreign policies the most important aspect of history in general.

Yet Ranke did have a concept of a Europe held together not by any laws of nature but by a morality which checked the power struggles of nations. Periods of harmony were produced by a balance of power between states and by a moral factor which limited the destructiveness of power. Again there was a combination of two factors: the struggle for power which was the crux of historical change (here Ranke was close to Hegel once more) and the moral factor which was part of that cosmic force's direct relationship with every historical period.

Given his view of history, he saw the problem of the nature of power as central to his analysis. Power was both an empirical and a moral force, for all power had a spiritual essence. This was applicable not only to those states which recovered from defeat and defended themselves from attack but to that power upon which the state itself was built. Power was, after all, the factor which had, again and again, created new and valuable forces in history, forces linked directly to God. Moral forces operate through the egoism of states, for states were the basic components of history. Ranke's definition of morality was obviously a very broad one which included "reason of state," the necessity of the state entering into and winning the power struggles of the epoch.

Ranke gave power a moral content. His view of the state was very close to Bismarck's for whom, as has been seen, morality meant the responsibility to preserve the state even through conventionally immoral means. Moreover, such a concept was related to that historical relativism mentioned earlier. Not, however, for Ranke himself. He believed in a cosmic moral force, God, and this cosmic force, he thought, would temper the power struggle itself. This was the force which stood outside the historian himself, beyond the data with which he dealt, and which infused history with a morality and with laws which had to be "intuited." In the end, Ranke may have glorified power by assigning it a morality but he sprang from the idealist tradition. To be sure, his idealism came to mean a justification of power; for some, this historian symbolized the glorification of the existing Prussian state. But even Hegel, for all his idealism, tended to make the processes of history self-justifying. The balance in this movement between realism and the moral forces outside of history was precarious. This is why German idealism, and specifically Hegelianism, did seem a conservative ideology, supporting the status quo. This was not always the case, as will be seen shortly, with the "Young Hegelians," but Ranke and his school belong to the conservative tradition centered upon the moral justification of the state. Cosmic reality had its earthly equivalent in a concept of national power.

Ranke's followers often forgot the idealistic element of his thought and veered toward a historical positivism. They emphasized historical data and the empiricism which had to evaluate this data, while ignoring the other side of Ranke's ideology. For him history was integrated into a general cosmology; for many of his followers it became divorced from any general meaning of life. The historical monograph triumphed, and history itself became enmeshed in that academic specialization for which Ranke's emphasis on rigorous scholarship had prepared the way.

Yet not all of his followers trod this path. The greatest of them emphasized the idealistic component and at the same time returned to the Hegelian inspiration. Friedrich Meinecke (1862–1954) praised Hegel as the founder of historicism.

Agreeing with Hegel's definition of the nation and its preponderant role,

Meinecke held that only the history of culture was valid history, culture signifying the production of unique spiritual values. Unlike Ranke he did not believe in the primacy of foreign policy but emphasized Hegel's concept of the nation as a cultural entity. In this way he posited a more direct "breakthrough" of the cosmic forces into the very existence of the state. "Culture is thus the revelation and the breakthrough of a spiritual element within the general complex of (historical) causality." Civilization lifted itself above nature (that is, earthly reality). Thus history was always related to eternal values. For Meinecke, at one point, these values lay in religion and art; but for him as for the other practitioners of historicism, only the state could allow such values full expression. National power interested these historians, and they infused this power with superior values. Thus historicism was reduced to a spiritualization of power. Ideally, they looked for a fusion of purpose. Protection of national interests would be joined to an explosion of cultural energies. They imbued national power with universal principles. Such historicism became German national history, and as such was important for two reasons. First, it defined culture once more as a universal principle of race or of *Volk* spirit expressed through the state. Secondly, it made a sharp distinction between culture and civilization.

Culture, as the integration of the nation's spiritual energies, was a direct expression of the world historical spirit, while civilization was viewed as shallow, individualistic, and materialistic, not linked to any constant cosmic principle. Hegelianism in this guise rejected pragmatic, material causes in history, and in life, as the mere surface realities of a deeper spiritual impetus. The result was that life was viewed in emotional and romantic terms. In this way Hegelianism squarely opposed the Enlightenment, and, indeed, it laid the foundations for the revolt against materialism and positivism at the end of the century. It did not lay these foundations by itself, for Hegel was, in a sense, a child of romanticism. In the end Oswald Spengler was to repeat this distinction between culture and civilization and again popularize the view that material things are unimportant, that it is the spirit which counts.

This was, however, only one aspect of Hegelianism. There was another more immediate side to it. While the professors were proclaiming their version of Hegel, a circle of young intellectuals, calling themselves the "Young Hegelians," also stressed the fact that outside history no reality was possible. But these "Young Hegelians" were not so much concerned with the "idea" which underlay history as with debunking the false notions to which man had ascribed his fate on earth. In the course of this activity they came to define the world spirit in different ways, but they were united in seeing Christianity as the force which blocked an understanding of history as embracing the totality of life. As a result they began to analyze Christianity in the Hegelian manner.

David Friedrich Strauss wrote his *Life of Jesus* (1835) to show that Jesus himself was a product of history and not of a sudden intervention of the Divine into the dialectical process. Strauss accepted the Hegelian "idea" which underlay history and he defined it, similar to Hegel, as the "folk soul." National culture climbed to victory on the ladder of historical evolution. In this Christ was merely a stage of development. For Strauss this was proved by his contention that Christ was not a fully-integrated individual in society. His relation to the state was a passive one. He spurned business activity; art and the enjoyment of beauty were outside his purview. Hegel maintained that the perfect integration of the individual with the nation's life was a prerequisite for the victory of a world historical people. It followed that Christ represented an incomplete stage in the final resolving of the dialectic. But had He existed at all? Strauss then proceeded to use canons of historical evidence to show that the Biblical account did not possess historical validity. In sum, for Strauss, Christ was a part of myth and legend, thus a reflection of the folk soul. Strauss's book created a sensation. Though he himself seemed to have destroyed the Divine basis for Christianity, he indirectly stimulated higher Biblical criticism.

Ludwig Feuerbach (1804–72) pushed such criticism still further. Originally a student of Protestant theology, he abandoned it under the spell of Hegel's philosophy. Christianity now seemed to him an outmoded cultural stage in the historical process. The importance of Feuerbach for us, however, lies in the fact that he went beyond Hegel to a materialistic view of the world. Idealistic philosophy was merely theology on another level, and both, he thought, reversed the reality of things. His *Nature of Christianity* (1841) was perhaps the first consequential denial of religion as well as of idealistic philosophy. Without hesitation, Feuerbach accepted the primacy of matter. Central to such a primacy was man himself. For Feuerbach man, not the world spirit or the world historical people, stood in the center of all historical development. Ideals must proceed from the reality of human development, from the individual's own journey through historical time.

Here the individualism of the age stands fully revealed. Religion was merely a phenomenon of man's development; in fact, Feuerbach entitled one chapter of his famous book "The Human Being: Beginning, End and Center of Religion." Religion was an illusion which man built to serve his own purposes. The love of God for man was but a disguise for the love of man for himself. In all religions, including Christianity, Feuerbach maintained that man created God after his own image. Religion becomes a fantasy, a wish fulfillment, a means by which man might better worship himself. Karl Marx summed up Feuerbach's thought well when he wrote that "this criticism of religion ends in the maxim that man himself is the ultimate higher being for man." To quote Feuerbach's own words: "God is what men are not ... but what they want to be and could be; God takes upon himself the sins of man; he is man's deputy; he releases them from the duty of being toward each other what He is in their place."

Underlying these ideas was Feuerbach's materialism. To say that God came before nature would be as ridiculous as to say that the church came before the bricks out of which it was constructed. Man was a material creature in a material universe. Neither history nor religion was an expression of the folk spirit, as Strauss had thought; they were a response to the needs of man. Yet, like Hegel, Feuerbach believed in the evolution of history, in progress. For him Christianity was a higher historical stage than that of the heathen: "... the heathens worshipped the qualities of man, Christianity man himself, his inner nature." The criterion of historical progress was clear: not the world spirit, not the folk soul, but man perceiving and accepting himself as the center of the universe. Heathens worshipped man superficially; Christians were merely more thorough worshippers at the same altar. It was time, said Feuerbach, to come to terms with the reality of materialism. "Christianity is an *idée fixe* which stands in flagrant contrast to our fire and life insurances, our railways and steamships, our galleries of painting and sculpture, our military and commercial schools." Small wonder that Friedrich Engels called the *Nature of Christianity* a "liberating" work. It exemplifies, for us, this particular Hegelian impetus in contrast to the patriotism of the professors. The idea of history remained, but now it centered upon humanity's progress within a materialistic context. Society, particularly its economic structure, was ignored. In short, Feuerbach's individualism militated against any historical theory which was not centered on man but was built upon social and economic forces; his conception of man as a material creature was opposed to a theory positing material forces standing outside of man himself. After having experienced the first liberating shock of Feuerbach's work, Marx and Engels became highly critical of this approach to history. Feuerbach himself refused to make common cause with Marx when the latter asked him to do so. Instead he reverted to ever more abstract and abstruse philosophical writings until he died, in 1872, forgotten and in poverty, thirty-one years after he had written his famous book.

Strauss had attacked Christianity from within the framework of Hegelian idealism; Feuerbach had replaced this idealism with an accented individualism; the third of this Young Hegelian trilogy came closest to the Marxist approach to man. Bruno Bauer (1809–82) was the closest friend of Marx's youth. He also, departing from Hegel, took the line suggested by Feuerbach. But his materialism was of a quite different order; it returned once more to a consideration of general principles operative in history. Like his friend, he started with the Greeks. Heraclitus held great interest for Marx; Bauer also accepted the Greeks' description of historical forces as the true nature or the "idea" in history: The individual was part of the totality of his material environment and yet he had the power to change that environment. Feuerbach's view of man was too extreme in both its individualism and materialism. Man had the power to choose rightly, to be united with the course of history, if only he could obtain an inner tranquility. For Bauer also, man was the "idea" in history, but man defined as a creature only partly material. The basis of man's strength lay, Bauer thought, in Roman and Greek ideals; for him Christianity was nothing more than a falsification of those ideals. The Gospels were an obvious plagiarism upon them. Marx, too, believed man, possessing free will, was far from being a creature of a totally materialistic nature as Feuerbach had thought.

The relationship of the individual to the environment was important for all the Hegelians, for Hegel had, as we have seen, advocated the totality of culture and the importance of man as sharing all the factors which make up a civilization. For Strauss man's role was played through the medium of the folk soul, for Feuerbach through materialism: "Man is what he eats" the latter once wrote. Bauer saw this total relationship in terms of an interplay between free will and environment. Karl Marx was to see it in similar terms. Yet his friendship with Bauer did not last, and for a significant reason. All these men saw in Christianity their adversary, the obstacle to a true realization of a culture. Bruno Bauer became obsessed with the struggle against Christianity and that led him eventually to play the state against the church. At that time Bruno became "holy Bruno" to an increasingly contemptuous Marx.

With the Young Hegelians the master's doctrine did become a "breviary of revolution." In order to fulfill history, to link man to culture, the existing religion and the existing suppression of man must disappear. This could have a socialistic content. Moses Hess (1812–75) combined Hegelian ideas with those of the early French Socialists. In order to bring about the triumph of the state as the embodiment of the world historical spirit, the proletariat must be freed; all classes must be made equal and private property abolished. Hess was much impressed with Marx, but eventually he saw in Marxism merely the shifting of the class burden from the proletariat to the bourgeoisie, and not true equality. Hess himself underwent many ideological changes, becoming best known as a champion of Jewish nationalism long before Theodor Herzl's Zionism. Obviously Marx learned much from his close association with these Young Hegelians. He became first a disciple of Hegel and then embarked upon a theoretical journey which, for a short time, paralleled that of the Young Hegelians, but he was to go far beyond the ideas discussed. Hegelian concepts thus bore a varied and many-sided fruit.

The so-called orthodox Hegelians interpreted his idealism as an essentially irrational world spirit, and combined it with his idea of a world historical spirit working through the nation. The Young Hegelians infused his ideas with a materialistic spirit, and turned them toward an attack upon Christianity and an exaltation of man himself. Both groups retained Hegel's idea of history and his dialectic as well as his definition of culture. Small wonder that Hegel must stand as one of the most important thinkers of the century—both for Marxists and for those bitterly opposed to Marx.

# CHAPTER TEN

# The Development
# of Socialism

*T*ODAY THE term "socialism" has become associated with a Marxist analysis of human society. Yet when this word was first used in England (1835), it was the most elastic of terms. Socialism was defined as the attempt to introduce greater equality into social conditions in the hopes that such equality would, in time, become reality in one way or another. To this definition can be added the belief in the principle of human association for the mutual benefit of all, as opposed to competition and free enterprise. As such, socialism was applied to Frenchmen like Saint-Simon and Blanqui, as well as to Robert Owen in England. The pre-Marxian use of the word "socialism" subsumed a longing and theorizing about social equality which had a long history behind it, about which we know too little. Long before Marx, the lower classes had felt a social dynamic which, at times, led to statements of class equality. From the late Middle Ages on, there have been such statements within the context of revolutionary situations such as peasant rebellions or urban revolts. This kind of impetus was, from a Marxist point of view, utopian. It was connected not with theories of history or with formulated dialectics but instead with a chaotic longing for freedom from social oppression. The basis was mostly scriptural and moral rather than scientific and historical. The poor would inherit the earth; the rich must therefore be stripped of their property and this property distributed to all. Such ideas, in revolutionary situations, were connected with millenarianism: that the time for Christ's return to the earth was at hand and that therefore the redistribution of property must begin at once.

In the sixteenth century this social dynamic found expression in the thought of Thomas Muentzer or in the Muenster experiment in equality. In the seventeenth century many Puritan radicals embraced these ideas in the English revolution. Nor were such ideas dead during the nineteenth century. They were operative among those whom E. J. Hobsbawm has called the "Primitive Rebels." Social banditry and millenarianism in rural Italy expressed much the same kind of longings among a people who had not yet entered the industrial age. The bandit who robs the rich to give to the poor is familiar through the legend of Robin Hood, but in rural Sicily of the nineteenth century he was a reality. The millenarianism of Sicilian and Andalusian peasant movements transformed these bandits into revolutionaries. All of these manifestations of social discontent did not possess a clear-cut social program any more than had their ancestors in earlier ages. Their goals were vague, sometimes expressing a longing to return to an idealized past, the legendary "good old times." Nevertheless, these archaic social expressions were important in the nineteenth century. The very fact that they survived into that century testifies to the continuing longings for a more thorough equality in these regions of Europe not yet caught up in modern industrialism. Social banditry continues, in Sicily, into the mid-twentieth century. The millenarian content prepared the ground for the acceptance of true revolutionary dogmas. God or Christ will reveal a new society; nothing is impossible under such a dispensation.

The traditional social dynamic of the lower classes was conservative. It tended to look backward rather than forward, but even so, it wanted to uproot existing society which was oppressive. Popular longings were therefore not unreceptive to socialist thought in its modern formulas. This kind of impetus toward social equality was, however, not limited to people living in preindustrial regions. When industrialism in its beginnings brought great hardships to the lower classes, such an ideology came to the fore as well. The Luddite riots at the start of the century in England and in parts of Germany (especially Silesia) are a good example of this. The Luddite riots occurred in England in the years 1811 and 1812, as well as intermittently for some years thereafter. At first they were a protest not against the introduction of new machinery but against the abuse of old machinery in order to manufacture shoddy goods which ruined the market on behalf of quick profits.

Whether Ned Ludd of Sherwood Forest existed or not is immaterial, for the Luddites were not one revolutionary organization but bands of workers who had joined together for action on an individualistic basis and without any overall plan. Indeed, the Luddites were archaic in the sense discussed above, wanting a return to the old, driven by a chaotic fear of the new. The Luddite riots in Silesia among the weavers (1844) were quite similar. Such riots were another expression of the deep current among the lower classes: the longing not for change as such but for stability and freedom which meant change in terms of going back to a preindustrialist, glorified past.

All of these movements were apt to have a strong religious base. The effect of millenarianism has already been seen. Trust in God was an often expressed sentiment among such men, and while this could be combined with millenarianism, it did not have to be so. Where it was not, such trust in God could lead to fatalism and indeed to pacifism. The Chartist movement in England was organized and did have a more or less coherent aim, but into it went many of the currents of social equality which have been discussed. The movement was directed toward seeking political cures, the suffrage was desired as a solution to economic ills; yet the religiously-oriented pacifism did much to rob the movement of its revolutionary impetus. The workers, the poor, however, were not left to their own ill-expressed and chaotic longings. Men of other social classes became increasingly aware that a social problem existed and that its solution lay in the direction of greater equality. Religion had played a leading part in the ideology we have discussed; it was Christianity in industrial England which at first tended to stimulate a greater awareness of the problem among the other classes of society.

The background of evangelicalism played an important role in this process. It has been seen that the evangelical movement was partly practical and partly emotional. The emotional factor flowed into the romantic movement, the practical into a developing Christian socialism. This practical orientation stressed charity and thrift in tune with John Wesley's exhortation "pray, work, save." As we know, it became a part of the liberal morality of the century. Evangelicalism, however, also stressed the experience of conversion, of coming to Christ. This led to an emphasis upon the inner man and his condition. If this could be rectified, social problems could be overcome. William Booth founded his "Christian Revival Association" (1859) in order to convert the poor of the London slums and through such a conversion make them useful citizens who could find their place in society. He started with a tent, his "conversion shop," and in 1870 the Salvation Army sprang from these beginnings. Booth's concern with the poor stayed within the limits of evangelicalism; the end result was to be an individual reformation, not a change in the class structure. Such ideas operated within the framework of liberalism—the belief that if man had the right spirit he could find a dignified place in society. Booth did, however, infuse his kind of Christianity with a social consciousness.

The early Christian Socialists retained this reformist direction. They did not want to upset the existing class relationships, but they did want to see greater social justice for the victims of the Industrial Revolution. In contrast to the Liberals, they realized that the workers' lot was not subject to automatic improvement, that not mere strength of character was needed to rise in the social scale. Christian Socialists desired some kind of greater equality, and they envisioned it arising upon a revitalized religious base. Charles Kingsley was typical of this movement. The author of *Westward Ho!* believed in a liberal morality of honesty, manliness, and courage, but he also wanted to bring Christianity into line with the Industrial Revolution. "We have used the Bible as if it were a mere special constable's handbook, an opium dose for keeping the beasts of burden patient while they are being overloaded." Religion as the opium of the people—that sounds as if it were written by Karl Marx. On the contrary, what was needed was the right use of Christianity and all would be well. The problem, as the Reverend Kingsley and his like-minded contemporaries saw it, was to bring the Church and the working classes together. In turn, this meant an increasing concern for equality and an increasing practical kind of Christianity.

As Kingsley put it "sanitary work is a sacred duty." How far removed this was from the romantic Christianity of the contemporary Oxford movement! The matter of equality was subject to more ambivalent interpretation. Kingsley believed in the existence of social classes. As for revolutions, these men would have been at one with Tennyson, who termed the French revolution of 1848 "the blind hysteria of the Celt." Kingsley himself told the Chartists to desist in their agitation.

The approach was always through religion; as the Christian Socialists put it in their manifesto of 1848: "There will be no true freedom without virtue, no true industry without the fear of God and the love of fellow Citizens. Workers of England, be wise, and then you must be free, for you will be fit to be free." Quite a different appeal was sounded that same year in the *Communist Manifesto*. In retrospect it might seem as if the latter appeal triumphed over that of the Christian Socialists, but, in fact, they cannot be so readily dismissed. In England the Christian Socialists did bring the Church closer to the worker, preventing that hostility between the Church and the working class so common on the Continent. The first Labor Prime Minister, Ramsay Mac-Donald (1866–1937), was a pious Scottish Presbyterian. Christian socialism vitally influenced the growth of the Labor Party, and it is small wonder that many of the founders like Sidney and Beatrice Webb came to socialism, in

Christian Socialists

part, via the route of a Christian social consciousness. This, in turn, tempered socialism in England. Christian Socialists, however, went beyond a mere wish for greater equality and practicality in Christianity's approach to man. Indeed, they themselves came to criticize one of the fundamentals of liberalism: free competition.

Kingsley, the advocate of a liberal morality, the believer in a class society, founded the Tailor's Association. Repulsed by the sweatshop conditions among tailors, a condition of "everlasting darkness and despair," Kingsley saw the roots of such oppression in free competition, the blind pursuit of profits. The Christian idea of human brotherhood dictated that the tailors should associate together and, as an association, compete on the open market. In this manner workers could produce and sell for their own benefit. This was not intended to upset existing society but to stress cooperation, not revolution. The workers in France had forgotten God; that is why they revolted instead of choosing the path of mutual cooperation as had the tailors. Kingsley's novel *Alton Locke, Tailor and Poet* (1850) made this clear. It had a huge impact on England largely because of its vivid descriptions of social misery. There was a moral to this tale—though Locke took part in the Chartist uprisings, he saw in the end that this course had been false. It was based upon the pursuit of abstract rights, and such rights were ineffectual: ". . . the same ideas of abstract rights do not (in America) interfere with the tyranny of the white man over the black." Christ died for all—here was the true equality. It was bound to be realized sooner or later in the course of peaceful change. Association in cooperatives was the first step in this direction.

The example of the tailors was followed by the weavers, and indeed it became the concrete program of the Christian Socialists. They even succeeded in getting such associations legalized. Nevertheless, as far as the Christian Socialists were concerned, in the end they proved a failure. Some in the associations felt that Christianity was superfluous to their existence and that cooperation was an ideology which could stand on its own feet. Moreover, the trade union strike of 1852, the first major strike in England, forced many a Christian Socialist to compromise his nonviolence principles. The idea of association was, however, far from dead. No trade union challenge could destroy it. Instead it continued but on a different footing. The figure of Robert Owen (1771–1858) became important in its further development.

Owen, a successful businessman and philanthropist, slowly became convinced of the necessity of a socialist society. As early as 1817 he had submitted to the House of Commons a report which advocated the principle of association as a cure for pauperism. Starting with his own mills at New Lanark and ending in New Harmony, Indiana, he constructed supposedly self-sufficient cooperative ventures in which all modes of production were held in common.

Owen enlarged the cooperative program of the Christian Socialists into a plan for completely self-sufficient cooperative communities. No longer were these associations to embrace only one trade whose members were a part of and competed in society; New Lanark and New Harmony were to be islands of self-sufficient virtue in the sea of competitive society. Virtue was important to Robert Owen, not in the sense of Christianity, but as part of a theory about environmental influences on human nature. Man's character depended upon the environment in which he lived. Christianity was no help here—rather, it was a hindrance, because it dwelt upon man's sins. Both capitalist society and Christianity were wrong. The solution was a society formed on the principle of association. The profit motive would disappear, and the movement of goods would take place through labor exchanges which would trade the value of labor for an equal value of labor.

Owen failed both in England and America. It was not possible to maintain only isolated units of a good society. In the end, he devoted himself to the labor movement as a whole. His "Grand National Consolidated Trade Union" attempted to call a general strike in 1834. He seemed to have learned the lesson of his failure. Owen extended the concept of cooperation into a theory of society which included morality but excluded a Christian base.

Owen's failures made more important contributions to the development of socialism than his lack of success would indicate. Like contemporary French Socialists he wholeheartedly accepted, rather than rejected, industrial society. His principle of cooperation stressed the necessity of that scientific industrial management which had made his own mills at New Lanark so successful. The industrial manager occupied a key place in his thought, for the kind of environment which would make men virtuous was an industrial environment led by industrial managers who had a social responsibility for the cooperative enterprise. Socialist leadership was defined not in terms of a vanguard of the proletariat but in terms of the social function of the captain of industry. Not only Owen, the businessman, but many French Socialists, as a consequence of their acceptance of a growing industrial society, were struck by the need for industrial management. They differed both from the Luddites who looked to a past age and from the Romantics. This was hardly "utopian." It foreshadowed the claim, which gained a general currency, that the industrialist, because he better understood the new society, should exercise social and, indeed, moral leadership. These Socialists were mistaken in believing that a capitalism which practiced this type of social control would support a cooperative society. Yet the key role of the industrialist must be added to the ideal of association or cooperation in order to complete the basic beliefs of this type of socialism.

The actual realization of the cooperation principle was to start on a much more modest base. Neither Christian idealism nor self-sufficiency was in the forefront when, in 1844, twenty-eight flannel weavers opened their cooperative store in Rochdale. They sold their goods at current prices and divided the surplus over costs among their purchasers. The idea behind the "Rochdale plan" was to acquire control over the means of production for the benefit not just of the workers, but for everyone. Much more modest in scope and ideals than the kinds of association we have discussed, the "Rochdale pioneers" succeeded in their venture. They are the beginnings of the cooperative movement as we know it today. It must be remembered, however, that they were part of an atmosphere which was created by the ideals discussed. In Germany a cooperative movement started at almost the identical time. Schulze-Delitzsch (1808–83) organized a system of consumers, producers, and credit cooperatives. Like the Rochdale pioneers he had no wish to inaugurate a fundamental change in present society. Through voluntary associations the individual would fulfill his obligations to society, and, in turn, society would espouse complete civil and economic liberty, as well as the equality of all before the law. Schulze-Delitzsch was not a Socialist but a Liberal in ideology and outlook. Through such voluntary associations, he wanted to harness the working man to the liberal state, an aim which was closely related to that of the English Christian Socialists.

The concept of association remained strong in movements for social improvement. Unlike Marxism, this attempt to gain control of the means of production was based not on the materialist dialectic of history but always upon a moral idea: virtue with Owen, Christianity with men like Kingsley. Nor was it supposed to change society through revolution, but instead it merely desired to modify competition through example.

Yet, in England Owenite utopianism and the Christian socialism of Kingsley did not stand alone. Movements more radical than either of these attempted, from the beginning of the century, to rally the working classes. In no other Western nation was there so much talk about "classes" as in rapidly industrializing England. Not only the working classes but also the middle classes used the language of class to identify themselves. In their attempt to win the working class to a liberal viewpoint, one pamphlet of the 1830s appealed to the identity of interest between the "middle and working classes"; instances of the use of this terminology could be multiplied. It was not Karl Marx who invented a view of life in class terms; it was generally held by many Englishmen before he ever came to write his works.

The middle class might appeal to the working class to come into the fold, but obviously their interests diverged. The Luddites had already thought so, and the fact that the working classes gained nothing from the Reform Bill (1832), which they had supported, seemed to bear out the contention that the working classes stood alone. The reform Parliaments had "united all property against all poverty." A trade union movement had developed from the end of the last century, as it had in all the industrializing European nations. In France unions had been forbidden by the Revolution (1791) and they were branded unlawful combinations in England at much the same time (1799). In both France and England, however, craft unions existed despite their illegality. In England unions were legalized within very narrow limits by 1825, while in France the final repeal of the law of the Revolution did not come until 1884, though it had been a dead letter long before that. Obviously, it had proved impossible to forbid entirely the organization of workers for bargaining purposes.

At the beginning of the nineteenth century, however, these unions were only bargaining units. Most of them were not concerned with changing society. Their relationship with both French and English socialism was tenuous at best, and more often than not, one of outright disapproval. Not only did the English unions rapidly organize most of the skilled workers, however; some of them, as the century wore on, advocated general change in society. Owen's Grand National Consolidated Trade Union has been mentioned, and this was only one of several unions dedicated to the subversion of the existing order. In England the growing sense of isolation among the working classes was increasingly directed toward equating social injustice with political oppression. The high hopes dashed by the outcome of the Reform Bill stimulated the feeling that in a parliament responsible to the people themselves, the necessary social changes could be peacefully legislated.

This desire for a representative parliament was the crux of Chartist demands. Marx and Lenin saw in Chartism the first militant labor movement. Yet, in its initial development, Chartism was not revolutionary—it sought instead to work through a parliament elected by universal manhood suffrage. The "Great Charter" (1837) demanded annual parliaments, manhood suffrage, and equal electoral districts, as well as greater social justice. At first Chartism was a local rather than a national movement and its social demands varied with the conditions of the locality. When Chartism did become a national force, by 1839, these local variations resulted in a platform which was inconsistent and in rival claims to leadership as well. Conditions of work in places where there was no factory system were obviously different and demanded different remedies from those of highly industrialized centers. Thus Chartism had to be both Luddite and sophisticated. Asa Briggs has quite rightly called its failure "inevitable." The high point of Chartism was reached in 1848 when Chartists from all over England gathered to present the Charter, in the form of a petition, to Parliament. The Duke of Wellington came out of retirement to defend the city against revolution. The danger proved nonexistent. The petition was presented, refused, and the workers dispersed peacefully. Unlike the rest of western Europe, England was not to have a revolution. Social upheaval remained, as Tennyson put it, the "madness of the Celt."

Yet the revolution was avoided not because of the English character, as English nationalism saw it, but because the Chartists were, from the beginning, disunited. What should have been the movement's climax became its disintegration. The remaining Chartists went into the cooperative societies or into trade unionism. For some, however, the failure of Chartism resulted in a shift of emphasis from political reform to socialist change. Nevertheless, the Chartists' defeat spelled the end, for a long time, of schemes by working-class organizations for the reform of society. Instead, the "New Unionism" took over: craft unions made up of sober and prudent men with a vested interest in industrial peace. Not until the end of the century would the demand for not only unionism but also social purpose be heard again. By that time, unskilled labor began to be unionized, and the pressures of their demands forced a reformulation of the trade union movement's goals. Yet the English labor movement retained its respect for political action through Parliament and its fear of violence and revolution. More of this will be seen when the English Socialists, the Fabians (who were to give that movement its typically English complexion), are discussed. Though there was much talk about class in England, there was, after mid-century, very little talk about class struggle.

These developments did determine the growth of English socialism and are the principal reason why, even among workers, Marxism as such had slight success. A different tradition had risen in the island nation. The classical country of early socialism was thought to be France. But the early French Socialists held in common this emphasis on association with those across the Channel. They differed in their greater elaboration of a cooperative theory completely divorced from Christianity. They built up a socialist theory which not only believed in association but also in a science of society. France was the country where Auguste Comte (1798–1857) elaborated his positivism, and this influenced French socialism in a manner quite alien to English socialism. As a result, early French Socialists like Saint-Simon and Proudhon assumed the possibility of a science of society based on incontrovertible facts which formed general laws applicable to everyone and everything. It was on the basis of such positivistic laws rather than on the principal basis of a moral ideology that these Socialists proceeded.

The Count of Saint-Simon (1760–1825) came to his socialism from an awareness of France's current problems. She was lagging behind in industrialization, and the depressions of 1816 and 1825 deepened his feeling that something was amiss. Saint-Simon believed that the basic trouble was too much individualism and too little social organization, not that industrial society was

167

an evil—indeed it was the highest stage of history. Saint-Simon believed that human society had passed through successive stages in history. What was now emerging was the final and highest stage—industrial society. This society could be directed for the good of all through an understanding of its underlying social and material phenomena, for this period of history was the highest, precisely because it allowed the realization of a social theory constructed from these facts. Truth, to Saint-Simon, rested upon knowable certainties which could be erected into a science of society. In short, society could be manipulated in the very way scientists manipulated nature, and from such manipulation universally applicable general laws would emerge.

This was an important affirmation. Auguste Comte concluded from a similar argument that everything that existed had therefore to be accepted, for the laws of society made whatever exists inevitable. But Saint-Simon linked such ideas to a theory of progress and to the development of history. France must go forward into the industrial age. How was this to be done? Through association, but also through a new ruling class—the industrial manager. He did not intend a mere shifting of the class structure, but instead a new society which would be managed by this elite for the benefit of all. Both the state and the existing class structure would vanish. Saint-Simon held that government was an anachronism in industrial society. If France lost her royal family and all her state officialdom she would be little inconvenienced, but if her industrial leaders were swept away she would indeed degenerate and become fixed in an earlier, more barbarous stage of history.

According to his theory of society, he maintained that no state was needed, only a class of industrial managers who, applying the general laws of society, would lead industrial society forward. Private enterprise would vanish. Under such leadership the people would control and enjoy the benefits of industrialism. It has been asserted that Saint-Simon's state was really a foreshadowing of the modern totalitarian state. The positivistic base upon which his elite rested made truth something certain and therefore enforceable. In such a situation the industrial managers seemed indeed supreme. Yet Saint-Simon, in his *New Christianity* (1825), did define, in the concept of Christian brotherhood, a moral basis for his society. This, however, did not contradict his deterministic idea of truth or the status of the managers. Saint-Simon's ideas were not very popular. They were couched in an abstruse language and vastly more complex than their essence given here. But he did relate a socialist ethic to social organization, making them interdependent. Liberty was not the direct outcome of the new society; instead there was industrial advancement under a managerial class. Efficiency was one of the hallmarks of this socialism. In the twentieth century, when interest became centered upon making the capitalist system work better, when the managerial class did come to the fore, interest in his theories revived. He foresaw what James Burnham has called the "managerial revolution," but in the name of a socialist, associative society. In this he was not unique. Robert Owen and Enfantin shared this kind of ideology.

Though Saint-Simon tried to retain freedom, especially in artistic creativity, his followers, the Saint-Simonians, began to emphasize the necessity of a social organization which would dominate all spheres of human activity. The economy was to be controlled by an "industrial priest," while "general priests" would rule everything in the name of the totality of social organization. Their ideology was a religion, but religion based on social fact. For them, Christianity was an integral part of the general laws of the science of society. They despised the masses as politically incompetent. The leader linked the masses to rational society and its laws. Undoubtedly these men developed Saint-Simonism into a systematic despotism. Though man was no longer exploited, he would owe strict obedience to his leaders. The Saint-Simonians focused sharply on several elements of their master's thought. Abolition of private property and of exploitation was combined with a social organization which was despotic. Their socialism pointed to a future where liberty would be subordinated to an elite of experts manipulating society.

One of Saint-Simon's followers did start an ideal community on such a basis. Enfantin in 1824 founded an association whose members lived out of a common purse in Paris. The concept of industrial managers was translated into a "hierarchy of the able." Not surprisingly, this utopia attracted, in the main, young men from the École Polytechnique, the scientific and technical school of the French university system. To such men Saint-Simonian ideas had an obvious appeal. This association quickly developed lax notions on marriage and sex. Not only money but women, too, should be shared in common. Enfantin eventually left for Egypt to look for a woman messiah to lead them. They continued a little longer under Bazard (1791–1832) who assumed the role of leader. That this group became the laughingstock and the sensation of Paris must not obscure the importance of the ideas set forth above. As with New Lanark or New Harmony, the building of islands of the good society in a capitalist sea was, in a sense, self-defeating. Instead of organizing and agitating to change society, the movement was thrown back upon itself; rather than a socialist movement it became a socialist sect. The utopia withdrew into itself, became preoccupied with internal politics, and sought to draw attention to itself by shocking bourgeois society. This development was to be repeated several times in socialist history, though without the exhibitionist element of these men. When the movement became so small that it felt itself an island in a hostile sea, it did exhibit sect-like inbreeding, wasting its energies in internal intrigues. The larger perspectives vanished. The history of the Communist parties in England and America provides good recent examples of this process.

The second French socialist thinker of importance was Charles Fourier (1772–1837). His attempt to combine the principle of association with freedom differed from Saint-Simon's. Fourier did not build his theory on the basis of positivism or history but rather upon a theory of human nature. His ideology did not involve a manipulation of society. It centered instead upon the principle of association. The universe operated upon a system of mutual attraction. Had not Newton discovered that the law of attraction governed the world? This must therefore be the will of God. Whatever was wrong with society was so because the will of God had been thwarted. From this Fourier drew a conclusion which Friedrich Engels was to call "liberating"—there must be a clean break with the past. All societal arrangements must be started afresh.

Fourier's concept of progress did not conceive of history as a seamless web. A break must occur so that God would no longer be hindered in His work. To the theory of attraction Fourier added a theory about the human passions. With Rousseau he felt that social passions could harmonize all human passions and actions into a constructive pattern. Thus these passions must be left free; but this could only be done in a new society where the principle of association was supreme. The phalange which he founded was therefore both the will of God and the medium by which evil passions could be corrected through social passions. This phalange started with small groups based upon mutual affinities and then merged into bigger groups, up to 400 families, all living a self-contained and self-sufficient life on the land. They lived on the land; there was in Fourier none of Saint-Simon's acceptance of industrial society as the highest good. The phalange seems a return to Arcadia, to the manor, a romanticism which looked to the past rather than to the future for the cure to the ills of industrial society. Inside the phalange, association would be complete, love would be free, work would be made attractive, and all would be equal—children from the age of five.

Yet, Fourier is more important than as merely the deviser of a singularly elaborate utopia. He did attempt to combine the principle of association with the idea of freedom. His phalange was organized from the bottom up and not, as Saint-Simonian society, from the top down. The basic social unit derived from a free association on the basis of affinity, and this Fourier viewed in terms of the family. The larger associations were built up on an equal freedom of association. He introduced the importance of the local body, the commune, into socialist thought. Moreover, as this new society was fulfilling God's will, these associations had a specifically moral character. Perhaps these were the reasons why the Fourierist communities flourished, for a time, in the United States rather than in Europe, in rural surroundings rather than in industrialized areas. Under frontier conditions, such free associations would have a special usefulness. Indeed, the extent to which European inventors of utopias saw the unsettled vastness of North America as an experimental station for their ideas is striking.

The phalange developed the same characteristics that had marked Enfantin's group; it became a sect plagued by an excess of the cooperative spirit as far as sexual morality was concerned. Against this sort of development Joseph Proudhon (1809–65) revolted. The outlines of this new socialist society seemed to him both utopian and immoral. Proudhon was not only moral to the point of prudery, he saw truth not merely in a science of society or in the laws of attraction but in the absolute moral truths of justice, liberty, and equality. The attainment of these truths for man lay not in the political but in the economic realm. Proudhon's economic theory used the labor theory of value of the classical economists not to bolster but to destroy the profit system; Karl Marx was to do the same thing. Capitalism was unproductive, simply a gatherer of tolls on those commodities which passed through its hands. Instead there should be equality of remuneration; a day's labor must balance a day's labor. Thus he returned to the idea of labor exchanges which Robert Owen had also advocated. In early socialism capitalism was pitted against the true value of labor in terms of labor itself. The whole principle of association excluded the profit system and made itself the criterion of economic values. Marx's labor theory of value followed this tradition. Here also labor was viewed as a commodity like machinery or raw materials. The worker was alienated from the commodity he produced by capitalism. With these attempts to restore the dignity of labor in an industrial society, Proudhon was in agreement. He summed it up in his famous work *What Is Property?* (1840) when he answered that property is theft.

How can society be transformed? Not suddenly, but through the ethical development of man. Now Proudhon traveled in the direction of Saint-Simon. He, too, used the ideas of positivism, linking them to ethics. Ethical progress rested upon discovering the laws of society: "a science, absolute, rigorous, based on the nature of man and on his faculties, and on their mutual relations; a science we have not to invent but to discover." Once these laws had been discovered man would have the maximum of freedom and the oppressive state which denied justice would become unnecessary. Society would run itself. Proudhon's conclusions were quite different from Saint-Simon's; they stressed justice and liberty in a free society. Out of this came his famous paradox of anarchy: the free development of society. The ethical development of man, the result of discovering society's laws, would abolish government. The state

171

would not, as with Saint-Simon, dissolve into an industrial management—it would vanish absolutely. Basic to Proudhon was his ethical impetus.

Karl Marx was to criticize him for this in particular. His *Poverty of Philosophy* (1846) pointed out that Proudhon started his analysis from abstract principles like justice and equality, and not from reality. Proudhon made an invalid distinction between the economic and the political; every social change must involve political change as well. For Marx, the Frenchman never comprehended the dialectic of history and thus remained a petty bourgeois. Proudhon's ethical approach was tied to a deterministic science of society. This science could not be based on history because it was an unalterable, universal, and ascertainable truth. The final liberation of man hinged on such discoveries but more than that upon the freedom which such discoveries gave to man's ethical development. Proudhon was an optimist in matters of human nature— take away the oppression of government and private property and man would order his life on the absolute truths of justice, liberty, and equality. Marx had reason to write against Proudhon; his anarchism proved a great rival attraction. Only one anarchist community ever existed, and that was among the watchmakers in the Jura Mountains. Unlike the other French Socialists, Proudhon's idea was not closely tied to any existing utopia. Workers saw in it a direct path to freedom from all oppression. The struggles within the Workers' Internationals toward the end of the century pitted Marxism against an anarchism now led by Mikhail Bakunin (1814–76). Marxism triumphed, but not everywhere. In the unindustrialized countries of Europe, Russia, Spain, and Italy, where oppression was especially heavy, anarchism became an important movement.

It became, increasingly, a direct action movement. If the state could be destroyed, then the new society could begin and the laws of society would be discovered. Thus anarchists became assassins of despots par excellence. Not only despots, but parliamentarian statesmen, too, became their victims. All government was oppression. The weakness of anarchism became obvious through such deeds. Once an assassination had taken place there was no anarchist party to take over power, no program to be put into effect, except that of no government. From the Proudhonist point of view, the difficulty was that the science of society had first to be discovered; that discovery, however, could not take place unless the oppression which prevented it was first destroyed. No political organization could be formed because there must be complete freedom after the removal of oppression; the future prime minister, Proudhon held, need only be an expert in those statistics relating to the laws of society. Perhaps it was the optimism, the clear-cut solution to present problems, and the ethical impetus which gave anarchism its popularity. Freedom, justice, and equality could be obtained without the tribulations of party organization or a transition period of dictatorship. Communism was, for anarchists, just one more form of oppression.

Proudhon's denial of direct political action could be utilized by those who sought a nonviolent solution and who emphasized Proudhon's idea of association through economic groupings like mutual credit societies and cooperatives. In this guise, Proudhon attracted many French trade unionists who carried his ideas into the First International. Later they withdrew from it because it seemed to be directed toward political violence. Yet, the direct action wing of anarchism persisted. It was never a group which shared a coherent ideology other than a certain moral passion and a belief in the violent overthrow of society. Bakunin, who became the leading anarchist of the second half of the century, combined his passion for violent action with a romanticism which looked to an agrarian society and rejected industrial progress. Peter Kropotkin (1842–1921), at the end of his life, went to unbridled lengths of individualism. No individual should be bound by his fellow men; man was a law unto himself even if thousands were injured through his actions.

Terrorism became a part of nineteenth-century socialist activity, though it was quite alien to both the theoreticians of socialism and those socialist parliamentary parties which quickly arose at the end of the century. Louis August Blanqui (1805–81) was probably the first man to consider violent social revolution not merely as a necessary and transitory phenomenon, but as an art, a profession, and a social science. He devoted himself to the founding of secret, revolutionary conspiracies against every regime in power during his long life and repeatedly attempted to seize power. Indeed, when he was not involved in projected *coups d'état* and conspiracies, he was in prison for these same activities. To many he became a living symbol of the long fight for the realization of socialism.

Blanqui's outlook was formed by two French traditions: the materialism of the Enlightenment and the political activism and equalitarianism of the communist element in the Jacobin revolution. He was a militant atheist who believed that the crushing of religion was a prerequisite for any socialist society. Science would discover the truth, and here he was in agreement with other Socialists of his time. Indeed, scientific positivism had a marked influence upon socialism even before Marx called his socialism "scientific." Blanqui's materialism was tempered, however, and in part contradicted by his emphasis on the power of ideas. Institutions were dependent upon the intelligence and sophistication of the masses; therefore the masses, at present completely ignorant, would have to be educated before they could participate in any socialist society. This could not take place before the revolution had succeeded.

Alan Spitzer has pointed out that in every period of his life Blanqui expressed a commitment to fundamental economic and social change through the violent triumph of the proletariat in the class struggle. But since the proletariat would remain ignorant until the revolution succeeded, they could play no role in starting it. Only conspiratorial cadres drawn from the vanguard of all classes could initiate the revolution. Blanqui opposed the system of parliamentary majorities; the people so long oppressed had a slave mentality and were therefore easy tools in the hands of the reaction. Because the masses had played leading roles in revolutions, the bourgeoisie had, in every case, been able to recapture their power. Conspiracy was of the essence in preparing and in initiating the revolution.

Blanqui's entire thought centered upon revolution. It was useless to work within present society; the goal must always be an immediate *coup de force.* Thus, he was totally uninterested in committing his organizations to a struggle for the improvement of the proletariat's condition. Concern for wages and hours was of little account before the immediacy and necessity of revolution. Not without reason was Blanqui known as the "living symbol of revolutionary action." He was a realist, however; Spitzer believes that he formulated what was perhaps the first socialist *Realpolitik:* "he who has arms has bread." What a contrast with Saint-Simon who waited for an enlightened industrial manager to finance his socialist schemes. Blanqui planned every one of his coups in great detail, eagerly exploiting the weaknesses of the existing state; the correct timing of the revolution became almost an obsession with him.

Even after the revolution there would have to be a dictatorship by the revolutionary elite to prevent the bourgeoisie from recapturing power. Only then could intensive education liberate the people from their slavery and open their eyes to the benefits of economic association. His end goal was similar to that of other French Socialists—association. Blanqui, however, differed from his fellow Socialists primarily in his stress upon revolution as the essential instrument of socialism, a difference which made him an eternal *Putschist.* He was never successful, even when he attempted such a *Putsch* in 1848 during that revolution; the other Radicals joined with the Conservatives to defeat him. The Paris Commune, which will soon be examined, seemed an ideal coup from his point of view, but he himself was not present though he had helped to prepare the event.

Nevertheless, his influence was greater than the number of those who joined his conspiratorial organizations might indicate (at their peak some two thousand men). Marx, though admiring Blanqui's devotion to revolution, fought him and his disciples in the First International's power struggle for the leadership of the socialist revolution. Apart from the loosely organized followers of Proudhon, Blanqui and his disciples provided the chief challenge to Marx's efforts at dominating the socialist movement.

Blanqui had been a French patriot and he believed that France carried within itself the seeds of world revolution. It was indeed in France that socialism got its chance for power in the nineteenth century, first during the revolution of 1848 and subsequently with the Paris Commune (1871).

The revolution of 1848 is a landmark in the history of socialism as it is in the evolution of nationalism, for in France the revolution against liberalism first veered in a socialist direction before it fell into the waiting arms of Louis Napoleon. The Socialist Louis Blanc (1811–82) influenced this phase of the revolution. His ideas differed in one important aspect from those of most other Socialists, though they partook of Blanqui's realism. The state was central in Blanc's thought; not industrial managers but state planning would lead to social reorganization. Political power could not be ignored; it must be on the side of socialism. In this, Blanc's thought resembled that of the Chartists, who also believed that a democratic state would use its legislative and executive power to solve social questions. Despite this, Blanc feared an all-powerful state. He, too, turned to that idea of association in groups, previously seen in the thought of other Socialists. These associations would be industrially organized, autonomous, and self-supporting. Again, this was similar to those corporative theories which were becoming popular. But in Blanc's view everyone would have an equal voice, and there would be no distinction between manager and laborer. The Social Workshops, as he called them, were perhaps closer to the English cooperative idea than to corporation itself. The state was to be above these Social Workshops though its power over them was to be limited. The state would establish them, providing the necessary funds. Though it could regulate the workshops for the good of all, such regulation must be minimal. In these Social Workshops Blanc saw a positive freedom. Everyone would be guaranteed work, and in the general participation in the economic and political affairs of society, the human personality would freely unfold.

The provisional government in 1848, of which Blanc was a member, did establish workshops, but they did so primarily to make work for the growing unemployed and not in order to initiate a socialist society. The result was a travesty on Blanc's ideas. The right to work was translated into hundreds of men aimlessly digging up the great square of the Champs de Mars in Paris. Moreover, the government quite consciously withheld funds so that the workshops would never be established on a viable financial basis. In spite of this, a few of the workshops did prosper until the whole project was scrapped as the revolution moved to the right. For one of Blanc's most important contentions, that a democratic state would be a socialist one, proved wrong. True, the Chamber was elected by universal manhood suffrage. But these elections brought, in agrarian France, a preponderance of rural representatives to the Chamber, representatives who believed that "in Paris they make nothing but revolutions" and who were dedicated to the suppression of radical experimentation.

In spite of failure, however, a socialist experiment had been tried by a national government for the first time in modern history. The second experiment, under quite different conditions, also took place in Paris. The episode of the Paris Commune made a more lasting impression than that warranted by its short duration. France had been defeated in 1870 by Prussia, and the regime of Napoleon had fallen. Adolphe Thiers (1797–1877) was conducting peace negotiations with the Prussians, but Paris would not countenance a Prussian peace. In the face of continuing pressure by Thiers, a bloodless revolution took over the city's government (Commune) and proclaimed itself sovereign (1871). What shocked Europe was not the nationalist resistance of the French capital but that this resistance was accompanied by what seemed to be a social revolution. This time members of the working class were members of the government itself, a still more frightening phenomenon. The manifestoes they issued proclaimed the treason of the ruling classes, and the rule of the proletariat. The proclamations of the Commune were indeed full of a revolutionary terminology which prior to this had never been uttered by a governing power.

Very little was actually accomplished. A few factories were taken over by the workers, but the Bank of France was left undisturbed. The reason for this was not only the state of siege under which Paris suffered but the fact that the Commune's leadership was divided and contested. The workers who sat on the council seemed to epitomize the history of the socialist movement for they, too, were disunited on fundamentals. Though the influence of Blanqui's disciples predominated, others were followers of Proudhon, others Marxists, and still others represented ill-defined aspirations such as those who called themselves "Garibaldian." They were opposed by bourgeois politicians like Clemenceau who attempted to calm their revolutionary ardor. The Socialists were no more in full control of the Commune than Blanc had been in 1848. Moreover, just as the rest of France had been determined to crush the Paris revolution in 1848, so now the elected Assembly meeting safely in Versailles moved to crush the Commune. This it did after much street fighting and bloodshed, and another socialist attempt at power had failed.

Karl Marx studied these events carefully and identified himself with the Commune. After it had failed he made a series of speeches on the subject (collected by Engels in *The Civil War in France*) branding Thiers and the Assembly as the "ghouls" of the past while the Commune represented the

176

future. Marx's analysis of the Commune's failure was to be important for the future of Marxism, one of the indirect results of this event. A manifesto had proclaimed that the proletarians of Paris had seized the governmental power. Marx believed that this was the crucial mistake: ". . . the working class cannot simply lay hold of the ready-made state machinery, and wield it for its own purposes." Marx reaffirmed the *Communist Manifesto* which in 1848 hopefully called upon the working classes to smash the existing state and not to use it. Lenin was to reemphasize the identical point. Thus the lessons of the Paris Commune pushed Marx and Lenin still farther apart from the Social Democrats. In the end they resulted in Lenin's break with German Communists like Rosa Luxemburg. The Commune played an important part in the internecine strife of Marxism, and reinforced its divisions.

But the Commune was studied not only by Marx. The fear of radicalism among the bourgeoisie, so obvious after 1848, was also reinforced. The general movement toward a new romanticism, toward nationalism as well as racism, was accelerated after 1870 as it had been after 1848. Socialism was not only a matter of theory; attempts had been made to put it into practice, however partial or unsuccessful. It had come to Europe to stay. This socialism was not Marxist. Neither the theoreticians nor Blanc nor a majority of the Paris Commune were Marxists. By 1870, however, the dominance of Marx in the socialist movement was rapidly becoming an established fact.

Early socialism erected its own visions of equality not directly related to Marx and indeed in competition with him. To be sure, he knew their work and at times borrowed from it. Yet, he was more influenced by Hegel than by these socialists. The maladjustments incumbent upon the industrialization of Europe had produced socialist solutions before Marx ever wrote; they were in the air. The word socialist was vague; as we have seen, it covered a multitude of theories. Socialists had in common an opposition to capitalist society, to the exploitation of labor in favor of private property. Socialists substituted ideas of a greater equality of property based on the principle of association. Aside from this basic agreement, they varied considerably. Some believed Christianity to be the chief ideological impetus; others saw it in the growing positivism of a science of society. Karl Marx brought order into this socialism though he fought constantly against these rival faiths. But it was he who was triumphant, so much so that today the word socialism is exclusively associated with a Marxist approach to society.

# CHAPTER ELEVEN

# *Marxism*

## I

IT WAS the strength of Karl Marx (1818–83) that, just as Zeus collected thunderbolts and then hurled them in different directions, he took the chief nineteenth-century ideologies and hurled them in quite a different direction than their originators had intended. German idealism, evolution, individualism, the urge toward collective society and social change were all combined in his works. Marx's education reflected this broad approach. He knew his classics. In fact, his doctoral thesis on the difference between Democritus' and Epicurus' philosophies of nature probed Greek thought. Friedrich Engels (1820–95) was to say later that he and Marx had returned to the font of Greek philosophy. In this instance Marx participated in the continuing impetus of the classics during the century, when they were still part of the equipment of every educated man. It was in his doctoral thesis that Marx raised the problem of free will and determinism which was at the heart of Marxist thought.

Marx contrasted Democritus and Epicurus. For Democritus, atoms move by force of circumstances alone which drives them to their logical goal, but Epicurus allows for free will on the part of the atom until it itself chooses the path to the heavenly bodies where all contradictions are resolved. This element of free will remained constant in Marxist thought; he himself never wanted to do away with the individualism in which he, as a child of the nineteenth century, believed. But, surely, Marxism is deterministic and the word "determinism" is found on almost every page of his writings. It was when Marx came to work out the factors shaping the individual that he redefined individualism from its liberal base and sent it, as it were, in the opposite direction. But for Marx it was always the individual who stood at the center, and he himself called his theory "Socialist Humanism." Yet Marx's individual was no free agent in the sense of Epicurean atoms. Freedom was drastically modified by the influence of the environment. But what were those influences? Marx criticized both Feuerbach and Hegel, for the former made the individual merely a part of nature and the latter saw in him a servant of the state. Moreover, and here is the crux of the matter, both these philosophers made man an "abstraction." For Marx it was wrong to talk about a human as a "genus" or about the "human essence," for each person was a concrete individual entity and had to be treated as such. " ' The human essence' is no inherent abstraction in each individual. In reality it is the ensemble of social relations." Man's individualism is not limited by nature or by the state, but by a combination of all the social forces which act upon him. That is what Marx and Engels called "realism." The individual operated in concrete situations, and these situations drastically limited free will.

But what produced these situations? To say, as some mistakenly do, that the human situation is produced solely by economic necessities, is to grossly oversimplify Marxism. Friedrich Engels talked about the "endless maze of relations and interactions" which made up nature as well as the history of humanity: The essence of these was change. Marx made the same point when he inveighed against the materialism of natural science as "abstract" because it omitted history. For if all is change then any analysis of the human situation must be historical, that is, an attempt to make sense out of this maze by arriving at a theory about the workings of this change in the past and projecting the nature of the change from past history to the future. That is exactly what Marx attempted to do. Social relationships were a part of this change. At first, Marx wrote, the forces of nature confronted man as alien and inexplicable but soon social forces began to be active. When this happened the forces which confronted and limited man were no longer hostile and inexplicable, but instead they acquired social attributes. At this point Marxism became a philosophy of history and the individual was seen through social relationships as determined by the workings of history.

Marx called these workings of history "dialectical materialism" or "historical materialism," terms he used quite interchangeably. The dialectic was that method of reasoning fashionable among the Hegelians. History moved from thesis to antithesis until the final synthesis of the classless society. What determined the thesis-antithesis relationship was the class structure of society. Thus feudal monopoly, the dominance of the feudal classes, was a thesis in history opposed by the antithesis of free competition advocated by the commercial classes. A struggle ensued which was won by the commercial classes who now formed a new thesis in their turn. The engine of history was the internal contradictions which existed in any ruling class and the pressure of an "inevitable" new and hostile class from below. The internal contradiction of the ruling class of the bourgeoisie was that, on the one hand, it presupposed competition, and on the other that, through the formations of monopolies and cartels, it excluded competition. The new class was the proletariat upon whom the bourgeoisie was dependent but who would also be its "grave diggers." History was, therefore, a struggle between classes. Friedrich Engels concisely summarized this in 1892: "And thus I hope even British respectability will not be overshocked if I use, in English as well as in so many other languages, the term historical materialism to describe that view of the course of history which seeks the ultimate cause and the great moving power of all important historic events in the economic development of society, in the changes in the modes of production and exchange, in the consequent division of society into distinct classes, and in the struggle of these classes against one another."

This struggle was fought over the control of the means of production—the factor which Marx thought lay at the root of the dialectic. The means of production were, for example, the plow in older agrarian societies and facories and machinery in Marx's own era. The class that controlled these means had an iron grip upon the whole of the economy, ruling the rest of the population who were dependent upon them for their very existence and livelihood. Only when the people come to control the means of production would the class struggle for their control cease, and with it the workings of the dialectic in history. The proletariat were the people and thus, with their triumph over capitalism, class and class warfare would disappear. Marx, perhaps wisely, looked back rather than forward and was interested in the historical dialectic rather than in spelling out the classless society itself.

So much for a brief sketch of the dialectic. What about the materialism? For cultural history this has a special importance because it determined Marxist attitudes toward modes of cultural expression. Was it an economic determinism inasmuch as classes in history struggle over the means of production? Not only this but changing means of production determine the emergence of new classes and the fall of the old. Marx did believe that such changes as that from plow to tractor were the bedrock reality of history. But he also held that to make this the sole factor in the dialectic was to transform it into the kind of "abstraction" which Feuerbach had used when he talked about "nature." Granted that the means of production were at the base of change, the superstructure of ideas and events which grew out of this base could also have a determining influence on the course of history and therefore upon the individual. It was this interaction of means of production, ideologies, politics, and religious beliefs which Marx called the decisive element in history: the production and reproduction of real life. Here also individualism entered, for people could make history within the framework of the dialectic and the interactions of reality. Perhaps this is best summed up by saying that the superstructure of history was the interaction of the individual and the totality of his environment—an interaction where the means of production were only decisive in the last instance. As Marx summarized this: "... the history of ideologies is to a large extent explained by the rise, modification and breakdown of associations of ideas under the influence of the rise, modifications and breakdown of definite combinations of social forces."

What are the consequences of this for Marx's view of art and literature? This must be dwelt upon at some length, for Marxism like romanticism was a total view of life. Attitudes toward artistic and literary creativity clearly illuminate the complexities of this ideology, for both Marx and Engels were vitally concerned with this aspect of human endeavor. Their attitude can be briefly described as a desire for realism. Such realism was, in turn, defined as the interaction of the individual, his ideology, and the social forces surrounding him. But there must be another important ingredient in addition to these. Realism must be set into the context of history, for all is change. But this working of history was "determinist," that is, history really worked this way and no other. Therefore categories like "tragedy" and "comedy" must be modified, for events do not turn on the free will of the individual alone but on his position in historically-determined change. Engels criticized one novel as not realistic enough, though it had the promising title *City Girl*: "... realism to my mind implies, besides truth of detail, the truthful reproduction of typical characters under typical circumstances"—and we have seen what such typical circumstances must be. Just so, Marx criticized the German Friedrich Schiller for his plays in which tragedy was linked to the individuality of the hero and therefore led to "the exaggerated reflection of the individual about himself." Marx rejected the whole classical idea of tragedy just as Hegel had rejected it, and for the same reasons. Man stands within the inexorable dialectical process of history which is reasonable. To revolt against it is not tragic but puerile.

In the debate with Ferdinand Lassalle (1825–64) about the latter's drama *Sickingen*, Marx returned to these ideas. Sickingen was a revolutionary who failed, but this must not be seen as a tragedy—no more than the failures of the Jacobins or of Thomas Muentzer were tragic. These were premature revolutionaries whose failure could not be linked to their individuality as such. It was instead to be linked to a concrete historical situation which was not yet ripe. Omission of this factor distorted the picture, since the human situation for Marx was never isolated but a part of the "maze of interactions" that have been described. It may have been necessary to conduct the struggle even though it failed. Such failures, however, should lead to self-criticism helpful to future revolutions rather than reflections on the tragedy springing from within human nature. Whether a revolutionary leader goes down in the name of a drowning class or of a class of the future is not immaterial. Sickengen was, after all, a feudal knight. History had already doomed his class.

The romantic hero was rejected in the name of historical materialism. Romanticism was, for Marx and Engels, an escape into a dream world. Romantic themes were reinterpreted; thus Engels tried to isolate the essence of the Siegfried legend. For his romantic contemporary Richard Wagner, Siegfried symbolized the hero who would redeem the *Volk,* leading it back to its genuine roots. Engels, however, rejected the importance of the actual legend; to him, Siegfried represented German youth, a youth consumed by an urge for action and the will to free themselves from the fetters of society. Moreover, he represented a youth which sought escape from the prison of contemporary education. Indeed, such a youth did exist, and it will be discussed later. Its revolt, however, was not Marxist but romantic and Nietzschean.

Engels's attitude toward that medieval literature so popular among Romantics was similar to his interpretation of the Siegfried legend. He recognized the importance of such literature if it opposed the aristocracy, demanded freedom, and rejected the aesthetic ideal of pietistic religion. The Romantics, he said with contempt, treasured only the poetic content of such works. This was only partly true; the Romantics, too, found a political and social ideal imbedded in the art and literature of the Middle Ages. Into this Franz Mehring (1846–1919), later to be a leading Marxist literary critic, had a clearer insight. For him, the knowledge of medieval literature led to an understanding of the transformation of yesterday's "devilish injustice" into today's equally oppressive "Divine law." He saw something positive in romanticism, in the joy of contemplating the fatherland's past, and, above all, in the pleasures derived from medieval folk song and poetry. But this was to vanish from his later, negative attitude toward the Romantics.

Marx rejected the romantic cult of the individual, and, like Engels, he condemned the primacy of poetic form among the Romantics. He linked this with the idealism of romanticism which was far removed, he thought, from the realism he desired. "Categories of thought are not aids which man has constructed for himself but expressions of the laws of nature and man."

These laws were a part of history's dialectic. Yet he did not reject all romantic authors; for example, Marx liked Sir Walter Scott. He accepted Scott for aesthetic reasons and because of that romantic realism previously mentioned. The Marxist critic Georg Lukács (1885–1971) later praised both Scott and Manzoni as "democratic" artists because their heroes originated in the people and were molded by them.

Romanticism, however, as a literary and ideological expression was rejected as diametrically opposed to Marxism, for ideas, instead of reality, dominated its interpretation of man. Yet, so all-pervasive was the romantic impetus of modern times, that for some, the "humanism" of which Marx spoke was infused with a romantic attitude toward the masses. Lenin was forced to denounce this as the "cult of the proletariat" but, as will be seen, Marxism never did rid itself of this attitude. For all this, Marxism emerged as the chief opposition to the romantic or "inner-directed" concept of the individual and the world. That is why it has been important to analyze what Marx and Engels thought of the Romantics and why they rejected this poetry of life.

But once again one must not fall into the trap of interpreting Marx's approach to literature and aesthetics as a mechanistic one. Man as an individual was never excluded from Marx's thought. One factor in the interaction of the individual and environment was what Marx called the "permanent motives of human action." Man does have an inner life of his own. But unlike Sigmund Freud, for whom this inner life came to be an explanation for the outward world, for Marx the outward world acted constantly upon the human mind. Self-knowledge and the knowledge of the world cannot be separated; they must go hand in hand. Honoré de Balzac was his favorite author because he saw in him the delineation of characters with a life of their own combined with an awareness of the importance of social life. Balzac, for Marx, "saw the necessity of the downfall of his favourite nobles, and described them as people deserving no better fate, and that he saw the real men of the future where, for the time being, they alone were to be found . . . ," namely among the republican heroes. Balzac combined the highest level of social analysis with character portrayal. Marx's admiration for him was unbounded. Shakespeare was his favorite dramatist for the same reasons. Unlike Schiller, here the tragedy never centered on the individual hero, but was concretized within the contradictions of the dominant society depicted in the play. Thus Marx believed that Shakespeare was criticizing the vanishing feudal order and the triumphing capitalist society as well. Indeed he produced "typical characters under typical circumstances." With Shakespeare and Balzac as his models, Marx would have been appalled by the naive realism of most modern Marxist art.

184

Basic to Marx's view of literary and artistic production was his concept of the intellectual's role in society. Here he was concerned with the idea of the division of labor which he and the classical economists thought essential to the working of a class society. Marx separated intellectual workers from the rest of the working classes, since those engaged in the daily struggle for existence have little time for intellectual endeavors. The intellectual, the artist, is therefore removed from the working classes and forms a category of his own. Yet as far as their function and therefore their status in the class hierarchy were concerned, they served the dominant class and furthered its aims. Again this was not just a simple equation between intellectuals and the ruling class, for he believed that tensions existed between the two. But at the crucial moment the identity of social interests between them would be victorious. Marx was imbued with a suspicion of his fellow intellectuals. His analysis of many writers aimed at exposing their supposedly antibourgeois leanings as a mere façade for their basic subservience to that class. Even though the Saxon "young Socialists" wrote poetry against the injustice of the Prussian police system, this was solely for Marx the complaint of the petty bourgeoisie. The Saxon Socialists had forgotten that such police brutality would not be possible in England, a country far removed from socialism. They had therefore not touched upon the real workings of capitalism which is the same everywhere within the changing context of history.

In his attitude toward the artist, Marx's suspicions of exaggerated individuality cropped up once more. The exclusive concentration of artistic talents in one person, thanks to the division of labor, meant the further suppression of the masses, for they had no chance to partake in such endeavors. Moreover, no artist really had a monopoly on genius; therefore, if such is thought to exist it must be built upon the exploitation of others. He cited Raphael's paintings as evidence of this, for they were finished by other and anonymous artists. The same he thought was true for Mozart's *Requiem*. Again this is far removed from the romantic genius. Men, said Marx, are not artists in order to be men, but they are men and incidentally artists, musicians, and painters. Artistic or intellectual genius did not make a man an exception in a world where *"la condition humaine"* circumscribed the freedom of his actions.

It was in the classless society that the "human condition" would radically change. Up to that point literary content and form were largely determined by the necessity to clarify the progress of man in the context of historical materialism. But with the victory of the proletariat a true "socialist humanism" would come into being by the resolution of the tensions growing out of man's interaction with his environment. Above all, the human desire for freedom, frustrated in a world governed by historical necessities, would be realized by abolishing private property and its concomitant class struggle. Property estranged man from himself by placing his sense of possession above his other senses. Again, this was not a crude economic determinism, but instead the realization that the individual's perceptions were governed by the struggle for wealth or by a wish to maintain personal wealth against all challengers. The classless society would free man's perception of these blinders and thus release his creative energy.

Here Marx attacked the liberal ideal that it was the free competition of ideas which produced important literary and artistic results. John Stuart Mill strongly adhered to this concept; his *On Liberty* became a classic even in Marx's own lifetime. Enthusiasm for the beneficent effects of competition was, for Marx, a part of the dominant ideology of capitalist society which was as misleading in appearances as the poems of the young Saxon Socialists had been. To free true individuality the basic mechanism of the historical dialectic must come to a standstill. As Georg Lukács put it: ". . . the social revolution can only get its poetry from the future. Then man will be liberated and the limiting factor of the environment, which produces tensions interacting with man, will vanish."

Marx felt that until the coming of the classless society, all must be judged relative to the workings of historical materialism. Change, in these terms, would become the governing factor in cultural judgment. Thus Marx did not condemn religion at all times as the "opium of the people." In the Middle Ages the belief in religion was strong, a consensus, and therefore it made sense within the medieval framework. But in modern times it had become simply a device of the exploiting classes who themselves were cynical about their faith. Religion now, Marx maintained, was a part of the bourgeois ideology which is designed to exploit the masses; but this was not always so. Yet in this relativism a cultural problem of some importance arose. If ideas thought to be eternal can become the device of the ruling class, are there no cultural constants apart from the mechanism of historical change? If eternal justice led to bourgeois law, the social contract to the bourgeois democratic republic, what about those cultural manifestations whose appeal has been a constant through history regardless of class change? Marx once again turned to the Greeks, for their literature did have a continuing appeal. He asks why this should be so: ". . . where does Vulcan come in as against the Roberts & Co.; Jupiter as against the lightning rod; Hermes against the Credit Mobilier?" The Greeks were out of date—and yet they still lived. Greek culture was based on Greek mythology—here was the clue. The continuing love of Greek culture was the charm exercised by the childhood of our civilization. "Why should the social childhood of mankind where it had obtained its most beautiful development, not exert an eternal charm as the age which will never return?"

Here relativism was tempered, just as we saw it limited by aesthetic standards which cut through the dialectic. Marx inveighed against what he called the *Grobiansliteratur* of his age—that realism which ignored aesthetic values for rudeness and bad language. Marxist realism had to be distinguished from that naturalist realism in art and literature which will be discussed in the next chapter. Naturalism, inspired by the sciences and epitomized in Zola's desire to apply the methods of the laboratory to literature, laid stress upon the environment which seemed to exclude the workings of the dialectic. Marx thought this naturalism, like contemporary science, purely descriptive and mechanical. The artistic and literary creativity of Marxist realism should center on an exact reflection of that totality of social relationships which had determined the past and would determine the future. The problems involved in such a realism were to haunt Marxist intellectuals. Could this standard be fulfilled in practice?

Marx thought that some artists had come close to it. Shakespeare and Balzac were his models because they combined awareness of the dynamics of history in relation to man with high aesthetic standards. His favorite poem was Goethe's *Faust* which, again, had no ties with Marxist theories. Marx himself, therefore, did not share the rigidly dogmatic crudeness of many of his successors.

This flexibility on the part of Marx and Engels, however, must not disguise the fact that both believed that their theories were founded not on speculation but on fact. Marx had criticized the mechanical nature of contemporary science because it left out the dimension of history. But once he had built dialectical materialism into history, this was to him scientific. There was nothing relative here. Both Marx and Engels felt they had insured the scientific nature of their theories in two ways. The first was the collection of the widest possible range of data. Economics, philosophy, culture—all was grist for the mill of historical analysis. Marx believed that historical materialism fitted the data. In this he proceeded just as any modern historian would proceed in building upon the data available. It must also be remembered that Marx was a contemporary of Ranke and of Henry Thomas Buckle (861–62). With Ranke he believed that it was possible to tell the story as it had actually happened; with Buckle he held that it was the historian's business to explain the workings of the totality of history. With the political economists of his time he also held that economics was not a factor which stood apart from human history, but indeed it could only be explained through it. There is nothing extraordinary in Marx's method or approach; it was his results which were revolutionary. Ranke, too, believed that historical analysis must be "scientific."

The second scientific method was, once more, a general phenomenon of his time. Engels specialized in anthropology. In his *Origin of the Family*

(1884) he tried to prove two important points by turning to the research of the anthropologists: First, that no political institution like the state was eternal because primitive society did without them; second, that the contradictions which emerge in the course of the dialectic can already be found among primitive peoples and especially in the primitive family organization. "The modern family contains in germ (that is, origin) not only slavery but also serfdom, since from the beginning it is related to agricultural services. It contains in miniature all the contradictions which later extend throughout society and the state." This use of anthropology also served to explain religion as originating in myth; it could serve to clarify the material origins of supernatural beliefs. Engels was not the only one who made such use of anthropology; Sigmund Freud provides another example. By the last quarter of the century the science of anthropology had become an alternative explanation for supernatural belief. Sir James Frazer in his *Golden Bough* was to explain the origin of religion in Italy through the myths of primitive Italians. Darwinism was not the only scientific onslaught on religion and the supernatural in Marx's time. Both methods of proof which Marx and Engels used were not unusual in their time, and most all-encompassing theories about society felt the urge to take on a scientific character. After all, a theory as irrational as racism tried to do the same. It is not astonishing therefore that Marx's view of history was not merely based upon dialectic materialism but that it also claimed to be scientific. It was this claim, however, which was to lead to a dogmatism much stricter and, in the end, much cruder than that of Marx himself. Where Karl Marx had struggled to reach his conclusions after much doubt and contemplation, his successors found them ready-made. With many of them, his subtle ideas became slogans and the impulse of an eventual "socialist humanism" was diverted into the maintenance of Marxist orthodoxy.

Marx himself, as he became absorbed in the unremitting struggle to establish his doctrines among workers, became increasingly dogmatic. Competing theories of socialism had to be discredited and their influence nullified. This struggle took place within the first workingmen's international organization founded in 1862. The International was a loose federation of independent workingmen's organizations from diverse countries. Its members adhered to many of the socialisms discussed in the previous chapter and to others besides—a veritable "tower of Babel." This awkward and unwieldy tower Marx wanted to dismantle. He only succeeded in dismantling the whole organization.

Though fighting Blanqui's influence, the principal target of Marx's ire was the diverse followers of Proudhon, the strong anarchist federations. The struggle within the International became polarized in the enmity between Marx and Mikhail Bakunin. This Russian eccentric who had passed through

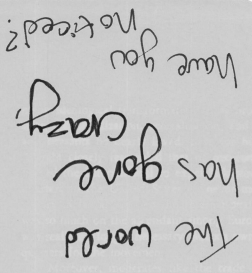

laimed his hatred of the modern
udaism. Intellectuals he detested
rejection of the state, Bakunin's
inticism. Marx subsequently per-
(1872) and to remove its head-
again. In spite of his apparent
By that time, however, Marxism
ean workers that an International
house in London served as head-

ion leaders had left the Inter-
national before this. It was too radical in its denial of the possibility of
collaboration with the bourgeois state. The International's support, under
Marx's leadership, of the Paris Commune seemed especially shocking.
Moderates were willing to concede that perhaps the International was synonymous with the "red terror." Though the First International had failed, a
Second International was formed in 1889, composed this time entirely of
Marxist socialist parties. Stronger than the First International, it had, however,
hardly any centralized authority, and it went to its unlamented death at the
outbreak of the First World War. Rather than serving as effective organizations for socialist action, the Internationals served merely to frighten the
bourgeoisie. Only the Third International, founded in 1919, was effective—
precisely because it was not an autonomous international federation but
became an instrument of the Soviet Union by the middle of the 1920s.

Marx fought for the worker's allegiance not only against competing
socialist systems but also against the diverse interpretations of his own doctrine which arose within Marxism itself. In his formative years Marx's ideas
had a subtlety which did not necessarily lead to a materialist dogmatism. He
had stressed, after all, not only the scientific nature of his thought but also
what he called a "new humanism." The latter idea evoked an impetus toward
Marxism which tended to underplay the dialectical and materialistic elements
of his thought.

Until the 1930s, part of the attraction exercised by Marx's thought was
humanitarian and ethical. It is important to understand this, for it accounted
for much of the position Marx attained among certain intellectuals. This was
true before the First World War when for some socialist leaders Marxism
provided an ideal of compassion for the downtrodden masses, a compassion
which coincided with the moral teachings of a nontheological religion.
Jean Jaurès, the French socialist leader, combined his Marxism with pantheism. In his writings, God was often mentioned—not the God of the
churches, but a God who was justice—and it was justice which Marxism

sought to achieve. Léon Blum, who was Jaurès's secretary, was later to write that for Jaurès socialism was "the sum of the heritage of all that was virtuous and beautiful in man since the beginning of civilization." Similarly, Beatrice and Sidney Webb in England combined their Marxist analysis of society with a strong moral imperative, and here Christian morality seemed to coincide with a reform of society based on Marxist social analysis. The First World War strengthened this appeal, as Marxism came to be a part of the humanitarian revulsion against the horrors of war and the cruelty of the emerging fascist societies.

Ignazio Silone's famous novel *Bread and Wine* (1937) provides a good example of this. Here the priest Don Benedetto resolved the contradiction between Christianity and Marxism. Both have the same object, namely to transform the present hate-ridden and deformed society so that "truth and brotherhood will reign among men in the place of hatred and deceit; living labour will reign in the place of money." The French novelist André Gide (1869–1951) gave an additional example of this idealism. It has been rightly said that he reached communism not through Marx but through the Gospels. Gide stated, and Silone implied, that if the Church had fulfilled the teachings of Christ there would be no need for communism—indeed the social problem would not exist at all. Neither of these men was a professional Communist, but this kind of approach to Marxism can also be illustrated through a communist leader of the twentieth century. Antonio Gramsci (1891–1937) was one of the founders of Italian socialism, and he played a leading role in its activities until Mussolini imprisoned him. For him Marxism was a moral passion, an ethical impulse, which would be fully revealed by the communist future. His thought fastened onto the "leap into freedom" which Marx had prophesied with the abolition of the class struggle. This freedom he viewed as a new humanist culture whose values would inspire the leaders of the proletariat. By humanism he meant the same thing as Marx: the full unfolding of the human personality. But he believed that the communist leadership (totalitarian as he conceived it to be) must stress the power of man and individual initiative in preparation for the new society. Gramsci thus emphasized the factor of man's power in his interaction with the environment, something which Marxism tended to neglect for a deterministic view of historical materialism.

Basically, this kind of Marxism tended to make a distinction between socialist theory and socialist values. The ethical impetus found in these men became more important to them than the historical theory upon which the new society was to be based. For them Marxism was a movement of liberation and freedom, and it is small wonder that when Silone and Gide came into contact with Soviet reality they left the party. There were many more men like themselves and the fact that this original impetus went sour in the actual "new society" of Russia explains the defections from communism on the part of the intellectuals, a problem to which we will return.

II

*Marxism is coupled and contradictory.*

The tension between determinism and flexibility, dogmatism and humanism, was inherent in Marx's subtle relationship between human power and interaction with dialectical materialism. Apart from socialist humanists this problem came to the fore in the development of social democracy. By the 1890s it had become the conviction of Engels that power resided in parliamentary action. He had always held strong convictions about the inevitability of progress and the unilinear development of history toward its inevitable socialist end. Engels became increasingly materialistic at the expense of the "human condition" which had been central in Marx. Historical evolution was for him a part of natural evolution: dialectical materialism embraced both nature and history. Engels was the real founder of social democracy and his ideas were compatible with capitalism which was showing no signs of collapse. Once engaged in the "game of politics" socialist tactics had to be geared toward attaining tangible benefits for the workers. The question was how Marxism should proceed in the face of the dialectical certainty of history, involvement with parliamentary politics, and the continued expansion of capitalism. A theoretician like Eduard Bernstein was driven by such considerations toward an outright Fabian position.

Before an analysis of the social democratic answer to this question is attempted, it is important to understand how Lenin, writing later than Marx, tried to answer it, for his answer, so different from Bernstein's, throws important light upon social democratic attitudes. Lenin also realized that capitalist society was not, on the face of it, declining but instead was "growing far more rapidly than before." But this growth did not mean that a Marxist must become more flexible in dealing with bourgeois society. For the growth of capitalism was in reality capitalism in transition—in the process of dissolution through its internal contradictions. Lenin saw this exemplified through the age of imperialism. Imperialism was "dying capitalism" for here the bourgoisie had become totaly parasitic—living off the colonial nations abroad just as at home the bourgeoisie had become increasingly a *rentier* class. Monopolist possession of colonies was a part and, in fact, an extension of monopolist capitalism at home. Imperialism meant the increasing exploitation of the many by the few who, through this development of capitalism, were becoming even fewer. Marx was not wrong in his forecasts; the stage of imperialism was necessary in order to develop and bring to a climax the contradictions within bourgeois society. Within the dialectic, the dominant order had to develop to its fullest extent before it could be destroyed by the forces which it had set in motion: "... new higher relations of production never appear before the material conditions of their existence have matured in the womb of the old society." In viewing contemporary capitalist development, Bernstein and the Social Democrats had abandoned Marxist analysis. Yet Lenin himself was a "revisionist." The young Marx of the *Communist Manifesto* blended with a Russian populist emphasis upon agrarian upheaval: the conscious proletariat became the professional revolutionary elite. Those "Marxists" after 1918 who paid allegiance to communism of Bolshevik inspiration were themselves not in the pure stream of doctrine.

Lenin drew a further consequence from Marx's analysis of the decline of capitalism. Marxists must not compromise with but strike out against the state which was the repressive force used by the bourgeoisie against the exploited. Dictatorship of the proletariat was still a revolutionary necessity. But unilke the Marx of the *Communist Manifesto* for whom the dictatorship was a short-range necessity, for Lenin it became a long-range totalitarianism. With this the Social Democratics disagreed, just as they rejected Lenin's thesis about imperialism as the last stage of capitalist development. Most social democratic parties could never formulate a consistent policy toward the empires of their respective nations.

Their answer was to proceed by evolution rather than revolution— through flexible tactics rather than by a sharp confrontation of Marxism and bourgeois society. This in turn meant working within the framework of the existing state, through parliamentary action, and not outside it. Anything else was, for Bernstein, utopian. The workers wanted concrete gains within society and to deny them was in practice to isolate the Marxist movement from the working classes. Social democracy became a political party, and the great attraction of this kind of modified Marxism is witnessed by its growth into the largest political party in Germany and France at the turn of the century. But was such a modification merely a matter of procedure? It obviously cut at the root of the concept of the class struggle. Not that Social Democrats meant to abolish this concept; on the contrary, they believed themselves to be the leaders of the proletariat. Yet, in practice, these parties tended toward what Marx called *embourgeoisement*. Collaboration for Marx meant contamination and the questioning of the basic workings of the dialectic.

His growing bitterness against Ferdinand Lassalle, the founder of the German socialist workers' movement (1863), was typical. Lassalle was a complex personality. Like so many of the early working-class leaders, he came from a middle-class environment full of German romanticism and nationalism. He died fighting a duel for an insult which had been offered him.

More important, the whole conflict with Marx over his drama *Sickingen,* of which mention has already been made, showed his leaning toward the romantic hero and toward romantic tragedy. Lassalle was no Marxist, but the heir of the democratic tradition of 1848; he wanted to couple universal suffrage and working men's associations with the kind of national feeling which the revolutions of 1848 had tried to encourage. When Marx once told him that "I care the devil for the judgment of your German public," he was rebuked, "Do not forget that you are a German revolutionary and that you must act and think for Germany." Odd sentiments to address to the author of the *Communist Manifesto.* Yet the judgment of the German public was bound to be important for the future of Marxism operating as a political party, and that public possessed national consciousness.

The Social Democratic party resulted from the fusion of Lassallians and Marxists, yet the party was closer to Lassalle than to Marx. This meant Marxist rhetoric but a policy which stressed parliamentary democracy and concern for the German nation. August Bebel (1840–1913), the most important leader of the Social Democrats before the First World War, was typical in his belief in the defense of the fatherland, the virtue of bread-and-butter trade union organization, and the suspicion of intellectuals with their theories.

Not only in Germany, but in the rest of Europe as well, social democracy moved ever closer to a national democracy. At the outbreak of the First World War Socialists voted for war credits and supported the war effort. The war itself did not arrest this development. Afterwards, many Social Democrats held that Marxism and the class struggle were no longer adequate for the needs of twentieth-century socialism. Hendrik de Man (1885–1953), the leader of the Belgian Workers party, became the leading spokesman for this point of view. Though class war no longer compelled the workers' allegiance, de Man maintained that psychological cravings of the workers for an ethical and emotional significance in socialist doctrines still had to be satisfied. Patriotism would satisfy these cravings. Such ideas became popular particularly in the French Socialist party, but de Man himself went even further. The working class must forget its specific interests and collaborate with the bourgeoisie in the development of social planning which embodied the interests of the entire national community, ignoring the differences in class structure. Emphasis upon the nation had led to the virtual abandonment of Marxist theory. Instead men like de Man or the French Socialist Albert Thomas became advocates of that national planning to which the future, in fact, belonged.

It seems clear that the *embourgeoisement* which Marx feared did come about when socialism faced the forces of nationalism. As socialist parties came to power the idea of national interest was defined in the traditional way, and no so-called socialist foreign policy has ever emerged. Even after the Second World War the Laborite Ernest Bevin in England and Socialist Guy Mollet in France found themselves carrying on and advocating the traditional foreign and imperialist policies of their respective countries. National interest consistently triumphed over socialist aims; the enemies of the nation had to be defeated rather than the enemies of the working classes. In this development the year 1899 played a decisive role, for this was the year when, for the first time, a Socialist joined an existing bourgeois government. The government which Millerand joined in France was led by the *haut-bourgeois* Waldeck-Rousseau and included as minister of war the general who had played a decisive role in suppressing the Paris Commune. Alexander Millerand (1859–1943) did not ask the permission of his party, but in that same year the party congress tacitly condoned his action. That same year also the Italian Socialists praised the "inescapable necessity of liberty and the prudent tactics of alliances"—liberty could be defended and socialism advanced within the very citadels of bourgeois power. Marxism was enmeshed in the bourgeois state —even if Jaurès at the party congress of 1899 thought that this was only a matter of temporary tactics.

At this same congress of the French Socialist party Jaurès was challenged by Jules Guesde who, in 1875, had brought from London the platform for French socialism written by Marx himself. He now asserted with commendable orthodoxy that where the consent of capitalist society was required socialism could not succeed. In the inevitable class struggle participation in a bourgeois government and socialism are exclusive of one another, he continued, since socialism can only come to power through the total defeat of capitalism. Guesde on the one hand and Jaurès on the other represented a fissure in Marxism which was to be duplicated over all of the West. In Germany this was to be especially significant, for the German Social Democratic party was regarded as a model by the other socialist parties of Europe. From the beginning the gradualism of Lassalle and Bernstein had been challenged by Karl Kautsky (1854–1938) as well as by Wilhelm Liebknecht (1826–1900). At the "unity congress" of Gotha (1875), however, the German Social Democrats had found a consensus which guided the party along revisionist lines. Though as a national party the Social Democrats did not enter into coalitions with bourgeois governments, they did so on the local level. Between 1903 and 1914 such coalitions existed in Baden and in Wuerttemberg, and in the latter state even with the Catholic Center party. Though the north German Socialists were shocked at this, these coalitions showed that Socialists not only compromised with national aspirations but also tended to get involved in the game of politics played for the sake of power rather than for principles.

The crisis in the German party came not over participation in a government but over the use of the general strike. Georges Sorel (1847–1922) proclaimed the general strike the most effective weapon of disorganization in his
*Reflections on Violence* (1908). But some time before this the idea had
entered socialist discussion.

The concept of the general strike, an integral part of syndicalism, was an
alternative road to socialist action. Syndicalists were pledged exclusively to
economic action, emphasizing the Marxist contention that economic change was
the basic change which would usher in the classless society. The class struggle
was central to this movement and with it a belief in revolutionary violence.
They did not believe in political parties but instead organized themselves into
industrial unions which they hoped would eventually embrace all the workers
in every industry. Once again corporatist ideas became prominent, entering
this form of Marxism as they had entered conservatism and Catholicism. Here,
however, corporatism was conceived in terms of autonomous, worker-con-
trolled unions which would together constitute the state. Sorel was the theoretician of syndicalism, and in France it gained a great deal of strength, rivaling
the socialist party. In Italy it also gained followers, as will be seen. The general strike epitomized the syndicalist approach to socialism for it emphasized
the primacy of the economic factor and the class struggle; belief in its efficacy
automatically meant a rejection of evolutionary socialism.

Here then was an immediate method of precipitating society into that
class struggle which would result in the eventual victory of the proletariat. It
would do so because it would destroy the capitalist system which Marx had
regarded as parasitic in this stage of its development. A younger generation of
German Socialists led by Karl Liebknecht (1871–1919) and Rosa Luxemburg
(1870–1919) proposed such a strike as an alternative weapon to gradualism.
At first they were defeated (1904), but the Russian revolution of 1905
seemed to show, for a moment, that socialist society could come about without
facing the dangers of evolutionary socialism. That year the German party congress approved the tactics of a general strike. When the Russian revolution
collapsed, however, the party reverted to its former position (1906), stating
that "a general strike is general nonsense." The victory was won by the trade
union leadership which came to dominance in the German party as it already
dominated the party in England. Trade unionists were gradualists looking for
immediate benefits for their members, suspicious of long-range plans. As they
grew successful they tended to become bureaucratic, indeed wedded to the
existing society in which they now had a sizable stake.

In Italy also the question of the general strike provoked the great crisis
in the Socialist party. Here this idea took root in the south which was the poor
and neglected part of Italy. Arturo Labriola (1843–1904), who led this fac-

tion in the party, was successful in starting a general strike which spread from the south to the industrial north. For four days in 1904 the world witnessed the first nationwide general strike which in the next year was to be the prelude to revolution in Russia. The government broke the strike by promises to the moderate Socialists and by exploiting the weak organization of the strikers. But to Labriola "five minutes of direct action are worth many years of parliamentary chatter." The failure of the strike played into the hands of reformists. Here, as in Germany, the trade unions took a leading part in the victory of the evolutionary Socialists at the Congress of Florence in 1908. But here, unlike Germany or France, the dissidents walked out of the party. The man who led them out was the young editor of the powerful socialist paper *Avanti*, Benito Mussolini. This was the point at which some of Italy's leading intellectuals like Benedetto Croce and Gaetano Salvemini openly expressed their disgust with socialism—not because it had repudiated direct action, but because it had proved itself unable to cope with the grave economic problem of the Italian south.

In Germany Liebknecht and Luxemburg did not quit the party as yet. The practical and tactical orientation of the Social Democratic parties did present a problem for the more theoretically-minded Marxists. Much of Marx was modified through this flexible approach as has been discussed above. Trade union domination seemed in the end to typify the actual result of the original Marxist impetus. Rosa Luxemburg called any work with trade unions the "labor of Sisyphus" which would never lead anywhere. The First World War brought about the open break between Liebknecht, Luxemburg, and their group, on the one hand, and the party on the other. As Bebel's quotation foreshadowed, the majority of the Social Democrats voted for war credits and joined with the general patriotic upsurge. In opposition to this policy Karl Liebknecht and Rosa Luxemburg proclaimed in 1915 that "the enemy stands at home," and this enemy was not the Triple Entente but the capitalist class. In that year they founded the Spartacist society which called for revolution rather than evolution and which repudiated the *embourgeoisement* of German socialism.

This Spartacus society, named after the Roman revolutionary, was the origin of the German Communist party. It must be noted that it antedated the Russian revolution. Rosa Luxemburg rejected Lenin's advice even when Bolshevism had triumphed in Russia, for, despite their split with the Social Democrats, the Spartacists shared a mutual regard for the state—not the state as it existed, but the necessity for keeping the state intact even when it had been seized by the Communists. The state would not wither away but would be captured instead. With that Lenin could not agree. As he wrote in *State and Rev-*

*olution,* "the state as state" was a repressive force and it must be demolished by the "special repressive force" of the proletariat. Perhaps Rosa Luxemburg was too much of a German to want to demolish the German state; at any rate, she roundly rebuked Lenin for presuming to advise German Communists. In a sense, she was the founder of that movement, now known as national communism, which attempts to maintain independence from the new mother country—though after her death German communism was to come increasingly under Russian domination.

The developments we have discussed typified socialism's successes and problems—but only on the Continent. In England socialism developed differently, despite the fact that the Labor party can be termed a Social Democratic party. While in Europe the working classes wholeheartedly supported the Social Democratic parties as "their" parties, in England the assumption that the working class would consistently vote Labor was one which could not be made. One historian looking at the ineffectual Labor governments of the 1920s has written that "the weaning of Labour from Liberalism was a long and painful process." This is hardly surprising in a nation which had undergone a more intensive period of liberalism than the Continental countries, where the shadow and even some of the substance of prosperity had lingered on. Moreover, the Liberal party became, as the new century opened, a reformist party, introducing such measures as death duties and graduated income taxes. In England the political parties were flexible, even though a Labor party eventually came into being.

Liberal England took a long time dying, not just with regard to its political allegiances but also in its dominance over men's thoughts. Christian socialism had a strong liberal component, and even that socialism which was not principally Christian, which shared certain Marxist presuppositions, did not derive so much from Marx but from certain trends in liberal thought. Jeremy Bentham and John Stuart Mill also inspired those men who founded the Fabian society in London (1884). A society formed for debate, propaganda, and study, it attracted some of the best minds at the close of the century. People like George Bernard Shaw and Sidney and Beatrice Webb were its leaders, but at one time, H. G. Wells, Bertrand Russell, and Ramsay MacDonald also belonged to the inner circle of this group. Their thought was, at first, a mixture of Bentham's greatest happiness of the greatest number, and Mill's contention that such happiness could only result from human social impulses satisfying the desires of all people collectively. To the influence of Bentham and Mill must be added the great impression which Henry George had made on these men. His *Progress and Poverty* was published in England in 1881 and more Englishmen were brought to socialism by this route than by that of Marx. Taxation of rent and nationalization of land seemed the road to social salvation. The Fabians, however, progressed from these thinkers to a belief that the greatest happiness of the greatest number could only be achieved by a welfare state which controlled the means of production. Man's attributes were molded by the social pressures to which he was subject; personal activities were interwoven with the activities and necessities of the whole body politic. Such was the burden of the *Fabian Essays* (1889), edited by George Bernard Shaw.

This basic statement of Fabian philosophy had certain elements in common with Marx: the control of the means of production; man viewed, above all, in terms of his social relationships. Yet class struggle as the basic means for change was denied. The issue was not between the bourgeoisie and the proletariat but between the great mass of people and those who lived on surplus rent or on their capital investments. The solution was not revolution but the "inevitability of gradualness" whose goal would be the nationalization of the means of production. This belief in gradualness, shared with Continental Social Democrats, was based on the contention that Britain had the framework for a democratic organization; what had to be done was to persuade the people to participate in it. "The difficulty in England is not to secure more political power for the people, but to persuade them to make any sensible use of the power they already have."

This sounds reminiscent of Tocqueville's belief that political participation would cure all ills. Indeed, the Fabians shared this liberal doctrine to a large extent. Sidney Webb (1859–1947), the theoretician of the movement, combined such ideas with an emphasis upon education. Government must provide a minimum education, just as it must provide minimum standards of public health, sanitation, and wages. This required a reorganization of existing society and the Fabians were primarily interested in educating the public to an awareness of the need for such a change. They became experts in local government, conversant with every cranny of the governmental structure—pointing out faults and how they might be remedied. Sidney and Beatrice Webb (1858–1943) specialized in this approach, combining it with a belief in the social sciences. As Sidney Webb put it, ". . . reforming society is no light matter and must be undertaken by experts especially trained for that purpose."

Like so many of the French Socialists, the Webbs believed implicitly in the efficacy of scientific principles within the social realm. But in a typical English manner they combined this belief with a Protestant tradition, not the Protestantism of the Church of England, but that nonconformity which emphasized a Calvinist moral factor without stressing theology. Sidney Webb believed in a "righteousness" above and outside himself. The word "righteousness" was very apt, for in its name the Webbs accepted what this book has called liberal morality. They opposed the general insurance scheme of the Liberal party because to give money to the sick and unemployed without imposing a corresponding obligation to get well or seek employment was wrong. There would be no malingering in their socialist state. One of their associates said quite rightly that the Fabians wanted to achieve a socialist society without disturbing existing conventions.

In order to train the necessary experts the Webbs founded the London School of Economics and Political Science (1895), which eventually became a part of the University of London. The contribution of the Fabians, however, was not primarily institutional but rather widely diffused through their learned studies of government and their pamphlets. It was their influence upon the Labor party which gave them a lasting importance.

In 1890 the Fabians called upon the trade unions to give up their alliance with the Liberal party and form their own political party. Two years later, an Independent Labor party arose under the auspices of J. Keir Hardie (1856–1915). It sought support among trade unions and nonconformist chapels—support which the Labor party continued to rely upon. The appeal to nonconformist Protestantism was a part of that strong, moral basis which underlay the Fabians' call for collective ownership of production. At first the trade unions held back; as we know they had become nonpolitical craft guilds after the debacle of trade unionism in the first part of the century. But unskilled labor began to be unionized. The great London Dock strike (1889)—the Fabians took the side of the union—was a sign of this. Actually, a general attack upon unionism frightened the trade unions into political activity. In the Taff-Vale decision (1900) unions were held responsible for damage to any struck company. While the decision was in the making, the Trade Union Council approved the Independent Labor party's motion to form a Labor representative committee (1899). Thus the Labor party was born.

Fabians provided the ideology for the party, though at times they became impatient with its operation and leadership. Moreover, the crisis of 1930, the Great Depression, led some of them to admire the Soviet Union. The Webbs who previously had not had a good word to say for Bolshevism now wrote a book in praise of it. In contrast to England's depression they saw, in the Soviet Union, real social engineering upon a professed ethical base. George Bernard Shaw was equally impressed, but then Shaw could never resist iconoclasm, though of his earlier Fabian convictions there can be no doubt. Yet even in that period the Webbs disapproved of some of his plays because they tended more toward a negative criticism of society than toward positive solutions. His humor, his eccentricities, and, above all, his wit made him a social critic far superior to the heavy-handed Continental naturalists. He proved a supreme satirist of the bourgeoisie. Lenin, for one, was greatly impressed; he coined the phrase that Shaw was "a good man fallen among the Fabians." Shaw had that aesthetic sense which the Webbs lacked so conspicuously.

After 1900 Fabian influence was exercised through the Labor party, though the party was dominated by conservative unions and included all sorts of people from supporters of the cooperative movement to former Christian Socialists. Aside from the unions, its adherents were recruited from small tradespeople, the backbone of English nonconformity, and intellectuals influenced by Fabianism. The competition with liberalism for the workers' votes did not, as one might suppose, push the Labor party into more radical channels; its basic ideological foundation remained the Fabian ideal of gradualness. To Marxists this typified *embourgeoisement* at its most extreme. For example, Fabians split on the issue of the Boer War—many supported the war —and again they split on the First World War. Foreign policy and the Empire were two areas in which they could never get unanimity of opinion. Their imperialist stand was based on the assumption that it was more rational to govern the world through big rather than small states, for, the Webbs maintained, small nations were inefficient governmental units from a scientific and thus from a socialist point of view.

Marx and Engels despaired of English socialism, but they focused their attentions not on the developing Fabians but instead on the Social Democratic Federation (1881) of H. M. Hyndman and William Morris. Not the Fabians but Hyndman was the popularizer of Marx in England, though he was afraid to use Marx's name. His SDF was not a success. Hyndman quarreled with Morris and everyone else, and his Federation suffered one defection after another. Fabianism easily triumphed as the English form of socialism. It was the same story with the guild socialism advocated by G. D. H. Cole (1889–1959). He advocated control by self-governing industrial guilds of their own affairs within the wider framework of an over-all policy. Actually this guild socialism introduced Sorel's syndicalism into England. It wanted to "rouse the poor rather than to praise them." In spite of an active propaganda campaign this movement had almost no effect on the working classes. The failure of the general strike of 1926 and the growth of the Communist party led to its demise.

Fabianism monopolized English socialism until the Communist party split off from the Labor party after the war, a process duplicated over all of Europe. Even then, Fabian ideas maintained themselves. The importance of communism in England lay in the realm of intellectual influence rather than in politics; no mass communist party arose there as it did in the rest of

Europe. The reasons for the almost uncontested strength of Fabian socialism lay in the peculiar advantages the Fabians possessed. Solidly based, as has been seen, in a specifically English tradition which had grown up within the liberal age, they combined socialism and traditionalism to a greater extent than their Continental brethren. English institutions were becoming more democratic (universal suffrage was granted in 1918), and this reinforced that English nationalism which thought greater freedoms could be attained through the peaceful evolution of English institutions.

Traditionalism was combined with belief in social science; both would lead to a better world. The Fabians relied upon hallowed conventions and this gave them a high moral purpose and a rigid morality. The moral and ethical precepts of bourgeois society would never be abolished. In short, Fabianism gave Englishmen a socialism within the traditional framework they cherished; it meant security in the face of a changing world, an attractive prospect. Though Continental Social Democrats also believed in the "inevitability of gradualness" and in bourgeois morality, no Continental country had either a strong liberal tradition or that peculiar English nationalism which inculcated a belief in representative government. Their socialism came from Marx, not from Mill and Bentham. There can be little doubt that, through the Fabians, socialism through nationalization became rooted in the English ethos, as it did not on the Continent. Unlike the rest of Europe, communism could make little headway against this.

Concern with practical action had served to produce a split within Marxism. What began as a question of revolutionary tactics became an ever-deepening gulf separating Marxists from each other. Karl Marx was not entirely blameless for this state of affairs. He himself had changed his mind several times on the exact nature of the action needed to overthrow bourgeois society. During the revolution of 1848, Marx had, at times, felt that the classless society could be attained by peaceful means. More important still, the question of tactics, the practical problems of revolutionary action, had increasingly engrossed his mind. At times it seems that, in his writings, Marx forgot about that socialist humanism which at other times he tended to stress. The question of attaining power moved increasingly into the foreground and nowhere did Marx detail the nature of the classless society which was to be the result of the coming end of the class struggle.

For all these problems involved in Marx's writings, for all the subtleties of the interrelationship of man and society, the basic structure of Marxism was never in dispute. It was a formidable system built upon facts which must determine the behavior of man in the present just as they determined man's future. No longer was man a subjective creature whose attitude toward the world was determined by the struggles in his "soul" or by the eternal laws under which he was said to live. All men were not the same, they were each the product of the dialectical workings of history. The individual human being was oriented by his place in the historical dialectic, that is, by his status in the class struggle. This status was a part of the kind of interrelationship of man and social forces which has been described.

It was this ideology which did more than any other to further the crumbling of the old order in Europe. Though Bernstein believed that capitalism was not, in fact, declining, yet Marxism was, within another generation, to constitute a challenge which not only could not be ignored, but which was to have solid successes of the greatest magnitude.

# CHAPTER TWELVE

# The Science of Society

THOUGH MARX had emphasized the scientific nature of his ideas, he had, at the same time, criticized the mechanistic nature of nineteenth-century science. To him, this science was too much of an abstraction; it seemed to deny those subtle interrelationships between the individual and the environment upon which historical materialism must be built. Moreover, science denied the importance of history in the name of the immutable operations of the laws of nature. For Marx, therefore, the sciences of his time lacked the subtlety and dimension necessary for a true science of society. Yet, despite this criticism, he believed his theories to be scientific in the sense of being the result of the application of scientific method to historical analysis. There was such a thing as a reality which could be grasped in this fashion, and therefore, within this reality, determinable truth existed. Underlying such a view was Newtonian science, which predicated a universe governed by laws which man could, through a scientific method, discover and grasp—and which, when so understood, were the "truth." In spite of Marx's criticism of mechanistic science, this concept of scientific truth underlays his own historical materialism. But Marx was not alone in positing a body of knowledge about society upon its parallelism with a similar body of knowledge about the scientific universe; during the century many social theories had such a base. There was an urge to transfer scientific laws to society and thus to arrive at proven truths about the nature of man and his place in the world. It has been seen that even an essentially irrational ideology like racism indulged in this scientism in order that it might claim its conclusions valid.

The tie with the eighteenth-century world view is obvious here. By the end of the nineteenth century, as political and social theories attempted to clothe themselves in the mantle of scientific truth, we witness, in a sense, the climax of the application of science to society. Yet this climax occurred at precisely the same time that science itself began to discard the idea that there is a discovered truth which was irrevocable once it had been discovered. In the end, scientific development itself was to erode the Newtonian concept of the universe and substitute for it the relativism of most scientific phenomena. At the same time many sensitive men were to rebel against the rigidities of a "science of society" and turn back to a preoccupation with man's own consciousness. Emphasizing introspection and the reality which lay beyond the scientifically explicable, they denied what was called the positivist" outlook upon the world.

In order to grasp the complexities of this scientific approach to society, it is necessary to return to the beginning of the century and to Auguste Comte (1798–1857), who is sometimes called the father of positivism. For him, social laws were directly analogous to the physical laws which govern the universe; both were discovered through the collation of observable data. These data were all-important; Comte believed that scientific truth was arrived at through the description of individual phenomena. First causes and last causes were not the business of science; instead, continuous observation of these individual phenomena would yield similarities which, upon collation, would in turn become valid natural laws. Exactly the same procedure was applicable in the social sciences—indeed it was scientific method which led directly to the truth about society. Here Comte adapted a method which is found in contemporary science. For example, Buffon's *Natural History* (1749–1804) was based upon a rigid classification of individual data. The same was true of Sir Charles Lyell's *Principles of Geology* (1830–33), which tried to deduce the history of the earth from a wide variety of painstakingly collected facts.

Comte, then, held that the laws which governed society could be discovered in the same manner that Lyell tried to deduce the principles of geology or Buffon the history and laws governing animals. So far this has an eighteenth-century ring about it—society and the universe were connected through the inexorable workings of natural laws. Yet Comte's positivism rejected the synthesis which the Enlightenment made of science and society. In that age the cement which linked man and nature had been man's reason—

reasonable man and reasonable nature formed one unity. Comte believed such a view to be "negative" rather than "positive," and this for two reasons. First, because it lacked an empirical base; it believed certain things to be "self-evident." He would have rejected the premise of the United States Declaration of Independence, for nothing could be self-evident; all had to be based on the description of individual phenomena. Second, the Enlightenment held that man himself can change his condition, that, as Adam Smith put it, "free individuals could fulfill their own needs." Reason ruled the world and men could change obsolete forms of government and society. This Comte denied. Natural laws moved through natural, not human necessities; man could discover these laws, he could not change them. They were no more susceptible to human legislation than the Newtonian laws of gravity.

Positivism was rigid in applying science to society and it lacked the eighteenth-century belief in reason as well as that century's optimism in the potentialities of man. Comte denied that man could alter his social institutions in accordance with his rational will. He believed that his sociology would prepare men for that discipline required by an obedience to the existing order of the universe. Comte called this "resignation" to things as they are. It is significant that he wrote after the French Revolution which demonstrated to him the folly of utopias. He believed in progress but not in the same way that the Liberals believed in it. Progress was achieved by formulating laws which accorded with the results of empirical knowledge. Such formulations would define progress as away from religious, "abstract" ideas toward positivism. Man cannot influence the laws he deduces in this manner, but in discovering these laws he arrives at the truth about society. Positivism believed that the truth existed absolutely for both the world of men and the physical world, and this truth was to be discovered through the application of scientific method. With Comte this led to resignation toward an existing order, but this was not necessarily the result of such a scientific approach.

For example, John Stuart Mill, though he believed in the inductive approach, held that any general judgment must be the résumé of individual observations. The historian Henry Thomas Buckle exemplifies this tendency. He wanted to apply the scientific method to the study of history and to formulate from the empirical observation of detailed historical data general laws. This task required, he believed, a certain amount of skepticism: ". . . the greatest enemies of civilisation are a priori thoughts." Thus, the Positivist's empiricism swept aside not only the "self-evident" conclusions of the Enlightenment but also the Romantic's emphasis on sentiment. It also challenged the individualism of the liberal universe. An absolute determinable truth was possible; it could be discovered through scientific method and once found it put an end to the part man could play in the process of change. This was a sober doctrine but one which had a great deal of appeal; any theory could claim validity if it applied science to the study of society. It gave man certitude even if it denied him freedom of action. Proudhon believed that government was unnecessary since both the universe and society functioned according to laws which science could perceive. All that was needed was an office of statistics which would gather the necessary data upon which laws expressing truths could be formulated. Thus, the rationale for both anarchism and conservatism could be founded upon such a science of society.

Just as the Newtonian universe was a static universe ruled by inexorable and changeless laws, so positivism meant a static concept of society. In fact, Spencer was to call Comte's ideas "social statics." He approached the science of society from the vantage point of the doctrine of evolution. For it was this doctrine which, by the middle of the century, modified positivism without negating the essential foundations upon which it was built. Evolution was also looked upon as a binding law which could be transferred from the world of natural phenomena to human society, binding not only upon society but upon the individuals within that society. It also was a truth arrived at through the analysis of data, of observable facts, and not through metaphysical ideas derived from man's consciousness itself. For here man's progress was not of his own making: it was the concomitant of the inexorable process of the universe.

The idea of evolution had entered scientific thought before Darwin. The eighteenth century's preoccupation with the mere classification of scientific data had been challenged by Jean Baptiste Lamarck in his *Philosophie Zoologique* (1809), a work which combined evolutionary ideas with an environmental explanation of evolution. Once again, science was not concerned with any inner life forces of men, plants, or animals but rather with observable material explanations of how life on this planet evolved. But even so the idea of evolution seemed to clash with the static, older concept of a natural world whose manifold varieties had been created by God in their present forms, a world that could adequately be explained in terms of the classification of these same life forms. These two views led to a famous debate before the Paris Academy of Sciences (1830) in which the evolutionary concept of life won out.

Yet Charles Darwin (1809–82) was probably influenced to a greater extent by certain social theories than by the scientific developments which preceded his discoveries. Above all, the liberal concept which saw life as a continual struggle and the Malthusian hypothesis that more people are born than can survive had a marked effect upon Darwin's formulation of his own theory. Moreover, ideas of evolution had been deeply ingrained in German idealistic philosophy. For Hegel such evolution was evident, but it was explainable only in terms of the clash of ideal essences. Never could the material world's imperfect reflection of these essences, outward and observable phenomena, yield up evolution's secrets. The central concept of Darwin was, therefore, a part of the intellectual atmosphere of the century. This is not to belittle Darwin's importance, for he gave to the idea of evolution scientific respectability and therefore a new dimension of "truth." In doing so he seemed to make a synthesis between science and philosophy of a kind which Comte would have rejected. For Darwin was concerned with cause and effect and not merely with the classification of data. Despite Darwin's own personal abhorrence of the application of his scientific ideas to social theory, it was this unity of science and society which appealed to his fellow men.

Darwin's *On the Origin of Species by Means of Natural Selection* appeared in 1859. The main points of his theory can be stated in four propositions without elaboration, for it was these propositions which impressed contemporaries. First, there were more individuals of every species born than could survive, and this meant, second, that within each species as well as between species there was a constant struggle for survival. The scope of this struggle was enlarged to a battle between a species and its environment. Third, there were differences or variations among members of the same species which made some better fitted to the environment and therefore better able to survive. Fourth, and last, all this resulted in the survival of the fittest. At first, Darwin talked about plant and animal species solely; he was not at all concerned with humanity. Only much later did he study man with those ideas implied in his *Origin of Species. The Descent of Man* (1871) was meant to be read in connection with the earlier work. In it Darwin argued that man originated in an ancestral type from which the anthropoid apes had also sprung. Stimulated by this book, Thomas Huxley began his search for the "missing link" which, in turn, gave great impetus to the growth of anthropology.

What is of interest here is not the spectacular assertion read into the book that humans were descended from apes, but rather Darwin's environmental explanation for human evolution. Once again, as with Lamarck earlier, immaterial forces within this process were denied and here this denial was applied to man. His moral sense, for example, was not "innate" but a part of the necessary process of evolution, something determined by the environment. Any animal would acquire such a sense if its evolution had progressed as far as that of mankind. This meant not only a denial of the human soul in a religious sense but came close to the kind of positivism already discussed. While Darwin was always cautious in his statements, the positivism implicit in his theories was made quite explicit by his popularizers. Of these Ernst Haeckel was the most important. His *Riddle of the Universe* (1899) sold a quarter of a million copies and was translated into twenty-five languages. In it he attempted to apply the doctrine of evolution to philosophy and religion. The science of nature, he told his readers, offered a substitute for religion. The origin of all matter was a universal substance that ruled through natural and eternal laws which can be grasped scientifically. Because man is composed of this substance man is an integral part of nature. Haeckel was a pantheist who talked about a world soul. This soul determined the attraction or repulsion of matter and did not go beyond the material universe.

Haeckel founded the German Monist's League in 1906. This league denied the existence of a personal God. They thought of God as the sum of the forces of nature, expressed through the unchanging law of cause and effect. The attraction of Haeckel and the league was clear: man was a part of nature; individualism was downgraded while man was enabled to grasp the cosmic forces of which he was a part. God could be worshipped, but this worship was really a recognition of the laws of science and matter. The age of economic acquisitiveness, nationalism, and *Realpolitik* had found a world view much to its liking.

Surprisingly, this kind of materialism came to be regarded as a symbol of strong-mindedness as opposed to the sentimental "mush" of the romantic epoch. It was said to stand upon reality just as the much admired *Realpolitik* of statesmen like Bismarck seemed refreshingly free of cant. It has been rightly said that after the idealism of the early nineteenth century, men "were filled with a devouring hunger for reality, but they had the misfortune to confuse this with matter." Darwin's concept of evolution through struggle furthered this confusion, for it fitted in with liberal preconceptions. Here was an explanation of progress which made this prime tenet of liberalism respectable by converting it into a scientific truth. Herbert Spencer illustrates this well.

The evolution of man was progress away from primitivism. For the Liberal, the key to this evolution was man's individuality which must be left free to unfold. Rousseau also believed this, but now this unfolding took place against the background of a continual struggle for the survival of the fittest. Such a "war against all" had led earlier theorists like Thomas Hobbes to call for a strong government in order to protect those who might go under in this struggle. But now, on the contrary, this struggle was held to be good because it was the "natural" way to progress. Those who fell by the wayside were not fit to survive. Though even Malthus had been hesitant to make value judgments, with Spencer this process of selection became, in fact, a moral imperative. If the state interfered to protect "pitiable Jones," it was, in reality, perpetrating an act of aggression upon "hardworking Brown," who was fit to survive. The whole liberal attitude toward poverty, originally linked to a Calvinistic point of view, was now sanctified by Darwin rather than by Calvin.

"Protection of the vicious poor involves aggression against the virtuous poor"; it hindered the process of evolution by natural selection. The state must remain aloof; as for socialism, it was a "coming slavery" which could only have a retrograde effect on man's evolution. It was Spencer, and not Darwin, who coined the phrase "survival of the fittest."

In these stark terms, human evolution became a part of European thought. Spencer, however, combined this view with ethical ideas which tended to temper this dog-eat-dog concept of people and society. Human conduct, he believed, evolved with man and his environment; here, too, there was progress. The less such progress was hindered, the more the evolution of human conduct could serve to protect the individual. Gradually, as the strong were preserved, insuring the survival of the species, conflict between individuals would be replaced by cooperation. War would be eliminated and industrial society would progress peacefully. Thus, Spencer grafted Tennyson's vision of peace and progress onto the survival of the fittest. He was, after all, a Liberal. Moreover, as the final definition of his ideal clearly showed, he lived in the shadow of Benthamism: the largest amount of purposeful activity freely and cooperatively pursued by the maximum of individuals.

The ethical consequences which Thomas Huxley (1825–95) drew from Darwinism were more popular, however. For him the survival of the fittest revolved around a conflict between the cosmic and the moral order. The qualities of goodness and virtue defined by traditional morality seemed opposed to those qualities needed in this struggle. Thus Huxley's Darwinism impelled him to postulate a transmutation of accepted values; Nietzsche (1844–1900), too, arrived at such conclusions, though from quite different premises. Now the hero was no longer the romantic genius fettered by his emotions; instead the superman survived because he was best fitted to survive. He gloried in those qualities needed to win the struggle.

Such ideas on survival of the fittest were subject to a wide variety of adaptations. Two of these ideas are worth mentioning because of their importance. They saw the process of evolution by natural selection in terms of groups rather than of individuals. Walter Bagehot in his *Physics and Politics* (1873) wholeheartedly accepted Darwinian presuppositions. He saw in war the primary instrument of social evolution since it determined which group was most fit to survive. Such ideas could easily be adapted to racial thought. Karl Pearson (1857–1936), one of Darwin's principal popularizers, transferred the idea of natural selection to the struggle for survival among racial stocks. In order that his (the British) race might survive, it was necessary to rid the race of its unfit members; thus, he proposed for the first time a program of natural eugenics.

It is difficult to estimate the degree to which racialists like Houston

Stewart Chamberlain or Paul de Lagarde were actually influenced by Darwinism. Though the survival of the fittest was central to their thought, such ideas were, after all, not necessarily Darwinian, and their stress on the "inner" coherence of racialism placed them in the antipositivist camp. Even the concept of race assumed a scientific garb which, as has been seen earlier, was related closely to phrenology and anthropology rather than to evolution, for what was the end of a superior race's evolution? It was already the *summum bonum* on earth. Here, evolution could provide no answer.

Though consequences of Darwin's thought and his diffuse influence are at times difficult to pin down, one must not lose sight of the kind of positivism which underlay his as well as Comte's ideas. By the end of the century, this positivism no longer firmly denied man any control over his destiny. Obviously Spencer's adaptation of Darwin involved more than environmental forces, for Spencer thought a liberal morality necessary for survival. The hard-working poor were, to Spencer, fit candidates for survival. Huxley's stress on those human qualities which marked the fittest returned to man that individuality Comte had denied him. Darwinism bolstered the cause of individualism rather than that of the statistician-ruler. Francis Galton had already made this still more apparent. On the basis of a statistical analysis he demonstrated that within a random sample of the population, eminent men had a greater number of eminent relatives. From this he posited the inheritance of ability in his *Hereditary Genius* (1869). Galton believed that Darwin had exaggerated the importance of environmental factors. In turn this led Galton's successors to stress the possibilities of education as a device which would stimulate these abilities.

As the rigidities of the positivistic approach were modified, an optimism about the possibilities of the individual could develop. This optimism was based upon the belief in a science of society—whether through struggle or through education, the future could be forecast by applying scientific criteria to human society. The soul, the consciousness of self, did not enter the picture. Its rather spectacular denial of religion as a factor determining human evolution has obscured, in our day, the fact that this thought also denied romantic and idealistic introspection any role in the on-going course of human history.

Not only were religious men part of the coming revolt against scientism; sensitive men who had no clearly-definable religious faith participated in this rebellion, for religion had already been challenged by the time Darwin appeared. The growing science of anthropology had led, even before Darwin, to an analysis of Christianity in the context of primitive civilizations. As man evolved, he would outgrow this primitivism. To be sure, Darwin's influence may have been important at a later stage of the development of anthropology.

Possibly Sir James Frazer was under his influence when, in his *Golden Bough* (1890), he traced the evolution of religious modes among the ancient Nenni in Italy. Frazer's famous thesis that primitive religion originated in magic was applied to religion in general. Thus, Darwin's statement that man originated in primitivism rather than in paradise came at a time when anthropology had already laid the foundations for such ideas—ideas used not only by Feuerbach but also by Friedrich Engels. Neither Darwin nor Frazer shocked Europe as they did America. Moreover, no religious thinker in Europe was influenced by evolution as much as Theodore Parker was in the United States.

If Positivists thought that they had superseded religion and romanticism, what was positivist influence upon literature, which Romantics had conceived of as being an expression of man's soul? The realist and naturalist movement cannot be ascribed to scientific influence alone, but there is little doubt that these writers saw in science a welcome support for their literary viewpoints. By the end of the century some naturalistic writers aimed at closing the gap between science and literature. Hippolyte Taine (1828–93) substituted "scientific" literary criticism for a subjective criticism based upon individual intuition. Literary problems became mathematical problems as Taine sought to weigh the author's race, milieu, and moment of composition in order to arrive at a definition of his talent. For Taine, as well as for many writers themselves, the truth lay in environmental factors, which could be observed and chronicled, rather than in the inward sentiment of the soul.

In Germany such environmental literary criticism can be found in Georg Brandes (1842–1927), who explained north European literature through an examination of its milieu. Nor did the writing of history stand aside from this influence. The historical works of Karl Lamprecht (1856–1915) attempted to see the evolution of history through social conditions and environment. Treitschke, the worshipper of race and heroes, called this, ironically, "history without people."

With Lamprecht, such concepts did lead to determinism and had a very stultifying effect upon literature. Only one writer really did fuse an environmental approach with the expert delineation of character. Balzac's *La Comédie Humaine,* which one critic has called the entomological memoirs of an observer of human society, set a high standard. The environmentalism which we have noticed in the development of positivism was faithfully reflected here. Small wonder that Balzac was Karl Marx's favorite author! Émile Zola represented the climax of this literary school. Relying upon the observation and classification of human reality, he wanted to apply the method of the laboratory to literature. At times Zola wrote about types rather than living characters; yet Zola's great artistry lay precisely in the fact that he did not consistently follow his own method. There was a point in his novels when he did abandon the sheer naturalist approach, and then his characters sprang to life. He himself, however, proclaimed triumphantly in the year 1900: ". . . as I finish the century, I open the next century. All this is based on science and the dream which science allows."

Zola's dream held to an optimism in the perfectibility of man, the kind of hope which science had offered in the eighteenth century. With others, however, the world which they dissected so painfully led them to pessimism and despair. J. K. Huysmans in his *En Rade* (1887) wrote about an ill-assorted couple imprisoned in their villa in the country, full of hate for each other, without purpose in their life. The plot is reminiscent of Sartre or Kafka, but it sprang from an attempt at realism and naturalism mixed with an almost hysterical sensualism. As one critic put it, after such a novel Huysmans had only two alternatives: he must either put a pistol to his head or lie at the foot of the cross. He took the latter road with his conversion. Realism, unrelieved by optimism about humanity or by a belief in a necessary evolution, led to such feelings of despair. At the end of the century those who opposed positivism and this literary trend also shared this despair about society, but they fell back upon their own inner selves and found new strength to face the future. Writers like Huysmans, however, could not deny the outward reality in the name of man's consciousness of himself—externals were all important to them.

Huysmans's conversion to Catholicism showed an uneasiness with his approach to life. Similarly, the restlessness of de Maupassant, when faced with the reality he felt he had to describe, led to feelings of "incompleteness" and pessimism. Obviously it was not enough to grasp human reality by closing of the gap between science and literature; these men of letters saw the problems created by this scientism more clearly than the philosophers or those concerned with social thought. Literary photography of life was, after all, not as true to reality as a photograph of man's bodily structure. Émile Zola, in his best moments, realized this. No wonder that literary men like Proust and Gide came to be in the forefront of the antipositivist revolt.

The literary school of naturalism treated man as a product of his environment, thus emphasizing the conditions under which men lived. The favorite subjects were those in which Zola excelled—the struggle of the disinherited within their squalid environment. In this manner such realism was connected with a drive toward social reform at the end of the century. The humdrum and miserable life of the masses became the reality illuminated by a thorough examination of the environment, not of the soul. In his cycle *Les Rougon-Macquart* (1871) Zola constructed characters who acted according to their social and economic environment, without any free will. Through such naturalism, the tendencies we have discussed became social criticism.

This was a type of social criticism which Marxism rejected. The Marxist critic, Georg Lukács, attacked Zola's description of artistic endeavor: ". . . a corner of nature viewed through the human temperament." This implied, to Lukács, a mechanical view of nature, for the naturalist beholder, in his carefully-maintained position of observer, stood outside of life. He was isolated from that totality of life which was implicit in the Marxist dialectic. Zola's works represented simply a mechanical reproduction of a segment of life arbitrarily divorced from the whole. As a result, this art became abstract and alien to reality. For reality, in Zola, was "abstracted," and Lukács felt that naturalism suffered, as had other bourgeois literary movements such as romanticism, from a similar alienation from reality as he defined it. This was the Marxist view, though in practice Marxist realism built upon and approximated this naturalism. Nor must it be forgotten that the Naturalists did call attention to the social problem. They broke, as has been seen, with the romantic attitude toward life.

Yet, such naturalism could be used by reactionary forces. In literary criticism the stress upon environment fused with the idea of the importance of the right kind of country suited to great literature. Thus Joseph Nadler entitled his gigantic literary history, *A History of Germanic Races and Landscapes* (1912). Only the German landscape fusing with the German racial ideal could produce true creativity.

Such emphasis on the milieu also had great influence on the theatre. Gerhart Hauptmann (1862–1946) used stage directions to create an environment which would tell a part of his story. No longer did he merely want the stage "dark" or "light," but he required the most detailed execution of the scenery, down to the color of the walls and the objects in the glass-fronted cupboards. Putting up pictures of Darwin and Haeckel on one wall of the scenery and Biblical representations on the other told the audience something about the conflict within his hero. His most famous play, *The Weavers* (1892), showed one family completely dependent upon their environment, the loud and restless spindles which dominated the scene. But above all, in painting, this naturalism broke with the romantic tradition.

Instead of mystic landscapes or romanticized heroes, painters turned to the reality of coal fields, railway stations, or factories. The figures themselves tended to be mere ciphers surrounded by a world of machines; they were not characters possessed of a force of their own. The necessity of man to obey his milieu led to the love of interiors from which man cannot escape into the wide landscape, interiors in which man fused with the furniture and the walls. Max Liebermann in Germany best typified the artistic reflection of this theory.

The science of society led to a dehumanization which was well expressed by the artistic consequences which flowed from it. The statistician, the gatherer of facts, was closer to the truth than the intuitive man who would never comprehend it. Any theories about the nature of the world or of man had to be based on this kind of scientific data. To be sure, this did lead toward an invigorated social criticism, but a criticism which never really became social theory. It had an affinity with Marx, however, and Marxist literature was to take over this kind of realism. Yet it may be symptomatic that Marxist literature was always better at analyzing the faults of the present environment than in forecasting the future. Such a handicap was an integral part of this naturalism's stress upon present environmental factors.

Scientific methods and concepts were here applied to literature as they were applied to society in general. This urge to extend scientific truth everywhere came at the precise moment when science itself was becoming more specialized and technical. Not surprisingly, the scientific amateur, so popular in the eighteenth century, no longer had any place in nineteenth-century science. The increased compartmentalization of knowledge in all fields was especially manifest in science. The fact that the layman was increasingly removed from scientific research did not influence attempts to create a science of society. It did mean that such attempts proceeded for a long time upon a basis which scientists themselves had left behind. Social scientists were still to believe in the possibility of immutable scientific truth when scientists themselves no longer believed that there was any such thing. The attempt to found a science of society was still based on a Newtonian concept of the universe at a time when physicists stressed that everything changed and that the machine never was a copy of nature.

The men we have discussed believed such a truth existed. It was not a revealed truth in a religious, Christian sense, but the truth of observable phenomena or the truth of evolution through natural selection. Moreover, this truth was a material truth in the sense that it could be grasped only through observation and statistics and not through intuition. This materialism in the intellectual realm was linked by many sensitive people to the materialism which dominated all compartments of life. The importance put upon outward good manners, upon moneyed wealth, had in their eyes its counterpart in the materialistic approach of the social scientists. Max Nordau's *Conventional Lies of our Civilization* (1883) and his *Degeneration* (1892) typified this "positivism" for the *fin de siècle*.

The cornerstone of Nordau's world view was a belief in ordered progress through the natural sciences. Those who understand the working of science will also have an unobstructed view of the future of mankind. Science operates through physical laws which apply to people as well as to nature. The law of cause and effect is basic to all other laws and it depends upon sharp observation and clear formulation. Both, in turn, are based upon mental discipline. Discipline means hard work and acceptance of the liberal morality. Those who do their duty will survive in the struggle, for Nordau was a convinced follower of Darwin's science of evolution. Such evolution is defined as "disciplined progress." Here there is no room for the free flow of the imagination or for artistic sensitivity. Nordau thought most literature "degenerate" because it refused to stick to clear and unambiguous ideas and falsified the observation of phenomena: "A clear-head poet calls a cat a cat." It is degenerate to trifle with knowledge based on scientific law and observation.

The result of Nordau's contentions is an emphasis upon artistic realism and upon normality defined in terms of liberal or middle-class morality. The unusual is the degenerate, and here we might recognize why even during the twentieth century those who departed from the norm in dress and appearance were also thought immoral and a bar to progress. Nordau based himself upon the dominant school of psychology which supported this kind of positivism. Man's feeling and his conduct of life were determined by his physical condition as reflected in his bodily structure. This materialism was reflected in Cesare Lombroso's *Genius and Madness* (*Genio e Follio,* 1863), which saw genius as reflections of the pathological condition of the body. Moreover, genius, which the romantics had revered, was the opposite of science and normality which alone meant progress. Both the genius and the madman have in common a distaste for order, a lack of understanding of the practical realities of life: they are dreamers which lack a steadfast character. Lombroso went on to analyze the sickness of supposed genius from Dante to Schopenhauer.

Liberalism seemed to have climaxed in a positivism which denied human individuality and creativity, which put up the stereotype of the "clean cut" Englishman, German, or Frenchman as the man of the future. Physical appearance had always been stereotyped, and we saw how the Aryan type built upon an ideal of Greek beauty which ran deep since the rediscovery of the ancients during the eighteenth century. Liberalism adopted this stereotype and the classical idea of beauty for which it stood: here as clarity and symmetry corresponding to the laws of science. Those mentally degenerate would also possess an ugly body far removed from the Apollonian ideal. Such a stereotype further limited liberal ideals of freedom and individuality: they joined hands with moral respectability in restricting the dignity of each human being and thus further deepened the linkage of human stereotype and a preconceived aesthetic which most Europeans came to share and to direct against those who were different.

But this liberalism soon came under attack from a new generation which had grown up in the *fin de siècle* and found the atmosphere of conformity stifling. These young people suffered frustration in developing their individuality and blamed it upon the "positivism" of their elders. They began a change in the nature of European thought which was to have far-flung consequences, most importantly because this change, hostile to existing society, denied the materialist universe. It was to be an anti-positivist revolution. As such, it built upon the forces of romanticism and idealism already analyzed, reinvigorating a world view which saw truth not in an environmental or material reality, but instead searched for the "genuine" beneath the appearances of the moment. This neo-romanticism, as it is sometimes called, lacked the urge for definition characteristic of the original romanticism (even if today we find its search for a definition of emotions somewhat comical). The second wave of romanticism seemed to exalt the imprecise, the mystical, and the sentimental. To be sure, such changes in the public spirit of Europe produced much literature and art, but it also gave support to a political irrationalism and emotionalism which would in the end, suppress these very literary and artistic aspects of the movement.

# FROM THE NINETEENTH TO
# THE TWENTIETH CENTURY
## 1870-1918

# CHAPTER THIRTEEN

# Change
# in the Public Spirit
# of Europe

BENEDETTO CROCE (1866–1952) saw in the years after 1870 a change in the public spirit of Europe which ended the nineteenth century and began the twentieth. In politics such a change was clear enough—the two nations of Germany and Italy were now unified, and within each nation, a strong and politically conscious labor movement arose. The decades after 1870 saw the founding of most modern fortunes and, in spite of some crises, a remarkable wave of prosperity engulfed society. The upper-middle classes, which benefited most by these good times, felt secure, and this smugness seemed, at least to the critics of bourgeois society, to climax the *embourgeoisement* of Europe. Though today we know that these decades spelled the end of this kind of security even as it reached its climax, many of these critics, who could not foresee the total destruction the First World War would bring, felt that these years were the beginning of a dreary prospect (bourgeois society) that stretched endlessly into the future.

National pride and bourgeois security went hand in hand during these years. They, in fact, urged on the drive for a positivist, scientific explanation of the world. Here reality was identified with matter. Materialism as discussed in the last chapter was used not only to give meaning to the aspirations of the working classes, but also to explain and support the acquisitive society. It is small wonder, therefore, that as man passed from the nineteenth to the twentieth century he was met by a variety of movements which attempted to revolt against this state of affairs. Some Marxists sought to temper their materialism through an infusion of idealism. In like manner, others, working from a bourgeois context, found their way back to a revived romanticism and attempted to find in the search for beauty a consolation for the drabness of their age. Chateaubriand, Matthew Arnold, and others had taken this road during the height of romanticism; Stefan George and many others would do so again in the new century. Young people tried to escape the prison of bourgeois convention by fleeing to the countryside and, with the *Wandervoegel* (Roamers), began the history of the modern youth movements. Though much of this repudiation of the material world was of an antibourgeois nature, middle-class society itself was not wholly materialistic and given over totally to books like Haeckel's *Riddle of the Universe*. For here, too, there was an escapism from the drabness of everyday existence, an escapism which manifested itself in the popularity of Wagner's operas or the acceptance of racial ideas and ideals. The bourgeoisie tended to fasten onto national themes and aspirations. Not in a cult of beauty or nature but in an emotional nationalism did the middle classes seek escape from a material society to which they paid apparent outward allegiance.

This change of public spirit after 1870 tended toward a recapturing of the irrational—a revolt against positivism which was later to form part of the totalitarian movements of our century. Many people accepted the positivist definition of the universe, to be sure, but the dominant modes of thought tended to become increasingly antipositivistic. This has led Stuart Hughes to write about an "intellectual revolution" as a number of thinkers, independently of one another, proposed views quite different from those society accepted. They all tried to penetrate behind the façade of the material world, to return to a preoccupation with man's consciousness of himself, placing a renewed stress upon the role of the unconscious in the formation of man and his society. Small wonder that this period not only saw a revival of romanticism and idealism but was also the age in which Sigmund Freud (1856–1939) did his most important work. As André Gide was to write, looking back over his life, "how much stronger are innate values than acquired ones." For him, "in spite of every kind of starching, dressing, pressing and folding, the natural stuff persists and remains unchanged—stiff or limp as it was originally woven." It was the changeless substratum of humanity which was important; the environment changed people in only a superficial way. It became the task of writers and artists to capture this basic human nature while political theorists like Vilfredo Pareto (1848–1923) attempted to manipulate it for the sake of strong government and Georges Sorel for the sake of revolution. Reality, material reality, was the "myth" beneath which man's irrational impulses worked.

The change from impressionism to expressionism in art provides a good example of this new definition of reality. The impressionist artist grasped reality's movement and color with his eye. What he painted was, to him, an actual representation of reality. The artist's form of expression was subjective, personal, but what he expressed about the world was what he could obtain through visual impression. The Expressionists did not want to picture the world as it seemed to the human eye; they wanted to penetrate beneath any visual reality to those forces which they believed to be behind reality. Real art was not the formal reproduction of visual experiences, but instead a projection of those basic urges, those soul experiences which underlay reality. Traditional form and beauty must be sacrificed for the expression of the tormented soul of the artist.

These Expressionists wanted to go back to the basics of human nature; they rejected actual sense impressions of the external world. Their inspiration was Paul Gauguin (1848–1903), and what he said about the women of the South Sea islands corresponded to their own ideas: "She is the Eve just after her sin, who can still walk naked without shyness, and who has kept her animal beauty as on the first day." They admired primitive African sculptures and for much the same reasons. Expressionism searched for a new dynamic; art was an expression of the basic drives of the soul. Here the usual forms of beauty and ugliness were irrelevant; what mattered was the spontaneity of expression. A transformation of the concept of beauty to the idea of ugliness was general not only in the literary world—it was exemplified in many of the expressionist paintings. Moreover, these painters were concerned with the "soul" of man, regarding reality as a myth which had to be penetrated. In revolt against rationalism and positivism the Expressionists claimed that they painted with the heart. The beginning of this movement occurred in 1905. In Paris that autumn a group of painters exhibited together and were promptly dubbed the "wild beasts" (*les Fauves*) by their enemies. In the same year in Dresden, a similarly-minded group of German painters exhibited under the name of "the bridge" (*die Bruecke*). The leader of the French group was Henri Matisse (1869–1954); in Germany Ernst Ludwig Kirschner (1880–1938) and Ernst Nolde (1867–1956) were among the most prominent.

Thus the visual arts made their contribution to this change in the European ethos. The French painter Maurice Vlaminck (1876–1958) summed it up when he talked about the "vital, instinctive painting" and defined this as concern with the "natural and basic." This was the theme that ran through so much of the thought around the turn of the century. The revolt against reason seemed to revive the primitive in man and to glorify it as the true reality. Not only in art but also in literature expressionism signaled a revolt against bourgeois culture. Kasimir Edschmid (1890–1966), one of the pioneers of German expressionism, talked about the "century with the capitalist façade." The age of classes, of lawyers, of officers, and of proletarians hung over Europe like fate, disguising the tragedy of the age through mask-like laughter. For these Expressionists, like their brother artists, held that creativity expressed itself not in photographic sense impressions but in visions which were the stuff of reality. It was the "inner meaning" which was important. Expressionist literature was abstract, exaggerated, and rhapsodic. Young expressionist writers were in revolt against society and this revolt expressed itself in their opposition to older generations. All of them lived in conflict with their families who could not be expected to understand their poetry or prose. This feeling of alienation was summarized by the dramatist Frank Wedekind's exclamation: "We artists are the luxury article of the bourgeoisie!"

Expressionism in literature was not a unified movement. With some of these writers the feeling of alienation became an orgy of pessimism and a conscious rejection of bourgeois values at all costs. They sought to shock, and as their work had to express a felt reality they did this by building their poetry around images of horror. The young Gottfried Benn (1886–1955) is a good example of this. As a physician, he took his themes from the most squalid details of hospital life or from life in the morgue. His revolt became nihilistic within the disjointed syntax of the visionary poet. For a few others, like Ernst Toller (1893–1939), expressionist criticism became social criticism. The unlimited social and spiritual freedom which was part of their revolt against the *embourgeoisement* of Europe became a revolutionary dream. Man must become the master of the factory, of the machine. Toller's drama *Man and the Masses* (1919) had considerable impact. When he became, for a brief time, one of the leaders of the Bavarian revolution of 1919, Toller proclaimed love and universal brotherhood in a series of expressionist manifestoes. His path was obviously a different one from that of Benn, who joined national socialism.

Yet, in all of these men, there was the same longing for reality in terms of an inner vision. The French poet Arthur Rimbaud (1854–91) summed this up well. The poet has to destroy his bourgeois crust in order to let the buried reality of the world erupt within him. Such expressionism was obviously part of the new romantic impetus at the turn of the century—that "neo-romanticism" which will be discussed in the next chapter. Both were a part of the same revolt. Expressionism and neo-romanticism shared the sharp reaction against materialism, but there were also some differences. The Romantics sought security, stressing once more the roots of the *Volk*, in contact with nature; while Expressionists did, at times, put forward a revolutionary utopia, one which would make a clean break with the past. But this very emphasis upon the unbridgeable gulf between past and future deprived expressionism as a revolutionary ideology of all contact with reality. Revolution tended to become a longing for "salvation," a spiritual and artistic momentum which led some Expressionists toward socialism but others into the arms of the Nazis who themselves emphasized a revolution of the spirit rather than social and economic change.

Expressionism shared with the new Romantics, and later with Spengler, a belief in the inevitable conflict between "mind" and "soul." Ludwig Klages, the author of a book with the typical title *The Mind as the Adversary of the Soul* (1929), was both an Expressionist and a new Romantic who took refuge in the Aryan myth. Gottfried Benn excused his adherence to Hitler with the thought that the simple idea of the *Volk* stood in opposition to the industrialism and intellectualism of the bourgeois epoch. With many Expressionists the revolt ended in neo-romanticism. Thus this movement must be put in another related context: that of the German youth movement. For all youth, the symbol of the oppressive society was the German school system with its Prussian discipline, its learning by rote.

The youth movement of the *Wandervögel* saw an escape from this in a spiritual contact with the landscape of the fatherland, in a kind of romantic patriotism. The Expressionists mercilessly caricatured the educational system. The most famous of such caricatures was Heinrich Mann's *Professor Unrat* (1905) which was made into a famous film, *The Blue Angel.* The intellectual tyrant of the classroom, seduced and destroyed by a shrewd but ignorant cabaret dancer, becomes in the end a pitiful clown, mocked by his former students. The school symbolized for Expressionists their alienation from society. The suicide of the student who cracks under the pressure became a recurrent theme in their works. The horror of school leads to failure when man has to confront life. Such pessimism contrasts with the vitality of the youth movement. While the youth movement revolved around the group, the poet or writer was fixed in his isolation. "The poet is one who is scattered among the nations . . . an exile. He is, in our time especially, a stranger dwelling in insecure domiciles." Many Expressionists had a feeling of hopelessness; they felt their isolated endeavors absurd in the face of a powerful and hostile world. Symptomatic of expressionist literature was its disregard for rules of syntax or grammar in the name of the personal vision of the writer. The artists exhibited a parallel tendency.

The expressionist revolt was part of the attempt to recapture human nature viewed in emotional terms. It did father an important art form. Man stood alone with his emotions, a reality which he expressed in words or on canvas. The image was usually dislocated, in isolation, as in the expressionist use of a nondiffuse light which highlighted the main theme or the hero. This was particularly prevalent in the early films; indeed, much of their initial artistic excellence was a result of the movement's influence. The term "expressionism" was German but this was more than a German movement. The French poet Rimbaud has already been cited as summing up its essence. The Italian Marinetti, in his *Manifesto of Futurism* (1909), demanded the creation of a dynamic personal experience as an end in itself. In England, Wyndham Lewis's *Imagist Manifesto* (1913) defined the aesthetic norms of expressionism. Cubism, in France, directed the reaction against impressionism along similar lines as the German expressionist movement. Pablo Picasso (1881–1973) said about cubism that "we only wanted to express that which was within us." There was no plan. Picasso continued that he found painting to have its own value, to be something in and of itself, independent of outward reality. A painting could represent the "idea" of something just as well as it could depict the object's outward appearance. Painting, in short, was the continuous expression on canvas of the "idea" in the mind of the artist. Georges Braque added that art must never be an imitation of anything— "senses deform, the spirit forms." Every painting was therefore a new spiritual adventure.

Especially in France this revolt shaded over into surrealism. This movement, whose full impact came only after the First World War, made full use of the discovery of psychoanalysis. Similar to expressionism was its accent on the subconscious of man, and this, together with the importance of dreams and dream fantasies, was stressed. André Breton, in his *Surrealist Manifesto* (1924), spoke of the power of dreams which could be used to solve the fundamental problems of life. He compared such creativity with the feeling induced by opium where the same emotions of exhilaration and spontaneity were experienced. Obviously, surrealism and expressionism were closely allied movements. Surrealism stressed the new discoveries of Freud and Jung, discoveries which were being made at the very time expressionism was born.

Expressionism in all its phases symbolized the reorientation of European thought at the turn of the century. It went hand in hand with the new romantic impetus. This was also true of surrealism, with its immense debt to psychology, itself a part of this reorientation. The same attitudes which

224

expressionism typified in the extreme will be seen in others like Gide and Wilhelm Busch, who were not Expressionists themselves.

Expressionism did not have to be pessimistic, and Toller is cited as an example, though it certainly tended that way. Others, watching the course of this revolt, also felt a sadness which added to the fund of pessimism about the world as it passed from the nineteenth to the twentieth century. This was especially true of those who were concerned with the retention of the humanistic tradition. Hugo von Hofmannsthal (1874–1929), writing about true love and a positive universe, thought that the contemporary world was moving toward bestiality. Thomas Mann (1875–1955) was later to chide artists for having lost contact with life. Would they ever recapture it? Here indeed lay one of the fundamental problems and tragedies of the intellectual in the new century, and this problem will be dealt with at length in a later chapter.

The divorce from reality experienced by the creative artist in revolt can also be illustrated through another important movement. In the 1890s *Art Nouveau* or the "new art" movement was launched in opposition to the sentimentalism and eclecticism of contemporary painting and architecture. Diffused through all the West, the Germans gave it a symbolic name: *Jugendstil,* style of youth. In Germany, the movement's magazine *Youth* carried a cover which depicted two young maidens hustling along a frightened and stuffy old man. William Morris in England inspired them with his contention that the artist should be a part of society, not a priest detached from it, and John Ruskin's thesis on the unity of life and art provided further support. But unlike these Englishmen, the *Art Nouveau* rejected a return to the romanticized Middle Ages as a model for the artistic integration with life. Henry van de Velde (1863–1957), the Belgian inspirer of the movement, talked about art adapting itself to social change, about "the engineer" who stands at the inception of every artistic style.

The protest of this "new art" against romanticism and imitative styles was supposed to take the form of rational construction; beauty was to be conceived of in rational terms. Yet, except in some of their furniture, which did substitute simple and clean designs for the Renaissance and Baroque imitations then in vogue, the results fell far short of early expectations. The trouble was that the element of protest swamped the rational and "modern" scientific ideal. By 1914 van de Velde placed individuality of the artist before any canon or any standardization. These men now thought acceptance of the realities of modern life, such as industrial mass production, to be stifling as the older eclectic art forms; they revolted against such acceptance in the name of individuality. Above all, this expressed itself in the use of the line, something van de Velde regarded as typical of the realism of the engineer in modern society. But with an ever greater emphasis on individualism the line ran riot as curve succeeded curve in designs which had to be individualistic and unfamiliar in order to lay claim to creativity. We can sum up the movement as an adaption to industrialism *manqué*. It became wholly detached from reality.

In the end, its difference from expressionism consisted mainly in a continued emphasis on form and design; the dynamic was here clearly expressed and not formulated through a more or less chaotic longing of the soul. Moreover, the "new art" was highly popular, and many buildings, both private and public, are the concrete examples of this vogue. From the Paris Metro stations to many a suburban villa in Germany, van de Velde's influence lives on. At least for the most part, an end was put to mock Gothic and mock Renaissance, however mock Baroque the style itself may seem today. This, then, is an interesting and significant example of how artists who wanted so much to be abreast of social change and modern technology ended up in turn by divorcing themselves from reality, even if this was not as self-conscious an impulse as it was with contemporary expressionism. The disassociation of the creative artist and the intellectual from the reality surrounding them came about during the change in the European ethos; with it came a search for individuality and values, an elusive reality, supposedly more true and genuine than that which met the eye. This is perhaps the greatest significance of these revolts.

This reorientation of European thought was accompanied by a pessimism about people and society. It was in this period that Schopenhauer's *World as Will and Idea* (1819) became important. Pessimism and the force of human will were the twin concepts which structured his thought. The force of human will moved the individual, but that will was blind, purposeless, and without direction. It hurled itself against a world of misery. Escape lay in a denial of will—a negation of it—and here Schopenhauer turned to the Buddhist ideal of nirvana. Yet nirvana was in reality impossible, and the best that could be done was to retreat from the world into scholarship and art. Schopenhauer had no faith in the idea of progress, in the materialistic construction of a better world; instead, the individual, driven by blind and purposeless will, could only retreat from the world. Man was not linked to society but was an island unto himself. Nietzsche's words illuminate this mood's belief in a chaotic reality: "...the value of a human being does not lie in his usefulness: for he would continue to exist even if there were nobody to whom he could be useful."

Thus life could not be grasped through reason or science; this seems reminiscent of the romantic "chaos of life" at the beginning of the century. The retreat of which Schopenhauer spoke became for some one way of meeting such a chaos. "Art for Art's Sake" was a slogan which appealed to many, and scholarship for the sake of scholarship became quite popular. In both cases this was the kind of retreat into aesthetics lampooned mercilessly through the poet in Gilbert and Sullivan's *Patience*. It is exemplified in the historian Jakob Burckhardt (1818–97), who refused a call to a prestigious professorship at Berlin because big cities made art "nervous." This belief that the aesthetic would provide meaning in a confused world led not only to a quest for individual isolation but also to a repudiation of mass society. In this it fastened onto a trend which was developing with the Romantics. Jakob Burckhardt wanted to get at the "spiritual essence" of an age, and such an essence was far removed from the aspirations and tastes of nineteenth century mass society. How different the world of the Italian Renaissance was, for Burckhardt, when even the state was a work of art! Such a withdrawal was not necessarily opposed to bourgeois conventions, and Burckhardt with his well-regulated life was nothing if not conventional. But for many, this view of life did seem to clash with the conventions of existing society. It meant a necessary transformation of values.

In the attempt to get to the true reality of man's consciousness of himself the rules of good behavior were bound to be thought of as merely external, and thus a part of the confusion of reality with matter. Henrik Ibsen shocked the *fin de siècle* by drawing a picture of society which not only stifled the passions but forced man to pervert his natural drives. Thus in *Ghosts* (1881) Captain Alving is a victim of society, forced into a secret life of dissipation which leaves behind a heritage of syphilis. Through this heritage his son is deprived of joy in life as he loses his eyesight and his senses. Ibsen was hitting close to home: syphilis was the scourge of the age and here the playwright was making public what had only been whispered behind closed doors. The theme of many of Ibsen's plays is that society is an evil hypocrisy in which reputation is the highest value corresponding to the granting of credit in finance. For example, *A Doll's House* (1879) contrasts the self-fulfillment of a woman with the repressive institution of marriage typical of alienating society. For Ibsen what society thinks of as great sins touch on great virtues (as in *Peer Gynt*, 1867) and these are closely related to the powers dormant in nature.

For Ibsen society is man's fate and it is not a pleasant one. André Gide, brought up in a strict French Huguenot household, wrote (1892) that he was torn between rules and sincerity. Bourgeois morality consisted of substituting a fiction for the natural creature, "the old Adam." For Gide reality was a myth beneath which lived natural man, a creature of emotion and intuition. In his *Immoralist* (1902) Ménalque put it this way: "... men go on imitating, yet they love life." What was needed was a "private and inward unconventionality." But this unconventionality was, with Gide's early contemporaries, neither private nor quiet; it had definite channels of expression. In England Aubrey Beardsley's *Yellow Book* (1894–97) mercilessly caricatured conventional society. An unfriendly critic has written that Beardsley was a satirist of an age without conviction, but that was only a part of the story. For Beardsley believed that aesthetic standards were primary and his caricatures revealed middle-class society at its hypocritical worst. Though superficially it paid homage to art, in reality it confused beauty with fashion and both with materialism.

In Germany Wilhelm Busch (1832–1908), whose influence and importance were to continue unabated into the twentieth century, became the satirist of middle-class life. His books of verse and pictures, like *Struvelpeter* or *Max and Moritz*, were often thought of as children's literature. This was not the case. They, like his famed *Humorous Treasure of the Home*, were a vigorous attack on bourgeois conventionality. He poked fun at the values which underlay these conventions: marriage, the family, religion, and the great hunger for respectability. The virtuous maiden widowed, the symbol of virtue in bourgeois society, fared badly at his hands. The pious Helen took to the bottle and came to a bad, if hilarious, end; another paragon of virtue was poisoned when she mistook medicine for liquor. Morality was in reality hypocrisy; only maiden aunts had virtue, for they had left "everything" behind them. But even their virtue turned out to be a sham. Schopenhauer provided Busch with a large part of his outlook; his creatures, too, strove through blind impulse, and their evil natures in this case led them to their doom.

Busch's satire was biting and cruel; he had this in common with Beardsley in England. But Busch's cruelty was not confined to his drawings; it was an intrinsic element of his stories. The pious Helen was burned to cinders, cats' tails were set aflame, and the jokes his characters played upon one another invariably gave the victims great pain. This pervasive cruelty in satire and humor was important, for it influenced the humor of generations of Germans. It is difficult to generalize about something so intangible, but perhaps in this manner a certain element of cruelty was accentuated in the German character. With Busch, death and pain were something to be laughed at, and, moreover, they were the just deserts of many a hypocrite. In England liberal morality was too firmly entrenched to give wide currency to Beardsley's satires, but in Germany the middle class laughed at its own hypocrisy. After all, as seen previously, the romantic urge with its distaste for conventionality had never been subdued in Germany the way it had in England or France.

Busch's satires were not entirely nihilistic. He himself was a pious, even moral, man; he despised materialism as the root of hypocrisy. Moreover, he believed in the restraints of society. Authority modified blind impulse rather than a negation of will through retreat into art or nirvana. Busch had a typically German respect for authority. Children were his favorite subjects, for society and authority had not yet modified the cruelty of their blind impulses. They possessed, therefore, a meanness and maliciousness far surpassing that of adults. Busch, a life-long bachelor, undoubtedly regarded children, other people's children, with a jaundiced eye; and his view of society and authority made him an enemy of what we like to call progressive education. Authority had to be asserted in order to tame impulse, and Max and Moritz suffered a great deal of corporal punishment. There was no room here for that optimistic kind of exhortation to virtue which Thomas Arnold had practiced at Rugby. Max and Moritz would not have understood the meaning of the term "Christian gentleman."

This kind of satire went hand in hand with a rejection of that pleasure derived solely from things which gave outward pleasure. Ruskin's aphorism, "great art dwells in all that is beautiful," was false; externals were always misleading. That was again confusing matter and substance, and from this a phenomenon already observed in romanticism as well as in expressionism was reinvigorated—the ugly and shocking became the truly beautiful—a conscious transformation of values. Baudelaire maintained that not only must the poet's imagination penetrate the hidden recesses of beauty, the poet must also powerfully evoke the beauty of ugliness and evil which appalled less imaginative minds. While penetrating to the essence of this revolt against positivism, Charles Baudelaire (1821–67) attacked the scientific concept of truth. "Poetry will die if it assimilates itself to science and morality. If it does not have truth as object it is not poetry. Truth can be demonstrated in all sorts of unconventional ways." We are reminded of Chateaubriand's passage upon the superiority of poetry over mathematics as a vehicle of truth. Now this truth was partly enshrined in a transformation of the usual concept of beauty. How two different generations confronted each other over this problem can be demonstrated by Matthew Arnold's comments on the poetry of Giacomo Leopardi. This poet was perhaps the earliest representative of this trend. The concept of ugliness as beauty permeated his poems, and in the end they expressed a kind of nihilism about humanity and the world. Arnold, the product of nineteenth-century romanticism, was shocked. Leopardi concentrated upon the "unhealthy essence, the bitter, unworthy, mystery of things," Arnold claimed. How superior was Wordsworth whose view of life was "healthful and true."

Baudelaire and his contemporaries went beyond the romantic preoccupation with the weird; they exalted the unusual as the essence of things. Swinburne's poem "Before the Crucifix" turns out to be concerned with a gibbet. Themes which society deemed tabu were used, and in the end, their

229

existence freely admitted. Thus Gide's *Immoralist* dealt partly with homosexuality, and Oscar Wilde's homosexuality did not denigrate him in the sight of his friends and admirers, even if it did eventually bring down upon his head the weight of English law. What if that which society called vice was a part of the "sincerity" of which Gide had spoken? The hero of the *Immoralist* was torn between the values of society: rootedness and love for one's wife, and the values which sprang from his own nature—restlessness and love for boys. And those latter values were equated with strength, vigor, and manliness while the conventional values seemed symptomatic of weakness. Marceline understood Michel but rejected his nature. She accused him of liking what is inhuman while Michel admitted "that the worst instincts of every human being appeared to me the sincerest."

But where did all this sincerity lead? In Gide's *Immoralist* it led to a gigantic boredom. "To know how to free oneself is nothing; the arduous thing is to know what to do with one's freedom." He never found out. Part of the difficulty was that nature could never triumph entirely over convention. In Gide, especially with his Huguenot background, the struggle for sincerity ended in frustration. *Strait is the Gate* (1909) was the story of such a conflict—of happiness denied in the name of holiness. Calvinist Christianity triumphed in Alissa over her real nature and feelings. In the end she died holy but forlorn. Alissa was not a hypocrite; she was sincerely devout, but it was a false sincerity, for it was opposed to self-fulfillment. Later, in *The Counterfeiters* (1928), Gide referred to a question which Dostoevsky's Karamazoff had asked—was suicide out of sheer lust for life comprehensible? Gide answered this question in the affirmative. For men like Gide there was no simple retreat to art or to scholarship; the conflict of man and society was always present.

The young Thomas Mann was similarly obsessed. He formulated the problem as the clash between the external demands of society and artistic creativity which stemmed from the individual's inner nature. In *Death in Venice* (1913), a sensitive artist finds strength in his homosexual tendencies, carefully hidden from the Philistine eyes of society. That one could never wholly detach one's private world from an environment in which one was misunderstood—this meant a reemphasis upon a theme first stated by Goethe in *The Sorrows of Young Werther* and further reemphasized by the pessimism of the Expressionists.

The Italian Luigi Pirandello (1867–1936) best summarized the pessimism and despair which these men felt. In his play *Six Characters in Search of an Author* (1920) he presented middle-class people who longed for conventionality but who were in a situation where they had to act unconventionally. The resulting conflict was never resolved; for Pirandello no norm was left by which society might orient itself. Indeed any ordered existence was an impossibility.

The frustration and conflicts which engulfed this group of writers is important beyond the kind of literary merit it gave to their works. This product of the revolt against a positivistic society became the distinguishing feature of a whole class of intellectuals who were the best minds of their respective nations. Concretely, it meant a withdrawal from participation in the concerns of their society. When later in life Gide wrote his *Journals* he expunged from them any reference to contemporary affairs lest they interfere with aesthetic judgments and form. What these intellectuals denied was the importance of drab, everyday political life. Though most despaired of ever attaining it, many idealistically held to a vision of a new society. This idealism was divorced from parliamentary democracy, however. The squabbles of political parties and their humdrum personalities seemed dreary, "external," and conventional. This attitude led such intellectuals into sympathy with totalitarian, if idealistic, concepts of society. Gide, for a time, joined the Communist party, and Benedetto Croce held the Italian Parliament contemptible—he fought fascism only from the moment when it seemed to oppose artistic creativity. Many others, despairing that man's internal conflicts would ever be resolved, doubted that society could be improved or, indeed, that it was worth improving.

The political attitude of these intellectuals was paralleled by a growing realization, on a more popular level, that there were human longings which established society did not satisfy. The feeling, especially strong in Germany, that romanticism had a greater validity than positivism has already been mentioned. Moreover, the racial movements which were gathering strength toward the end of the century symbolized an emotionally-directed undercurrent in much of Europe. The political successes of the Prussian Stoeckers' and the Austrian Luegers' combination of Christianity and race testify to the growing strength of these tendencies among popular aspirations. Though only the First World War brought these trends into prominence, their organization as political faiths, and their survival as such, took place during this period. Haeckel was read side by side with Houston Stewart Chamberlain or de Lagarde. On the nonpolitical level, popular taste had never accepted a positivistic explanation of life and of human emotions. The penny novel in England or the works of Courths-Mahler in Germany provided escape through romantic love, stimulating the heartfelt tears of many a servant girl.

This intellectual atmosphere had another consequence, though its true importance was revealed only after the First World War. A group of men attempted to find the reality behind the myth of the material world in a purely emotional and mystical direction. Where men like Pareto tried to harness emotion for the purposes of government, and all the men discussed saw a conflict between society and sincerity, this group turned to a kind of mysticism. They rejected existing society because it represented progress and therefore a material orientation. Instead they looked back to a past which had not been materialistic, a past whose reality they felt "intuitively." In Munich, Alfred Schuler (1865–1923) thought that conventional progress had led to a dark and evil goal; its course through history had obliterated those antique "times of light" which he himself still felt, and which in his own mind he relived so vividly. As early as 1895 he saw in the swastika a symbol of an era unstained by modern rationality and which, as the ancient sign of the wheel, signified the "open life" recalling a harmonious past. Concentrating around Schuler in Munich and on another group in Vienna, these men rejected modern intellectualism, reason, and progress for an intuitively-felt past. They combined this with anti-Christian ideas, for they felt Christianity had smashed this past in constructing the modern world. Moreover, Christianity sprang from Judaism which, in the name of progress, conspired to defeat the intuitive and harmonious life. Schuler believed himself to be the new embodiment of a never-extinguished ideal of the primitive and Roman past. In Austria, Lanz von Liebenfels founded a new order of Templars to keep the flame alight. He also proclaimed Judaism the enemy, and in his case the Germanic and Aryan past represented true, intuitive reality.

We may smile at Liebenfels's or at Schuler's symbolic mysticism, but these movements, though small and unimportant at the end of the century, had a double significance for the future. First, they supplied one basic element of Adolph Hitler's ideology. Secondly, they exhibited in an exaggerated fashion the lengths to which the revolt against positivism would go.

These men believed that their ideals possessed a tremendous magnetism for the hopeless, rationalistic world of the present, but pessimism seen in men of far greater intellectual stature also contributed to their ideology. Some took to the spiritualism of Madame Blavatsky or to the fad for Oriental sects which promised nirvana from the present. Only one thinker of great importance attempted to break through this pessimistic retreat into mysticism. Friedrich Nietzsche tried to extract from the intellectual atmosphere something positive: to affirm where others had merely despaired, to transform human values where others had either thought this transformation impossible or had looked for it in a revival of a mystical past. While the men already discussed searched for truth, Nietzsche rejected truth itself as a constant: "... *fiat veritas, pereat vita.*"

People were constantly modifying their values. In place of truth there are images only, Nietzsche held. Therefore humanity abandoning itself to the forces of life must be shocked into a conscious self-awareness. "God is dead," and the human situation will not be helped by creating gods in a vain search for security which, because no truth exists, must be artificial. Nietzsche's target was contemporary society. Despite what society believed, "happiness and virtue are no arguments"; they were self-deceptions, for there were also in society "the wicked who are happy and about those the moralists are silent." Many of Nietzsche's writings were given over to the destruction of this false security and its attendant self-deceptions. In reality chaotic man lived in a chaotic universe, and to master this reality man must detach himself from the preconceptions of society, indeed from society itself.

Society was, for Nietzsche, inimical to people; therefore any idea that the individual must lead a socially useful life was also misleading. Above all Christianity, with its tendency toward slave morality, was the enemy. To Nietzsche, slave morality was the idea of service to society and, beyond that, the concept of human equality. Christianity was the forerunner of democracy and thus, by burying man within the group, had defeated man's attempt to deal with the chaos of life. Christianity was the morality of the Old Testament in decay, a morality which Nietzsche saw symbolized in the old patriarchs—autonomous man, wicked and sensual. They were not inhibited and limited by the devouring urge for security. For Nietzsche, however, true man was embodied not so much in the Old Testament as in the classical tradition. He did not want to revive the past as did Schuler and his group; instead Nietzsche chose one part of the classical tradition as the true path for modern man's salvation. The barbarian was the crux of this tradition, for to Nietzsche, he was the true transformer of values.

The phrase "transformation of values" can, however, be misleading, for the barbarian totally discarded the values of society and created his own. Man was, after all, as Nietzsche put it, "suspended in a void." If this were true, how could man cope with his chaotic world? Nietzsche's answer was that man must live both in conflict and in harmony with this world. He must live "cosmically," revering life and life alone, but he must also master the chaos of life. Man could only master the chaos of the world by resisting it. His enemy was the maelstrom into which man was born in hate and violence. But this resistance could only be successful if man accepted life in a void and faced his own nature. Such a new barbarian was beyond good and evil as society had understood them since the victory of Christianity. For resisting meant abandoning yourself to the world, taking risks and making sacrifices. Nietzsche believed, with Darwin, that life was a universal and invisible force. Man must give way to this force if he were to cope with the world. This life force was a positive thing, and to give oneself to it meant the release of all positive passions—"pride, joy, health, sexual love, enmity and war." To accomplish this man needed what Nietzsche called the will to power, for the will to power reinforced man's will to life. Such a man Nietzsche characterized with the Greek term of "Dionysian man," a barbarian who created his own values, since, through his will to power, he entered fully into the force of life, mastering the chaos of the world by affirming it.

Man was at war, perpetually at war, but this war was won through the will for power and through becoming a Dionysian man rather than a bourgeois man. Nietzsche's individualism meant complete alienation from the mass of men. In Zarathustra he portrayed a man determined to convert the world to these ideas. He fails to influence the common people; he fails to form a coterie—only when he goes out into the world alone, by himself, is he the true superman. Nietzsche did come to believe in an elite of supermen, but they were all individuals suspended in the void. At the end of his life, just prior to his insanity, he discovered the incarnation of his barbarian in the Germanic sagas, but nationalism was as foreign to his thought as racism. Anti-Semitism was a feeble expression of the mass instinct for security, and in man's eternal struggle for mastery over chaos nationalism could play no part. Indeed one of his heroes was the Italian Cesare Borgia, not because Borgia unified central Italy, but because he seemed to create his own values.

Nietzsche's rejection of positivism led to an affirmation of life. From this vantage point Nietzsche called upon youth to rid itself of the burden of conventional learning. In his attack upon the German educational system he was at one with the Expressionists and the youth movement. The rote learning of factual knowledge, the idea of knowledge for the sake of knowledge, was sharply rejected. For Nietzsche such education was a part of that fear of life which led to a search for security, part of the instinct of a people whose "nature is still feeble and uncertain." How different this is from Schopenhauer's concept of nirvana or his retreat into scholarship! The will of man which Schopenhauer exalted and feared Nietzsche accepted unquestionably as the true expression of man. His attack on contemporary education inspired the revolt already mentioned, as did his rejection of the bourgeois age in general.

Nietzsche's influence was furthered by another facet of his work. His thought was never entirely clearly stated, for he wrote as if in ecstasy, especially in those passages which described life and its affirmation. As a result later movements tried to capitalize on his name. His sister gave Hitler his walking stick as a symbolic gesture of succession. Yet how Nietzsche would have despised a movement like national socialism, a movement founded on the manipulation of the "herd" which he abhorred! Others tried to use his ideas for national or racial purposes, emphasizing Nietzsche's stress upon ancient times in an attempt to play off the past against the present. But again, Nietzsche's individualism would have been appalled by such a misuse of his ideas. Above all, one group of men saw in him their founder, and this, once more, with only partial justification. These were nihilists who called themselves "revolutionaries without banners," those who despised all ideologies in the name of an undisciplined attempt to fulfill themselves. They will be met after the First World War in the German Free Corps, but, unlike their supposed master, they banded together in groups stressing a leadership principle quite foreign to Nietzsche's thought.

Nietzsche's greatest influence as a catalyst of revolt against the present was a vague one. Reading his ecstatic prose, generations longed somehow to free themselves of conventions and affirm life, to live it at its fullest. He sounded a much clearer call to arms than the tortured Gide or the other groups discussed. Nietzsche had grasped the illness of the times when he wrote that "the inhabitants of this Europe live in the midst of countless uncertainties and contradictions." But his solution was too extreme to produce a school of thought, though it did serve as an inspiration for other revolts against society.

It is useful at this point to contrast Nietzsche with that man who in France came to stand for the change in the spirit of European philosophy, Henri Bergson (1859–1941). The differences between the two men seem to summarize a difference between the temper of thought in Germany and France. Bergson also believed in the primacy of intuition, and in his *Creative Evolution* (1907) he equated this with an *élan vital*. This *élan* was close to the instinct of the animal world; it was a tremendous drive inherent in man which could enable him to overcome all resistance, perhaps even death itself.

Bergson's *élan vital* seems to run parallel to Nietzsche's lust for life. But this is not so, for the French philosopher did not negate the intellect. It led not to a denial but to a deepening of the life spirit. Only through his mental faculties can man comprehend the irrational stream of life. Intuition was redefined as "intellectual sympathy" through which man's mind must learn to grasp fluid concepts—the constantly changing reality as the *élan vital* drives man forward. The faculties of the mind were important to the Frenchman, and he called his ideas "not anti-intellectual but supra-intellectual"; they completed but did not destroy the intellect. Their result was to be a reinvigorating of the human spirit. At the close of his life Bergson intended to join the Catholic faith which seemed to penetrate deeper layers of consciousness with a similar emphasis upon reason (the intellect), as well as upon human spiritualization. The exuberance of the *élan vital* was drowned in both spiritualization and the stress upon the intellect.

This is quite different from Nietzsche. Bergson, for all his drives of the mystical unconscious, could not shake and did not want to shake the strong tradition of rationalism in France, a tradition which hardly existed in Germany and which had, in that country, been almost obliterated by romanticism.

Bergson also shows the strength of Catholic thought in France which retained intellectual vitality despite the rightist stances of the hierarchy. Bergson with his *élan vital* is a part of the changed European intellectual atmosphere, yet in France this change was never to lead to the excesses of a sheer ecstatic or mystical irrationalism like that of Schuler or of Nietzsche himself.

The last years of the century saw a change in the ideological climate of Europe. We have called it the revolt against positivism which became a dissatisfaction with society, an attempt at disassociating reality and materialism. Men tried to look beneath the externals into the depths of their own immaterial and irrational natures. In all of this there was something reminiscent of romanticism which, in reaction to the materialism of the eighteenth century, had attempted to do something of the same sort. In fact, did the specifically romantic impetus extend from the nineteenth into the twentieth century?

# CHAPTER FOURTEEN

# *Romanticism and Idealism Transmitted*

ROMANTICISM BEGAN as a mood which stressed sentiment and feeling; it had centered its attention upon the person as a creative being. Accompanied by an extreme individualism on the one hand, it made an effort to integrate man within the universe or the state on the other hand. Those men who, toward the end of the century, sought beyond positivism for man's own consciousness of himself seemed to share something of this romantic concern for emotion, creativity, and individualism. Yet, by their time, romanticism itself had evolved in a somewhat different direction. Sentiment became confused with sentimentality, and integration with the universe, group, or state tended to replace romantic individualism. Romantic realism, which had been a refreshingly unorthodox force at the beginning of the century, was now in danger of becoming escapist entertainment. Thus, while the romantic impetus was present among those who rejected positivism, romantic realism and individualism were by no means identical with their conflicts and longings. If Richard Wagner is representative of this later romanticism, his break with Nietzsche was indeed symbolic of that disparity in outlook between the two movements, both concerned with man's nature and its fulfillment.

Wagner's romanticism was sentimental. The soul was all-important to him, but he came increasingly to view this soul in terms of Christian love. Lohengrin, Parsifal, and the Flying Dutchman were heroes who had striven for self-realization, a goal only attained through integration with a higher purpose, through Christian love. Indeed, he took as his motto that "all understanding is possible only through love." Wagner, however, shared that pessimism about life so prevalent at the end of the century. True integration through love with a higher purpose could only be achieved in eternity. In this life there was only frustration; death was necessary for self-realization. With the earlier Romantics such a death as that of the young Werther was a tragedy, but with Wagner death became a logical necessity for self-fulfillment. It was the only way to escape human frailties. Thus the Dutchman was doomed from the start. Tannhäuser, an embodiment of human frailty, atoned through Elizabeth's and his own death, while Brünhilde movingly sings of Siegfried's "shining love, laughing death." The very fact that the human frailties condemned were the very ones Nietzsche found necessary for life—lust and joy—illuminates the contrast between Dionysian man and Wagner's hero.

Renunciation of human desires was Wagner's theme. Parsifal possessed titanic powers for resisting temptation, and Lohengrin, in the end, had to renounce earthly happiness. Not only must man fight his inner desires to attain self-realization but the temptation of outward riches and power as well. For Wagner, as for the Romantics in general, materialistic man had lost his "soul." Power itself was derided—"they hurry to their end who boast of such great strength." Siegfried, symbolic of the man of power in the capitalist epoch, lusted after power and riches, that is, the ring and the gold. But he was doomed, for he who possessed the ring and the gold was forever deprived of love. Brünhilde, realizing the nature of Siegfried's dilemma, saw clearly that only in eternity would he become a true hero once more. Death was the answer. Love and power cannot be married, for love means renunciation of power and riches, as well as of human desires. This criticism of materialism would have had the wholehearted approval of the men discussed in the previous chapter. But for Wagner, unlike Gide, holiness was not an illusion but the climax of existence. He would have approved of Alissa's sacrifice in *Strait is the Gate* and not seen it as a denial of human sincerity.

Romanticism in Wagner had lost its earthy element. It was far from Schlegel's *Lucinde*. It had adopted the Christian element within early romanticism and exalted it as an overriding principle. Where the early Romantics saw a constant conflict between human emotions and the environment, Wagner envisioned a solution to the frustrations of this world. Sentiment had become sentimentalized into chivalrous love; a comforting conclusion to the storms and stresses of the world had been gained. Wagner's Christianity, however, was combined with a romantic vision of the past. It was harnessed to the old Germanic legends of the Nibelungenlied. The heroes who knew the true Christian love were the epic figures of Germanic myth. In his essay *What is German* (1865–78) Wagner wrote that to be German was to understand Christianity as a religion of the soul and not of dogma. The characters of the Nibelungen saga could show modern Germans the real meaning of Christianity.

Nationalism, the vision of the past, and Christian sacrifice through love were intermingled in these musical dramas. No wonder that Wagner's son-in-law, Houston Stewart Chamberlain, believed that the prophet of a German, as opposed to an Oriental, Christianity had arrived. The emphasis on the hero meant stressing the leadership principle within Wagner's dramatic framework. Though this hero differed from both Werther and the superman, he had one thing in common with the preoccupation with vice at the end of the century. He derived his strength from his unnatural birth; he was selected in opposition to both human and Divine law. For example, Brünhilde was the child of a union of God and earth, while Siegfried sprang from an incestuous relationship. But this unlawful strength was not used to overcome convention but to reaffirm Christian love and sacrifice. Wagner's romanticism had, after all, become conventional. His Christian, chivalric love, his Germanic religion of the soul, was far from that revolutionary Wagner who had mounted the barricades of Dresden in 1848. This kind of romanticism did not intend a transformation of values. Vice stood at the beginning of the hero's career but not at the end of it.

Moreover, all of this was in danger of becoming sheer entertainment rather than a philosophy of life. Romantic unity was at the heart of Wagner's artistic conceptions and this meant that the staging was an integral part of the whole. Music, mind, and sight must all function simultaneously. At Bayreuth the orchestra was hidden so as not to detract from the effect of the whole. But the spectacular staging did tend to transform the music drama itself into a spectacle. The floating Rhine Maidens, the fire surrounding Bruennhilde, and the whispering forest in *Siegfried* were for Wagner an integral part of his music dramas. In spite of the dangers involved in such staging he may well have been right. The musical dramas were long, and with modern staging, which discounts the urge to the spectacular, they tend, despite the music, to become wearisome.

Wagner's romanticism was one the middle classes could understand. It was not disturbingly revolutionary but soothingly moral. It catered to nationalism and to the longing for group identification. Above all, it put forward a leadership idea: the hero as the redeemer of his people. In Wagner's hands romanticism had become political; indeed, the vision of a Germanic and Christian past offered an escape from the frustrations of the materialistic present. Siegfried, Parsifal, and Lohengrin pointed to a solution of conflicts which later, more sensitive artists like Gide and Mann thought were insoluble.

As one would expect, Wagner's appeal was strongest in the Germanic countries. Napoleon III could not get Wagner accepted in France. As mentioned before, romanticism had deeper roots in Germany than elsewhere, partly because of the strength of the German idealist tradition. Hegel had postulated that the ultimate reality of the universe lay in the "spirit" and "idea" rather than in what appears to our senses to have the attributes of reality. Appealing to that movement which rejected materialism at the end of the century, it was no coincidence that Hegelianism was introduced at this time into Italy by Benedetto Croce and that its role was enhanced in France. In Germany this idealism had always worked hand in hand with a romantic longing for a reality divorced from outward appearances. Though to many his musical dramas represented simply an escape from the dreariness of everyday life, Wagner did satisfy this longing, giving it a definite goal and direction.

The longing for this kind of attitude toward life went deep into the German consciousness and led to a variety of ways of fulfilling it which went beyond the Wagnerian romanticism. Many men came to believe that the process of German unification had been incomplete; to be sure the nation was politically unified, but it still lacked that true attitude toward life which would make it great. Materialism and rationalism threatened all that was German; the need of the hour was to "transform Germans into artists." The man who wrote these lines was Julius Langbehn, whose *Rembrandt as Educator* (1890) was of great influence. An artistic outlook upon the world would result in an all-encompassing national renewal. By an artistic outlook, Langbehn meant a world view whose essence was mystical—a life force dominated the cosmos and that life force sprang from nature. The romantic quest for the genuine led such men back to nature as the source of man's strength, and the stress upon "intuition" and feeling led them toward the mystical.

Only the inner nature of man counted: ". . . it is the soul which builds the body." This soul must be in tune with the life force and thus with nature. A man close to the movement called it the "new romanticism." From the very first this new romanticism had political as well as racial implications. In Langbehn's utopia class distinctions would have little importance, certainly no divisive influence, for all would be united as the "people." He did not desire the abolition of the class structure of society but instead advocated a romantic vision which would unite the *Volk* in an organic state. The organic nature of medieval society, expressed in the loyalty of the knightly gentleman to his king and generalized throughout that society in a web of reciprocal relationships between landlord and peasant, was to be revived once more. Langbehn summed this up: ". . . equality is death, a corporate society is life." The vision of the Middle Ages, so prevalent among Romantics, was resurrected and it gained new strength in the struggle against materialism. Both liberalism and socialism were declared the enemy, for liberalism atomized society into individualism while socialism exalted one class, the workers, above all others. The organic state would recruit everyone into a creative whole.

The ideal of the corporate society which Langbehn exemplified became one of the most important points of attack against liberalism. As mentioned earlier, the Conservatives at the beginning of the nineteenth century had already used the corporate ideal against the egalitarian consequences of the French Revolution and against liberalism as well. It was now used once more and for much the same purpose. Moeller van den Bruck in his *Third Reich* (1923), the most important work of the new German conservatism, attacked liberalism just as Langbehn had done. "Liberalism asserts that everything that it does it does for the people. But it is precisely liberalism which excludes the people and puts man's ego in their place." The corporate theory of the state and of the economy was for him the "German socialism." The ideal of the medieval guilds was put side by side with the "organic" and hierarchical state to form what he called a "socialism of sentiment" rather than the "socialism of reason." Langbehn, and Moeller after him, points to a third way between capitalism (viewed as liberalism) and Marxism. They, in Germany, adopted theories of the state and of the economy which were close to Catholic social and political thought. Various forms of fascism and national socialism, as well, were to adopt this third way of dealing with industrial society.

In Germany Langbehn's ideas of creativity came to be connected with racist ideas. It was the soul which counted, for the soul must express a genuine life force close to nature. These men interpreted this closeness as identical with the far distant, Germanic past. They felt that this past was more genuine than the industrial, materialistic, and positivistic present. In Vienna Guido von List (1848–1919) tried to rediscover this Germanic past through the "intuition" of his soul. Not surprisingly, this was highly congenial to the defensive mood of Germans in the multinational Austrian Empire. It was said that List's re-creation of the German tribal past exalted "holy Vienna" as the cradle of Germanism. In bygone ages the Aryan had ruled and he must rule again—this was the imperative underlying List's writings. Vienna was the cradle of the strong racial impulses infusing the new romanticism. Small wonder that in Vienna the young Adolf Hitler began his racist education.

All this had its absurd side. List believed the tales of an impostor who, as the self-proclaimed last leader of the *Voelsungen*, had related "ancient tribal memories" which confirmed his own researches. The stone of wisdom had come alive. The mysticism of the life spirit led these men to flirt with the occult, and some of their ideas parallel those of spiritualism in a striking manner. What was a fad in the rest of Europe became, in Germany, a serious world view. The life force was interpreted by many of the men associated with the "new romanticism" in spiritualist terms. It was always linked to racial ideas. Wagner's racism and his dislike of Jews are well known, but all these men shared it. The heroes of the Nibelungen saga were Aryan prototypes, while the Jew represented the materialistic element of modern civilization which threatened to drown the German soul. Given such an attitude toward life, it is small wonder that the revival of Gobineau's thought received its impetus from Bayreuth or that Houston Stewart Chamberlain wrote his works in the shadow of Wagner.

Paul de Lagarde was, together with Langbehn, the oracle of this trend of thought. De Lagarde's importance in the development of racial ideas has already been discussed. In pithy, easily remembered phrases, he advocated a return to "sentiment." He also despised industrial society as leading toward a materialism which would ruin the German nation. Instead, de Lagarde advocated a return to the medieval model of the corporate, organic state. But above all, his religious views received widespread acclaim. Like Wagner, he wanted a faith without dogma and without a church. His aim was the creation of a national religion for all Germans. Yet de Lagarde did not reject Christianity. But Christ was not to be confined within the bounds of dogma or a history fossilized in the Bible. History did not stand still, and thus Christianity meant the constant fulfillment of every man through faithfulness to his inner nature. Such fulfillment in turn meant individual integration into both a national religion and the *Volk*. Thus Germans would be spiritualized as Germans. Christianity, divested of the "Jewish poison" of dogmatism and historicism, would be generalized into a German and Aryan inspiration. These religious ideas sparked a new interest in German mystics of the fifteenth and seventeenth centuries like Meister Eckhart and Jakob Boehme. They displayed, for men like de Lagarde, a longing for fulfillment independent of the Bible, combined with a stress on Germany. Alfred Rosenberg, whose *Mythos of the Twentieth Century* (1931) was an important, if confused ideological guide for national socialism, used Eckhart as a central figure in his analysis. The mystic's ideal of freeing the soul from any foreign (that is, earthly) matter was interpreted by Rosenberg as a confession of faith by the *Volk* which found its spirit imprisoned by churches and Jews.

Germans must become artists. The new state of affairs was to be brought about by a leader. Langbehn wrote that "only the will of one individual can help us, not Parliaments or Laws." List talked about the "great one who will come from above," and Langbehn set Rembrandt as an example for future leaders. Thus the great painter was cast as a new prototype of leadership. Such longings for a new Siegfried permeated the movement. He alone could usher in the organic state. Representative government was obviously a liberal illusion, another way to atomize a society which should be organic.

The new romanticism was popularized in various ways. It was institutionalized through the rural boarding school (*Landerziehungsheim*), whose founder, Hermann Lietz (1868–1919), shared these ideas. But above all it was, in large measure, adopted by the German youth movement. The German youth movement set its revolt against society within a romantic context. This movement was to influence not only the generation which saw its birth, but succeeding generations of Germans up to the Second World War. With its new romanticism, the youth movement combined an emphasis on the leadership principle, not on the operatic stage but in real life. It has been pointed out how doctrines of the elite emerged as solutions to the dilemma of an all-engulfing mass society. Now there developed a doctrine not of group but of individual leadership based on what contemporaries called "charisma." This was a Greek word originally meaning the office of teacher, but then translated as the indefinable quality a leader, whose power stemmed neither from hereditary nor institutional right, possessed.

The definitive history of the *Wandervoegel* (Roamers) remains to be written. The movement has attracted more attention among sociologists than among historians. The *Wandervoegel* had their origin in the last decade of the century at the Gymnasium in the Berlin suburb of Steglitz where, for the first time, students were allowed to go on excursions without the supervision or even the participation of teachers. The slogan "Youth Among Itself" was broadened into a rejection of middle-class life and the manners of their elders.

The Gymnasium had provided a humanist education, and from it the concept of "eros" entered the movement at its beginning. The group of young men were bound to each other by the Platonic ideal of friendship. There were no mixed groups of roamers until 1907. This feature of the *Wandervoegel* excited the worst suspicions which were strengthened when a former member, Hans Blueher, the historian of the movement, wrote a special volume on the *Eros of the Roamers* (1913). It would be quite wrong, however, to consider this that retreat into vice common among others who rejected the materialism of the age. There is nothing of Gide's *Immoralist* at the roots of this movement. "Eros" was a central part of Greek culture, something they had been brought up on in school; the bond of male friendship cemented together young men discovering a world closed to their elders.

The world which they discovered was brought to them on their excursions which were the key activity of the Roamers. It was the world of nature conceived in romantic terms and opposed to the artificiality of cities and middle-class mediocrity. Of course this was reminiscent of those early Romantics who idealized the beauties of nature. For these young people this was an inward beauty also—man reacting to nature's genuineness. Simplicity in behavior and dress—the simple *Kluft* and the rucksack—became important. Nature also came to mean specifically the German landscape which they set out to explore, a landscape which held vivid reminders of the past through its ruined castles and the traditional way of life of the country folk. The German past seemed genuine, like nature itself, removed from the artificiality of industrial, middle-class society.

They revived the old folk songs and sang them as they marched along or as they sat around the evening campfire. Thus romanticism became connected both with a love of nature and with an idealized national past. These youth groups held their meetings at places like the Wartburg where the earlier youth movement of the fraternities had also met to dedicate themselves to German unification. But these fraternities had by now become dueling and drinking societies. The Roamers despised them; their world view had a puritan character, they did not duel or drink to excess. Nor was their nationalism at first as virulent as that of the older youth movement. The *Wandervoegel* rediscovered the German countryside and with it felt themselves linked to the German past.

In the cities in between excursions they continued this way of life; they gathered in their "dens" and sang folk songs. There developed an emotional outlook on life which valued the beauty of nature and the deep bonds of personal friendship above the mores of a society which seemed materialistic and therefore despicable. To all this must be added their strongly developed idea of leadership. The leading early personality of the Roamers was Karl Fisher, and the students at Steglitz who followed him were known at first as "Fisher's wild horde." As other branches of the movement were organized the direct relationship between leader and followers was preserved. The leader simply recruited his own followers. What made a leader? He was one of the boys, of the same age and one of the group. In this sense there was a democratic concept of leadership. His charisma consisted in being just a bit superior to the others of his troop. "When we shoot, he scores the most points; when we march his endurance far surpasses ours; when he laughs his example is most infectious, when we talk he talks the best." The leader's charisma required that he must not give himself airs; he talked as an equal with the weakest member of his band. Here was a leadership concept which was based on equality and yet on a difference of accomplishment. It was considered a democratic leadership. The leader was greeted with a revival of the medieval salutation: right arm outstretched and the word *"heil."*

To be sure, this salutation became the national socialist greeting. Indeed the elements of this concept of leadership were a part of the development of modern, totalitarian ideas. As a matter of fact, Fisher himself never got over this leadership experience. When he had outgrown the movement he sought adventure in China. This too became typical—the old boys who never grew up. The movement spread to the universities where, in opposition to the fraternities, the Free German Youth was founded—a name revived by the East German Communist Youth movement of our day.

The early stage of the movement reached a climax in 1913 when diverse groups met on the Meissner Mountain in Saxony. Nationalist overtones were present; the meeting celebrated the one-hundredth anniversary of the battle of Leipzig which had freed Germany from Napoleon. A continuity was thus established with the earlier national youth movement. The proclamation which came out of this rally, however, stressed the element of revolt rather than that of nationalism. Youth was determined to fashion its life on its own initiative. Bourgeois habits and comforts (including drinking) were denounced—all this in the name of sincerity as opposed to artificiality. Grandiosely, the proclamation ended, "truth is our program." The true nature of the gathering at the Meissner Mountain becomes apparent when one considers those men who were instrumental in organizing it. With few exceptions, they were the leaders of the new romanticism. Moreover, all the individual youth movements which attended made separate declarations; ideas of genuineness were mixed with concepts of nature and race. One of the speeches given in this connection restated such preconceptions. It was made by Ludwig Klages, a man intimately associated with the racist, romantic movement. He inveighed against that modern culture which atomized man. Instead man belonged to nature and must return to mother earth; he must return to the genuine, heathen past and reject contemporary Christianity. Only in this way can the "drowning of the soul" be arrested.

Small wonder that the national element of the Roamers gradually became dominant. The claims of historians of the movement, like Blueher, that such nationalism was absent in the pure, romantic, early stages of the movement cannot be maintained. As early as 1902 and 1903 the Roamers were the honored guests of the all-German patriotic organization at their celebration of the Germanic festival of the summer solstice. The celebration of this ancient Germanic rite was to become standard in the new romanticism. Moreover, from the beginning, Roamers read both *voelkisch* and anti-Semitic literature. It is significant that when the Austrian Roamers were founded, their constitution specifically excluded non-Aryans (1911). Here, once more, racial ideas were deepened by the specifically Austrian situation. Just as List tried to recapture holy and Aryan Vienna, so these Roamers took refuge in racial superiority against their minority status as Germans in the multinational Empire. There is, therefore, no doubt that in Germany and Austria the youth movement, if not aggressively patriotic, was filled with a *voelkisch* ethos which, like Langbehn, they combined with the new romanticism. After all, the romanticism of the Roamers worshipped not only nature itself, but the historic landscape: the specifically German nature of its ruins, hills, and valleys. The First World War gave this development its final impetus. When the youth movements met again on the Meissner in 1919 they proclaimed, "We young Germans desire to become individual human beings through the strength of our national spirit." The national spirit was now the "truth"; what had begun as a revolt against society ended up in part as a nationalistic movement. Romanticism became increasingly linked with the historic national spirit. As it became more involved in politics, the movement increasingly fell under adult tutelage. After 1918 most political parties had their youth movements, and in 1933 Adolf Hitler amalgamated all the youth groups into one and organized the whole movement under a Reichs youth leader.

The later history of the Roamers must not obscure their importance for the generations who participated in it. The original spirit remained alive even when politics dominated the majority of the youth groups. Concretely it did emphasize the exploration of nature and the superiority of the simple life. The International Youth Hostel movement (1907) was due to Roamer initiative. More important, it introduced a certain leadership ideal to German youth. Of equal importance was the romantic attitude toward life which was at the root of the movement. To be sure, this attitude was linked with a vision of history and with nationalism, but one should remember that it also rejected existing society and its institutions. This meant political institutions as well as manners and mores. Their revolt and their idea of leadership seemed closer to their own definition of reality. Here again is found that same indifference to existing society and parliamentary government already witnessed in many intellectuals at the end of the nineteenth century. One sought not to improve society but to sweep it aside in a search for beauty, simplicity, and true identity with the nation. The youth movement gave Germans an idealism, a longing which, on a different level, Wagner had satisfied. There is a link between the evolution of romanticism and the Nazi spectacles characterized by a sympathetic English observer as more glorious than the ballet of St. Petersburg. They capitalized on romantic longings by cleverly employing familiar, but awe-inspiring, natural settings, dramatic torchlight processions, and an oratory full of national idealism.

In England and France the youth movement never took hold in this manner. In England the public school set the tone and its kind of morality prized self-control and self-discipline. The Boy Scout movement emphasized both discipline and adult leadership. Liberal morality remained too strong for such romantic self-expression. In France a different tradition blocked its development. Positivism was never as widely rejected as in Germany. The French Impressionists like Cézanne combined a realistic portrayal of nature with an intuitive grasp of nature through man's consciousness of himself. Naturalism made a deeper impression on French painters than on the great German painter Kandinski, who called his craft an "art of the soul." He believed that painting must be as incorporeal as music (1911). The abstract school of painting, in full career in France, rose to dominance there as in Germany. But before the First World War positivistic and naturalistic ideas prevented the kind of romanticism which was expressed in Kandinski's statement.

Nevertheless, French impressionism had evolved from romanticism and it retained an emphasis upon the impressions imprinted on man's soul. Yet such impressions were not advanced with the kind of deep and irrational emotions observed in Germany. Not only were they combined with realism but their artistic expression was allusive, refined, and sensuous. Claude Debussy (1862–1918) provided a contrast to Wagner. Debussy's themes were consciously unhistorical musical impressions. Instead of that heavy, ideologically-oriented romanticism typified by Wagner, Debussy gave his music a realist base overlaid with many isolated romantic impressions. His romanticism worked indirectly and in a most refined way. The same cannot, of course, be said for the music of Richard Wagner. Debussy's was an intellectualized romanticism; so too had Bergson's philosophy concentrated on man's intellect. If France had a "new romanticism" it was expressed in this form or through the subtle search for sincerity in Gide and Proust. It lacked not only the pretentiousness of the German movement but also its political, historical, and racial base. In Western Europe at large the old romanticism had run dry, and only in Germany and Austria was it truly revived once more.

In Italy, for example, Mazzini had been a Romantic and so had the great novelist Manzoni. But the most important novelist of the last third of the century, Carducci, was not a Romanticist. Instead, he tried to imitate classical models. To be sure, these years also marked the climax of the Italian operatic tradition, and Verdi's music was certainly close to the romantic school. His operas were filled also with a glowing Italian patriotism. Nevertheless, there was a world of difference between Verdi's romanticism and that of Wagner. For Verdi, man was at the center of the stage; his interest centered on human character and not on the symbolism and ideological abstractions of the Germans. He could be criticized by Wagner as Berlioz had criticized Rossini: that he laughed too much and that his music was too light and devoid of the ponderous depth of true romanticism. Verdi's operas were folk operas understandable to the common people in their straightforwardness, dramatic content, and character portrayal. They ran parallel to the revival of provincial, folklore literature which came about after Italian unification. A new romanticism, of the German variety, did not become important in Italy—no more so than in France. Wagner's operas were religious rites; Verdi's were accompanied by applause for the singers' artistry as the audience hummed the popular arias which the singers presented. The ideological difference could hardly be greater.

These differences of the other nations from Germany are important; they served to separate Germany from the rest of the West. Not only Wagner but also the youth movement demonstrated the growing isolation of German thought thoroughly imbued with romanticism. Where else but in Germany could one professor, after the Second World War, advocate a revival of the original youth movement in order to secure his nation's future? Similarly, under national socialism, this same Jewish academic believed that the strengthening of a Jewish youth movement might lead the National Socialists to modify their anti-Semitism. Thus even those who had been disliked by the movement from its inception were influenced by its spirit.

No doubt the German idealist tradition encouraged this romantic impetus. Its appeal also reinforced attempts to arrive at the reality hidden beneath the "material" myth. It led in Germany to an even greater differentiation between the natural sciences and the so-called cultural sciences—those concerned with the mind and actions of people and thus not truly scientific. A previous chapter has noted the influence of idealism upon the way historians viewed their craft, how historical data were linked to the cosmic forces which were outside the historical process. Now the historian Wilhelm Dilthey confronted history squarely with the natural sciences. Though the collection of data kept the historian in touch with a certain kind of material reality, yet, to make sense out of this data, he must have something of the "fantasy of the artist." Understanding was only possible through a creative act; history must necessarily be the product of the historian's own consciousness. It could never be scientific or definitive in a Marxian sense, for materialism was excluded from historical truth. Jakob Burckhardt made this quite explicit when he wrote that it is the task of the historian to grasp the "spiritual essence" of an age. With Burckhardt this led, in the end, to a retreat into aestheticism, to an advocacy of a cultural elite, and to a fear that mass society would destroy true values. The external events of an age were merely the expression of an inward spirit. The historian had a specific task which distinguished him from the scientist, and that task was to penetrate beneath the façade of data to the essence of things, a task which depended upon the inner, creative act of the historian himself.

Benedetto Croce transmitted these ideas to Italy. He also felt troubled that the social sciences dealt only with data externally perceived. History, however, was dependent upon internal comprehension; it always filtered through the mind of the historian. It must indeed "vibrate" in his "soul" as he himself relived the events of the past "intuitively." Dilthey, Burckhardt, and Croce were historians of considerable standing. They did not ignore facts but they did reject the idea that history was just an accumulation of facts. J. B. Bury's optimistic nineteenth-century statement that if all the historical facts are assembled they will automatically tell a story seemed to these men superficial. Politics, economics—these were but surface phenomena of a deeper truth which had to be found.

Though historical truth was not necessarily romantic in character, it was idealistic in a Hegelian sense. Like the late Romantics these men brushed aside society as it existed in the name of a "spiritual essence" which lay beneath it. Not only man himself but every historical age had a soul. Thus this idealism shared a mood with the romantic impetus.

It was no coincidence that a man like Burckhardt lived in fear of the democratization of society, that he saw journalists and Jews as harbingers of this new age. Big cities were abhorrent to him, for here art became "nervous" and uprooted. Though neither Croce nor Dilthey shared such opinions, the idealist mood reinforced that emphasis upon national rootedness so prominent in Wagner and the youth movement. This in turn helped to transmit racial thought into the new century. The "genuineness" and "sincerity" of those who were linked in an emotional symbiosis with nature and history as against the materialistic artificiality of the big cities had been a constant theme of racialism. The leadership of a Siegfried or of a Fischer was a Germanic leadership. Houston Stewart Chamberlain and de Lagarde typified the increasing strength and popularity of racial ideas, meshing as they did with the rejection of positivism and with the moods which have been described in this chapter.

The mood connected with the change of the public spirit of Europe seemed to omit any serious consideration of orthodox Christianity. To be sure, many of the men discussed took Christianity and attempted to integrate it with their habits of mind, but these had little connection with historic Christianity itself. Nevertheless, Christianity did exercise a continuous influence from the nineteenth to the twentieth century.

# CHAPTER FIFTEEN

# *Christianity and Society*

ARLY in the century the romantic movement gave impetus to a Christian renaissance and this concern with Christianity remained an important factor throughout the century. Within this Christianity, however, there was a change from a primary concern with liturgy and "beauty" to an increasing preoccupation with the social questions. It has been seen that movements such as the youth movement, indeed the whole attitude of intellectuals toward the end of the century, were in some manner related to the social problems of the age. These movements tried to cope with an emerging mass society by advancing ideas of the hero, of leadership, or by retreating from bleak reality in the name of a revolt against it. Christian thought did confront the problems of society and, in the eventual founding of Christian political parties, attempted to work from within the realities of the contemporary situation.

This was the position of the Catholic church toward the end of the century. It wanted to meet the social, political, and economic problems in a realistic fashion and at the same time to keep Catholic dogma intact. The revolution of 1848 drew the Church into the mainstream of social and political activity, activity that had hitherto been limited to a mere support of restored reactionary regimes. It raised the problem of the Church's attitude toward the new forces of the century. Ultramontanism alone proved impracticable. Could Catholicism ally itself with the Liberals? Lamennais in France and Bishop Ketteler in Germany certainly thought so, and so did Pope Pius IX for a short while. For the first time since the onset of the reaction, the 1848 revolutions bestowed freedom of assembly on all groups, including Catholic groups.

Against this background Ketteler called the first "day of Catholics" in Germany (1848). Ketteler's speech that day was important, for it was meant to signal a change in Catholic thought. Catholics must emerge from their isolated position as collaborators in the reaction and confront the new forces of the age. The problem of labor, above all, was awaiting a Christian solution. Across the border in France Lamennais raised the same call. He added the wish that Catholics might also emerge from their cultural isolation. Why, he asked, can Catholics not write as good literature as Protestants? These men called upon the Church to reject the rigidities inculcated by men like de Maistre, encouraged, to their mind, by the growing force of Thomist scholasticism in the Church. Instead, the Church must relinquish supporting the moribund cause of kingship, face the social question, and align its thought with the new liberal forces of the age. Lamennais and Ketteler were the founders of liberal Catholicism. But what of the separation of state and Church which so many Liberals desired? These men desired a free Church in a free state and for them this implied the state's noninterference in Church matters, including Catholic education. Indeed, the freedom granted the Church was to allow it to solve the outstanding problems of the age in a Christian and Catholic manner. In social policy Ketteler set the tone by emphasizing medieval corporate ideas, and it is not surprising that he first concentrated upon the peasantry, a group, he thought, which reflected all that was good and healthy in society. He hated steam locomotives and factories. Once again, in the Catholic thought of Ketteler, is reflected that glorification of the rooted peasant in an industrial society.

Ketteler changed, however; he organized skilled workers in the Catholic Workers League, the ancestor of the Christian Trade Union movement. His aim was to give the worker status, to inculcate a pride in work as a counterweight to that divisive class consciousness popularized by the Marxists. Instead he envisioned labor as an "estate" in the medieval sense of the word. This became the crux of the Catholic approach to the working classes. The medieval idea of estates was translated into modern terminology. Each profession was considered an estate and would, as such, participate equally in national policy. This corporate ideal was already current in conservative thought, as has been seen, and it was to be adopted by the "new Romantics" as the preceding chapter has shown.

In becoming the crux of Catholic social thought, this ideal was reinforced and gained still wider currency. Indeed, it became a way of looking not only at society but at the state as well. The idea of a corporate society revived in this manner may well have been one of Catholicism's most important contributions to European thought in this period, and therefore something more must be said about it. It provided an alternative for those who deplored both liberalism and socialism.

This concept of social organization was based upon medieval tradition reinvigorated by the romantic movement. It was noted how Conservatives at the beginning of the century believed that feudal techniques could be applied to industrial society. Leo XIII in his encyclical *Rerum Novarum* (1891) clearly tied the past to the present. The ancient workers' guilds had been destroyed; workers were left defenseless before the callousness of employers. It is significant that the pope thought in terms of workers' guilds rather than in terms of an already flourishing trade unionism, for these guilds had been built upon a Christian basis of cooperation which viewed work as a craft and not as merely a necessary means to obtain a livelihood. Leo believed that by placing the workers' associations within this medieval framework the dignity of the laborer as a human being could be emphasized.

Employers must respect the dignity of the laborer as a person and a Christian. Their relationship must be governed by the Christian ideal of justice. This in turn meant that there was an interdependence, based on Christian love, between capital and labor—each had its duties, each required the other. Leo XIII's workingmen's associations were to work for mutual agreement between labor and capital, not for the class struggle. Moreover, they were to be instruments for cooperation among the workers themselves as the craft guilds of a former age had been. Piety and morality must be their foundation, just as Christian charity must govern the behavior of employers.

Thus Catholicism was the cement which would hold the divergent parts of society together. Such a society was arranged for mutual cooperation and here the workingmen's associations fulfilled an important function. The pope sanctioned an idea which has already been found in Ketteler. But the elaboration of this approach to the social problem went further than that. It envisioned a society where all people were organized according to the Christian cooperative principle—the workers as well as all other interest groups. There would then be a corporative society in which the various associations would define their place in the state through Christian principles. This thought must be sharply distinguished from syndicalism, which also predicated a corporate structure for society through the association of interest groups. These interest groups were also defined by their status in the economic structure of the state, but here the similarity ends. For Sorel this was a means to further the class struggle, and the emphasis was upon industrial unions (Syndicats) which would dominate the whole.

Though there was a superficial resemblance between the structure of Catholic corporatism and syndicalism, the basic differences of approach allow for no equation between the two. Catholic corporatism had great appeal: Christian trade unions were based upon it. Again interdenominationalism posed problems. Pius X, always a guardian of dogma, showed himself more of a latitudinarian here. In his encyclical *Singulari Quandam* (1912), better known as the Trade Union encyclical, he allowed inclusive Christian trade unions but made it clear that his sympathies belonged to Catholic unions. Meanwhile, Christian socialist parties like that of Austria flirted with the ideal of Catholic corporatism; it was instituted in that country after 1934. After its defeat by Germany in 1940 Vichy France was to adopt the idea of the corporate state through its Labor charter. Indeed, corporatism became linked with certain forms of fascism, though not necessarily so. The ideal spread outside a strict Catholic framework, though it was always inspired by it. A good summary of the corporative ideal occurs in an Austrian declaration of 1882 signed by both Conservatives and future leaders of Austrian socialism. Artisans and workers were to form vocational organizations, while corporative bodies representing trade, industry, agriculture, and forestry would, together with labor, advise the government on all legislation.

This was not socialism but an alternative to it. Pope Leo XIII saw in socialism the destruction of human dignity and that natural law which justified both the right to private property and the right to family life. Corporatism, however, was also opposed to liberalism, for it advocated the principle of association. The Catholic contribution to the solution of social problems was quite different from that of the Protestants, though the latter joined the Christian trade unions for a while. The medieval tradition could not be a determinant for Protestantism; its concept of social reform was based on a combination of liberalism and social action on behalf of the underprivileged. Liberal Catholics like Ketteler pioneered this corporate idea before it became the official thought of the Church.

The ideals of the liberal Catholics did raise grave problems for the Church, however, even if they gave to it a social policy of its own. In the end Ketteler opted for a socially-minded Christianity based on an alliance of all like-minded men, including Protestants as well as Catholics. Thus the problem of labor would be solved on a Christian basis. For the Church the danger was obvious; such liberalism and this approach to the social question might endanger Catholic dogma. Moreover, Pope Pius IX was returning to the Church's position at the beginning of the century. After his brush with Mazzini in Rome, the pope was convinced that liberalism represented as much of a danger to the Church in his time as the French Revolution had to his predecessors. Thus the *Syllabus of Errors* (1864) condemned Catholic liberalism as an impossibility and sought to tighten the rule of the Church against all heresies. Finally, the Vatican Council (1870) held that *ex cathedra* pronouncements of the pope were "infallible," something to which the Council of Trent had not given its unanimous consent. Even so, in 1870, many German and French bishops left the Council rather than assent. To Liberals, Pius, after having condemned liberalism itself, seemed to emphasize authoritarianism in the Church—and to desire it for secular states as well.

Pius's actions mark the beginning of fluctuating attitudes on the part of the Church which lasted for several decades. Whenever it seemed that Catholicism was accepting unreservedly the forces of the age, the papacy called a halt lest dogma be endangered. Catholic Liberals were opposed by the Jesuits and, on intellectual terms, by a Thomistic scholasticism which tended at first to isolate Catholic intellectuals from the movements agitating their fellowmen. All that Ketteler could do was to walk out of the Vatican Council.

But it was under precisely these circumstances that the first Catholic political party was founded. Ludwig von Gerlach (1795–1877) provided the formula upon which the German Center party was built. Political freedom could only be maintained in connection with Christian authoritarianism. Even here, though, adapting Catholicism to mass society brought dangers. In spite of Christian authoritarianism, which meant Catholicism, the desire for Protestant participation never vanished. It was actually fulfilled in the Netherlands through a combination of Calvinists and Catholics which called itself the Christian coalition. The coalition lasted until the papacy once more called a halt to such developments during the modernist controversy, which will presently be discussed. The value of such a Catholic poliitcal party was shown in Germany. The party's abilities were not only amply demonstrated in the realm of politics but in its confrontation with the problem of labor. It was no coincidence that Bismarck began his campaign against the party with a trumped-up riot directed against those priests who worked among the laboring classes of Berlin (1869.).

The so-called *Kulturkampf* showed that the pressures exerted upon a Catholic political party came not only from Rome but also from the state. This very fight against Bismarck guided the party along more liberal channels than the Christian authoritarianism of Gerlach. It now supported free expression, voting, for example, against Bismarck's antisocialist laws. Leo XIII applauded the party's course of action and gave it a greater freedom from papal control. Yet once more, after Leo's death, the Church attempted to tighten its control over both political parties and Catholic thought in general. Pius X had a saintly but intransigent personality. He believed that liberalism still constituted a menace to the Church, especially in its effect upon Biblical scholarship and the analysis of Church history. There were "Modernists" who wanted to do what Lamennais had advocated earlier: bring Church tradition in line with modern thought. They were especially influenced by Kant, by a rationalism which led them to revise Church history away from anti-Protestant polemics to a "scientific" analysis of the history of the Church in tune with German historical scholarship. This led some of them to question the pope's *ex cathedra* statements in the name of historical tradition. Once more, the introduction of "modern thought" into the Church meant a strong pull toward Christian interdenominationalism. Pius reacted with the syllabus *Lamentability* (1907), excommunicated leading Modernists, and made the clergy swear an anti-modernist oath (1910).

Once again the Church was driven into an intellectual isolation to which was added the confessional isolation of a Center party deprived of the benefits of interdenominationalism. Yet, after Pius's death, the pendulum again swung the other way and Benedict XV gave national, political Catholicism a lasting measure of freedom from Rome (914). In sum, these developments represent a sporadic, though ultimately successful, attempt to soften the rigidity of the post-Napoleonic church. Intellectually, this rigidity was built upon an ultra-montanist view of the papacy supported by the Jesuits and based on a revival of Thomism. Nevertheless, in spite of Pius IX's opposition to Catholic liberalism, what these Liberals had wanted did come to pass. The Church came to be directly involved in social problems, in parliamentarian politics, and in modern thought. The social ideas of Ketteler became, with Leo XIII, those of the Church. The founding of Catholic workers' groups and the advocacy of the corporate state went on throughout the end of the century. Indeed during the twentieth century Catholic social and political theory was to gain even greater prominence and, for example, to find adoption in the Austrian constitution of 1934. Thomistic philosophy, which most of the intellectuals in the nineteenth century had rejected, was, during the next century, to play a part which they could not have foreseen. It became the foundation for ideas of freedom which exercised a good deal of appeal in proportion as the nineteenth-century liberal basis for the maintenance of freedom declined. Thus Catholic ideology played an active part in Europe despite Pius X's objection to modernism or even his opposition to Catholic participation in Italian poltics.

The case of Italy clearly shows the direction which Catholicism took. The papacy was bitterly opposed to the Italian state which had stripped it of its temporal possessions. In unifying Italy, Count Camillo Cavour had attempted to use liberalism in order to win over the supporters of the Church. He had proclaimed as his formula "a free Church in a free state." He accompanied this by an active persecution of bishops, however, and by an extension of the secularist laws of Piedmont to the rest of Italy. This must be seen as part of the background for Pius IX's *Syllabus of Errors,* for such policies deepened the hostility of the Church to both liberalism and the new Italy. That new nation the papacy wanted to ignore.

The Church's official slogan demanded that Italians be "neither voters nor candidates" for political office. Even here though, under Franciscan guidance, an organization was founded which was at first called "Christian Democracy" and then renamed "Catholic Action" (1896). Under this name the movement survives to this day. In accordance with the Church's attitude toward the state, Catholic Action steered clear of politics and concentrated upon infusing the workers and peasant movements with Christianity. It became obvious, however, that in order to fulfill this task the state itself would have to be influenced. The school question involving the Church's control of education was as pressing an issue in Italy as it was all over Western Europe. It led Italian Catholicism to seek closer ties with Italian politics, for parliamentary support on the school question could be decisive. Thus, the Catholic Action began to exert pressure on Italian politics, supporting candidates on the local level.

Though "neither voters nor candidates" had not proved a feasible slogan, it was not until 1919 that Don Luigi Sturzo could found a Catholic political party, the "Partito Populare Italiano." Once again politics was coupled with social concerns. Sturzo envisaged his party as the party of the Christian proletariat. Suppressed by Mussolini, it was revived by de Gasperi after the Second World War under the older name of Christian Democracy. In Italy the Church, despite its enmity to the state, had penetrated national politics through the opening wedge of the social problems and the school question. In France, on the other hand, the Church could never reconcile itself to a hostile state, and here no Catholic political party developed. In France the Church had consistently repudiated republicanism and the revolutionary heritage of the French nation. The liberalism of Lamennais had attempted a reconciliation of the Church and this tradition, but it was defeated as was that of his pupil Montalembert.

This hostility to republicanism and liberalism drove the Church to take a definite stand during the Dreyfus affair. It allied itself with the anti-Dreyfusards, hoping, with them, to defeat the Republic. Priests led the rioting against Jewish shops and houses. The alliance between the Church and the military, both opposed to the Republic, became obvious when the Archbishop of Paris became the patron of a league of anti-Semitic officers and when the Archbishop of Toulouse denounced the campaign waged against military leaders. The Catholic paper *La Croix,* even before this event one of the principal disseminators of racial thought in France, asserted that republics were conspiracies of Jews and Freemasons against Christians. The use of such means to bolster its position is not a glorious chapter in the history of the Church, but as we shall see, Protestants also used such racial ideas when it suited their purpose. The victory of the Dreyfusards, however limited, was a defeat for the Church. Pius X's campaign against the Modernists gave the state its opportunity. When the pope remanded two French bishops to Rome for their modernist view, the French government raised the historic protest of an infringement of Gallican liberties. It considered the Concordat of 1802 broken and proceeded to pass a law which separated Church and state in France in 1905.

This separation had several important consequences. It meant that Church and state were rudely torn apart and this fed bitterness on both sides. In education there had always been, in France, a dual system of Church and state schools, but now the latter schools were strengthened through the completion of a network of free, compulsory, and secular primary and secondary schools. By 1925 over four times as many children went to state schools as attended the schools of the Church. The result was much strife and bitterness between the two systems, especially on the local level. The teachers in the state schools, facing hostility and pressure from the Church, tended to become ever more anticlerical and indeed left wing. They became the constant furtherers of anticlericalism in France.

On the political level the Church was linked to violently pro-Catholic movements which were also anti-Republic and authoritarian. The anti-Dreyfusard atmosphere was kept alive here as many of the bishops and clergy supported groups like the *Action Française* of Charles Maurras. It has been pointed out quite correctly that the separation between Church and state meant the end of the Gallican liberties which had given the state a say in the appointment of bishops. From now on the pope alone controlled the Church in France. But even those popes who wanted the Church to be reconciled to the Republic could not stem the tide of bitterness which remained. When in 1925 the *Action Française* was put on the *Index* many clergy changed their support to even more radical rightist movements.

Yet eventually it was from French Catholicism that the ideal of democracy received new strength. Those who wanted to reconcile the Third Republic and the Church were, at first, rejected. But their leader, Marcel Sagnier, spoke words which were to be heeded: "Catholicism contains the moral and religious forces which democracy needs" (1902). Péguy was to combine the ideals of democratic freedom and Catholicism in a way which appealed to many intellectuals and, after him, Jacques Maritain was to continue this tradition well into the twentieth century. These men put forward their views, however, in opposition to the hierarchy, an opposition which vanished only during and after the Second World War.

It has been necessary to sketch the changing relationship of Church and state, for only in this way can the role which Catholic Christianity played at the turn of the century be understood. Involved in national politics, it brought forth a view of the social problem opposed to both liberalism and socialism. That view was linked to the corporative ideal of society and state. The persistence of ultramontanism, especially under Pius IX and Pius X, enabled the Church to preserve a sharply defined identity of its own in approaching the problems of the new age, even though this meant periods of intellectual and political isolation. To be sure, insistence upon this identity evoked opposition both within and without the Church. The Modernists were excommunicated and the nation state opposed Catholic involvement in its affairs in Germany as well as in Italy and France.

On the popular level, this opposition meant an intensified anticlericalism. The distinction between the Church's visible, hierarchical structure and Christian Catholic dogma had deep historical roots. It was, after all, an ingredient of the Protestant Reformation. Such anticlericalism was perhaps stronger in Italy than elsewhere for here the temporal power of the papacy, its rule of the Papal States, had more often than not been highly unpopular. Roman citizens had often rioted against papal authority to which they had so long been subjected; other Italian cities had frequently, in their history, resisted papal territorial expansion. Moreover, Italian unity had been achieved over the violent objections of the papacy. No wonder the slogan "neither voters nor candidates" never worked, just as in our day the Church's prohibition against communism has been relatively useless in Catholic Italy. Traditionally, Italians made a sharp distinction between Catholic dogma and the politics of the visible Church, but by the end of the nineteenth century this distinction had spread to much of the rest of Europe as well. In France, for example, there were loyal republican and pro-Dreyfusard Catholics who, faithful to dogma, opposed the position of their Church. The tradition of Lamennais and Montalambert was officially condemned, but it lived on nevertheless.

The increasing involvement of the Church in politics and social action meant a corresponding increase of anticlericalism among many Catholics; an ancient historical tradition got a new and important lease on life. Not all Catholics voted for the Catholic political parties, indeed they were a minority among the faithful. It was only in those countries where Catholicism itself was a minority, fighting for its rights, that anticlericalism never took root. Especially in the United States this proved to be the case, for minority status was combined with the problems faced by immigrants. Here, too, the efforts of the Church in the political and social realm were not as clearly defined as they were in Europe. The very depth of European anticlericalism demonstrates that Catholic Christianity possessed a dynamic which had not lost its impetus. The problems of a mass age, of new political systems, were faced, and an attempt was made to solve these problems on a Catholic, Christian basis. Class warfare and individualistic liberalism were both officially rejected in favor of the ideal of a corporate society cemented by a "Christian authoritarianism."

Protestantism also tried to meet these problems of industrial society. It was for them not just a heritage of holiness which for André Gide prevented the true expression of man's nature. Christian socialism throughout the nineteenth century attempted to cope with the social problems of the age. Based on the evangelical revival, this socialism placed its hopes for a better society in a Christian "conversion" of present society. Instead of a corporative ideal, they stressed the application of Christian virtues to individual man in order to provide a fair chance for individual advancement in liberal society. Always combined with this was an ideal of social action. As every individual was a creature of God, no man must oppress another or allow him to live under circumstances amounting to slavery. Such Christian socialism, as seen in a previous chapter, had its home in England, and it was connected with a liberal, individualistic outlook upon the world. Social action and Christian conversion together could reform society.

In England this kind of Christian impetus eventually resulted in opposition to the acquisitive society. Fabian socialism had a strong Christian component. Beatrice Webb, for example, considered the common ownership of the means of production the inescapable outcome of the Christian principle of justice, and of an applied Christian morality. The true dignity of the Christian individual could only flower in the coming of a socialist society which would abolish private property, something sacred under natural law to Catholic reformers. This paralleled the "Marxism of the heart" so important on the Continent. There, men like Ignazio Silone joined the Marxist movement because its goal seemed to correspond to the Christian ideal. This co-mingling of Marxist socialism and the Christian impetus of the century gave this Protestantism a clearly-defined social and political goal. Thus, a Christian transformation of society required for some the abolition of the present order.

Even the Anglican Church was affected by this thought. Gilbert Cope's pamphlet on the *Church and the Working Classes* (1935) tried to make the dogmas of Anglican theology and the goal of a classless society compatible. Indeed, he believed Marxist ideas an extension of true Christian theology, for the mass was both a liturgical act and a symbol of the equality of all Christians at work. Yet, concern with social questions did not have to take a specifically

Marxist direction in order to be critical about the fundamentals of capitalist society. The Oxford World Ecumenical Conference in 1937 exemplified this trend. Summarizing its proceedings, it stated categorically that Christianity was a social faith, that social action was binding on all Christians. The idea of "charity" was condemned, for poverty was the fault of society and not a moral failing of an individual. The liberal view of society was rejected. Both socialism and the acquisitive society were condemned in the name of the Christian principle of justice. Property rights were not absolute but relative.

This criticism of the rights of property was extended at the Anglican Malvern declaration of 1941 inspired by Archbishop William Temple during the crisis of the Second World War. Private ownership of essential resources, it stated, might be an obstacle to human welfare. This declaration is far removed from a reformism centered on the individual—from the nineteenth-century Christian socialism to the advocacy of a basic change in society. Only this would restore Christian justice. It is against this background that the pro-Soviet attitude of Dean Hewlett Johnson of Canterbury or the flying of the red flag from the steeple of the parish church in Thaxsted must be understood. Nor is it beside the point to remember that Archbishop Temple was appointed by a Labor government. Yet, all this represents a tradition of Christianity combined with social radicalism which may still be of importance. Some Protestant churches in the present communist world, like those of Hungary and Czechoslovakia, found this pattern useful.

But this kind of Anglican tradition was secondary to the continued impetus of the less radical "social gospel" which stressed individual conversion and ameliorative social action without the overthrow of existing social or property relationships. In England, after all, the liberal tradition possessed a strength which lasted into the new century. Moreover, the Anglican church was an exception; as a state church it had more actual freedom from state control than Protestant state churches in the rest of Europe. These state churches, however, also tried to solve the problems of the contemporary world through Protestant Christian ideals.

Their approach was that of building a Christian state which would confront its problems in a Christian manner. Perhaps the term "building" is exaggerated, for they accepted the state as it was and sought to influence the course of national policy in a Christian direction. Such state churches combined an authoritarian approach in politics with ideals of social betterment. Typical of these attempts was that of the Prussian court preacher Adolf Stoecker. He formed a political party loyal to the Emperor and dedicated to a Christian authoritarianism, not an authoritarianism exercised by the pope but by the emperor who, as king of Prussia, was also the head of the state church. Stoecker's social program included the establishment of a regular ten-hour working day, progressive income and death taxes, high taxes on luxury goods, as well as reform of the stock exchange. All this would restore Christian justice to the Christian state. It soon became obvious that such a reform program had little appeal to the Prussian working classes who remained loyal to a strong Social Democratic party. Indeed, with the exception of England, this kind of Christian social program aroused no enthusiasm among workers. Social Democratic and Marxist solutions to their problems offered the European worker a more clear-cut goal.

Thus, the kind of Christian action which Stoecker proposed appealed not to workers but to the lower rungs of the middle classes and to the peasants. As time went on, Stoecker increasingly stressed the equalization, not abolition, of property and the idea that this Christian goal could be attained if non-Christians, namely Jews, ceased their speculations on the stock exchange. Anti-Semitism became the center of reform; elimination of Jews from commerce would set all aright and bring justice to Christians. The small middle-class merchant who feared Jewish competition, the peasant who disliked the Jewish cattle dealer, were attracted to such an anti-Semitic program. Thus the Christian impulse toward social reform became interwined with racial ideas and anti-Semitism. In Prussia, however, Stoecker's activities were brought to a halt by that very emperor whom his Christian authoritarianism had exalted. Persuaded by Bismarck that Stoecker was a potential threat to the nation's tranquility, William II dismissed him from his court post in 1889. William, who disliked such political independence as Stoecker's in his court circle, commented that his preacher had ended as all clerics who stick their noses into politics must end. But Stoecker's formula for popularizing Christian action survived its author.

In Catholic Austria Karl Lueger, long the Lord Mayor of Vienna, founded the Christian Social party. He, too, combined social reform and Christian goals with anti-Semitism in a party platform that appealed to the lower classes. Once more the emphasis was put on a more equal distribution of property in the name of Christian social justice, and here Lueger came close in Catholic Austria to adopting the idea of corporatism. Once more it was the non-Christian Jew who was said to conspire to prevent this. We have written about Lueger at greater length in the chapter on racism, but, in this connection, it bears repeating that Adolf Hitler absorbed his anti-Semitic ideas in Lueger's Vienna. Though Hitler admired Lueger for the rest of his life, he realized that the Lord Mayor himself was somewhat cynical about his program. Nevertheless, whether applied cynically or not, this was the successful formula for power used both in Vienna and in Berlin.

Stoecker and Lueger show the Christian impulse at the turn of the century caught up in the racial movements of the age; something similar happened, we know, to French Catholicism at the time of the Dreyfus affair. Thus the unrest, especially on the part of the lower-middle classes, could be captured and channeled in the name of a Christian authoritarianism. In Germany, however, one man made an effort to apply Christianity to the problems of mass society in a more democratic fashion.

Friedrich Naumann (1860–1919) was a liberal who might have been at home in English Christianity but who attempted his reform within the Prussian Church. From 1890 on he organized groups of young Protestant clergymen who pledged to support labor against capital. Naumann believed that Bismarck's social policy had failed and he coupled this with an attack on Bismarck's conservatism for its restriction of political freedom. He looked to the 1848 revolution for his political ideals. In this way Naumann combined political liberalism with the social gospel. Yet he did not do this in the English or American manner, for there was a strong element of nationalism in the German tradition in Naumann's thought. His purpose was to reconcile the worker to the state and thus destroy that class consciousness which saw in the state one of the enemies of the working classes. Naumann was sincere about his social policy and about his liberalism, but both were grounded in a nationalist tradition. For Naumann that tradition was best typified by the Germany of 1848 and not by the Germany of Bismarck. Even in a mass society the state could be maintained and strengthened if the best of the German tradition was combined with political freedom and a greater social equality.

Yet for all of Naumann's attempted combination of liberalism and the national tradition, at times he became obsessed with ideas of national power. When it came to German expansionism at the turn of the century, he gave wholehearted support and seemed to put such imperialism above any Christian concerns. As Naumann himself wrote: "Nothing—but nothing will avail culture and morality in world history if they are not protected and furthered by power! Whoever wants to live must fight."

In the face of such ideas, the ideals of 1848, the liberalism was bound to be jeopardized in the name of national power. There is, therefore, a basic contradiction in Naumann's thought which led him into a contradictory political course. He supported many of the emperors' foreign policies, yet in 1919 he welcomed the young Republic and founded the Democratic party to maintain it. All of his thought was advanced in the name of a Christianity synonymous with freedom and justice. To many contemporaries Naumann's ideology provided an alternative to both socialism and the Bismarckian state—an ideology, again, which called for a liberal Germany that woud dispense a Christian justice to the working man, without, however, overthrowing society or abolishing property relationships. Above all, his ideas reconciled many to the new-born German Republic, and his death in 1919 deprived Germany of a man who might have, had he lived, made a positive contribution to the new German Republic.

Whether this Christian approach to the problems of society and politics could have diverted the course of German authoritarianism is a matter of speculation. With Stoecker and Lueger, Christianity had already allied itself with this movement and this alliance was furthered on another level by the Christian thought of Bismarck himself, for the founder of the Second Empire was a devout Protestant. Yet his Christianity never seemed to interfere with his talent for "real-politics." Bismarck believed that Christianity meant executing one's responsibilities; his own responsibility was that of maintaining the power of the German state. Thus, at times, it became the duty of the Christian to act "unchristianly" in the political realm. Bismarck typifies the division of private and political morality, so much a hallmark of Western history. Moreover, this division was sanctified by Christianity itself. Here again, the Prussian statesman partook of an important tradition in Christian thought.

Bismarck rationalized his kind of Christianity, as had so many statesmen and theologians before him. The world was evil and full of sin; one triumphed over it through courage and a sense of realities. Only in this way could the statesman discharge his God-given responsibility to preserve the state. There can be no connection between the Sermon on the Mount and the reality of politics. One is reminded of the favorable comparison between Machiavelli and Scripture which Cardinal Richelieu made to justify both his faith and his politics, or of the eighteenth-century Calvinist theologian who asserted that "if God sat down with scoundrels even He would have to resort to a lie." Bismarck echoed these sentiments when he maintained that a statesman must "fit himself into the requirements of the state" because of the duty which God had laid upon him.

Thus the Christian impulse became directly connected with national power, and such ideas resounded from the pulpits of the Prussian State church. The Christian ethic was not manifested in outward actions, which could result in resistance to the state; it was a purely inward experience. Expressing this attitude, German boys sang a song from the Thirty Years' War: ". . . what does it matter if my body is imprisoned, if only the spirit is free?" To the peasants of the past the song had revolutionary implications, but for contemporary Germans it commemorated the division between the real world and that inner ethic which did not need outward manifestations. This Christianity was no bar to authoritarianism and no call to social action. It was not until national socialism was upon them that many ministers realized this and supported the fine, if belated, statement at Barmen in 1934. The Prussian church now declared that Christians must obey God rather than man to maintain Christian ethics against totalitarianism. Body and spirit could, after all, not be divorced from one another.

The basic problem facing Protestantism developed from its involvement with the state. Ernst Troeltsch characterized it as a religion more conservative than Christian. In Germany especially, Protestantism tended to become a legitimization of social inequality and this was its meaning for William II when he said that "religion must be conserved for the people." Yet this Christianity did try to face mass society, in Germany with a kind of Christian authoritarianism, in England with a more genuine concern for social equality.

Compared with the beginning of the century, interest in theology declined, for the challenge to Christianity from the new Biblical criticism and from the Young Hegelians was still very much alive. One German writer proclaimed that culture could do nothing better than bury religion among the dusty ledgers of history, and he was not a Socialist. A strong current of Protestant theology was present from the beginning of the century, however, and Biblical criticism was very much a part of it. Friedrich Schleiermacher in his *Speeches on Religion* (1799) had, in contrast to the rationalism of the age, emphasized piety and salvation. He had done so, however, by defining piety as individual self-consciousness of the Divine, not knowledge or deeds. For Schleiermacher the truth or falsehood of the Bible in historical terms was beside the point.

This kind of impetus was furthered by the most famous Lutheran theologian of the late nineteenth century, Albrecht Ritschl (1822–89). With him piety became an ethical imperative centered on the redemptive power of Christ. Though Ritschl did emphasize the New Testament, he eschewed the idea that it was divinely inspired. No theological criticism could touch the person of Christ, however—there was a fundamental difference between a worldly understanding of religion and the insight given by religion itself. Ritschl gave full freedom to higher Biblical criticism for this could not affect the evangelical books of the Bible if they were grasped through an act of religious cognition.

Ritschl's important student Adolf Harnack (1851–1930) attempted to combine such ideas with an emphasis on history and scholarship. These were not beside the point to him; they enabled the Christian to distinguish between the true and the false—the message of Jesus himself and what Paul and the Apostles had interpreted it to mean. What is important for our purposes is that both Ritschl and Harnack, as Schleiermacher before them, rejected a strict theological framework for Protestantism. This liberalism tended to broaden the faith and to support criticism of theology and the Bible from a historical point of view.

Such an approach to Christianity could, and did, at times go to the length not only of rejecting a historical framework as irrelevant to faith but also of seeing in such a framework a hostile force which had perverted the message of Christ. Christ was not the personification of the Divine but merely an ethical imperative. Thus he could become the monopoly of those who were, in their own eyes, the only true ethical people: the Germans or Aryans. De Lagarde advanced such an interpretation of Protestantism, opposing it to the "Jewish poison" of a historically-conceived religion which was the work, not of Christ, but of the Jewish convert (Saul) Paul. Arthur Drews's book, typically enough entitled *The Myth of Christ* (1909), became important to those who opposed traditional Christianity for reasons of race; Christ could never have been a Jew living in Palestine. In such ways this trend of thought integrated Christianity with racial and national ideology.

In art, the image of Christianity tended to the impious, to the view that religion was hypocrisy, a trend which led to a new kind of realism in religious representations contrasting with that of the Romantics. This could also contribute to a return to an older Christian morality, however. For the moment a picture like Max Liebermann's *Twelve-Year-Old Christ in the Temple*, a poorly dressed child standing amidst proletarians and old furniture, created a sensation in 1879. Such paintings protested the appropriation by the wealthy and the state of Christianity. They confronted Christianity with the social problem. Fritz von Uhde's *Christ* is depicted as a helper of the poor and oppressed, an apostle to the laboring man. These paintings were a part of that Christian social consciousness which tried to disentangle the faith from the capitalist state. They are representative of one element in Protestantism, at the turn of the century, which later led many to a Christianized Marxism.

Yet the revival of Christianity in the twentieth century came on a somewhat different basis. The as yet unknown Dane, Soren Kierkegaard, was more typical of this development. Man must learn once more to confront God directly in the dilemmas of his existence; he must go back to the Word and to the God who gave it to him. It follows that any connection between Christianity and external forces should be repudiated. This was to be the doctrine of Karl Barth, so important in the twentieth century.

The great question confronting Christianity in the twentieth century was its attitude toward totalitarian society. How well it did or did not meet the challenge subsequent chapters will show. Christianity was also challenged by competing ideologies, however, as it has always been in modern times. The change in the public spirit of Europe at the turn of the century meant increasing concern with the inward man as a protest against positivism, science, and industrial society. It was not until after the First World War that Christianity ordered itself into this kind of European ethos; it was then that Protestantism was to make an appeal quite different from that discussed in this chapter—not toward the solution of social questions but with the neo-orthodoxy of Karl Barth and his disciples. By that time another movement, also concerned with the "inward man," confronted Christianity—one which, springing out of a scientific context, became a way of penetrating man's being and, beyond this, an explanation of man himself in metaphysical terms.

# CHAPTER SIXTEEN

# Freud and
# Psychoanalysis

THE BEGINNINGS of modern psychoanalysis are a part of that transformation of the European ethos that has been analyzed in earlier chapters. This concern with man's mind as a part of a general reaction against the period's positivism and materialism Stuart Hughes has recently characterized as the "rediscovery of the unconscious." Writers like Proust probed deep in the unconscious and artists like the Expressionists felt they were reproducing the spontaneous emotions of the soul. This atmosphere encouraged a conscious longing for the primitive which was equated with the genuine. Men like the German Langbehn longed for a return to nature, to the Aryan past; Nietzsche exalted the primeval as a principle of life. Assaulting the traditional culture from every side, these longings undermined the supposed security of the great bourgeois age.

Sigmund Freud seemed, on the face of it, diametrically opposed to such a cultural atmosphere. His life was that of a bourgeois of settled habits and enlightened views—enlightened views in an eighteenth-century sense, for the ideology of that age had never vanished from middle-class consciousness. Freud combined a belief in toleration, in rationalism, with a Positivist's faith in the possibility of developing a science of society.

Science woud unlock the door to a better life. What, then, could this dedicated scientist have in common with a cultural atmosphere so opposed to everything he held dear?

In his own emotional outlook he had little in common with the antirationalists until after the First World War. However, there was a growing correspondence between his own thought and that of the antirationalists already discussed. But even before this it was precisely Freud's accomplishment that he emancipated the study of the mind from purely anatomical and physical considerations. With the master himself this made the human mind all the more subject to scientific studies, but with a disciple like Carl Gustav Jung (1875–1961) psychology became entangled with concepts of primitivism and race. After 1918 Freud himself began to isolate the human mind increasingly from factors of environment and, indeed, from the realities of this world. Thus the developing science of psychology was integrated into the cultural atmospheres of Europe before and after the war.

Up to 1918, however, the basis of Freud's examination of the human mind was anchored in the natural sciences. He himself had started upon a medical career and his interests were centered upon clinical neurology. The study of the human brain was not new, though in Freud's youth it was conceived of largely in functional and physiological terms. Such investigations had progressed beyond Franz Gall's phrenology, especially in the direction of anatomical investigations. Thus Broca had discovered the importance of the front lobe of the brain, a dislocation of which would cause severe speech disturbances (1861). From the years 1882–94 Freud developed a different approach to such problems in collaboration with another Viennese doctor, Josef Breuer.

The landmarks in the founding of modern psychoanalysis can be easily discerned. The first breakthrough came with the case of "Anna O," a patient of Breuer's suffering from severe hysteria. This hysteria seemed to vanish after she had, in free association, related some disagreeable events of her youth (1882). This was the beginning of the "talking cure," though it took Freud another decade to rid himself of a reliance upon hypnosis as a method of making patients talk. By then he had discovered the value of uninterrupted free association. This was only a first step, for the question arose why this association was important in the first place. It was this question which led to the greatest discoveries, and it did so because Freud was a rationalist and a positivist at this stage of his development. There must be some reasonable, scientific explanation for this as for all other phenomena in the world. In turn this meant that there must be a determinable cause which produced the effect. There is nothing here about the deep mysteries of the soul, about a cosmic life force and a natural "intuition," only the scientific search for the determinable truth.

The next significant step in Freud's analysis proceeded directly from this attitude which led him to probe deeper into free association. In 1897 he was sure that the stories patients told were simply not true, that they had no relationship to reality. Freud came to realize the importance of fantasies, their origins in childhood, and their intimate relationship to early sexual experience. The main outlines for psychoanalysis were now set and formulated in the most important book of that period of Freud's development, *The Interpretation of Dreams* (finished in 1900). Through scientific observations of many cases Freud had, in his own mind, found the origins of dreams and fantasies in concrete human sexual experiences. This is worth pointing out, for such phenomena had usually been ascribed to folk or racial memories as the brothers Grimm had done with their fairy tales earlier in the century. Freud took dreams and fantasies out of their romantic setting and gave them a determinable, human base—one, moreover, which he thought of as scientific. This was bound to be considered revolutionary by both those concerned with the unfathomable and therefore beautiful depths of the soul as well as by those who held to a liberal morality. It spelled a reversal of the "onslaught of respectability." Moreover, those medical men who thought their function confined to the physical and anatomical part of man's nature also disapproved.

Freud became a lonely figure surrounded by a band of disciples. He seemed overwhelmed as he contemplated the limitless revelations which science might make in exposing the essence of human nature. This could explain why he gave such serious consideration to the ideas of his close friend, the Berlin doctor Wilhelm Fliess. In an attempt to explain scientifically the whole of the cosmos, Fliess related the periodicity of all human activities to the periodicity of women's sexual activities. From this he calculated mathematically when men and women should or should not perform the tasks of life. His work was another attempt to provide scientific certainty in a disorganized world. Freud's temporary acceptance of Fliess's theories illuminates his own scientific insecurity. It was Fliess's growing dogmatism which led to the final break between the two men.

What, then, were Freud's own theories? At the end of his life he set down a short summary in *An Outline of Psychoanalysis* (1940). The point of departure was the relationship between bodily organs (including patterns of behavior) and human consciousness. Older theories had seen a direct relationship between the two, but this Freud rejected. There was a mediating structure which lay between the body and the consciousness. This layer of the "unconscious" was characterized by those special laws which Freud had attempted to grasp scientifically: symbolic expressions and images (fantasies), free flow of sexual energy in its broadest connotation (libido), and, above all, an absence of distinctions between past and present, subject and object, fantasy and reality.

How was this world governed? First, there was the "id," the primary instincts which were inherent in human beings. Second, the "ego," that part of the id which had become organized through adapting to environmental influences, was responsible for self-preservation. The relation of the ego to the id Freud compared to that of a rider to his horse. The ego stood for reason and the id for untrammeled passions. In this analysis the ego was all-important, for as the rider, it had to control the horse. The ego had to maintain an equilibrium between those forces which impinged upon it and threatened its function. Such forces were unpleasure to which anxiety was the response, as well as the instincts which were buried in the id. The ego confronted another danger from the "superego" where parental influences were prolonged. The effects of cultural inhibitants were reinforced, for man spent a long and vital part of his life in childhood. The greatest danger, however, came from the id itself. Its primary instincts expressed the true purpose of life and caused most of the tensions.

The id, too, had a core which Freud thought he had grasped. The libido caused most of the trouble which the id gave to the ego. Sexual drives did not begin in puberty but were an essential part of the primary instincts. This in itself was a revolutionary statement. Educators like Thomas Arnold had believed that sexual drives must be overcome as boys grew to be Christian gentlemen; they were the bad habits of boyhood. Others had followed him in this; throughout the nineteenth century, sexual enlightenment had taken the form of punishing those bad habits overcome by every moral person. Freud made the sexual drives central to man's evolution from the cradle to the grave. Increasingly, he saw the function of the ego as that of defending itself against the id by restraining sexual energy. How did the ego defend itself? The answer to this led directly to the illnesses from which Freud's patients were suffering.

The ego's defense took the form of repression: storing up unpleasant matters in a layer removed from man's consciousness. It sublimated, by deflecting sexual drives toward other aims; it used "narcissism" by directing the libido toward the human being's own ego. The neuroses which resulted from all of this were substitutes for some denied sexual satisfaction, a measure to prevent such satisfaction, or a mixture of the two. Such neuroses usually had their origin in childhood, especially in the sexual attachment to either mother or father. Freud called this the Oedipus complex, after the Greek drama of incest. In modern society these were longings which the ego had to counter and suppress. It was apparent, however, that neuroses could be prevented by simply giving full rein to the id.

Men like Gide and Proust were also concerned with problems of sexual aberrations. For Freud's literary contemporaries such phenomena as homosexuality were regarded either as a revolt against bourgeois conventions or as true expressions of an inner sincerity which must not be repressed. But here again Freud differed; it had to be suppressed. The central function of the ego was, after all, adaptation to the environment. That this was an environment of bourgeois morality Freud accepted without question. His whole effort was designed to effect cures, that is, to produce "normal" reactions to the realities of life. In this he was as far from being a revolutionary as he was in his personal habits or outlook on life. One of his chief ambitions was to be a professor at the University of Vienna, and he was delighted when he finally obtained the title of honorary professor. To be sure, the attempt to gain respectability for psychoanalysis played a part, but it also fitted into his general outlook upon the world. The whole edifice of his theory was built around the conflict of reason (ego) with the passions (id). The passions must be curbed. Erich Fromm has summed this up well: "Freud's psychoanalysis is the attempt to uncover the truth about one's self . . . the aim of the cure is the restoring of health, and the remedies are truth and reason."

Naturally these attitudes determined Freud's view on the nature of human culture. Culture's primary task was to suppress the aggressiveness of man, to help the ego fulfill its function. Extensive controls and restrictions upon sexual life were, therefore, necessary. Once again, Freud fused his discoveries with the dominant morality of his time; there was nothing of the libertine about him. Such restrictions meant, however, a release or diversion of energy into other channels which lead toward cultural creativity. Culture obtained a great part of the mental energy it needed by subtracting it from sexuality, he believed. Civilization thus obtained mastery over the dangerous love of aggression in individuals by enfeebling and disarming it. Freud's scientifically-based view of the eternal struggle between reason and passions became a functional interpretation of culture's ends and means.

Culture, then, was based upon coercion and renunciation. Freud warned against utopias and panaceas because of this. He was close to the Existentialists in his awareness of the tension between man's nature and his existence in the world. Here, too, man might liberate himself by understanding his own aggressiveness and irrationality; he was not the victim of history or of society as Marx had thought, but of his own unconsciousness. Man's condition, however, was not hopeless—his ego could be strengthened, he could be cured through science. Culture was a part of this process. By the First World War Freud's thoughts on culture became more pronounced at the same time that men felt the disillusionment that was sweeping over Europe. He came to see the ego and the id as the life instinct and the death instinct in man, and the death instinct was stronger—a reflection of the war, to be sure—but Freud had always been preoccupied with death, believing that he would die in his fiftieth year.

In *Civilization and its Discontents* (1930) he stressed the aggressiveness of man, *homo homini lupus,* in a manner which would not have occurred earlier in his career. At the same time he demonstrated his increasing disillusionment with democratic principles by emphasizing the necessity of leadership. But the most important change was of a different fashion. The importance of the environment on the mind was increasingly denied. Making social conditions better, changing them, would have little effect upon the state of the human mind. He criticized communism, the abolition of private property, from this point of view. Such an isolation of the mind from other factors had been implicit in the very way in which Freud treated it: as a universe with its own laws. Yet the ego functioned within society, adapted itself. It was not society which was important, however, but the struggle between the ego and the id within the mind. The implications were made explicit. The Oedipus complex and feelings of aggression were important and unrelated to society or culture at large. The result was that his scientific approach became ever more determinist and mechanistic. This was the way the mind worked as a separate mechanism; nothing else mattered.

But coupled with this aggressiveness was a despair about the possibility of firmly knowing anything outside the mind. Science, which would unlock the door to a better world, became a mere hypothesis. It could not lead to a knowledge of the real state of things, as everything must be translated into the language of man's perceptions from which he cannot free himself—". . . reality will forever be unknowable." Perhaps the difficulty was that a man who believed in what he called "passionless science," was suddenly thrown into the chaos of the postwar world. Yet Freud never lost his belief in reason, but its scope had diminished to that of explaining solely the processes of the mind. Even here reason faltered, for from this explanation Freud derived, in the end, his pessimism, his view of man the aggressor, his despair of ever really knowing reality. At this point psychoanalysis came close to being a metaphysic.

Rationalism and science could no longer fathom a world in which the Existentialist Heidegger defined man as ". . . a finite creature, placed between birth and death full of anxiety and guilt." Such people immersed themselves in the irrational and rejected any rational manipulation of it. They accepted it on its own terms. This Freud could not do. He was never a philosopher. He brushed aside Nietzsche, so important for his contemporaries, by saying that "I have never been able to read abstract philosophy." As revealing were his narrow literary tastes, indeed the absence of any real feeling of aesthetic judgment. Literature interested him only insofar as it seemed to pose a psychoanalytical problem. He could not seek escape from postwar chaos through aestheticism or philosophies like existentialism. Yet Freud laid the groundwork for psychoanalysis as a metaphysic, as holding within itself an explanation of the world, as that total cosmology embraced by many of the next generation.

Freud clearly rejected philosophy, but his attitude toward religion was a far more complex thing. He did put up a rival faith—at least many took it as such—but this did not mean that he ignored religion as a force in human affairs, indeed related to his concept of the mind. His analysis of obsessional neuroses was an integral part of this concept. Repressed sexual impulses had to be kept at bay, but the repressing of antisocial impulses was also a definite function of culture. Religion was connected with the latter; Freud saw parallels between the behavior of the obsessional neurotic and such practices as kneeling and praying. Once more he sought the answer to religion in a scientifically-determinable proof. But religion was also connected to the sexual essence of the id. In *Totem and Tabu* (1911–13) he stated it this way: ".... the beginnings of religion, morality and social life meet in the oedipus complex." Freud postulated that when man was little better than the apes, a condition of complete promiscuity existed in which the sons fought and killed their father in order to possess his women.

Again, Freud's religious views were related to a general tendency of his age. Engels, like Freud, was familiar with anthropology and used it in order to prove that the primitive family originated modern property relationships. In a similar fashion Sir James Frazer traced religious ideas back to the primitive customs of the Italians. There was one side of positivistic thought which strikingly paralleled Freud's own ideas. For Darwin himself, human consciousness was a product of biological evolution; to Freud it was a product of the laws of the unconscious which could be determined by science. These alternatives to religious thought have been examined elsewhere, but it must be noted here that through Freud's analysis of religion, psychoanalysis became enmeshed in such positivistic thought. Freud himself pushed this kind of analysis into literary genres such as biography. Leonardo da Vinci's supposed homosexuality was explained through childhood sexual experiences which formed his character (1910). Literary criticism itself became involved. The story "Gravida" by the Dane Wilhelm Jensen was analyzed by Freud who saw repressed childhood memories in the love of an archeologist for a girl represented upon a Greek relief and in his subsequent delusion that she died at Pompeii (1906). Freud thus extended the results of psychoanalysis to religious and literary life. Small wonder that it eventually became a complete cosmology.

Here Freud's onetime friend and pupil Jung was of great importance. Where Freud had been a rationalist to the last, Jung moved in the direction of the neoromantic and irrational movements of his time. Jung came from

Switzerland and, like Freud, from a respectable bourgeois milieu. The life of the middle classes in Basel or Zurich was not so different from that of the same classes in Vienna; such differences cannot have been fundamental enough to produce the break between Freud and Jung. There is little doubt about Jung's brilliance; his early work on the importance of the free association of words confirmed Freud's researches. Indeed Freud called him his "crown prince." But Jung was of an independent mind and given to dogmatism. Moreover his training had not been solely scientific; it had included philosophy and, particularly, the study of archeology. His father had been a pastor of the Swiss Protestant Church and Jung grew up in a morally high-minded atmosphere. Such differences in background led to different emphases in research into the unconscious mind. Jung proceeded to modify Freud's conclusions about the importance of sexual drives to the laws of the mind. In 1912 he wrote his essay on the "Symbols of the Libido" which made sexual ideas merely the symbols of higher strivings. With this he broke with the master who had regarded him as his successor.

What direction did Jung's thought take? This is perhaps best described by the title of a book he published much later, *The Reality of the Soul* (1932). The word soul came to describe the subconscious, and this soul represented the "collective experience" of mankind, of ancestors and peoples. Jung likened this subconscious, this soul, to a sea upon which the ego floated like a ship. The superego was broadened to include ancestors as well as parents. The sexual ingredients of the id and superego were relegated to a relative unimportance. Such a reinterpretation of psychoanalysis reflected Jung's studies of primitive peoples which, in turn, led him to emphasize group consciousness. Freud too, after 1918, had stressed this. With Jung it was not merely a device to restrain man's drives but part of man's soul. Jung called this the herd instinct; it led to man's desire to persecute the stranger, the different, the heretic.

Neuroses were not, therefore, connected so much to sex but to the alienation of man from his soul. The moral factor was central to neurosis. Jung attempted to illustrate this through the story of one of his patients. This man had a neurosis after having been on vacation at the popular Swiss resort of Saint Moritz. The key to his trouble was that a poor teacher who was in love with him had paid for this vacation. The patient's "moral posture" was at fault. Such factors, he charged, Freud had ignored, for they were part of the soul of man. It is not surprising that religion played quite a positive role in such psychoanalysis. It was part of the collective subconscious of man, part of the collective experience of mankind. Jung saw neurosis developing from an attempt to split the unity of the subconscious—it was not possible to dissociate religious and philosophical conviction on the one hand, and political and social concerns on the other. The sickness of his age was, for Jung, the dissociation of the ego and the soul. There was no image here of a rider curbing a horse. The ego must not attempt to split that subconscious which was, on the whole, a good thing and with which man must live in harmony at all times.

Yet Jung believed in great individuals who could emancipate themselves from the herd instinct through "destiny" or the "inner voice." They, like Goethe's Faust, had a private demon within them, but such men were not necessarily doomed. Indeed they are indispensable, for the masses wanted a leader; they longed for a personality of their own, to escape from the collective subconscious. It is significant that Jung cited Mussolini as an example of such leadership. But Jung came ideologically closer to national socialism than to Italian fascism. As he elaborated his theories, the collective subconscious became transformed into a racial unconscious. The collective experiences of mankind which included his ancestors and his peoples were now unified as racial experiences. Not only did Jung's psychoanalysis and racial thought fuse; he himself took over an "Aryanized" psychological journal in national socialist Germany.

No wonder that Jung linked human creativity to a naturalness of man which has not dissociated the ego from the soul. This he found, typically enough, in the life of the peasant "... whose work is so rich and full of change ..." contrasting with that of the town dweller. These he called "modern machines" far removed from the unconscious satisfaction which was the lot of the peasant. Here Jung fused with the glorification of rural life, close to the soil, which was so much a part of the transmission of romanticism from the nineteenth to the twentieth century. Spengler was to deplore in quite similar fashion the "intellect of the City," and in the last stage of its life his "cultural organism" developed into the world city or Megalopolis. Jungian psychology connected with this type of thought. Yet it must be said that at times Jung's closeness to racial thought was tempered by an emphasis on environment. Thus he wrote about the American immigrants who had been bodily and mentally changed by the environment of the New World.

But here again a kind of mysticism intruded. Jung wrote about certain Australian primitives who believed that one could not conquer foreign lands, for in foreign soil lived strange ancestral spirits which would inhabit the newly born. Jung concluded that there is great psychological truth in this legend; the strange land assimilated the conqueror. Jung's influence was great; the idea of the split personality, the moral factors, the collective subconscious all became popular expressions. Jung may have fulfilled a service to psychoanalysis by repulsing the scientific determinism of Freud. In doing so, however, he upset the balance in favor of a racial mysticism which, in turn, derived some scientific respectability through its incorporation in his psycho-analytical theories.

Jung was the most famous of those among Freud's former students and admirers who broke with the master. Alfred Adler (1870–1937) represented another significant development in psychoanalysis, partly because he demon-strated, once more, how much the "passionless science" was a part of the cul-tural atmosphere which surrounded it. This has already been seen reflected in Freud's own development and in Jung's connection with the new Romantics. In a similar manner, Adler reflected Nietzsche's will to power. At first he, too, stressed the sexual factor, connecting feelings of inferiority with the feminine in man's makeup, which was compensated by the masculine "protest." Soon, however, the will for power itself, man's aggressiveness, became the nucleus of his analysis of the mind. Sexual intercourse was not compelled by sexual desire so much as by pure aggressiveness, by man's will to power. Of all the early followers of Freud only Adler took part in political activity. He was an ardent Socialist and therefore took a more positive attitude toward the en-vironment than did Freud or Jung. An individual should be analyzed and understood in terms of his present purposes and life goals rather than in terms of his childhood. Once so understood, the will power could be curbed through a therapy which emphasized social feelings and community interests as life goals.

If Jung departed from Freud toward the mysticism of the soul, Adler traveled in the direction of social consciousness. His was a frontal attack on the master, not just in terms of rejecting the sexual factors but also in denying that the mind was a self-functioning mechanism which had to be adjusted to the environment without being a part of it. The break came a year before that with Jung (1911), and Freud was still bitter when Adler died twenty-six years later. He regarded Adler's theory as a direct attack upon psychoanalysis, and his life-long disciple Ernest Jones brushed off Adler's ideas in his great biography of the master. To be sure, Adler, like Jung, had followers, but above all he bridged the gap between external reality and the mind, for Adler be-lieved that reality structured the all-important internal life goals of the indi-vidual. Belief in the will to power linked Adler not only to Nietzsche but also to Pareto and to those who viewed life in terms of power struggles.

A history of culture cannot treat all the scientific and clinical deviations from Freud; a recent book counts no less than thirty-six of these. What should be noted is that psychoanalysis was involved with the problems of society every step of the way, and that even when it denied such involvement it re-flected widespread attitudes. Not only Adler but Otto Rank as well stressed the actual connection between mental illness and the state of society. The human will was the creative aspect of human personality and it was blocked by the dependency strivings of the individual. Such strivings took the form of a pathological wish to return to the womb. Man sought security in an insecure world. It is small wonder that such a need came to be emphasized by those psychoanalysts writing in the 1930s—a need certainly felt by many as much of Europe was entering upon totalitarian experiments. Erich Fromm stressed the individual's search for meaning in a period when many people found themselves alienated both from their society and their fellows. Self-fulfillment could be achieved either through building a better society or through retreating from freedom into submission to authoritarian society. Fromm reflected that feeling of the atomization of man which had occupied so many minds from the new Romantics to the present time. Increasingly, the most productive psychoanalytical thought involved itself with man's state in existing society.

Both Karen Horney and Fromm believed that man could only develop his personality and obtain true security through a society which was free. By a free society they meant attitudes toward freedom which were positive and institutions which would allow man to participate in his society. They did not believe that solely fundamental social and economic changes could end man's alienation from society and his consequent neuroses. Wilhelm Reich represented a left deviation from psychoanalysis which became revolutionary. He was, in reality, Jung's opposite pole. Reich believed that there must be a revolution of morals and of the economy in order to effect a cure, and that it was not only a specific individual but the vast majority of society who were sick. The clue to this state of affairs was that sexual repression which Freud had tried to cure by adjustment through the ego. For Reich the response to this repression was the building up of an artificial character as armor against sexual drives. In order to free humanity this "moral character" had to be destroyed, and it could only be abolished through sexual liberation. Not adjustment but sex liberation was the cure; education, marriage customs, and morals had to be adjusted to the human sex drives, not the individual to them.

A transformation of all society, not just its moral components, would result from such an adjustment. Men, restored to sexual health and to animal spirits, would no longer be satisfied with the existing economic order. They would balk at doing routine jobs, at obeying imposed authority. Repression was the reason people put up with a society of inequality, with rigid moral laws and irrational political authority. An unrepressed people would change all this. Reich was a Marxist and his psychoanalysis tried to combine that science with a Marxist dynamic. Where Fromm believed that the modern industrial system was basically opposed to irrational authority and thus would lead to a moderate, free society in which the individual is no longer alienated,

Reich came to the opposite conclusion. Industrialism under capitalism was a society built by the repressed personality of basically sick men. Freeing men sexually would change that society. Reich did not mean by sexual freedom un-restrained license, for man so freed would regulate his emotions, use modera-tion in all things, for he was now free from artificially imposed tensions.

All of this is far removed from Jung's "soul" or from Freud's "death wish" which Reich deplored. Reich himself was expelled from the psycho-analytical association (1933) and toward the end of his life became something of a mystic. His particular obsession was connected with the "Orgone box" which was supposed to renew man's sexual potency and thus rid him of his repressions. The psychic energy from the cosmos was supposedly trapped in the walls of the box, and sexual energy was one form of the cosmic psychic energy. But these later developments of Reich's ideas must not obscure his im-portance for the historian of culture. He attempted to transform Freudianism into a creed of social revolution, and he certainly influenced men like Arthur Koestler with whom he, at one point, shared membership in a Communist cell.

Adler, Rank, Horney, and Reich as well as Fromm represented a de-parture from Freud himself, for they espoused a psychoanalysis sensitive to the realities of society. From this point of view Jung was closer to Freud than the others discussed. Psychoanalysis had, through Freud, become a science, but one singularly responsive to the intellectual currents of the age, indeed, mir-roring them in its development.

The influence of this movement was quite enormous. Some of it was by indirection; Jung, as has been noted, tended to support the racial and irrational movements of his times. For many it became as valid as any of the other attempted solutions to the problems of the time—the more so as Freud, by concentrating upon the laws of the mind and questioning ideas about improv-ing society itself, gave his science a metaphysic of its own. Several uses could be made of this—curing the mind would lead to reasonable adjustments to existing society. Society did not need to change but man needed psychoanal-ysis. Especially in the United States this came to have a widespread applica-tion. From another point of view opposite conclusions could be drawn. Jung once likened Freud to Nietzsche as the great destroyer of the Victorian age of sublimation. It was not Freud's intention to destroy the morality in which he had been brought up, but his theories could be used to do just that. Man must get rid of his repressions, and this was taken to mean that sexual and moral restraints (which Freud himself had advocated) must go.

Once again this had little to do with the structure of society or the ame-lioration of social conditions. Frustration and unhappiness were due to sexual repression. A whole body of literature, with the novel in the forefront, took up this theme. Character analysis received a Freudian interpretation. Without doubt this movement did much to change the morality of Europe. Here again psychoanalysis was not unique. Writers like Proust and Gide, imbued with the change of the spirit of Europe at the turn of the century, had already begun the trend. Freudianism became a part, a most important part, of the revolt against bourgeois positivism and morality.

Yet there is one great and important difference between the search for sincerity by writers like André Gide and Freud's psychoanalysis. However much the latter tended to become a metaphysic in the popular mind, it had been shown that the area of the subconscious was large. Science has verified this basic discovery. Though Freud and his disciples may have strayed far from science in subsequent speculations, in the last resort their work was set upon a scientific and not an emotional base. No one could ignore the existence of man's subconscious mind for it had a reality in scientific terms as well as being a part of that change in the public spirit of Europe which rejected science for the "recovery of the unconscious."

The centers of the movement were Vienna, Berlin, and, through Jung, Zurich. It soon spread throughout Europe, however. In England Ernest Jones tried to introduce the movement against great obstacles. Both Freud and Jung had lectured in the United States, and there, too, psychoanalysis soon found a home. By the 1930s New York had replaced the European centers as the movement's focal point.

The spread of national socialism caused this shift in the focal point of psychoanalysis, for it had exiled most of the important personalities of psychoanalysis, who were almost exclusively Jewish. Both Jung and Ernest Jones were the exceptions, and there is little doubt that Jung's growing racialism was bound up with the fact that Freud and his disciples were Jews. It is difficult to explain why psychoanalysis should have been so attractive to Jews in particular. Viennese society, at Freud's level, did not ordinarily mix Jews and Christians, and therefore almost all of Freud's friends were likely to have been Jews, but this explanation is not sufficient. For many Jews of Freud's education and background, Judaism as a religion had little importance; it seemed antiquated in an age of science and assimilation. They searched for new approaches to man, and were thus more open to new ideas than the Christian bourgeoisie. They were especially attracted to ideas which divorced man from a traditional context which Jews, emancipated for barely a century, did not share. This has nothing to do with a special talent for science as is so often asserted without any proof, for young Jewish men were soon to be seen flocking to the banner of the poet Stefan George whose view of humanity had also disentangled itself from the fetters of a historically-oriented traditionalism.

After all, what Jews sought was an emancipation which was more complete than that which nineteenth-century society had given them, and this required a search for alternatives in viewing man and the world.

Psychoanalysis was a part of the preoccupation with consciousness which indicated the change in the public spirit of Europe. By explaining the workings of the human mind it tended to give to the individual a feeling of security. Society might be undergoing rapid change and people might be confused and disoriented, yet this could be remedied. The workings of the mind were known and from out of this knowledge people could overcome their difficulties and arrive at an explanation of life itself. Freud's scientific discoveries had become an ideology, and ideologies were badly needed. For, with the First World War, the certainties of life and of the universe were rapidly dissolving.

# CHAPTER SEVENTEEN

# Dissolving Certainties

*T*HE TRANSITION from the nineteenth to the twentieth century had seen the rise of new syntheses of European thought—new rather in emphasis than in substance. Romanticism inspired much of the change in the dominant European ethos; Christian contributions, too, had their source in nineteenth-century developments. No important ideology is ever entirely new; Freudian psychology, for instance, had ties both with the older positivism and with the new interest in man's unconscious. Moreover, it must be remembered that ideologies like liberalism and Marxism lived on into the twentieth century, Marxism, indeed, with renewed strength. It remained isolated from the change in the public opinion of Europe and we therefore analyzed its growth up to the First World War in the chapters dealing with its origins in the last century. Yet even here the "Marxists of the heart" were inspired by a new romantic impetus.

The First World War was one of the great cataclysms of Europe which divided one epoch from another. Yet this was not quite so, for the change in the public opinion of Europe was a more important dividing point. The First World War completed a process started much earlier; it opened the doors wide for the dominance of those habits of mind discussed in the last chapters. Certainties were vanishing on all sides, and here the changes in science went hand in hand with those produced by the war itself. The result was a deepening search for roots, for authorities, and for some hope which might lie beneath the realities of events. Liberalism and the bourgeois age were shaken to their foundations, but they had been eroded before the war ever started. It will be well to illustrate this through the social scene by taking another look at the life of the bourgeois classes before the war. Just how secure was this life in the minds of those who lived it and in actual economic fact? After such an examination the vanishing certainties will be seen more easily through war and through the direction of science.

Today life before the war seems almost unreal; for some, it represents a golden age of security and freedom from fear. From the standpoint of the upper bourgeoisie it was indeed an age of comfort. The massive, bulky furniture enjoying a vogue then symbolized something of this feeling of permanence, as did the social life of the wealthy with large and elaborate dinners where much the same people met each other in an unending round. A life without servants could hardly be imagined, even for the less affluent middle classes—to have a good cook was the epitome of a housewife's desires.

Middle-class tastes were both eclectic and conservative. Throughout Europe both the houses of the rich and public buildings imitated Greek and Roman styles. In Berlin buildings like the National Museum attempted to re-create the style of Greek temples, and in England, where the Gothic impetus was still strong, the railway stations resembled either Greek temples or Gothic cathedrals. Bourgeois taste craved for identification with the past, just as the newly-grown cities identified themselves with the traditions of a more glorious municipal past. The popular style of painting also evidenced this longing for historical continuity. Historical and mythical themes were part of that patrician culture that the *nouveaux* desired to claim as their own.

In Germany it became the fashion toward the end of the century to paint prosperous businessmen in Renaissance costumes. This urge toward historical identification was epitomized by the German architect Gottfried Semper (1803–79). The style of every building was to be determined through its historical association. A barracks must be built like a medieval fortress, the city hall like the Doge's palace in Venice, and every house should have a "Renaissance room" and a "Gothic room" as well. Unfortunately this did not remain theory. Nothing in this monumental art's classical and historical allusions reminded the beholder that he lived in a world of rapid industrialization. The realist and naturalist literature of the period had no popularity in bourgeois homes and its ideas were not used to decorate public buildings and monuments. As seen earlier, it was against such tastes that the *Art Nouveau* rebelled. This new style did come to rival in popularity the historical and romanticized art forms. Yet, in turn, the "new art" became fanciful as well as escapist, and this may have accounted for its considerable vogue among the bourgeoisie. By idealizing their existence, such classes were retreating from the problems of the present.

France constituted an important exception to this. The realism so much a part of novelists like Zola and painters like Honoré Daumier never ceased to appeal. The rationalist tradition continued to assert itself throughout the century. Charles Morazé neatly illustrated the force of this tradition when he contrasted the imperial eagles of the First and Second Empires. Napoleon I's eagle was copied from a heraldic tradition, Napoleon III's from an actual example in the botanical gardens. For generations the German bourgeoisie listened religiously to the music dramas of Richard Wagner; in France Wagner was a failure. Even a philosopher like Bergson, whom the Germans saw as a congenial example of the rejection of science and positivism, would not have agreed with this use of his ideas. His intuition was meant to be an addition to science, not its replacement. After the First World War the tradition of rationalism remained alive in France when in other parts of Europe men thought that they now faced the "end of reality."

The gap between the life-style of the middle classes and reality was clearly visible, not only to historians equipped with hindsight but to contemporary observers. The very drive for historical identification symbolized an uneasy awareness of this, as did the drive to penetrate outward reality. The popularity of the new romanticism and idealism has already been discussed. This search was coupled with attempts to escape from the hypocrisies and rigidities of bourgeois life. In France writers like Proust and Gide typified this, and in Germany the children of bourgeois parents sought to escape the youth movement. There was ample reason for this feeling of insecurity amidst opulence.

In the last decades of the century the whole European economy was undergoing change. Big business and big banking were squeezing the smaller entrepreneur to death. These were the decades when industrial dynasties like the Krupp family in Germany came into their own. Large banks not only controlled smaller banking establishments but also utilities and far-flung raw materials. Indeed, Lenin had called the tendency toward the concentration of capital both capitalism's apotheosis and a sure sign of its coming destruction. The bourgeoisie which could no longer compete was hard pressed. We have seen how it rallied, not to socialism, but to the Christian socialist parties of Stoecker in Germany and Lueger in Austria. For certain segments of the economy this development meant increased state interference. Railways were being constructed at an accelerated rate and private enterprise did not find them profitable enough for investment. Thus, in Germany, Prussia controlled three-quarters of the railway mileage, and in France the Western Railroad was nationalized in 1909. The liberal ideal was being sapped by economic necessity.

The workers were organizing in all European countries and everywhere socialist parties were successful. At the same time, mechanization created unrest and unemployment among the workers, especially in the textile industries. Gerhart Hauptmann's famous play, *The Weavers* (1892), was set in the 1840s and portrayed poverty which still existed among weavers in his lifetime. The workers did not organize quietly; each crisis brought a new outburst of unrest. Emperor William II was nearly blown up by a bomb in 1889 and the French Chamber of Deputies had a similar narrow escape in 1898, while King Humbert I of Italy was assassinated in 1900 and President Carnot of France in 1894. Though these anarchist deeds were condemned by the Second International, they forcibly reminded the propertied classes of the dissatisfaction among the masses which would stop at nothing.

The monopoly of the bourgeoisie was challenged in another area as well: that of education. From 1870 on there was a general debate in Europe about the necessity of extending and reorienting the educational system.

Compulsory elementary education was introduced all over western Europe. England was the first to initiate such legislation (1870), and France the last (1882). Ending, in general, with the pupil's tenth year, compulsory education was distinct from the better private schools which insured admission to expensive secondary schools. Nevertheless, almost the entire population of the West was taught reading and writing with considerable effect upon the literacy rate of each nation.

Moreover, industrial society demanded more technicians, engineers, and managers, and they could only be recruited from those classes hitherto excluded from higher education. In Germany educational innovations had advanced beyond the rest of continental Europe, while in France they lagged far behind. French higher education was fragmented in specialized professional schools while the lycée remained oriented toward a classical and literary curriculum. However, change was apparent—the École Polytechnique was established earlier in order to train scientists and engineers.

England established such a specialized institution by founding Imperial College at Kensington. Yet in England as in all of Europe there was a general resistance to such new developments. A classical education was a mark of status, and many of the best minds refused to study scientific or technical subjects. The change had to come from those excluded from such an education earlier, and here England made the greatest strides. Oxford and Cambridge lost their academic monopoly after 1870, and the provincial universities were allowed a greater amount of freedom. Many of them began to emphasize science, which the older universities were reluctant to do. Yet a worker's child could hardly take advantage of the new educational opportunities; he had to earn a living. This problem was not really attacked until after the Second World War, but in the 1880s and 1890s a new departure was made.

The role workingmen's colleges played in the liberal scheme of things has already been observed. Men like Thomas Hughes proselytized the workers with the doctrine of the "manliness of Christ" so that they, too, might rise in the social scale through strength of character. But in the 1880s the University of Cambridge began a university extension movement which prepared the worker and lower-class student for eventual entrance into the university itself. In France and Belgium the *universités populaires* brought knowledge to men and women who could not afford an education. In this manner the educational status of the bourgeoisie as a class was undermined partly by the need for trained industrial personnel and partly through a diffusion of knowledge by university extension movements. The change in the economic system, the growing strength and unrest of the working classes, and, at the same time, the spread of education—all this contributed to the insecurity felt by the middle classes. The age of comfort reflected in what Harold Nicolson has called the "sedative benevolence" of the bourgeoisie was, in reality, the beginning of an age of insecurity.

From a purely physical standpoint, however, life was becoming more secure. The nineteenth century saw a rapid advance in medicine well above the accomplishments of any previous age. Theoretical accomplishments, like the description of diseases and the perfection of medical statistics in France by Alexandre Louis (1787–1872), were the first to appear. The tangible benefits of medical research became obvious in the last decades of the age. Anesthesia was certainly a blessing for the patient and so was the introduction of the antiseptic principle in surgery (1867). Perhaps the most signal and important advances were the new emphases upon hygiene and cleanliness (pioneered by Pasteur and Lister) and the discovery of the contagious nature of puerperal fever. Through this discovery, Semmelweiss in Vienna (1847) eliminated the greatest hazard of childbirth. To these very selective examples must be added the improvements in nursing care associated with Florence Nightingale's work in the Crimean War.

Advances in public hygiene paced those made in personal hygiene. The renovation of Paris which Baron Haussmann undertook for Napoleon III involved an improvement of its sewer system, eliminating the sewer stench of the Seine which, prior to this, had plagued the whole city. Similarly, London obtained a new drainage system finished in the same year as that of Paris (1865). For centuries members of Parliament had with difficulty conducted their business amidst the odors that wafted up from the Thames. It was no coincidence that death rates in both cities declined after such a change. Personal hygiene's greater emphasis upon cleanliness triumphed over popular prejudices. The bathtub was introduced as a household fixture during the century. As late as 1782, one manual still advised against washing the face in water for this was bad for the skin, and in the new century a candidate had been refused admission to the ministry in Germany because he bathed too often.

All this began to change. Among those classes who could afford it, it became good form to be clean. Fresh air was no longer considered detrimental to health and open air sports became popular, including skiing and hiking. Resorts like Saint Moritz in Switzerland became the rendezvous of fashionable society. The love of the open air did not, of course, infringe upon that decency which bourgeois morality still held sacred. Yet the new Parisian fashions of the last decades of the century did try to break with that complete disguisement of the female body which the century thought "modest" (and which can still be seen in the uniform of English schoolgirls). Dresses hung from the neck to the feet but they did attempt to follow the contours of the body—a mild protest against the dominant morality. Yet as we penetrate below the morality of the bourgeois classes, the gap which divided them from the mass of the population once more becomes apparent.

Women of the poorer classes were driven into prostitution, and the statistics tell the same tale for Victorian England as for the rest of Europe. In Berlin, a middle-sized city, there were 20,000 prostitutes. In Munich nearly 50 percent of the births between 1854 and 1864 were illegitimate and similar figures could be given for other cities as well. The rise of criminality was rapid throughout the century, largely due to the cheap alcoholic beverages with which the poor consoled themselves. No doubt the rapid urbanization of Europe was, at least, partly responsible for this. Though in England this process was more rapid than elsewhere, by the end of the century Germany was catching up, and this in a precipitate manner. Between 1871 and 1877 urbanization had progressed from a rural-urban ratio of 64 to 35 to a ratio of 2 to 3.

The great medical and hygienic advances of the century had no real effect upon the insecurity felt by the possessing classes. In Germany these feelings were not allayed by Bismarck's social insurance scheme which made these medical advances available to all classes of Germans, despite the fact that in no other country did the masses enjoy such benefits. Greater physical security and hygienic advances did not markedly affect habits of mind—certainly not among the bourgeoisie.

Yet there was one class in Europe which still seemed to feel itself secure. European royalty was a close and insular society living in virtual isolation from their subjects, except in public functions and on ceremonial occasions. Though many had lost their authority, historians have written them off too lightly as a force in events. Queen Victoria was, of course, an exception to this, but her popularity was not due to the fact that she understood the forces of her age, and this can also be said of that esteem given her equally long-lived colleague, Francis Joseph of Austria. Both were symbols of security. The effect of supranational family relationships on Victoria and her son are worth noting. The Queen did not hesitate to pass on matters of state to her uncle, King Leopold of Belgium, and later, family concerns often swayed her political judgment. The same was true for the Austrian emperor and the minor princelings of Europe—all related to one another or to Queen Victoria. It was a closed society living in its own circle without much outside contact. It has been said quite rightly that even someone endowed with a social conscience like Queen Mary, the wife of King George V of England, could never grasp what socialism was all about except that it was somehow evil.

The bourgeoisie lived in a similarly closed society and one in which rank again played an important part. Titles and professions were graded according to their distinction; a judge was obviously better than a mere lawyer, and those shopkeepers subject to the public's whim were the lowest of the low. One circulated within a circle of acquaintances and relations. It was difficult for any stranger to gain admittance. Though "polite" society had always been organized into small, discrete, and insular groups, by the end of the century among both the aristocracy and the bourgeoisie the membership of these groups had become static and frozen. It was a comfortable existence but also a sheltered one. It is worth remembering that in 1850 domestic servants formed the largest occupational group in London. Only a few European cities had a larger population than the 121,000 London domestics. Yet, fears and insecurities could not be laid to rest; even in Victorian England they were but thinly disguised. This can be illustrated not only through those who openly revolted against society but by the fact that society itself adhered to the new romanticism, the nationalism, and the racism of the period. The new forces of the age were incomprehensible and evil. They sought security in those movements which stressed the maintenance of some kind of historical tradition.

Unlike those who had been squeezed out by economic change, the economically secure middle classes, whose mode of life was described above, deplored violence and "upsets." They did not want to lead the people but wanted to be left alone by them. Movements like the Christian social parties were without appeal. But in a more genteel fashion they also supported movements like racism and romanticism whose underlying implications would have shocked and horrified them. With the First World War the life they had built up for themselves came crashing down. The economic situation after the war no longer allowed them to ignore the demands of the dispossessed. The revolution of 1848 and the Paris Commune which frightened these classes were still considered temporary interruptions of an otherwise great tranquility. The chronic, violent unrest of the postwar era, however, assumed a terrifying air of permanence. The war itself smashed not only the concept but even the desire for the sedate life of an elder generation, a life which was secure only on the surface of events.

Life in the trenches of Flanders led a whole generation to question their ideological heritage. What remained? Marxism emerged strengthened in spite of the fact that Social Democrats in all countries had joined the war effort. But the Russian revolution and the longing for a new, better, and different society gave Marxism added strength. Liberalism was most badly damaged by the war. The idea of progress, of individualism, and of advancement through morality seemed outdated; this was no time for optimists. The economic crises of the postwar world completed what the war had begun. In the last resort liberalism was too closely associated with an outmoded society, a society which had not prevented war but had slid into it. Liberalism was in rapid decline as an important and dynamic ideology; it survived as an ideal in the minds of intellectuals concerned with freedom. Indeed, the great question which intellectuals asked themselves when the war was over concerned the problem of whether freedom, in the liberal sense of the word, could survive without the rest of the liberal credo.

Liberalism's decline posed a serious problem to all those concerned with individual freedom. Not only had Marxism emerged strengthened from the cataclysm but the search for the unconscious had also survived; indeed it dominated much of European thought. Though the change in the European ethos came at the turn of the century, the war gave a great impetus to ideologies founded upon irrational premises. Reality was, after all, far from pleasant, and the idea that the truth was hidden in man's own emotions gave a new meaning to life amidst the ruins of war. Coupled with this trend, another attitude gained prominence. The only reality was existence itself, and all ideological speculation was beside the point. Ideas similar to those of Nietzsche gained popularity. What were hopes for the future in comparison with life in the trenches? The only reality there had been survival; the individual was thrown back upon the primacy of his very existence in a hostile cosmos.

For many, the only alternatives were either Marxism or the new romanticism and nihilism. Upon the latter attitudes toward life the emerging totalitarian society could and did build its ideological structure. Caught in the middle were the intellectuals concerned with freedom. These are the complex themes which the following chapters will analyze.

The interplay of these themes must be seen against a background of a still further dissolution of certainties during the postwar age. Egon Friedell (1878–1938), who wrote his *Cultural History of Modern Times* (1927–32) in these same years, termed the contemporary epoch "the end of reality." Nothing had a real meaning any longer; nothing was certain. The cosmos itself was enveloped in the greatest uncertainty. On the one hand science had shown that in its totality the cosmos stretched into infinity; on the other, the very stuff of the universe, atoms, were too minute to be seen by man. Stars were no longer fixed in the universe; instead they raced through it at a speed of hundreds of miles a minute, while the only way to grasp the nature of an atom was through an abstract mathematical formula. Here there could be no reality, no fixed point from which man could understand the cosmos in which he lived. For Friedell, as for many other thoughtful men, the new discoveries of science emphasized an uncertainty which permeated the human condition of postwar man and which, in turn, strengthened the dominant ideologies mentioned. Positivism in its nineteenth-century form suffered the same fate as liberalism, not through the war but by the very progress of science. Positivism appealed still less to postwar man than to the antipositivist rebels of the turn of the century. The decline of positivism was thus one more factor strengthening nihilistic and neoromantic thought.

Not only was the cosmos relativized through science; time itself lost its fixed nature. Albert Einstein's theory of relativity (1916) maintained that time depended on the location of the beholder. The concept of space also was revolutionized by Einstein's findings. No more than time could it be divorced from the consciousness of man, no more indeed than shape, size, or color. Neither time nor space had any determinable reality. Together they constituted a fourth dimension which Einstein postulated in a mathematical formula. Not time and space but the speed of light was the only constant in Einstein's theory. For him, nature operated upon a mathematical principle, a natural law which could be discovered through the solution of mathematical equations.

For the nonscientist, the theory of relativity meant that what had been thought of as constants within the universe were now beyond comprehension. The more so as Einstein, and indeed modern physics in general, destroyed the basic belief in the orderly sequence of cause and effect. Werner Heisenberg proved by 1927 that small particles did not conform to the cause and effect sequence. If the universe did not conform to causal laws, what was the use of prediction, attempting to determine its future course on the basis of the scientific method as the Positivists had tried to do? The new physicists believed that no causal theory could predict without doing violence to their own recent discoveries. Yet it was only in Germany that scientists themselves rejected the validity of causality and with it the ideas of fixed natural laws. They took such a position not only because of problems which they faced as physicists or mathematicians, but also because they confronted an intellectual atmosphere saturated with a distrust of reason. Scientists were always influenced by the world around them, but after 1918 in Germany many capitulated to those who accused them of destroying the human soul, and to this accusation they sacrificed the concept of lawfulness on behalf of the idea of freedom, spontaneity and the will of a higher power.

The revolution in modern physics has been defined by J. Bronowski as the replacement of the concept of the inevitable effect by that of the probable trend. The positivism of the last century believed in inevitable effects, in fixed natural laws which, once discovered, would inevitably lead to causal relationships which could then be applied to society. Modern physics rendered this obsolete. Its own relativism paralleled the emphasis upon uncertainty within contemporary thought, and the impossibility of defining precise causal relationships corresponded to an approach toward the future for which science could give no prophetic evidence. Here again irrationalism was strengthened indirectly for men did want to prophesy the glorious future which would emerge from the chaos of the present. Yet it must be remembered that science as a guide for society had never gained general acceptance during the nineteenth century. Science had been used as a court of appeal, as a slogan which denoted "truth," but even this was difficult to maintain with the new direction which science was taking.

The Newtonian universe of the seventeenth century had led to ideologies based upon it in the eighteenth and nineteenth centuries. It was difficult, if not impossible, to build a consistent ideology upon the new scientific developments. Not only had inevitability given place to probability, the very unity of the universe seemed fragmented. Max Planck's Quantum Theory (1900) went far toward destroying Newton's world machine. Energy was not a continuous stream but consisted instead of discrete units which he called quanta. To the layman this meant a further disorientation of what had been a harmonious universe.

There were philosophers who did try to build an ideological system upon these new advances, but their influence was slight, except in certain academic circles. It was slight, not merely because the new physics denied them the necessary ingredient of all ideologies—inevitability—but also because they sought to stem the tide which attracted men to ideologies. Surrounded by a Vienna torn with ideological rivalries, Rudolf Carnap (1891–1970) attempted to counter them by trying to define truth. However, it was common that ideas of truth varied widely according to what world view men embraced. Desiring to stop this "vanity of dogmatizing," Carnap analyzed language; truth had to be defined through the actual meaning which sentences, the means of communication in language, possessed. He came to the conclusion that there could be only two kinds of sentences: factual, describing the things observed, and linguistic, formulating a rule about language itself. Though there could be sentences with social or psychological content, they did not express thought but commands to action. Logical positivism thus denied truth to any system of thought which was also a world view. As far as determinable truth was concerned, ethical and social problems were beside the point and so were formulations about future utopias.

The intention of Carnap and his disciples was to show where truth could lie and to demonstrate the relativity of all ideological speculation. It is significant that this Viennese school gained its widest popularity in England and the United States, nations which had strong pragmatist traditions. For most Europeans it seemed to remove philosophy from any relevance to problems of society, if only because of its penchant for mathematical formulas. Logical positivism did, however, consider itself relevant to society and, especially in England, it still thinks itself so. Nevertheless men would not deny ideological commitments embodying, for them, the one and only truth; they would not circumscribe the limits of truth after the Logical Positivists' pattern. We are still in an age when Europeans needed an "enthusiasm" and ideology to live by. Social and economic chaos only intensified this longing.

Logical Positivists could not apply their methodology to the problems of European life in a manner which would remove man's need for ideology—even the warring ideologies of the postwar era. Scientists themselves did not attempt it. They tended to see themselves as mere reporters of scientific observations. For Newton, science had been at the same time a philosophy of life, a consistent world view; modern scientists not only destroyed his concept of the universe but also his linkage of ideology and science. What was left is an important paradox. Science itself rejected determinism, while scientists seemed to become ever more factually deterministic in their outlook as did the philosophy based on this science. As their determinism could no longer embrace the universe as a knowable truth, however, they became ever more limited in their thought about the world. For Logical Positivists, ethical and social problems, as defined by ideology, were not susceptible to scientific solutions.

Not only did this approach divorce science from ideology, strengthening unscientific, irrational ideologies; it resulted in another important phenomenon. Scientists themselves supported and sometimes ardently believed in irrational or nihilistic totalitarian ideologies. German Nobel Prize winners became rabid National Socialists and devout believers in racism. Scientists attempted to build an atomic bomb for national socialist Germany, and among them were men of great scientific stature. The same can be said for fascist Italy. It is difficult to envisage early scientists like Newton or Boyle in such roles; to them science was connected with a definite rationalist view of man and the world. For them science meant a belief in the dignity of man and in the development of his potential through the use of his reason. It is ironic in this connection that national socialist students of science at Heidelberg claimed that the "Jewish" theory of relativity had destroyed that Nordic feeling for nature which they maintained was the basis of Newton's cosmology. Even national socialism had to come to terms with the new physics. A party memorandum of 1944 blamed the backwardness of German physics on its rejection of the theory of relativity and divested the theory of its "Jewishness" by simply crediting Einstein's predecessors with its invention.

Science was no longer a world view with certain necessary emphases upon man's dignity and rationality. Scientists increasingly thought of themselves as technicians—not all of them, to be sure. Albert Einstein was an exception to the rule, but there were few like him. As most important scientific work in our day is connected with national security, the scientist is encouraged to be careful in his ideological predilections.

This development of science does not stand alone nor is it confined to the twentieth century. It is a result of the increasing scientific specialization of the nineteenth century, a specialization made necessary by the advances of science itself. The humanities, after all, went through a similar development at the end of the century. The monograph triumphed everywhere; historians and literary scholars who sought to relate their task to the present were scorned by their professions. The so-called unpolitical historian or classicist was as common as the scientist who kept his science locked in the laboratory. Nevertheless, nonprofessional historians and literati could and did bring their task to bear upon the present, supporting or constructing ideologies. But it was quite another matter to be a nonprofessional scientist. Every man of culture could write history, but it took years of special training to make one's mark in science. Science therefore tended to remove itself further from being a force in the culture of Europe than the humanistic discipline. It could not provide a world view equipped to handle the great longings of the age, and did not intend to do so.

Instead of a new scientific positivism, the years between the wars marked, for many Europeans, what Friedell called the "end to reality." To this the new sciences had also made an indirect contribution. The United States chose a different path from that of Europe. This age was, for a philosopher like John Dewey, the age of rationalism, for now the spread of intelligence through education would make a pragmatic approach to social problems possible. No sensitive person in Europe would have thought himself living in an age of rationalism, though he might have been concerned with how rationalism could be preserved in an irrational age.

Nor are differing attitudes toward technology beside the point. The interest in technological advance was shared by Europe and America. But while in the New World technology was admired, almost at times being an ideology which by itself would lead to a better life, this was not quite the case in Europe. Technology was feared more than admired, as German films from *Homunculus* (1915) to *Metropolis* (1927) demonstrate. *Homunculus* told of a man artificially created through technology, a Frankenstein, "a man without a soul, servant of the devil—a monster." In *Metropolis,* robotized workers were, in one of the most striking sequences, swallowed by the machine itself. Such nightmares were more common in Germany than elsewhere; they were an added spur to Germany's desperate flight into a new romanticism away from the industrial age, but such themes appeared in the films of other European nations as well.

Technology was never a substitute for ideology but rather it was used by ideologies like national socialism without being exalted into a rival faith. These examples show the difference in texture between American and European thought in this period, though many of the intellectual trends also obtained a footing on the other side of the Atlantic. In Europe reality was not something to accept and improve, but something to overcome. Marxists wanted to actualize the basic truth of the dialectic against existing society; others wanted to change society through actualizing the basic truths of race or of the stream of history. Whatever the viewpoint, acceptance of society, the reality of the present, was rare; and where it was found, hesitant.

The uncertainties mentioned often pushed ideologies toward concepts of leadership in their search for authority. An elite was to lead the people to ordered government, exemplify the basic truths of society, and give the people security and hope for the future. In the postwar world elitist ideas had an obvious appeal as one way to deal with chaos. It is such thought that must now be examined.

# THE TWENTIETH CENTURY

# CHAPTER EIGHTEEN

# Theories of
# the Elite

HE IDEAL of an elite guiding humanity toward a better life in a new society has played a role in many of the theories that have been discussed. Marxism had its elite in the Communist party, and Nietzsche longed for an elite of individualistic supermen. It is important, however, to distinguish between ideologies which contained elites as part of their superstructure and those which centered upon the elite itself. A Marxist elite, for example, leads the masses because it has grasped the nature of historical materialism; it is the servant of the ideology rather than its master. Much the same can be said for the doctrine of leadership in conservatism or in liberalism. But the theories of elite which must be considered now are those in which the elite itself constituted the center of thought, in which a class of leaders determined not only its own ideology but directed the course of politics and society.

Broadly speaking, there were two conceptions of the importance of such an elite. First, that concept of leadership which had evolved from the image of the hero in nineteenth-century thought, the idea of an elite setting an example for the rest of humanity, and through that example redeeming mankind. Matthew Arnold wondered how standards of excellence could be preserved in a mass society and had answered that only an intellectual elite could preserve them. Such an elite would keep itself undefiled by popular influences, hoping that its standard would eventually lead mankind to better things. This concept of the elite was an intellectual one. In the 1920s Romain Rolland (1866–1944) in France talked about the duty of the intellectual to transmit humanistic values in an age of iron, while Julien Benda (1867–1948) accused intellectuals of abandoning their function as an elite and of coming down into the marketplace. In Germany the group which gathered around the poet Stefan George (1868–1933) had similar ideas. It conceived of itself as an elite which would lead Germany toward a better life by separating the good and the beautiful from contemporary materialism. We might call this an aesthetic elite in contrast to that elite composed of technicians of power. These men also believed in elite leadership, but they were unconcerned with the true and beautiful; they intended to use their insights into the nature of power in order to assert their leadership. Eventually, this preoccupation with power culminated in a worship of power for its own sake, a belief reinforced by the experiences of the First World War.

These were the two kinds of elitist groups which will be considered. Both contrasted with one another, though both were to lead into that 1920s atmosphere so congenial to the rise of totalitarianism. The most important theoretician of the power elite was Vilfredo Pareto (1848–1923). Born in Italy, he taught for most of his life in Switzerland. It is significant for the direction in which this kind of thought tended that Mussolini made Pareto, at the end of his life, a fascist senator. It was his book *A Treatise of General Sociology* (1916) which made him famous almost overnight. Hardly a "tract," it was a monumental work of two volumes, full of dull prose and endless facts. Why did such a ponderous work gain such great fame? The answer is a familiar one; here again, a whole system of thought was advanced under the guise of being scientific. Positivism was still strong, in spite of the challenges to its dominance, and like Comte, Pareto believed that human behavior could be reduced to a science. But there is another factor involved in Pareto's popularity. The challenge to positivism had accused it of ignoring irrational man, for its critics believed that to understand man one must delve into his essential nature which was irrational. Pareto took full account of this criticism.

Pareto's basic concern was to distinguish between reality and appearance to arrive at the essence of man. He also believed that essence to be irrational, as distinguished from rational, behavior. In his terminology this meant distinguishing between rationalizations which are artificial and impermanent called "derivations," and the constant, irrational elements in man, the "residues." Through the derivations, the residue took on constantly changing forms. An example will make this clear. Both the sailors in ancient Greece and those in modern Christendom had a need for Divine comfort—this was the residue;

but the Greek prayed to Poseidon and the Christian to the Virgin Mary and each would hold the other's belief in abhorrence—this was the derivation. Pareto thus took into account the search for fundamentals beyond appearances. And yet he was a Positivist, for he believed that both residues and derivations could be listed and that from such a listing conclusions could be drawn which would be serviceable to those desiring power over their fellow men.

Pareto's system of classification led him to a doctrine of power. The worship of Poseidon and the worship of Christ held the same value within the "scientifically" determined relationship of residue to derivation. It was the residue which mattered. In a quite unscientific leap of thought he concluded that these residues must be essentially good because if they were contrary to the welfare of society, society itself could not exist. Thus these residues must be furthered by those in control through encouraging the right kind of derivations. For example, a strong residue in man was his resentment of every disturbance to society and to himself. There was, therefore, a constant attempt to maintain the present order, and this attempt must be furthered even if the rationalizations for this were irrational. A lynching may be absurd—even the wrong person may be lynched—but it was a correct expression of a residue: the "residue of the integrity of the individual is satisfied." Disguised in scientific and sociological jargon Pareto justified irrational acts in the name of conservatism.

It was not conservatism in general which Pareto's system furthered, but the concept of an elite of leaders. The main business of this elite must be to manipulate residues through controlling their derivations. Here propaganda came into its own, for the residues were irrational and thus the derivations had to appeal to the irrational in man. Only the elite, the practitioners of Pareto's system, knew that all this could be grasped scientifically and therefore manipulated. Thus if meat inspection was desired, the appeal could not be to civic pride but instead to the fear of death through poisoning. Once again it must be pointed out that idealistic considerations did not enter here. It was human nature which had to be manipulated and not "abstract" ideologies.

What was the underlying motive? A longing to grasp and maintain power. Pareto bolstered this line of thought by formulating, as a climax to his work, a specific theory about elites. History—in his famous statement—was the cemetery of aristocracies. Yet an elite was necessary if basically irrational man was to be governed. But what had happened to elites? They were constantly being undermined by two interconnected phenomena: the accumulation of inferior people in the aristocracy and the equal accumulation of superior people among the lower classes. Sooner or later this resulted in a revolution. What, then, did he mean by inferior and superior people? Those who had or had not the ability to manipulate successfully the "residues" of the population.

No society could be governed by reason; it had to be governed, therefore, by propaganda and force. In Pareto's analysis of society there were basically only two classes: the rulers and the ruled.

Here, then, was an elite firmly wedded to the sole principle of power; they possessed no abstract ideology, only the skill to use and guide people through manipulation and, if necessary, force. This elite was not confined to a "happy few" with aesthetic sense; indeed it could be large. The connection between Pareto and fascism was close, though there is no evidence that Mussolini read Pareto and many other factors contributed to fascist thought. Nevertheless, the idea of an elite wedded to power alone and the concept of government through propaganda were given systematic expression by Pareto. He combined the new consciousness of society with the older tradition of positivism in his desire for a deterministic, scientific formula that would control man's irrational nature. Such an urge was not confined to Pareto. Earlier Sigmund Freud had attempted to make science serviceable in the analysis of the unconscious, basic human nature. But the approach and the results of the genuine man of science, of the Viennese bourgeois, were at first far removed from Pareto's science of society. It might, however, have been significant that late in his life Freud also turned to a concept of the strong man, also voiced suspicions of the irrational mass of mankind. The scientific impetus, combined with an irrationalistic world view and the revolt against positivism, often turned to ideas of an elite as an expression of a belief in man's inability to determine his own fate.

Pareto wrote his book during the First World War, and this catastrophe seemed to emphasize the validity of viewing the world in terms of power. The power aspect of this elite theory was important here rather than its direct involvement with fascist ideology. For after the war, ideas of power tended to detach themselves from those sociological and scientific considerations which had dominated Pareto's work; instead of an elite dedicated to power manipulation, there emerged a leadership intoxicated with the very idea of power. This power began to represent, in itself, a conscious rejection of ideological values, a kind of nihilism, while the "residues" not only remained irrational but were also viewed as primitive. This intoxication with power was thought to rest upon the primitive instincts of man.

The most important popularizer of this power concept was the German poet and novelist Ernst Juenger through his war diaries called *Thunder of Steel* (1919). In the war experience he saw the beginnings of a new age. Man's "residue" had freed itself from the overlay of bourgeois civilization. Thus Juenger stripped the concept of its sociological terminology, ignoring its scientific formulation. For him this residue was the primitive instinct of man. He described it in a charge of the shock troops:

The turmoil of our feeling was called forth by rage, alcohol, and the thirst for blood. As we advanced steadily but irresistibly towards the enemy lines I was boiling over with a fury which gripped me—it gripped us all—in an inexplicable way. The overpowering desire to kill gave me wings. Rage squeezed bitter tears from my eyes—only the spell of primeval instinct remained.

This, then, was the real nature of man, of humankind for whom the war experience had begun a new age. The dominance of primeval instincts was part of Juenger's protest against old values, a protest in the name of a dangerous, adventurous life whose essence was a quest for power.

The age of middle-class security was over. The search for safety and security was a dead end, for the bourgeoisie had achieved this security through their notion of infinity, an infinity in which the individual lost himself and in which all contradictions were resolved. For Juenger this led to what he called a "blur," a certain "vagueness" which culminated in compromise. In political life this meant that all responsibility was whittled away, atomized into small units until all responsibility vanished. What was needed was leadership, a return to the experience of the war in which the leader would lead his storm troops against the enemy. Juenger exalted this idea of life as unending war into a philosophy of life. Out of this would come a new man whom he called the "worker." This was Juenger's elite.

This new man would not shirk reality—that is, the natural tendency of his instincts to seek danger. He would not negotiate like a bourgeois; he would fight instead as a natural part of life. And he would do so in the name of power only: "This is the new man, the storm soldier, the elite of central Europe. A completely new race, cunning, strong and packed with purpose . . . battle proven, merciless both to himself and others." The war had not ended. It provided a continuing call to power.

Yet, in one sense, the war was over, for the means of power had changed. No longer did the elite give expression to their instincts merely through fighting the enemy in the trenches. A new factor entered Juenger's thought, for, like so many of his contemporaries, he was obsessed with the advances of technology. "Where machines become the symbol, all other forces must flee." Here, too, the bourgeoisie were wrong. They had used technology as a means for progress; in the new reality technology was a means to power. The war made this only too obvious; it had revealed "the power factor of technology, exclusive of all economic and progressive elements." Once more the quest for power was viewed as desirable for its own ends. Juenger's elite used technology as Pareto's elite used social science. It is important to realize that for Juenger, too, there was no future ideal toward which the elite could lead mankind. Indeed man was conceived of as having neither ideals nor ideology, only the dynamic of his primeval instincts. This can be summed up in Juenger's phrase: "... we shall never understand why we are born into this world. All our goals can only be pretexts. It matters only that we exist." Life was a struggle for the possession of power: "... war, the father of all things is also our father." A new type, the "worker," would form the elite of central Europe —warriors who would know how to use technology to gain power.

In Germany Juenger's popularity was greater than that of Pareto, not only because he wrote in a readable and fascinating manner. The war generation, fresh from the trenches of Ypres and Verdun, freshly disillusioned with a sacrifice which seemed in vain, could understand his kind of philosophy. Juenger gave to this generation a rationale which seemed to make sense. In addition, the preoccupation with power and technology was widespread in society.

The film between wars, especially in Germany, can illustrate this preoccupation. It was replete with the idea of power and the problems growing out of this for man. The Frankenstein motif first appeared in the film *The Golem* (1915), which centered upon the creation of a powerful monster by Rabbi Loew of Prague, a monster which escaped his control. In such motion pictures as *The Cabinet of Dr. Caligari* (1920) or *The Testament of Dr. Mabuse* (1932) the quest for power was combined with the use of technology —a technology which escaped the grasp of man and became his ruler. The tyrant was he who sought to master this new force, as Dr. Mabuse sought to master it. Juenger provided a solution to this dilemma, this fear of the new monster. The definition of man as a creature of chaos and elemental drives was reflected in the films of the 1920s—and here, again, the theme that reason could make no sense out of life, that life made no sense at all, was repeated. Once more, Juenger echoed and, at the same time, built upon this feeling. In effect he said: Let us grant that all is chaos, that life does not make sense. What is needed, therefore, is an elite which accepts such presuppositions and concentrates on sheer power alone. This elite would be, in his words, "revolutionaries without banners."

Such ideas enjoyed more than an intellectual existence; they found a solid expression in the realities of postwar Germany. The German Free Corps after 1919 is a pertinent example. Military units recruited from the old imperial army after the armistice. They directed their first efforts toward crushing the leftist uprisings in Germany, and then turned to the task of reconquering the Baltic lands. The remarkable fact about these Free Corps was the absence of any ideological longings; they were activists and nothing more, even an expressed nationalism was lacking. This is best illustrated by the reaction of Hermann Ehrhardt, the most famous of the Free Corps leaders, to the murder

302

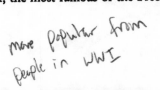
more popular from people in WWI

of the German foreign minister, Walter Rathenau (1922). One of the murderers came to Ehrhardt after the event in order to gain his approval, but Ehrhardt refused it. His reasons were that Rathenau was a Jew and that rightist nationalist groups were involved in the attacks upon him. Not that Ehrhardt had any objection to anti-Semitism; on the contrary, and not that he thought the Nationalists wrong. The murder, however, had assumed ideological overtones through this anti-Jewish association, and this Ehrhardt could not approve. More to the point was the motivation of another of the murderers: "I went into the adventure without a clear goal."

We can see the Free Corps's anti-ideological predilections mirrored in the postwar German youth movement. A part of that movement, which had started as a romantic revolt against the bourgeois life of an older generation, evolved toward activism after 1918 under an increasing disillusionment with the postwar world. As one leader, Eberhard Koebel, wrote: "... we are an army of those men who *must* act." Action itself was the one constant of a world in flux; it constituted the permanent revolution. The elder leaders of the youth movement called Koebel and his group the desperados of the movement, but they exercised a great attraction for German youth. The early romanticism of the *Wandervoegel* was no longer enough. But this activism was confused by its lack of goals. Koebel became a Communist, then a National Socialist, and ended up as a Communist party functionary in East Germany. Perhaps it was a fate symbolic of that restless generation. From the inspirer of German youth to the bureaucrat—was that the end of the undisciplined urge for action?

Hermann Rauschnigg summed up the consequences of such doctrine in his *Revolution of Nihilism,* published in 1938. This was the revolution of an elite without doctrines or ideologies, who wanted to attain power solely to maintain power. This was the underlying reality of their revolution, and the programs and manifestoes which this elite issued were, in Pareto's terms, merely derivations. Rauschnigg saw such a revolution taking place with the rise to power of national socialism. Yet, as will be seen, that movement did have a strong ideology which no tactic of expediency or manipulation of power could obscure. Rauschnigg's analysis could better be applied to the rise of fascism in Italy, for there the quest for power came first and the construction of a program occurred only when power was about to be achieved. The Fasci were very much like the Free Corps: associations of former soldiers without ideological trimmings whose object was power and who hired themselves out like mercenaries to anyone who could aid them in achieving their purpose.

These ideas did not vanish with the development of totalitarianism; indeed, they provided one of its ingredients. Yet such elitist ideas seemed especially attractive after the catastrophe of war, especially for the defeated. After the Second World War these concepts once again came into vogue. Juenger was no longer the prophet; he had recoiled with horror from the excesses of national socialism and returned to a Christian view of the world. Instead, it was one of Juenger's early disciples, one of Rathenau's murderers, who now sounded the trumpet. Ernst von Salomon's *Questionnaire* (1946) became a best seller in Germany after the Second World War, as Juenger's *Thunder of Steel* had been after the First. Ideologies were again repudiated. There was really no difference between Hitler and the democracies; both created a situation where man was atomized. The only solution was to join a power elite. Thus he condoned his friend's joining the national socialist movement; thus he also painted a picture of the SS in an American detention camp. They could take it, for they stuck together in an elite formation; they were not encumbered with thought. All this was second-hand Juenger applied to a later situation. Nevertheless, Salomon represented a new development in this kind of thought, for there was a note of despair when he faced the excesses of national socialism. Unlike Juenger, he did not return to a Christian foundation for his thought. Instead, he came to the realization that "to do nothing" was the only realistic attitude, the only thing a man of character could do. Bravery and stupidity were really the same thing.

Salomon accepted the world view of the early Juenger, but he himself was no longer convinced that there was any way out. The revolution of nihilism had become the nihilism of despair. Yet his attitude was ambivalent, as in his nostalgic portrayal of the SS elite. In Salomon, as in the works of the 1920s, technology played an important part. It had reduced man to a cipher; it conquered him as it had conquered Dr. Mabuse, but this time the conqueror came in the guise of the social sciences, of questionnaires and IBM machines. The note of despair deepened when he realized that the "worker" might not, in the end, be able to conquer this monster. Here, then, was the same preoccupation noted in Juenger, the same analysis of society in terms of the dynamic of power, of "residues," with a note of resignation that is absent from his master. But then, Salomon had experienced totalitarianism in action as well as another world war.

After the Second World War these ideas were not merely German; they could be found throughout western Europe. Curzio Malaparte's *Kaputt* and Virgil Gheorghiu's *The Twenty-Fifth Hour* were very similar to Salomon's work. The latter book showed a still greater preoccupation with the struggle for power between man and technology. Many of the works of Arthur Koestler also belong here, especially his novel *Thieves in the Night* (1946), which dealt with the struggle of the Jews for Palestine. Koestler's hero patted his gun, "That's the new Esperanto ... surprising how easy it is to learn. Everybody understands it from Shanghai to Madrid." The doctrine of force was made necessary by human fears and insecurities; it was a global infection, and one's only defense was to become contaminated oneself. Here again ideologies did not matter. The hero slapped a boy who refreshed himself by reading the Talmud instead of paying attention to his rifle. Unlike Juenger or Salomon, however, there was in Koestler, at this point, no elite theory but a reliance on the individualized hero.

From Pareto to Salomon, from the First World War to the middle of the twentieth century, such ideas touched a responsive chord among many men and women who had lived through times of war and social disorganization. These doctrines of the power elite were, in turn, related to the ideas of a contemporaneous existentialism. Here, too, there was a rejection of ideology and a concentration upon the "residue" of man's actual existence in reality. They echoed Juenger's phrase that it matters only that we exist; but in existentialism there was at once a greater despair and a greater sophistication. Neither led to an elite of power as a solution to the dilemma, but rather to the acceptance of the human dilemma of existence in a chaotic world. In both the thought discussed and in secular existentialism there was an opposition to ideology, to a preconceived system of values, indeed to any system of permanent values whatever. This reaction to the nineteenth century was understandable; the ideas of morality, of progress, and of hope for a better world seemed to have ended up in the bloody battlefields of France. The chaos and insecurity of the postwar world seemed to demonstrate conclusively the idiocy of causes. Only existence, only power, mattered; force and war were not isolated events temporarily disrupting the even tenor of human history—they were the reality. Those who were the elite accepted this and the predominance of power above all other values.

Opposed to such a point of view were those elitist ideas mentioned at the beginning of this chapter. To a world of nihilism and power they opposed a world ruled by beauty and by an aesthetic principle. To the "worker" they opposed the image of the "poet." The men who subscribed to this ideology did not react to the problems of the postwar world by withdrawing from it, seeking to deepen their individual sensibility through aesthetic contemplation. Such was at times the attitude of André Gide who sought to separate the world of politics from that of aesthetics. In contrast, men like Stefan George believed that their spiritual principles could revive a prostrate nation. Thus they exalted the poet even higher than had the expressionist revolt against society. One of them, Leonhard Frank, had compared the poet to Christ. Persecuted as Christ had been persecuted, the poet would inherit the kingdom of the elect. For the Expressionists the poet stood above society, endowed with a "truth" which, if men would only listen, might transform them. With some Expres-

305

sionists this resembled the Nietzschean concept of the superman, for the poet, too, was beyond good and evil. In one of their plays the hero decided he had the right to kill a bourgeois because he disgusted him. George never went that far, though in the first period of his activity he also exalted primeval forces as the truth and the poet as its divine harbinger. For George, moreover, the poet had always been the regenerative force within politics and society.

Stefan George symbolized this viewpoint as the century wore on; his personality drew into its band some of the best minds of Germany and his *Star of the Covenant* (1914) was a bible which many took with them into battle. The concept of the elite which George and his circle advanced must be understood against the background of both a continuing romantic impetus and, with Pareto and Juenger, a renewed emphasis upon the irrational essence of man. But here this "residue" was defined in a quite different manner. Man was irrational, to be sure, but among the elite this irrationality was an apprehension of the beautiful, of the poetic.

The poet was the intuitive "seer" from whose pen flowed the truth, who elevated suffering and chaotic humankind to heights of new understanding. In George's first period of activity (1904–14) this world view was linked with the desire of some German intellectuals to return to a purity of nature and a poetic exaltation of primitive forces. Intermingled with this were dimly perceived ideas of blood and race. The whole tendency was surrounded by an almost Nietzschean ecstasy, something which impelled George to prophesy a great catastrophe that would smash the existing order. This was an intoxication with power as well, but poetic power—the power of the seer who foresaw a great change toward spirituality, toward beauty. This change would renew the nation. Manifestly, at this stage, George had ties with that group of men who provided the mystical and romantic ingredients for national socialist ideology, men like Ludwig Klages, who combined ideas of romanticism, race, and leadership, and his pupil Ernst Bertram, who used Nietzsche to exalt the Aryan.

But George went on to become the poet of a new humanism rather than of racial nationalism. Because of his growing admiration for Hellenic culture, his work recaptured a kind of balance and harmony quite different from the ecstacy of his earlier period. Prophecies of impending catastrophe gave way to an optimism; the good and the beautiful would triumph and lead Germany, indeed the world, toward a new humanism. This was to be accomplished through an elite built upon a master-pupil relationship. The leader and his pupils would form a nucleus and their teaching as well as example would bring about change in society. He constructed a model of such a leader in his *Myth of Maxim*. Maxim represented the beautiful and the good; he was a symbol of heroic youth.

George believed that beauty of soul was mirrored in physical beauty. The correspondence between the inward nature of man and his outward visible nature was commonly held throughout the century. It permeated the ideas of those who thought of this correspondence in racial terms. George, rejecting racial ideas and inspired by the Greeks, based his identity of body and soul on an ideal of beauty. Thus he chose his disciples by a rather unusual method. George would sit before the window of his house in Heidelberg and collar any young man whose figure and bearing seemed to reflect his ideals. Many others sought admission to his circle on their own.

This was a male-centered elite, and in this George reflected a phenomenon already seen in the youth movement. It, too, had been originally an exclusively male society. The kind of eroticism involved in these associations drew its inspiration from the Greek *eros*, a platonic concept of male friendship which was familiar to generations brought up on the classics. This eros was the cement which held the George circle together, while the concept of beauty permeated the whole relationship. George himself was without question the center of this circle. His personality was overpowering, and he encouraged this leadership mystique by wrapping his very movements in secrecy. The disciples swore an oath of obedience; they also promised to live chaste, frugal lives without luxury or indulgence. The men who joined, who became, in George's words, the "direct nobility," were intellectuals, and the influence of the circle was spread when these intellectuals attained some of the most important academic appointments in the nation. One special phenomenon with regard to the George circle is worth pointing out. Many of his prominent disciples were Jews. At a time when Jews were being increasingly excluded from movements which sought the renewal of the nation, they were welcomed here. George's humanism knew no racial thought. When the National Socialists offered him the presidency of the German Academy he contemptuously sent his refusal through a Jewish disciple. George died in self-imposed exile in Switzerland.

It is difficult to clarify the profound effect that this circle had on all of those who passed through it. In one sense the membership was diverse: for example, Friedrich Gundolf, the great scholar at Heidelberg, and Werner von Stauffenberg, who, in 1944, made an unsuccessful attempt on Hitler's life. But in a deeper sense all the disciples were alike; all were an elite whose looks conveyed an inward beauty, leading a life imitative of their master. They shared a belief in what George called the "secret Germany," that is, those Germans who sought national renewal through culture. They were an intellectual coterie opposed to materialism, to bourgeois complacency, to the crude manipulation of power. They were apolitical in the same sense that the youth movement was apolitical. They cared not at all for political parties, economic theories, the left, or the right. What mattered was the aesthetically-defined "residue," the true spirit of man. Not the politician's, but the poet-seer's concept of beauty would reinvigorate society. George did not think of taking over the state, as did the adherents of an elite of power. Rather the "secret Germany" would provide guidance and inspiration, would be an order of Templars in the body politic.

While it may seem chimerical to those living in the second part of the twentieth century to seek national renewal in this way, its significance within the framework of German ideological development must be remembered. As far back as 1890 Julius Langbehn had called for a national transformation of Germans into artists. He believed that this transformation would be effected through a cult of nature and of race. The rather large movement which followed this trend of thought, and the youth movement as well, show that, for many Germans, the spiritual imperative was far more important than a political, social, or economic one. In spite of his repudiation of race, his humanism which saw Germany as part of a family of nations, George's elitist concept fitted neatly into this framework. Many came to him directly from the youth movement. This idealism which, with George, became an aesthetic idealism may, in the end, have been tragic for Germany. The idealist attempts to transcend reality enabled ruthless technicians of power, through their focus on concrete problems, not only to gain an easy victory over the idealists, but to make use of part of the idealist's elite concept for their own ends. Perhaps, in the last analysis, it was the profound course of German romanticism which turned some of the nation's best minds in this politically futile direction.

In one other nation there existed a parallel conception of the elite, though founded upon a different basis. The Italian poet Gabriele d'Annunzio (1863–1938) also believed that poets were of prime importance in society, for they were the acknowledged legislators of mankind. He too believed in the cult of beauty, but this belief was not tempered by the Hellenism of George. D'Annunzio held that in his quest for beauty the poet was above ordinary morality. Unlike George, he was also influenced by that literary movement which had seen the beautiful in the bizarre and the exaggerated. Such exaggeration led him to dramatize both the degeneracy of his fictional characters and his own debaucheries. Nevertheless, he believed order to be a part of beauty.

D'Annunzio believed that he had revived the simple and unadorned style of the ancient Romans, but whatever simplicity his writings may have had was swamped by the sonorous phrases and grand rhetoric that characterized his works of horror and death. Thus, the Italian poet was far removed from George's admiration for the Greeks, and he was unwilling to influence events indirectly through a "secret Italy." Instead, he took a direct part in politics. His ambition to revive a Roman Empire, to "see in all men of foreign blood the reincarnation of barbarians," encouraged in him a strident patriotism. The splendor and excitement of imperial Rome would be recaptured under the leadership of the poet. His ideal of beauty was transformed into a new style of politics to control the masses when d'Annunzio set out with his band to capture Fiume for Italy (1919–20) and ruled that city for over a year.

As an active political figure, the ruler of Fiume became a master in using symbols and myths. He dialoged with his masses of followers. This episode was a dress rehearsal for fascism and Mussolini took due note of the nature of d'Annunzio's rule. Fascist propaganda learned from the festivals at Fiume. Aesthetic leadership had become political leadership. This was far from the kind of "secret Germany" George desired, though it shared something of the ecstasy of the early George. This aesthetically-motivated elitist idea had found a political place for the poet, but it either distracted intellectuals from immediate tasks or became political and nationalist rhetoric.

In France there was nothing that quite paralleled these ideas. A possible exception to this was Mallarmé's salon in Paris. For Mallarmé also, poetry was the sole truth and the sole religion. For him such thought had no political or social aims; it was art for art's sake alone. Mallarmé's poetic universe had none of the nationalist goals so typical of elitist theory.

The two systems analyzed are a study in contrast—different approaches to the twentieth-century problems of war and insecurity. In central Europe a third analysis of the human dilemma was even more influential than either of these systems, and it also posited an elite. Having written it before and during the war, Oswald Spengler published his *Decline of the West* in 1922. The impact of the book was little short of enormous. Like Pareto, Spengler offered a complete explanation of the world, but unlike Pareto he based this explanation not merely on science but also on the majesty of the historical process. His end result approximated a Nietzschean exaltation of the "new barbarian" elite while his value judgments on civilization recognized, as George had done, the importance of the metaphysical impetus. Spengler thus combined in his work diverse strands of thought, each of which had proved its appeal.

No single part of Spengler's thought was of greater importance than his distinction between culture and civilization which has previously been mentioned. A culture was a living, growing organism which had at its center a metaphysical impulse. Civilization was culture's moribund stage; it was an "external and artificial state," materialistic, and therefore without a dynamic of its own. Once again there was a rejection of materialism on behalf of the inner impulses of man, and that life force was defined as philosophical and religious. The tie with idealism and with romanticism was clear; again there emerged an opposition to rationalism, with a recapturing of the inner dynamic of man. For many this involved a rejection of the superficialities of life which they defined as the social and political realities of the moment. Thus, Thomas Mann wrote during the war: "... the difference between the spirit (Geist) and politics involves that between culture and civilization, the soulful and the social ... the idea of the German is that of culture, the soul, art, not civilization, society and literature." Spengler's system enabled man to look beneath these realities to the essence of things, as did the other elitist theories. But Spengler's clearer formulation had a deeper general impact.

Spengler took account of science; indeed, he was fascinated by biological imagery. His historical approach to the rise and fall of civilizations rested upon biological analogies. Briefly stated, history was for him a biological process impelled by metaphysical impulses. Adopting a romantic symbol, he placed what he called the Faustian man in the center of Western civilization. Such a man was eternally restless, always longing for the unattainable. His was the art of endless vistas—the medieval cathedrals, the Renaissance inventions of perspective and music dominated his life and thought. This dynamic creature came to maturity in the sixteenth and seventeenth centuries with the Reformation, with free inquiry and scientific speculation, but maturity was followed by old age and decline, as in every biological organism. The autumn of Faustian man began with the stale rationalizations and destructive criticisms of the eighteenth century, while the winter of his decline fell in the nineteenth century when the metaphysical impulse had exhausted itself. The triumph of money, the hostility of the dominant middle class to aristocratic virtues, the absence of vitality and dynamism in the West, and the growth of a philosophy of resignation, of materialistic socialism, made all this manifestly apparent.

It was above all the lengthening shadow of materialism, the quest for gain, and rationalistic philosophies which brought about Faustian civilization's decline. But the twentieth century had witnessed a new development which might yet have revived the processes of biological evolution in the West. Pride and instinct were about to triumph over money and civilization. An epoch of perpetual warfare had begun. This was all reminiscent of Juenger, even though Spengler's formulation of the West's decline preceded the composition of *Thunder of Steel*. For Spengler, Western culture's new beginning would once more revive the principle of an aristocratic elite—as it had flourished in the heyday of Faustian man. This perpetual warfare meant that future wars would be fought by followers grouped around a leader—a generation of new Caesars would arise. Racked by armed conflict, life for the rest of the population would descend to a level of mere subsistence. Only a handful of cities would survive and their inhabitants' existence would consist of a meaningless repetition of mechanical tasks and brutal diversions.

But this new primitivism would possess the seeds of future development.

Men would find solace for their miseries in a revived appetite for the supernatural and metaphysical. In the immediate present, however, society would polarize around the leaders, the "new barbarians," and the masses. All this was cast in a deterministic mold; no nation would escape this fate and man himself could not change it. Spengler also captured the feeling of his contemporaries that they were helpless before the catastrophes of war and crisis, but he used a historical biological system to prove it to them. Moreover, this was history reinforced by scientific analogies made scholarly by a wealth of footnotes and therefore seemingly more authoritative, as well as more easily understood, than Pareto's turgid prose.

Once he had published his *Decline of the West,* Spengler went on to elaborate some of his ideas in order to make them as relevant as possible to Germany's situation. He sought to do this by more clearly defining the new elite, and in so doing, the prophet of the "new barbarians" finally revealed himself as a great admirer of Prussia. His *Prussianism and Socialism* (1919) was as popular as his previous work. In it he redefined socialism. Socialism was not Marxism, for Marxism was too idealistic in this age of perpetual war and crisis. Of prime importance was the ability to govern. Spengler had come to the conclusion that the new elite had to do more than fight their way across Europe; they must be the governors of a strong state. For him this meant that the new Caesars should exemplify the Prussian spirit, for here strong government was combined with a concern for the whole nation.

To find a prototype of this new elite he returned to the eighteenth century which once he had condemned as the autumn of Faustian man. Frederick the Great, while believing in strong, authoritarian government, was still the "first servant" of the state. Here was the model for an "instinctive socialism." Frederick William I of Prussia, his father, the "Potsdam Fuehrer," as a modern historian has called him, was the first Socialist and not Karl Marx. He believed in an organic state where the welfare of the whole was guaranteed, not by the dominance of one class and not by an idealism of the future, but by strong government. What a contrast, Spengler thought, to the democracy of the German Republic and to its bourgeois, acquisitive society. Spengler characterized contemporary politics as the "continuation of private business by other means." In the end, Spengler's elite were not "new barbarians" similar to Juenger's "workers" but supposedly efficient rulers like the eighteenth-century monarchs of Prussia.

All these elitist theories opposed contemporary politics as they did concentration upon social or economic theory. They were groping toward a new approach to the seemingly insoluble problems of their time. In this search they were aided by that change in the public spirit of Europe which has already been discussed. Important to them was the basic nature of man, which Spengler put into a deterministic framework of a historical system, Pareto into a straitjacket of scientific formula, and George into an abstracted realm of the poet. Salvation lay in recapturing or at least understanding this human nature which required the elimination of rationalism, the common enemy of all these men. But not total elimination, for, as pointed out, some of them were concerned with science and all feared the Frankenstein of modern technology while trying to devise means of controlling it. For all of them the solution lay in the growth of an elite which could provide leadership and which would manipulate those forces which seemed inexorably to plague modern man. With Juenger, Pareto, and Spengler this search for an elite culminated in doctrines of power and in the belief that the modern age was the age of the barbarian. George was the exception, though some of his ecstatic poetry did come close to a glorification of power.

Such new departures menaced the democratic process, and it is significant that these doctrines were strongest where this process was weakest—in Germany and Italy. Though neither George nor Spengler joined the National Socialists, d'Annunzio became a Fascist and Pareto a Fascist-appointed senator. And though Juenger repudiated modern totalitarianism, his ideas did provide some of the foundations for national socialism. After all, totalitarianism climaxed the search for the leadership advocated in these theories. Yet even in the Europe of elitist aspirations some men were engaged in trying to maintain a liberal position.

They, too, were intellectuals, but they were men who believed that the "religion of liberty" was of primary concern. To the sociologist Karl Mannheim, such an elite of intellectuals was relatively free from class ties and therefore able to see reality in more objective terms. This observation seems untrue for the intellectuals about to be discussed. Though class ties did not play an important role in their thought, and though they tried to be objective, their final ignorance of the realities imparts a pathetic quality to much of their thought. They had the right intentions, but they seemed to have ended as Benedetto Croce did, proclaiming a return to a liberal past in his palace at Naples—a palace which was an island amidst the totalitarian sea of fascism. Similarly, Thomas Mann was swept into exile by the fascism of Germany. Even if men of the *respublica literaria* were excluded from consideration, scientists showed no deeper grasp of reality. The task the intellectuals about to be discussed set themselves was a noble one—the preservation of freedom. But twentieth-century Europe was not the reality in which their type of individual freedom could find a congenial home.

*312*

# CHAPTER NINETEEN

# Freedom and
# the Intellectuals

IN 1927 THE Frenchman Julien Benda published a book which created something of a sensation. Entitled *The Betrayal of the Intellectuals,* the work was a reaffirmation of the ideals of rationalism and liberty in contrast to the passions of the age which he felt were destroying both. Racial hatreds and political factionalism had usurped the place of that humanistic reason and morality which once had set universal standards impervious to the passions of an age. Benda attempted to exalt, once more, the image of a free, reasonable, and moral man who rejected the petty hatreds of an age of antihumanism and unchecked passions. "The condensation of political passions into a small number of very simple hatreds, springing from the deepest roots of the human heart, is a conquest of modern times." Thus, Benda disavowed that whole development which has been analyzed with the change of the public spirit of Europe at the turn of the century. The neoromanticism of men like Nietzsche and Bergson was sharply attacked; so, too, was the pragmatism of the masses. Both these developments seemed to have led to the present decline of liberty.

What, then, was the "betrayal of the intellectuals"? These men partook of the two chief evils. They had espoused the passions of the age, and they were, to Benda, pragmatists, for they were neo-Romantics on the one hand, and, on the other, were Positivists blinded to all but material facts. As a result, doctrines of arbitrary authority had been substituted for the spirit of liberty. On these twin accusations Benda rested his case, but he went on to suggest an alternative to the present position of the intellectuals. Benda envisaged the intellectuals as a class apart, dedicated to transcendent concerns. Though it was easy to follow his contention that intellectuals should not be pragmatists, one can make the objection that neo-Romantics had also made transcendent concerns their chief argument. For Benda, however, such ideology meant involvement in the passions of men. The only true concerns of intellectuals were those of liberalism and humanism. Instead, intellectuals had become spokesmen for irrationalism and thus intensified the hatreds of race, classes, and nations. Seen against the background of Europe's cultural evolution, Benda's condemnation of the intellectuals made some sense. The "rediscovery of the unconscious" did further the trend toward totalitarian society in Benda's period.

His solution could not be so readily accepted, however. Intellectuals were to be a class apart, according to Benda, uncontaminated by passions or by the urge for pragmatic action to improve society—an ivory tower of rationalism amidst an antirationalistic society. Such a simplistic formula, though easy to state and appealing, tended to be self-defeating. Seen in the context of the ruthlessness of twentieth-century political and social movements, it implied a withdrawal from society, a retreat and half-acceptance by intellectuals of those forces inimical to liberty. Though Benda's intellectuals were, ideologically speaking, the opposite of George's elite, they, too, would have comprised an elite. Nevertheless, Benda's intellectuals reflected the strength of French rationalism's opposition to German neoromanticism. But this ideal of reason and liberty led to a withdrawal from society in contrast to the drive for national regeneration of George's "secret Germany." Benda's ivory tower no longer existed, except perhaps at the École Normale Superieure, the summit of the French educational system. There pupils were selected by rigid competitive examinations and, unlike other universities, the students lived and ate together. In contrast with the development of higher education in general, the École Normale still emphasized intellectual excellence combined with a rationalist outlook. Benda had passed through this education, but so had Bergson and Péguy, both of whom had turned away from this rationalist outlook upon the world.

European universities gave little aid to intellectuals in their effort to maintain this kind of liberty. They typified the two trends which Benda had castigated. On the one hand, both students and professors were engaged in searching for tangible, ascertainable facts within ever more specialized definitions of subject matter. On the other hand, the lecture room became a platform from which certain professors encouraged the passions of the age. What little general education there was took the form of national propaganda. Specialization was not confined to the sciences. The trend at the end of the last century for all subjects to cover themselves with the mantle of science has already been seen. This meant, in all disciplines, an increasing reliance upon the discovery of new facts. In history, for example, the monograph triumphed over general works addressed to the lay reader; the footnote documenting each statement became as important as the text itself. Useful though such efforts were in ferreting out new sources upon which to base historical interpretations, these interpretations themselves stuck close to the evidence contained in the sources. Professional historians tended to hold generalized historical interpretations in disrepute, and they deplored any speculations upon the nature of society and the world based upon history.

No longer did there exist the sweeping formulations of a Vico of the eighteenth century, or even the effort which Buckle had made in the nineteenth century, based as it was on careful attention to material facts. A recent historian clarified this when he wrote that most professional historians agreed that the purpose of history was to "... find out the truth about this or that, not about things in general." For Benda, this was the kind of specialization which led intellectuals toward pragmatism. It could hardly lead intellectuals toward a renewed humanism. History was not the only discipline which, in this way, withdrew from the general concerns of the world into a scientism. In the last century both literature and the classics had provided a general inspiration; indeed, Benda spoke of a Hellenic rationalism which enlightened the world. In schools and universities, classicism bogged down in philological monographs could no longer fulfill this function. A similar situation existed in literature. During the last century Shakespeare, for example, had provided the inspiration for much of the romantic world view, but this also had passed. Philology had been victorious over literature conceived as inspiration.

In literature the search for the exact meaning and history of words became important. It seemed of greater importance to put literary figures into their historical setting than to talk about the ideals they might provide for the present. Professors and teachers of literature became historians or philologists. The classics were now taught by rote as grammar rather than for their meaning. Generations of students were under the mistaken impression that the irregular verb had dominated ancient civilization. To be sure, this scientism led to a revolt against this view of the classics and literature. But this revolt came from outside the universities and schools, indeed, in opposition to them. Both the youth movement and George embraced a revived classical heritage. The concept of eros was quite alien to the grammarians. This reaction had its undesirable features, but its extent and depth were partly due to what these men termed the "pedantry" of the educational system. The victory of philology in the schools and universities stimulated an ominous neoromanticism.

In this regard the secondary schools were no better off than the universities; indeed, these same trends were reflected in the education they provided. The Expressionists and the youth movement were violently opposed both to the sterile learning of the schools and the underlying assumption of this education which Nietzsche had already denounced as the idea of knowledge for the sake of knowledge alone. As in the universities, many teachers in the secondary system either attempted to drill the facts into the bewildered heads of the students or took patriotic stances. Teaching was not improved by the fact that many secondary-school teachers were men who had wanted to become university professors but had failed in this and had to take the second best. Teachers were often embittered and disappointed men who took their misfortunes out on their students. Bad teaching went hand in hand with an ever greater specialization of subject matter and a heavy dose of patriotic propaganda.

The increasing specialization, the urge toward scientism, robbed humanistic subjects of their inspiration in the cause of liberty; those who revolted against this abandoned ideas of liberty altogether for an emphasis upon the passions. Professors who wanted to reach a more general audience ignored the ideals implicit in Benda's concept of the intellectual and became, instead, propagandists for nationalist causes. They were, of course, state employees and thus not apt to take unpopular stands. The more so as in their selection, political beliefs had played a very definite role. Not only men like Karl Marx could never hope to become professors, many Liberals were also barred. The faculty, therefore, usually consisted of either nonpolitical specialists or patriotic professors. Some, however, tried to preserve ideas of liberty within a university atmosphere of patriotism and specialization. That they failed does not make their quest any less significant.

Max Weber (1864–1920) is the first example, though he ceased active teaching as early as 1897. Weber opposed the increasing narrowness of specialization; he believed that there was a cosmic order which individual research could help to illuminate. The meaning of knowledge, he tried to tell his students, was the "rationalization" of the world, our desire to organize, explain, and control the forces of nature and the functioning of society. The task of sociology was to provide a conceptual framework which would make human society, and through this the world, understandable. Weber's famous "ideal types" were analytical tools with which abstractions like "economic man" or "Protestant ethic" could be examined in a more meaningful way. Such ideal types would focus attention upon generic concepts which might include all levels of abstraction and might be arrived at through empirical data or historical investigations. Weber thought of the results of this method as a unified analytical construct formed by the one-sided accentuation of one or more points of view and by the synthesis of concrete individual phenomena.

This method was to have a profound influence upon the development of social analysis. It tried to capture through scholarship and data, as rationally as possible, the "ideal type" of what had been vague concepts like capitalism or kingship. Yet, significantly, the ideals of men played an important part in making up such types. When Weber wrote about the relationship of religion to capitalism he reversed Marx. It was not so much capitalist development which produced the superstructure of ideology, but it was the Protestant, puritan ethic which drove the "ideal type" on to provide the dynamic of acquisitive society. Ideology was as important to Weber as it had been to the whole school of idealism and neoromanticism. He, too, was concerned with irrational man while trying, at the same time, to capture him within a rationalistic "type." This led Weber into a dilemma which was symptomatic of the difficulties encountered in preserving and transmitting ideas of liberty in this manner, for he believed that politics had no place in the classroom. His stand, when contrasted to the nationalist professors, more nearly approximated the liberal view of academic ethics. He believed this, however, because a teacher should distinguish between personal judgment of values and statements of fact. It was a mistake for the student to demand from academic teachers positive guidance either in the moral realm or in the making of decisions.

Yet was his sociology enough of a science to allow such distinction between judgment and facts? Were the facts clear enough to lead a student to repudiate irrationalism and to base his actions upon the kind of ideal of rationalism and freedom in which Weber believed? Was it, in other words, enough to present a sociological analysis of world problems to students, without proposing a solution, and then to hope for the best? It might have been at least a possibility that such students would have become democrats, but Weber's own intellectual dilemma made this still more difficult, for he was no Benda with a consistent rationalism at the base of his thought. It has been mentioned that idealism based upon an irrational human nature played an all-important role in his sociology. In his political analysis of contemporary times this became predominant.

More sensitive than Benda, Weber had an increasing awareness of the real problems of his times. He saw the growth of the state and the increasing complexity of society as a menace to liberty. But unlike Benda he did not recommend that intellectuals withdraw into their ivory tower. Instead he believed that a "charismatic" leader might offer the way out, for such a leader's "extraordinary" qualities and personality would mobilize people. Charismatic leadership rested upon "magical powers, revelation, hero worship," and one can recognize in charisma the kind of personal power which distinguished the leaders of the youth movement. Here Weber captured in his "ideal type" a man like Fisher, the founder of the *Wandervoegel.* Weber himself was close to the youth movement.

Thus Weber, with all his dedication to the cause of freedom, meshed with neoromanticism and the leadership cult of Germany at the beginning of the century. Yet this charismatic leader was democratic in the same sense that the leadership of the youth movement was so. This led to another interpretation of Weber's "charismatic" leader. Perhaps he was only advocating strong leadership within a parliamentary framework, for there could be little doubt about his allegiance to free institutions. He realized that democracy in Germany would desperately need strong leadership. His definition of "charisma," however, did give the concept totalitarian overtones, though he may have meant it to be democratic, for did such a leader really fit in with a representative form of government? Here Weber used one concept to strengthen another, but the emphasis was on the leader, not on parliament, as the dominant element in government. It was, at best, a roundabout defense of representative institutions, one so typical of those intellectuals who tried to maintain freedom in Europe.

Weber too was a Nationalist, if not with the violence of some of his colleagues. How, then, could he square the desire for a charismatic leader with ideas of freedom and rationalism? On one level he could do so by using his own concept of those limitations imposed on man which social analysis made obvious. Sociological analysis could demonstrate how unfree man really was, and this realization might be used to defeat man's irrational longings. In this way, a democratic society could be built by harnessing man's irrationality through his understanding of the social sciences. But Weber promptly smashed this hope by infusing social sciences with an idealism of their own, and using this idealism as a basis for a belief in the charismatic leader.

Intellectual freedom was Weber's highest value, yet he thought this freedom could only be maintained by having a charismatic leader. The massive emotional tensions generated by this conflict induced his long illness and his unhappy death.

Education on the Continent did not halt the march of irrational and totalitarian movements. After all, a disproportionately large percentage of the SS held Ph.D. degrees and Himmler himself had been a school teacher. The leaders of Italian fascism were, for the most part, highly educated men, as were those Frenchmen who looked to a totalitarian society. Where, then, did ideals of liberty still live amongst intellectuals? Looking at Europe in the year 1931, Benedetto Croce summed this up:

[Liberty] ... lives in many noble intellects in all parts of the world, which, no matter how isolated and reduced almost to an aristocratic but tiny *respublica literaria,* yet remain faithful to it and surround it with greater reverence and pursue it with more ardent love than in the times when there was no one to offend it or to question its absolute worship. . . .

This *respublica literaria* existed outside the seats of learning; indeed, Benedetto Croce became one of its symbols. He turned to his formulation of liberty, after having mirrored in his thought most of the influences affecting intellectual development since the end of the nineteenth century. He grappled with Marx, Freud, Sorel and German idealism. More important for him than all those influences was the view of history he derived from the eighteenth-century historian Vico. In Vico he found a mixture of philosophy and history and he fused this with Hegelian insights; he, in fact, was the first to introduce Hegel into Italy. History, for Croce, was the sum of human knowledge, and all philosophy was merely the judgment which men made upon history. The processes of history can be grasped by man's reason, for history was both supremely rational and the only reality. Croce did not stop here, though some of his pupils did.

For a man like Giovanni Gentile (1875–1944), this combination of history and rationality came to mean that "all that is real is rational." This meant the acceptance of the real, the thing that was in being, and thus led to the statement that "action and truth are mutually convertible terms." In the hands of Gentile these ideas formed a part of that nihilism of power which became Italian fascism. Mussolini was to sum it up in the phrase: ". . . outside history man is nothing." The very processes of history produced movements whose actions had to be accepted in terms of this historicism. Such a philosophy was little fitted to protect liberty.

Croce, however, went on to fuse this relativist view of history with German idealism. History was not just manifested through action; it strove through "internal" comprehension to gain its goal. It must vibrate in the historian's soul. Reality lay deeper than appearances; what the historian needed was a kind of "intuition" which would make possible the comprehension of a spirit of an age. Here Croce was close to Burckhardt. But how was this spirit to be defined? Croce believed that it must center on man's highest aspirations in art, religion, ethics, and theories of politics. The result was that his own history was quite consciously subjective. He loved the Renaissance because its aspirations were high; he condemned the Baroque because here men's aspirations tended to degenerate into sensuousness and a narrow acceptance of reality. Such comprehension of history in idealistic terms was for Croce not opposed to rationalism. He believed that through such a study man would become more rational, that his irrational drives would be harnessed. Yet the link between history and reason was shadowy at this stage of Croce's development. Only after the advent of fascism was he to construct a closer and well-defined relationship between these two forces.

Yet once again this did not seem to bear upon the problem of liberty. Indeed Croce was at one with many leading Italian intellectuals in his disillusionment with parliamentary institutions. The great upsurge of the *risorgimento* seemed to have ended in political corruption and petty party intrigues. A similar feeling was expressed by many Germans who believed that the great deed of national unification had not been reflected in contemporary politics. Like them Croce blamed this upon positivism, scientism, and the acceptance of a sordid reality. Unlike many of his Italian contemporaries, he did not withdraw into a nihilism; instead, he viewed his philosophy of history as a means to prepare men for a greater future. At this stage of his development, Croce saw this future grounded on ethical rather than on liberal principles. Machiavelli was his Italian hero, a man who had ennobled the art of politics by a splendid vision of the end toward which the nation should strive. Using Machiavelli as a touchstone, Croce foresaw an ethical and moral, rather than a liberal, end implicit in history. Thus Croce's attitude toward the advent of fascism was ambivalent. It was a part of historical development and it was directed against the sordidness of parliamentary squabbles. At this point in his development, Croce was not truly one of those intellectuals who made the preservation of freedom a central concern of their lives. But in the next two decades he came to stand for that *respublica literaria* in which the desire for freedom survived.

Croce's opposition to fascism developed from his ever stronger realization of the individualism implicit in his own theories. It was through the individual historian's mind that history must pass in order to form meaningful patterns. Individual criteria of moral aspirations, those possessed by the historian himself, determined the spirit of an age. This, coupled with Croce's aestheticism, became of ever greater importance. High aspirations meant a consciousness of aesthetic factors in art and literature, a consciousness which could not be divorced from the freedom for artistic development. He saw in fascism a direct menace to true aesthetic expression. This was what he meant when he told young Italians, "work for culture, he who works for culture, works against fascism." Croce's concern for freedom in this explicit manner differentiated him from many of his fellow intellectuals. It was based not on a primary concern for social justice or even for political freedom, but on an aristocratic definition of culture. The historian and the artist must be left free to develop their historical intuition and aesthetic expression. Croce was free, therefore, from the "cult of the people" which brought other anti-Fascists, like Ignazio Silone, for a while to communism. More consistently than any of the other men discussed, he now came to advocate individual freedom for the creative man as a cultural necessity. Through this preoccupation he found his way back to a thoroughgoing liberalism whose benefits would be extended far beyond an artistic and cultural elite.

History itself was viewed in its totality as the "history of liberty." Its aspirations were crystallized in the struggle between the "religion of liberty" and its enemies. Croce documented this in his last major work, the *History of Europe in the Nineteenth Century* (1931). At the same time he called for a closer link between history and reason, for it was the tragedy of the French Revolution that it had divorced the two. History and reason must be linked through the concept of liberty; once achieved, this would constitute the "moral soul" of Europe. In this manner Croce stood for a liberty which most of Europe had long rejected. His vigorous espousal seemed, for a short while, to give it new life. Yet, in the end, this proved misleading. When, after the war, Croce briefly assumed the reins of Italian government, he was ineffective. This was partly due to his advanced age, but also due to the fact that his vision of liberty seemed inappropriate and impractical in the twentieth century; its day in Europe seemed over.

Croce was not harmed by Mussolini. Living in Vico's old palace in Naples, he felt himself an island of freedom in a totalitarian society. His example served to inspire many an intellectual who searched for freedom in a world where defenders of liberty were becoming ever less vocal. Yet such a concept of liberty seemed strangely isolated in the postwar world. Was it really feasible for intellectuals to return to the classical liberalism of the previous century? Some who shared Croce's attitude recognized the hopelessness of ever again recapturing the pure ideal of liberal freedom. Paul Valéry, in his book *France Wants Freedom* (1938), based his liberalism on the older idea of France's mission to spread freedom in the world. He was also conscious of the social problems which faced mankind, however—of a chasm between these problems and the ideal of freedom which could not be bridged. Modern man was not only victimized by laws which limited his freedom but also by progress and technology. The only way to preserve freedom would be to found monasteries which would rigorously exclude modern technology. "There one will go on certain days in order to see some examples of free men through the bars." The majority of mankind was outside the monastery gate; the free man glorified by Liberals of the last century was like an animal in a zoo. Croce did not share this pessimism, perhaps because he was much less conscious of the problems involved in social progress. Surrounded by a totalitarian society, he seemed to be the kind of specimen Valéry described. Yet both the Frenchman and the Italian were concerned with the idea of complete human freedom, and, however irrelevant this seemed to contemporary problems, it was still a concern shared by many intellectuals.

One leading intellectual did attempt to fuse the idea of freedom with an appreciation of the social forces which were reshaping his times. Romain Rolland said that Jean Christophe, the hero of his great novels, would always have his fists clenched "against every tyrant who tramples upon humanity and oppresses the working people." He sympathized with the Soviet Union and defended it against critics who were, he thought, bourgeois capitalists and thus the oppressors of humanity. But the point is that Rolland was not a Communist. He accused the Communists of a blind rationalism which ignored the powerful currents stirring the depths of humanity: "... woe to those who scorn the forces of the heart." These forces Rolland saw exemplified by the individual striving to attain his spiritual freedom. Here was a truly revolutionary spirit which transcended social and political transformations, transformations which, in any case, were never final. He did not deny the necessity of a change in the class structure, but he did deny the contention that this necessity should lead to a new enslavement of the spirit through Marxist dialectics.

He defined his relationship to the revolution in which he also believed: "I wished to bring into the camp of the revolution these great eternal forces we had rescued, though tattered and bleeding, from the war of the nations." The power inherent in the ideal of the freedom of the spirit, the "high moral legacy of bourgeois society" would become a revolutionary weapon. In his controversy with the communist writer Henri Barbusse (1922), he championed individual conscience as against the collective forces supposedly dominating man's fate. The "social geometry of revolution" was rejected on behalf of an eternal struggle for freedom by all humanity. Rolland denied the necessity of force in the revolution and attacked the basis of current revolutionary strategy. The end did not justify the means. Moral values must be upheld, even more so during a revolution than in ordinary times. How did one fight for the revolution then? For, as Rolland told Barbusse, they both wanted the identical thing, an end to the oppression of the workers. Rolland saw a correct means not in force and deception but in the civil disobedience of Gandhi who was just becoming known in the West. Indeed, Rolland became the great popularizer of Gandhi's ideas.

Unlike Croce, Rolland did not return to a liberal inspiration but accepted revolution as a necessary cure for social ills. Unlike the Communists, he believed neither in Marxist dialectic nor in revolutionary force and strategy—the freedom of the spirit was always uppermost in his mind. It is no wonder that Rolland was, at times, depressed, and that his enemies on the right and left castigated him for joining no party in the struggle. But what is especially significant about Rolland's thought is the way he viewed himself, as an intellectual. Like Croce he talked about the "Republic of Letters," and like Benda he believed that it had betrayed its heritage—not, however, by entering the passions of the age (he did so himself after all) but by discarding the primary task of the intellectual.

The primary task of the intellectual was to carry on the "intrepid struggle of the spirit" by criticizing society. Voltaire and the Encyclopedists did more for the downfall of the *ancien régime* than "the handful of hotheads who took the Bastille." Together with this, the intellectual must keep the spirit of free thought alive in an age of iron. The intellectual must not stand in isolated impartiality; "brain workers" have to free men from the ties of race, caste, nationalism, and superstition—a task complementary to that of the workers who were organizing themselves for this purpose. But this organization must not, in the end, forge new chains to replace the old ones now imprisoning man's free expression.

Romain Rolland is practically forgotten today. Perhaps his ideals seem more utopian than Croce's because they combined sympathy for social revolution with an emphasis on freedom of the mind. It could be argued, however, that he is more germane for the present world crisis than the liberalism of Croce. Of all the intellectuals, he alone grasped the full implications of the social crisis of his time, and he alone refused to abandon the freedom intellectuals must have while resolutely accepting a solution which involved the destruction of bourgeois society.

Not surprisingly, the voice of freedom in Germany was much more hesitant than that of the South. Thomas Mann, in spite of himself, became the great symbol of freedom's defense and of democratic institutions. Before the birth of the German Republic, Mann was an integral part of the neoromantic stream. Like Croce he came to his liberalism only after the war, but with less confidence. Earlier, Mann had, in his *Buddenbrooks* (1901), been a novelist of decadence, of the death of an older bourgeois order. In the preface to a book whose young author had died (1914), Mann wrote ironically about the regeneration of youth. Viewing their freshness, he likened this to tuberculosis whose victims always look the picture of health. Youth could cry out how beautiful life was, how strong, but to what avail? Life was often on the side of him who denied it. Mann was a stranger to the urge for life which was sweeping contemporary German youth up into youth movements, of the worship of beauty and strength which seemed to capture their imagination in opposition to the stuffiness of bourgeois life. Mann's answer to bourgeois stultification, at that stage of his development, was not the activism of the Nietzschean youth but the bitter revelation of the Buddenbrooks's decadence. Subsequently, he began to retreat into an aesthetic detach-

*323*

ment from life, as in his novelette *Death in Venice* (1913). Mann shared that fascination for the morbid and unusual so common at the *fin de siècle*. All of this led him to accept Spengler's distinction between culture and civilization so symptomatic for this trend of thought. The *Remarks of an Unpolitical Man* (1918) pictured Germany as a nation of culture; it rejected democracy, indeed all politics, as "un-German" occupations. There was no concern for freedom here.

By 1922 Mann had repudiated these lectures and was fast becoming a symbol of liberalism both within and without Germany. In *Mario the Magician* (1929) he painted a picture of a magician-hypnotist who, tyrant-like, bent people to his inexorable will. The parallel between such a man and mass leaders like Adolf Hitler who wanted to destroy the Republic was obvious.

Yet Mann's position cannot be so simply defined. The great work of this period of Mann's life was the *Magic Mountain* (1921–24), and in this book the complexity of his position became manifest. Mann called this famous book a "leavetaking," a renunciation of much that he had loved. He intended, according to his own analysis, to advocate the attainment of an inner balance for man whose ideas must encompass both the spiritual and the natural. The artist must reach such a balance, and he implied that in a world free from excesses, true freedom could at last be found. This equilibrium was upset by the pull of three antagonistic world views. The first one was that view held by Settimbrini, the rationalist and pragmatist, whose liberalism was an expression of both. Such a world view divorced the artist from a reality which included the irrational in man and the world. The equilibrium was also upset by Naphta, the totalitarian—a Jew who had become a Jesuit and who defended medievalism as well as the authoritarianism of cultural control through the Church. The third man who symbolized unbalance differed from the others in that he nearly triumphed. Peeperkorn was a personality who typified naked, natural force. There was in him something of the primeval man, and he was much less ridiculous than either Naphta or Settembrini, for they were both hypocrites. The aesthete Naphta, who worshipped poverty, lived surrounded by luxuries; the liberal Settembrini was in reality a patriot. In the much more sympathetic Peeperkorn there was reflected a love for the genuine so prominent in neoromanticism. But Mann overcame this by having Peeperkorn commit suicide; he, too, did not have the answer to life.

In the end, the central character of the book, Hans Castorp, left the Magic Mountain in order to fight for his fatherland in the war, believing that he was fighting to save culture. The setting itself, a tuberculosis sanitarium surrounded by snow, isolated from the world, had a symbolic meaning. Can one achieve the kind of balance Mann wanted in a place so removed from the stresses of life?

Mann's answer was obviously in the negative. No longer could art and life be divorced from one another. The interpretations of a novel written with symbolic meaning have been legion. A Marxist critic has characterized it as the swan song of the bourgeoisie, a bourgeoisie removed from reality, dancing toward Armageddon without knowing it. It seems doubtful, however, that this was the message Mann wanted to preach. The theme of decay, symbolized by the very nature of tuberculosis with its outward appearance of health and inward decay, was long congenial to him. This theme was combined with a plea against philosophic excesses in an age when totalitarianism was closing in on so much of Europe. It is possible that this theme was muffled, in the *Magic Mountain,* by the atmosphere of general decay which pervaded the book. There was a concept of freedom through a balance of thought, but it was indirect and, because of the novel's tone, quite inconclusive.

Mann himself was to say that his real position was given in his prose essays rather than in his novels. But even these bore little resemblance to Croce's clearly defined liberalism. To be sure, essays like those on Schiller and Goethe were full of liberal confessions, but they were mixed with a neoromantic emphasis on feeling and culture. Mann was an interesting and significant example of the strength, in Germany, of that neoromanticism which he himself had wholeheartedly accepted up to the end of the First World War. After the war he attempted to fuse this with a concern for freedom, but never on the explicit rational base which Croce used. He hesitated between the inspirational image of Tolstoy or of the Goethe of the Enlightenment. Thomas Mann was not an example so much of the decline of the bourgeoisie as he was of the German Liberal's dilemma and of the timid liberalism of the German Republic which was never able to rid itself of the strong current of romanticism—of the distinction between culture and civilization.

Significantly, those writers who did defend freedom on a rational basis in postwar Germany were much less famous than Thomas Mann. He disliked his brother Heinrich, but Heinrich Mann tried to uphold the tradition of the French Revolution and of the Enlightenment in Germany. Hermann Hesse (1877–1962) called upon Germany to accept her defeat and to reject the neoromanticism which he believed had led the nation into the war. Hesse thought Germany needed a moral purification and a new attachment to liberal ideals. There existed a thorough humanism and rationalism among many German intellectuals; yet viewed against the background of the postwar world it seemed curiously detached from the world's problems.

Stefan Zweig (1881–1942), a very popular novelist, can serve as a good example of this detachment. One of his novels, *The Right to Heresy,* deals with the struggle of Sebastian Castellio against John Calvin in sixteenth-century Geneva. Castellio, the humanist, was seen as the archetype of what an intellectual should be. He spoke moderately and with clarity of mind, being concerned more with justice than with victory. Calvin was the typical zealot, filled with hate and concerned only with winning his victory. He was partisan and such men ". . . are never concerned with justice, but only with victory. They never want to concede another's point but only to uphold their own. . . . Eternal is the contrast between the disposition of the humanist and that of the doctrinaire. . . ." Zweig believed that Castellio had triumphed in the end. The idea of toleration had spread over Europe, and, with the French Revolution, the rights of the individual were guaranteed. By the nineteenth century the notion of liberty had been "accepted as an inalienable maxim by the civilized world." This must seem a gigantic self-deception, but it was part of an optimistic tradition which had its roots in the liberal humanism for which Zweig stood.

It might seem that after the war, especially in Germany, such optimism would be difficult to sustain; doctrinaires were winning victories on all sides. But Zweig, like most of these humanists, had little conception of the force of social change, of the restlessness of the mass of men. Not only Castellio but also Erasmus seemed to him a guide for the present. He cited with approval Erasmus's indifference to the mob, indeed, to the depths of human passion. No doubt the rationalism, the great learning of this humanist, evoked intellectual sympathy—but what example could he provide to the postwar world where human passions demanded appeasement? Zweig clung to his optimistic humanism even when national socialism, in the hour of its triumph, had driven him out of Germany. But there came a moment when he could no longer do so, for the world around him seemed to acquiesce in the triumph of the doctrinaires. Zweig died a suicide in far-off Brazil.

Zweig's tragedy highlights the dilemma of the rationalist-humanist outlook in the postwar world. This dilemma can further be illustrated by considering Benda's own attitude once fascism had triumphed in much of Europe and threatened to triumph over all of it. At the end of his life (1948) he sadly rejected the idea of the detached intellectual. Confronted by communism or fascism, he chose to be sympathetic toward communism, for fascism was the ideology of the oppressors while communism, at least, wanted to free the oppressed. But in the same breath he contended that communism would never give man freedom, because it was based on the principle of organization. Only democracy had been able to maintain freedom, because it had never been able to organize effectively precisely because it was liberal. Marxism meant merely a change in masters. He finished by proclaiming that he gave communism his stamp of approval because he had no other choice. But Benda reserved the right to judge Communists and at the same time the right to guard the freedom of his own spirit. This was not the kind of commitment Rolland had made nor was it the lofty humanism of Zweig. The old Benda gave up in despair, and this touches the essential dilemma of these intellectuals.

The concern with freedom was difficult to maintain and led to tragedy. But men like Croce, Rolland, Hesse, and Zweig did make freedom their primary concern, refusing to bow to the dominant illiberal forces of their age. In Germany, however, Thomas Mann's hesitancy was more symptomatic than the appeal of such men—Germany eschewed Hesse's moral purification or Zweig's humanism and raced toward a new catastrophe. Men read Stefan Zweig and Hermann Hesse (who, like Thomas Mann, received a Nobel Prize), but they did not believe in freedom defined in terms of rationalism or of liberalism.

Yet a thorough defense of freedom could exist apart from rationalism; it could be rooted in a coherent moral philosophy based upon a Christian inspiration. Such a concept of freedom arose not in Germany but in France. It was symbolized by the discovery in the 1920s of the importance of Charles Péguy. He had started his intellectual pilgrimage as a Socialist impassioned by the Dreyfus affair. Péguy then became one of those Marxists who was interested in an ideal of freedom rather than in historical materialism, and, when the Socialists came to power, he broke with them. Péguy's love of freedom made him oppose all compromise in politics, and he rejected any kind of forced unity. An insistence upon socialist unity destroyed, for Péguy, the whole content of socialism.

Inspired by such an absolute idea of freedom, Péguy founded a literary review which, as Romain Rolland said later, "kept us from asphyxiation." The *Cahiers de la Quinzaine* was not a commercial success, however, and Péguy spent his last years in poverty until, joining the army, he was killed at the battle of the Marne. He had, meanwhile, firmed his philosophy of freedom by giving it an ever stronger moral content. He, too, sought a union of thought and feeling centering on the idea of liberty. Péguy did not arrive at this, like Croce, through an ever greater stress on rationalism, or like Mann, through an inconclusive struggle between feeling and a spiritual balance. Instead, Péguy's quest led to his conversion to Catholicism in 1908. This became for him an *approfondissement,* a deepening of the heart—and through this he thought he had gained a true fusion of thought and feeling. The Church represented a perfect union of freedom and tradition, a fusion originating in liberty. Liberty was the precondition of Divine grace; it required an initial faith. Catholicism taught a profound respect for everything human.

Free will was for him the essence of Catholicism. It was this faith which supported ideals of human freedom and combined them with a deepening of the moral impetus in man. Péguy continued, however, to criticize the Church as it existed. By permitting tradition to harden, it had come to oppose all that was new; the real Catholicism of freedom did not put authority above free will. The moral beauty of Christianity was for Péguy something apart from actual historical development. He sharply rejected the idea that "all is history":

> Clio spends her time looking for the imprints of the past, vain imprints; and a little Jewess, a little nobody, a child, Veronica, takes out her handkerchief and makes an eternal imprint of the face of Jesus. This is all the explanation needed [for the world].

This was not a call to withdraw from life but a spur to political action. Both left and right had the same metaphysics; they both denied free will in the name of a quest for power and unity. Only the moral faith of Catholicism, as Péguy understood it, could save freedom.

These ideas sparked a Catholic renaissance in France. Here was a decisive break with the pessimism about the world which Péguy saw in nineteenth-century Catholicism. As he put it: To the Catholic bourgeoisie, Christ's passion was more important than his grandeur. In this grandeur lay that equilibrium between human nature and Divine grace which meant freedom. This freedom Catholics must defend against the power-seeking left and right. Led by Claudel and Bernanos, a young generation of French Catholics took up the challenge. It seemed as if, after a century, Lamennais was finally coming into his own. Such liberal idealism penetrated the thought of French Catholicism, distinguishing it from the Catholicism of other European countries which held more closely to the nineteenth-century tradition.

A revival of Thomist philosophy gave ideological strength to this Catholic renaissance. Thomism had become, in the previous century, the foundation of Catholic orthodoxy, and it tended, then, to divide Catholic thought from that of European intellectuals. But now Thomism came forward as a protector of individual freedom and as a philosophical system which could provide basic truths in a chaotic world.

Jacques Maritain (1882–1973) wanted to return to the basic Christian philosophy of Saint Thomas and to reemphasize the concept of human personality contained in that thought. Man was made in the image of God; he was, in himself, a reflection of the spirituality of the universe, possessing freedom of choice and thus confronting the world as an independent self-contained being. This thought had been lost by an emphasis upon the glory of man himself, by making man into a god instead of a reflection of God.

Man's freedom rested upon a transcendent, religious principle and not upon the volition of society. Christian fulfillment of the individual personality must be put first. Therefore society must provide freedom, for man could only fulfill himself through freedom as he was endowed with free will.

Maritain first formed his ideas in an attack on Henri Bergson (1913). He believed that Bergsonian philosophy rested upon wrong premises because he saw it as fundamentally anti-intellectual. Maritain wrote ". . . Thomist philosophy establishes the freedom of man in the very terms of intellect and being." The human will was not an irrational driving force as it was with Schopenhauer or indeed with the early Bergson—it was filled by God. But man could control it, for through human freedom man participated in a similitude of Divine freedom and this, through his intellect. As Saint Thomas said, "Man is free by the very act of his rational nature."

This was a philosophy of freedom based on man as a rational creature as well as upon man as a reflection of the Divine. It followed that freedom was indeed essential and that the state must grant it. In considering how this freedom could be realized in society, Maritain returned, again, to Catholic corporatism. Society must be pluralistic and the state must guarantee the freedom of voluntary associations beginning with that of the family through the various social communities. For Maritain's freedom was not the individualism of liberalism which for him would come close to a deification of man. It was the freedom of man within a social and political system which assured him the greatest freedom of development toward a true reflection in himself of the Christian cosmos. Man's choice was not between evil and good, but only between various goods, because evil had only a negative existence. Neo-Thomism, as it was sometimes called, gave man security within a traditional philosophical system and combined this with a strong emphasis upon freedom. From this position neo-Thomists could and did combat both emerging totalitarian society as well as the irrationalism of contemporary thought.

The contrast between this Catholic and French renaissance and the contemporary Protestant renaissance must be noted. Protestantism went back not to Thomism but to Luther, as reinterpreted by men like Kierkegaard in the nineteenth century and Karl Barth in the twentieth century. It stressed the complete abandonment of man to God and the irrelevance of society to faith Once more the rationalistic and Catholic tradition of France led to a wide difference between it and those regions in Europe which did not share either of these bases of thought.

Summarizing the efforts of all the intellectuals discussed, it can surely be said that their efforts were noble, their dilemmas severe. Was the rationalistic ivory tower the way to proceed? Could the liberalism of the nineteenth century be recaptured? Was there a possibility of finding a balance between the world of neoromanticism and the freedom of the individual? Did Catholic liberalism provide the answer? These are the questions which these men raised and debated.

Did the dilemma of these intellectuals reflect a corresponding decline of representative government—of those parliamentary institutions which the Liberals of the last century had regarded as essential for the orderly advance of freedom? Some of the difficulties which intellectuals experienced were due to the problem of linking freedom and representative government, the desire to make the participation of all in the state the crux of a definition of freedom.

After the war, economic necessities and social disorganization bulked too large for such an institutional definition of liberty. It is significant, however, that many movements which wanted to reorganize society still maintained the idea of representative government intact. The Socialists were an obvious example, but even advocates of a corporate state did not want to do away with parliaments, they only wanted to organize their representation along different lines. Yet the search was a search for a freedom which would have a deeper ideological and social base than was possible with a government concentrated upon parliamentary forms. That this was a dangerous threat to the existence of representative government will become clear in subsequent chapters.

Men were prone to think democratic machinery of little consequence and to concentrate upon the spirit behind it. Thus, in the end, they sacrificed the institution for the spirit. Others, however, like the Socialists, provided the only real defense in Europe of representative government after the war, for a democratic form was an integral part of their vision of a better society. Where parliamentary government was strongest, as in England, it was a part of the national ethos itself.

In considering nationalism it was seen that the development of representative government was the very crux of the developing English nationalism. It would be correct to say that in England parliamentary government was taken for granted in a manner unknown on the Continent. When the Second World War came, the defense of parliamentary government was basic to England's defense of freedom. Though the dilemma of the intellectuals did not reflect in any simple fashion the decline of representative government in Europe, it did symbolize an uneasiness about the liberal foundations such a government implied. Change was desired on the Continent, but that change did not always result in the destruction of this representative type of political organization.

Yet parliamentary government was on the defensive against a host of proposed alternatives, Marxism and facism being the chief challengers. For intellectuals, moreover, the search for the new had to go beyond a defense of institutions, and that was, perhaps, why so few of these men felt impelled to defend parliaments vigorously.

The majority of intellectuals in Europe not only failed to rally to the defense of parliamentary institutions, but in addition they did not make liberty, in terms of individual freedom, their chief concern. Some followed the times and sought to adjust to totalitarian ideas. Others looked at the world as it was and attempted to arrive at an explanation of reality as it existed outside the "superficial" political or social institutions. Their goal was to place man not in a framework of hope but instead into the context of the reality of existence itself. The latter group—the Existentialists—must now engage our attention.

# CHAPTER TWENTY

# *Existentialism*

HOWEVER SUBTLE in its thought, existentialism was one more reaction to the chaos of the postwar world. It stressed the evil in man, the hopelessness of his situation on earth, and enveloped both in a feeling of despair. As Jean-Paul Sartre (1905–1980) maintained, "We should act without hope." From this the Existentialists drew the conclusion that only the reality of things mattered—to quote Sartre once more, "I must confine myself to what I can see." These ideas were reminiscent of the nihilism of Ernst Juenger, and they document once more the pervasiveness of this atmosphere. As in Juenger's early works, the enemy was science and rationalism. Man was viewed as an essentially irrational creature. The German philosopher Karl Jaspers (1883–1969) had harsh words for Sigmund Freud's attempts at understanding the human mind through science.

Existentialism was not confined to one official dogma, however, nor was it a static philosophy. A distinction must be made between the Christian and the secular Existentialists—between those who were inactive in society and those who tried to introduce a note of social activism into the movement, for unlike Juenger, this movement was concerned not with nihilism but with finding a solution to man's despair. Indeed, it shared certain elements with idealism, but unlike Hegel the Existentialists rejected reason.

For Georg Lukács, writing from a Marxist context, this rejection of reason symbolized the bankruptcy of bourgeois philosophy. He accepted Lenin's thesis that the crisis in bourgeois thought would evolve into irrationalist tendencies. Such tendencies in European thought developed long before the existentialist movement, which itself built upon a neoromantic tradition. It differed, however, from the new Romantics in its stress upon the primacy of the individual. In this regard it was close to both nihilism and those ideals which had survived the liberal decline. Though Lukács castigated this individualism as antisocial and asocial, Sartre did attempt to give social and even revolutionary meaning to his brand of existentialist thought. Yet, he also rejected the optimism which an emphasis on reason entailed. Materialism was ". . . the subjectivity of those who are ashamed of their subjectivity." Idealism in the sense that man had to transcend his existential reality lay at the base of the whole movement.

The Christian Existentialists had, perhaps, the most lasting influence. The movement merged with Protestant neoorthodoxy, for these men wanted to return to the essentials of the Reformation as they understood them. At the same time, such Existentialists were intent upon disentangling Christianity from the toils of Church and state so that it might return to a truer purpose. Each nation had claimed Christ as its very own, as its shield in war. What was left of Christianity if God was only on the side of the strongest battalions? Neoorthodoxy and Christian existentialism revolted against that institutionalization of Christianity which had been accelerated by the war.

The catalyst for this development was a man who had died almost a hundred years before, all but forgotten by the world. The Dane Soren Kierkegaard (1813–1855) was elevated to the status of a patron saint. He had rejected all the ideological systems of his time: rationalism, nationalism, and institutionalized religion. Kierkegaard was contemptuous of the crowd in an age when the worship of the masses was on the lips of so many constructors of ideology. But for this worship he did not substitute an optimistic individualism or the idea of an elite. Individual man was stupid and self-deceiving: "It is not truth which rules the world but illusions." Pursued by his illusions, man tried to escape from his own misery by merging with the crowd. Of course this was vastly appealing in an atmosphere which decried the illusion of life's externals and maintained the primacy of its underlying essence.

What then was the right path for man to take? In his *Fear and Trembling* (1841), Kierkegaard set the stage for much of later Christian existentialist thought by reinterpreting the story of Abraham's sacrifice of Isaac.

Abraham was both committing a murder and making a sacrifice to God. He loved Isaac and yet wanted to kill him. Kierkegaard developed his thought through such a love for paradoxes and he later was widely imitated in this. The final paradox of this story occurred when God gave Isaac back to Abraham. The father now acted as if nothing at all had happened; he was as joyful with his son as before. What did all this mean? Abraham had drained the cup of despair and thus knew the bliss of the infinite. Faith had taught him the lesson that life was absurd and not reasonable, for "he has resigned everything infinitely and then grasped everything again by virtue of the absurd." The faith which had taught him this lesson was far from the comforting faith of the churches; it was the "dread" which led to "fear and trembling" before God. Through this faith he had comprehended life and has was thus able to joke with Isaac immediately after trying to murder him. "Humble courage is required to grasp the temporal by virtue of the absurd, and this is the courage of dread."

Abraham's rediscovery of his true individuality was manifested in his ability to make decisions. Sartre was quite right when he said later that existentialism was not a quiet despair, though he himself openly admitted to just this feeling before the Second World War. Kierkegaard believed that individualism would express itself in action; he had in mind, however, not merely outward acts but particularly mental decisions. Not the nihilism of the *Thunder of Steel* but the inward commitment of the individual was advocated. Such an inward commitment had spurred Abraham's decision to follow God and Luther's confrontation of his God as well. This decision must precede a true understanding of the world, as it had in the case of Abraham. Faith was a prerequisite for individuality. How different this was from the secular existentialism epitomized by Simone de Beauvoir's saying that "man fulfills himself within the transitory or not at all." Kierkegaard, then, confronted that same dilemma which had impressed the postwar Existentialists as the crux of the human situation—man lived in an absurd, illogical world, enveloped by illusions and driven by despair. Escape lay in grasping and accepting the absurd. This could only be accomplished through a decision of faith which required a total resignation, a resignation which signified a recapturing of life. In this manner man, grasping his true individuality, would be able to make future decisions.

Kierkegaard's thought led into that religious revolt which sparked a revival of interest in religion among the intellectuals of the 1920s and 1930s. Karl Barth (1886–1968), the central figure of neoorthodoxy, seized many of the Dane's ideas. He, too, stressed the "dread" with which man must face God and equated this dread with original sin. Indeed, this stress upon the sinfulness of man was not confined to Barth; it was also found in works of theologians like Reinhold Niebuhr. Man was as nothing before God. Barth thought this sinfulness had destroyed man's faculty for perceiving God either in creation or in history. Man therefore must return to God's revelation in order that he might come to terms with his own existence, and God was revealed in Christ, "the word made flesh," and in Scripture itself. Thus Barth and the neo-Orthodox returned to the original inspiration of the Reformation: the absolute sovereignty of God and His revelation through Christ and the Holy Word.

Barth related this return to the contemporary crisis of man's existence which was generated by man's sinfulness and his consequent alienation from God. This crisis could only be resolved by overcoming this alienation not through critical reason but through "dread." Faith was needed; the Biblical depiction of man's humility and the joys of faith were recalled. No more than Kierkegaard, however, did Barth suggest that this faith in a sovereign God could solve the dilemma of human life, transforming it into an orderly and rational progress through history. Barth, as did all Christian Existentialists, offered a way of grasping life's brutality, of bearing it with an equanimity derived from a deeper understanding of life itself. There were no final answers for alienated humanity. It must not be forgotten that his efforts were directed toward disentangling Christianity from the all-devouring concerns of the world. How foolish, in a world of war and misery, to ask if God was righteous; how wise to stand in awe before a sovereign God.

In 1934, with national socialism triumphant, he reminded the Germans that the reformers were concerned only with faith and not with culture or civilization. Yet, under the stress of Nazi pressures upon German Lutheranism, Barth abandoned his quietism and became the spiritual leader of the Lutheran resistance to Nazi encroachment. The declaration of the Prussian Reformed Church at Barmen (1934) reflected his views upon the state's pretensions to jurisdiction over the Church. It sharply rejected the idea that the Church should recognize any revelations either from men, states, or ideologies, aside from that of God alone. The declaration attacked the contention of the national socialist state that it represented the sole, true ordering of the totality of man's life. Finally, and this was the crux of the matter, the Church could not subject its divine message to the changing intellectual and political ideologies of this world. This opposition was rooted in Barth's constant attempt at returning to a "pure faith" unencumbered by human considerations. He once wrote that, after all, God was not the servant of man, man was the servant of God.

Barth's solution, or rather his analysis, of the existential dilemma of man led, in the end, to an opposition to totalitarianism, not because it was a wrong political order (Could there ever be a right one for sinful man?), but because it destroyed that faith which signalized man's "dread" of God. Faith so defined involved a confrontation of God and man in which no third power could be allowed to intervene.

In both Kierkegaard and Barth the theme of confrontation played an important role. It was, in reality, the crux of their approach to man's existence. Through such a confrontation man, in "dread" and "faith," was led to accept the absurdities of life. This theme was common also to secular Existentialists. Their confrontation, however, was not with God but with nothingness. In Sartre's story *The Wall,* one of the doomed characters reminisced about his involvement in the Spanish Civil War: "I took everything as seriously as if I were immortal." By the end of the story he had come to the conclusion: ". . . to hell with Spain and anarchy: nothing was important." But one fact was still important—the death which awaited him at the "wall." Such a confrontation did not result in that "dread" about which Barth and Kierkegaard had written; it was, instead, a kind of carefree despair. Of what use is it to take life seriously if you are going to be stood up against a wall and shot in the end?

Sartre also considered man a lowly creature. "Consciousness is a being, the nature of which is to be conscious of the nothingness of its being." Even such consciousness was part of a self-deception. Again, life was regarded as an illusion, an unremitting pattern of self-deception. For Sartre this pattern was a screen between existential reality and man, a kind of security which men erect to mask the horror of their true liberty of commitment, for men have freedom of choice; all Existentialists stressed this. But one must choose without any illusions, without that cowardly self-deceptive screen behind which an individual could retire in supposed security. The anti-Semite was such a coward; his prejudices enabled him to escape the dilemma of freely-made commitments. "Man makes himself."

Sartre also thought that a decision must initiate the penetration of reality's illusions. This was all the harder to do because there were no signs to guide man. Sartre rejected the supernaturalism of Kierkegaard's story of Abraham. As a skeptic he wondered where the proof of the Angel would be—was he really an Angel? Am I really Abraham? His decision forced man to realize the hopelessness of his situation but at the same time it was this understanding which liberated man. Again, all this ended with an existentialist paradox. Camus expressed it well in his story of the "Myth of Sysiphus." Sysiphus became a happy man because he knew despair; it was a Greek story with a happy ending.

These existentialist solutions to the dilemma of postwar man seem, at first glance, oddly unsatisfactory. "Dread," death, and despair were written large in their works. These men sought escape from their difficult age by denying objective reality. Being was "thought," being was "faith," everything was intellectualized and objective reality was repudiated. The initial and all-important decision took place in the mind. The philosopher Jaspers summed this up: ". . . the purpose and meaning of a philosophical idea is not the cognition of an object, but rather an alteration of our consciousness of BEING, and of our inner attitude toward things." Obviously such attitudes were in sharp contrast to the brutal nihilism of contemporaries like Juenger.

This existentialist solution was not a nihilistic acceptance of reality but rather a repudiation of it as an illusion. The goal was the recapture by man of his true individuality. Yet this solution was paradoxical. True individuality required both a discovery of reality as absurd and at the same time an acceptance of this reality. One had also, however, to be above, or rather beyond, the battles of life, just as the Christian church for Barth was beyond them. Though the great theologian fought the national socialist state, it is well to remember that existentialist philosophers did not act so resolutely. Martin Heidegger, the most famous existentialist philosopher, collaborated. Here was the danger of the existentialist paradox.

To be sure, under the impact of totalitarianism and the Second World War some of the Existentialists tried to arrive at a more positive attitude toward a free society. Jaspers concluded that true "self being" could only be realized in a community where others were also free. Sartre came to the same conclusion through a different approach. He attempted to temper man's free decision by stressing, in addition to freedom, man's responsibility. The result was that man did not, after all, make choices free from any external system; instead, he must accept responsibility for his actions. Man's free decision had to take into account his responsibility toward society and freedom. But were these not the kind of illusions Sartre had deplored; how could man's decisions be made with an objective reality in mind if this reality did not exist? Responsibility could be only to one's existential condition, not to any social or political system. Sartre attempted, after the Second World War, to impart to elements of objective reality a deeper meaning so that man's responsibility to society could be reconciled to an existentialist world view.

When he published, in 1943, his *Being and Nothingness,* the world was still seen as hostile toward individual self-expression. Respect for the freedom of others resulted only in the repression of one's own freedom. The freedom of every man encroached upon that of his fellow men. By 1948, however, he had changed his view. The liberty of one now depended upon the liberty of all. Political and social systems were no longer something extraneous to man's self-fulfillment within his existential condition. "Man makes himself," but he could only do this under conditions where all men were free. The individual, in creating his own values, created the values of all, and he must act as if the whole human race would regulate itself by his example. For Sartre, commitment to social and political action for the sake of freedom became imperative.

The world was no longer a tissue of self-deception. Whether this ideal became the "Baedecker of the left-wing intellectual," as one admirer has written, is questionable. This theory of commitment brought Sartre closer to the Communist party for a while, until the Hungarian revolt.

There was, however, an inevitable tension between Marxism and the individualism of existentialism. The tension between an emphasis upon the existential, inner-directed situation of the individual and the necessity of being a part of the Marxist mass movement introduced an ambivalence into Sartre's thought. He himself, in 1957, admitted this contradiction in his thought but maintained that it was an inevitability. The movement lost much of its force once it attempted to link itself with a social theory and to relate itself to that mass society against which it had revolted in the first place.

Sartre's situation was exceptional among existentialist thinkers. Jaspers talked about freedom but withdrew, nevertheless, into a kind of futility about the existentialist dilemma. Neither Jaspers nor Heidegger were, in the end, concerned about whether even their students understood them—and Heidegger never changed his philosophy, even after the war. Apart from the France of Sartre, the movement was not concerned with external commitments to society but with man's internal sense of bewilderment.

This internalization of the human existential situation, this sense of futility, was best expressed by a novelist who had been discovered in the 1920s, Franz Kafka (1883–1924). It is difficult to interpret any of the Existentialists, and for the same reasons—their thought was often embedded in ambiguous philosophical and literary forms. This has led to endless works of interpretation; it has been part of their appeal. Though the literature on Kafka is enormous, merely the essence of his thought will be considered here. For Kafka, life's problems were unfathomable; he depicted the dilemma of the human situation without providing any solutions. Indeed, Edmund Wilson called his writings a "verbalization of futility." In *The Trial* Kafka constructed a novel around a man who was tried for a crime whose nature is never discovered either by his remote judges or by himself. During the nightmare of the trial the accused comes to feel that he is guilty, though he has no idea what he is guilty of. The individual is the plaything of the existential dilemma.

Perhaps the contemporary critic Austin Warren has expressed it best: Kafka was not deluded into thinking that the soul and its choices mattered in the City, that is, in the complex, modern world. No kind of synthesis was possible between man and God, good and evil. There was a confrontation, but it was frustrating and futile, a nightmare burlesque of an actual trial. Action and even decision were useless in solving anything, for the quest was so much greater than man himself. Kafka agreed that the world was built upon illusions, "built on lies." Within these illusions man was hopelessly trapped. "But the multitudes are so vast; their numbers have no end"; man could never reach the "open field." He would always remain imprisoned in the City. The negative qualities of existentialism found their purest expression in Kafka.

Kafka was not alone, however; another writer who enjoyed a delayed popularity also expressed this negativism. Rainer Maria Rilke's (1875–1926) poetry has also been subjected to a wealth of interpretations. He piled image upon image until all clarity was lost in a search for form, in a verbal symbolism. He played with poetic nuances until all was dissolved into a kind of relativism. Rilke was under the spell of impressionism which he had absorbed during his stay in Paris. He accepted the movement's main contention that the world could be understood through its assimilation to one's own experiences and visions. Thus, artistic reality became an "expression" of the individual. For painters this meant a rejection of merely photographic and representational art; for Rilke it meant that nature and the world had to be assimilated and, through one's own individuality, transformed into visions and poetry. The poet, however, was aware of the nature of reality. He drew attention to the misery of great cities and the hardships of the poor.

There was bound to be a tension between such a reality and this reality transformed into art. In his famous *Duineser Elegien* (1912–22) this tension between art and life became manifest. To this tension was added the dilemma of life and death: the conflict between vision and poetry, which were life, and reality, which led to death. For Rilke the only escape lay in reaffirming both; the dichotomy could never be overcome. What mattered was survival; just to be, to exist, was wonderful. Thus Rilke accepted the paradox between life (art) and death, but he, too, thought man's situation hopeless. There could be no mediation between these twin poles of life, no God and no Christ. But once this reality had been accepted, Rilke could become more affirmative than Kafka. He dwelt on the exhilarating challenge of existence once he knew that, in reality, "survival is all."

Rilke's popularity was, of course, primarily due to his poetry, just as Kafka's rested largely on his superb literary craftsmanship. Beyond this, however, Kafka's resignation was at one with a weary generation's own attitudes, while Rilke accepted the reality of life and yet saw beauty in the existentialist paradox. Like those Christian Existentialists whose thought was taught in many theological seminaries and preached from many pulpits, their ideas are still influential in the second half of the twentieth century. Sartre's type of despair has not fared so well. He eventually tried to turn in the direction of a free society, but without great success.

Whatever one might think of existentialism as a philosophy of life, it expressed a mood more widespread than that of those intellectuals who glorified a personal, external freedom. The view of life as an absurdity also found expression in the visual arts, without, however, any existentialist apparatus. Dadaism in Germany derived from that revolt against old art forms which had found its greatest expression in the Impressionists as well as in the Expressionists. To the Expressionists, in particular, rationalism had been the enemy of art which must be a spontaneous expression of the heart. Central to the Dadaist's endeavors was the truth and beauty of absurdity.

The dadaist manifesto (1920) described rationalism as a "bourgeois bluff" while a dadaist novel proclaimed: "La vie est une chose vraiment idiote" (life is really nonsensical). The very name of the movement was illustrative: it meant hobbyhorse in baby talk. As far as dadaism was concerned it did not want to be related to any other artistic movement. The dadaist painters no longer emphasized figures in motion as did the Impressionists, or the love of space and color as did the Expressionists, but simply confusion. If life was absurd, only nonsensical representations could adequately portray its actuality. Dadaism did not last; it never founded a school or received widespread support. In fact, seldom has any literary and artistic movement vanished so quickly and without a trace. Yet it did share the basic world view of the Existentialists and pushed it to its logical conclusion. In its abhorrence of theories and ideologies it also closely mirrored the vague despairing mood of the postwar generation.

Existentialism had many ties with those habits of mind already discussed since the change in the public spirit of Europe. Both the individualism of expressionism and the search of the neo-Romantics are related to it. Of Kafka it has been said that he belonged to a time "whose torture lay in the fact that all its conflicts lay outside the visible world." That the habit of mind which denied reality by looking for truth beyond it was widespread in Europe has been seen. Where neoromanticism sought for tangible authority in nature or race, the quest of the Existentialists ended in renunciation. "Eternity flees from fulfillment," the poet Franz Werfel wrote in the twenties.

Existentialism was a faith for intellectuals; men in general wanted not renunciation in the face of life but security and hope. No more than the philosophies discussed in the previous chapter could existentialism fulfill such longings. While the intellectuals were trying to meet the challenges of the postwar world in this fashion, different and ruthless forces were taking events out of their hands. Totalitarianism was on the ascendant in Europe at the same time that these intellectuals were talking about the need for freedom and reason, or the necessity of man's confrontation with God. In many parts of Europe fascism was the wave of the future. It could take care of man's search for authority, his need of belonging, and it could do this in terms of hope for a better world which rejected the reality of the present. Fascism was to climax many habits of mind which grew up after the age of romanticism which was discussed at the beginning of this book.

# CHAPTER TWENTY-ONE

# *Fascism*

**A**FTER 1918 parliamentary government, so precious to Liberals, was under attack everywhere. The attempt of men in the postwar world to reorient themselves in society led to a disregard for outward forms of government in preference to a concern with man's "soul." The definition of reality, which has in previous chapters been traced through many movements, regarded the external world as a myth beneath which coursed the true principles of life. Representative government, a purely external matter, was not of the essence of life and was thus dispensable. The relativism of values, the revolt against logic and reason which had shaken the foundations of nineteenth-century liberalism, also led to a rejection of parliamentary government. But despite this rejection, there was no lack of preoccupation with the forms which a true government should take. The people should have a part in their government, but one responsive to their own nature.

Men who were antiparliamentarian were not antidemocratic. Their redefinition of democracy was divorced from ideas of representation, for representative government seemed to lead to rule by vested interests or to corruption. As Spengler put it, "Politics is merely the continuation of private business by other means." Men prided themselves on their aloofness from the melee of political parties. The new romanticism, in particular, searched for a form of government that would knit people together, that would be politically solid. For example, the German youth movement demanded a national renewal which was not based upon antiquated political organizations, that is, the traditional political parties. The search was viewed in terms of the people's direct participation in the state. The influential German writer Moeller van den Bruck summed this up: ". . . not the form of the state makes a democracy, but the participation of the people in the state." Representative democracy was thought to be out of tune both spiritually and socially with the times. Carl Schmitt, whose *Cultural Position of Parliamentary Government* (1926) impressed many scholars, put it very simply: Parliament, as a bourgeois institution of the nineteenth century, lacked foundation in an age of mass industrial democracy.

Not only Germans were in the forefront of this attack on parliamentary democracy; in Italy the same current of thought was at work. As was seen in a previous chapter, Croce attacked parliament, and some of Italy's best minds followed his lead. Italian intellectuals were also searching for new forms of political expression. The nihilism of the Italian poet Giacomo Leopardi prefigured the despair engendered by an Italy which had failed to fulfill the high hopes of the *risorgimento*. Gabriele d'Annunzio's popularity was part of a feeling of revolt which was, at that point, too confused to have a well-defined direction. Like the youth movement in Germany, d'Annunzio's writings symbolized the revolt's confused but romanticized political program. In his writings one discerns a Nietzschean disgust with bourgeois society coupled with neoromanticism. This mixture resolved itself into a longing for new national leadership.

The attack on representative government was not confined to theorists—the politicians soon joined in. In both Germany and Italy parliamentary government was not overthrown by revolutionists; it committed suicide peacefully —and with the blessing of the parliamentarians. All members of the German political parties, with the exception of some Social Democrats, voted for the Enabling Act of 1933. This gave Hitler plenary powers, powers which everyone knew meant the end of parliamentary, representative government. Similarly in Italy, the parliament signed away prerogatives to Mussolini which it had refused other prime ministers. He, like Hitler, was granted these powers only for a limited time (twelve months), but here again there was no doubt that this marked the end of constitutional rule (1922). To be sure, this took a little longer in Italy, but the electoral reform giving any party polling 25 percent of the vote an absolute majority (1923) transformed the Italian parliament into a Fascist party meeting.

The most important fact about fascism's triumph in Germany and Italy was that it came to power legally. The disgust at party politics in contrast to the grave problems crying for a solution had affected politicians as well as intellectuals. Moreover, the danger that socialism might succeed where bourgeois parties had failed was a powerful persuader. In the Italian senate the liberal Albertini summed this up when he pointed out that Mussolini's government had given Italy "freshness, youth and vigor." Moreover, "He has saved Italy from the socialist danger. . . ." Albertini, a Liberal in the classic, nineteenth-century sense, illustrated how far the repudiation of existing governmental institutions had gone.

If fascism came to power legally it was only overthrown by a lost war and not through internal revolution or conspiracy. That also is a fact worth noting. There can be little doubt about the popularity of fascism, especially in the beginning. Millions of Germans and Italians voted for it in their last free elections. In Italy, men like Toscanini and Puccini joined the movement and Benedetto Croce gave it his tacit support. Repudiation came afterwards—for Toscanini, within a few years; for Croce, somewhat sooner. For many it never came at all. Underlying the social disorder and the voluntary liquidation of representative government was the constant feeling of disillusionment and frustration.

Just as in Germany there were men who believed that the attainment of political unity had not brought with it a corresponding spiritual revival, so in Italy the patrimony of the *risorgimento* seemed shamefully wasted. But what were the political alternatives? There was Marxism; Croce flirted with this ideology for some time. Its attraction will be discussed subsequently. The longing for an organic state emerged also as a choice in this continuing romantic era. It was this alternative to parliamentary government which became of prime importance in the growth of fascism. The organic state retained the class structure but it fused the population into a whole through the ideology of the *Volk*. This concept expressed the prime importance of a common feeling and history regardless of the outward form of government. It condemned parliamentary democracy in particular because instead of knitting together a nation it atomized the individual. The real spirit of the *Volk* must be expressed through a "natural aristocracy" and through a leader. An elite would express the shared spirituality of the nation as its "ideal type"; the leader, in turn, would lead this elite, and through it the people, to the fulfillment of their true personality. Ideas which have previously been dealt with thus come together here: the organic state, the elite, and the leader.

The new leaders would depend not on the shifting allegiances of political parties but on "intuition." As has been pointed out, intuition played a large part in those movements transmitted from the nineteenth to the twentieth century. Intuition would guide the creation of a state in tune with the "spirit" or the "race" of the people. Sorel termed this whole process that of the creation of a "myth" which gave a group cohesion and enabled it to fully utilize its energies. Human beings acted upon illogical premises; therefore the creation of a "myth" would stimulate their will for action. Pareto, basing his thought on similar premises, had tried to teach the ruling classes how to use such myths for the sake of power. Thus the intuition involved in the construction of an organic state was thought of as the ability to use and create "myths" fusing governments with the irrational mainsprings of human action. Ideas like those of Sorel and Pareto did not influence fascism directly. Yet fascist ideology was built upon the use of such thoughts as an alternative to parliamentary governments. Spiritual renewal and political forms would meet in a national revival. The organic state, reaching full flower in fascism, was the alternative to Marxism; both built their strength upon a disillusionment with representative government.

The ideal of an organic state in which everyone could participate through national myths seemed well suited to the age of mass politics. From the very beginning the rise of nationalism in the early nineteenth century had coincided with the beginning of mass politics, and national symbols had served to unite masses of people and to give them a sense of political participation. National hymns, sacred fires, and flags were some of the symbols which led men into festive action. There were processions and meetings at which folk dances or gymnastic exercises were sometimes performed. There is a direct connection between such festivals of the nineteenth century and twentieth-century mass meetings and mass politics. In reality fascism was never a simple confrontation between leader and led, but instead a secular religion, replete with national myths and symbols, a bridge between people and leaders, providing at the same time an instrument of social control over the masses.

Fascism differed in its diverse manifestations. In Germany the ideological content of the organic state concept was of prime importance from the very beginning; the corporate restructuring of society which men like Langbehn had forecast never became reality. Austria, Portugal, and Spain infused the ideal with a different ideological content, that of Catholicism, adopting a corporate political structure which had, for almost a century, been an integral part of Catholic social thought. Italy diverged from both these forms. The corporate state, where both workers and managers were to cooperate within each profession, was meant to meet a pressing problem: the taming of Trade Unionism. For even after Mussolini had created a compulsory fascist trade union, it tended to be militant, upsetting the employers. The corporate state, finally set up in 1939, took care of their problem, for the state mediated between workers and employers within each corporation and thus could bend both to its will. All fascism integrated labor into its system by stressing the hierarchy of function but not of status: the worker had status as an important member of the *Volk* community even if he had to obey his employer when at work. The attempted division between function and status accounts for much of fascism's success in avoiding disturbances which might affect the smooth course of industrial development.

The worker was given a sense of belonging to a community which appreciated his work. Such a national community was generally symbolized by the political liturgy and rites of fascism, as well as by the orgy of uniforms which raised the status of the most humble when he was decked out in this manner. But for workers fascism created the *Dopolavoro* as an extensive program of social paternalism. The worker was provided with cheap vacations, theatre, opera, as well as adult education in his spare time. Hitler imitated the Italian example in his "Strength Through Joy." There is ample evidence that this solicitude was appreciated, even as the worker's real wages declined and nothing was done in either Germany or Italy to improve his housing.

Italian fascism had, at first, an explicit pragmatic base which it was never to lose entirely. Mussolini's early career in the socialist movement had centered upon an urge toward activism more than upon an acceptance of Marxist theory. He made his mark agitating for intervention on the side of France in the First World War, for such an intervention might bring about revolution in Italy. During the war itself Mussolini came to believe that a new force was needed to act as guide to the masses, and he now saw this as an alliance of men involved in economically productive activities and war veterans. He had been expelled from the Socialist party and therefore had to find a political terrain which was not preempted by his former brothers.

Thus fascism was born and moved slowly but surely to the right of the political spectrum. The earliest fascists were both Nationalists and radicals; they wanted to satisfy Italy's territorial aspirations and to support the workers. Gabriele d'Annunzio during his occupation of Fiume (1919–21) had similar ambitions. The poet was a master of the use of myth and symbol and public festivals which he used to maintain a dynamic within the occupied city. But he also made an alliance with the radical union of seamen. Mussolini and his followers, however, could not keep up such an alliance for workers tended to be preempted by socialists.

The first fascist program (March 1919) points to the future. Nationalism was to be the essence of the "myth" of government; Italy's unfulfilled aspirations at Versailles the new goal. But another approach to political organization now came to the fore. Syndicalist doctrines were cautiously affirmed. The leaders needed for the management of labor could be recruited from the masses. Men from the working classes should acquire managerial skills, but they should also realize that it is not easy to run industry and commerce.

Fascism was on the way toward a corporate organization which would actually keep the class structure intact while uniting laborer and employer in the nation's service. Thus, a greater concern for the rights of labor coud be displayed along with a support of management; both were combined in a monolithic unity dedicated to the higher purposes of nationalism.

Along with the development of a corporate structure, the ideological foundations for Italian fascism were more explicitly laid. Mussolini later gave much of the credit for this to the inspiration provided by the pragmatism of William James and Sorel: particularly to their idea that all theory originated in practical action. Mussolini's activism, however, grew out of the historical situation in which the Fascists operated and out of his own ideological orientation. His alliance with the Futurists was close from the very beginning of fascism. These intellectuals saw reality as a continuous and unpredictable process of creation which could only be lived intuitively. The Futurists wholeheartedly adopted Bergson's *élan vital*. Mussolini, who had earlier infused his socialism with Nietzschean ideals, found futurism equally congenial. In fact, all of fascism stressed activism, the ideal to live life to its fullest, and for many followers this might have served as substitute for a firmer world view. Certainly this activism was well attuned to a movement which all over Europe attracted youth rather than the middle-aged. No doubt the war experience added to such a love of activism, for it was in many minds bound up with the true community which had existed in the trenches—the camaraderie absent in the postwar world.

When Fascists talked about the organic state and the *Volk* community they thought of camaraderie basic to close-knit groups: not a society held together by coercion but a *Bund* (as the Germans called such a group) which was dynamic and at the same time provided shelter for the members. Fascism took up what the sociologist Ferdinand Tönnies, at the beginning of this century, had called community as opposed to society, the voluntary group as against an imposed togetherness. Tönnies formulated an attitude which had its roots in the opposition against positivism during the *fin de siècle* and which had found reality in the groups of the German and other European youth movements. Fascism was the inheritor of such a political theory but could not accept it without modification, for such a principle of organization could lead to anarchism instead of discipline and order in which fascism believed. The key to fascism is not only the activism and the longing for a community of affinity but also the taming of these ideals into a system of hierarchy, discipline, and order. In Germany concepts of race, rootedness, and the *Volk* were used to accomplish this taming; in Italy the ideological foundations provided by men like Giovanni Gentile and Alfredo Rocco accomplished this purpose.

For Gentile the nation was the sole reality in the Hegelian sense, and man was only fulfilling his moral self when he integrated himself with the nation. He combined with this Croce's early ideas on the process of history as the only reality. The state was the product of a progressive, historical evolution, and thus a true expression of this reality. Man must not stand in the way of its triumph. Success became its own justification, for the process of history justified success as an absolute good. Moreover, the state had always triumphed through the use of force. Gentile's argument reached its climax in the statement that freedom meant submission to state power, for true morality consisted not of defiance but of accommodation to that history whose essence was the progressive triumph of the nation. "Always the maximum of liberty coincides with the maximum power of the state . . . every force is a moral force for it must always be an expression of the will," and, it should be added, of history.

History expressed the will of the people; it was the "myth" which fused political forms and the "spirit" of the people together. With Gentile, that "myth" was a history whose will the nation expressed by its use of force. Mussolini agreed with him when he proclaimed that "outside history man is nothing," that the state was the true reality of the individual. For the Duce, all this was part of a myth created by fascism. "The myth is a faith, it is a passion" and its content was the greatness of the nation. The task was to translate this myth into reality. Mussolini believed that a myth was necessary before reality could be transformed. Ideology was a primary consideration in fascism, just as it had been for the new Romantics earlier in the century. Mussolini was anxious to integrate activism and ideology; no nation could be transformed on the basis of undisciplined action.

Though Gentile, for a time Mussolini's Minister of Education, provided part of the necessary myth, Alfredo Rocco (1875–1925), his Minister of Justice, did much to systematize fascist thought. He stressed the organic nature of the state in contrast to the mechanical and atomistic concepts of communism which viewed the nation as merely the sum total of individuals. This, to him, was anti-historical and materialistic for it was the soul of the people which had to be stirred. The fascist state was at one with the passions and strivings of countless generations. Society was the end and individuals the means, for in such a state the daily lives of organized humanity had a scope and direction which transcended the trivial struggles of individuals. Thus, the highest ethical value of fascism lay in the duty to the state so defined.

Not surprisingly the "myth" as both a faith and a passion fused into a kind of mysticism. Gentile wrote that ". . . we all participate in a sort of mystic sentiment. . . . The new Fascist society will be born through a creative faith which germinates in our heart." That faith was tamed into order, hierarchy, and discipline through the theories of Gentile and Rocco but not without considerable difficulty. Youth continued to be in ferment, especially in the 1930s when many of them charged fascism with having grown fat in power. Fascist youth attacked a fascism which was no longer open-ended and activist but seemed bureaucratized and institutionalized. There is some evidence that Mussolini welcomed the Ethiopian War as one means of distracting rebellious youth who held that "fascism is not a state, it is a dynamo."

Such fascist youth was apt to be found as students in the university: they were the intellectuals of the future. Fascism also attracted mature intellectuals, famous men like Ezra Pound or T. S. Eliot. Such intellectuals saw in fascism the guardian of ultimate values in society at a time when these seemed to have vanished. Such intellectuals envisaged fascism as resurrecting Greek and Roman values as against bourgeois culture which they despised. Moreover, they connected ancient values to a purity of literary style which seemed sadly absent in the bourgeois dominated world. For a poet like Ezra Pound opposition to capitalism played a part, a capitalism which symbolized the middle-class society: once capitalism had been introduced by the Jews, "art thickened. Thereafter design went to hell." Fascism gave intellectuals a pride in belonging to an ongoing movement, to fuse themselves with the nation and symbolize it through their literary form and production. What a contrast with their isolated status in the bourgeois world where they had faced the danger of becoming rootless like the Jews.

Some intellectuals believed that fascism would support the avant-garde in art and literature. As one architect put it: fascism called itself a revolution; we wanted a revolution in architecture and therefore we became Fascists. Such intellectuals were largely doomed to disappointment, less in Italy than in Germany. While National Socialism annexed the unchanging genre of popular art and literature, Italian fascism left greater room for artistic creativity. The Futurist element in fascism made it possible to patronize modern art as well as some of the most advanced architecture in Europe. Yet the fascist regime attempted to introduce a traditionalism into artistic creativity which would continue the Roman past. "Romanitá" was the word before which the moderns were supposed to retreat. Moreover, just as internationalism was condemned in politics, an attempt was made to eliminate foreign literature from the schools and universities. Things foreign were equated with moral perversion throughout fascism wherever it appeared: nationalism meant provincialism in art and literature. This restrictive view of the world succeeded better in Germany than in Italy, for in the South the humanitarian and enlightenment traditions were too strong and had played too decisive a part in Italian unification. Though an effort was made to exalt rural and small-town rooted virtues, in reality "Romanitá" was confined to archeological excavations. The ancient monuments of Rome were set off within the planning of Rome in order to remind present Italians of historical continuity.

Censorship was chaotic at best and it may well be true that artists and writers had more difficulty evading the censorship of the Church than that of the state. As far as scholarship and the universities were concerned there was, in contrast to Germany, little disruption. The oath of allegiance to the regime was not enforced until 1934 and most academics took it in Italy, just as their German counterparts went along with National Socialism. But here it was easier: no one was as yet dismissed for racial reasons and the ideology of the state was sufficiently vague to allow latitude. Mussolini always preferred the carrot to the stick, in cultural matters as well as elsewhere.

Primary and secondary education never fulfilled the promise of equality and social mobility which the fascists were so fond of making. The class structure of education remained intact and the majority of the population still left school at the age of fifteen, perhaps edified by the compulsory course in great men and heroes of Italy which represented the only real change in the curriculum.

The principal new art form which fascism perfected was the secular religion of myth and symbol which expressed itself in mass meetings and public festivals. D'Annunzio had pioneered these in Fiume and Mussolini took them over, including the balcony from which it was possible to dialogue with the people below. But it was later, in Nazi Germany, that this cult reached its perfection with the silent marches borrowed from the workers' May Day parades, the speaking choruses, the leader's lonely march to the sacred flame, the huge flags, and domes of light. Politics had tended to become a drama as soon as the age of mass politics dawned in mid-nineteenth century, but now this was perfected through conscious *mise-en-scène* which did not lack a certain beauty. Perhaps through this drama fascism could symbolize its "tamed" dynamic, the order as well as "movement" symbolically acted out by all participants through their hands and their bodies as well as communal song and speaking choruses.

But what of the leader? He benefitted, no doubt, from the hero worship which runs through European culture. We have seen how from time to time men longed for a leader who would solve their dilemmas. But as a part of modern mass movements fascist leaders did not stand in isolation, for as Gustav Le Bon had rightly forecast they must share the ideas of the crowd and cannot be innovators. The conservatism of crowds which Le Bon had observed during the Boulangist episode in France (1886–89) seemed true enough and nationalism fulfilled such longing for it and provided a meaningful tradition which was expressed through living symbols. The leader and the masses must be united in ideology but it is equally important that the national mystique through such myths and symbols mediate between leader and led. Max Weber believed that only a charismatic leader could stop society from disintegrating. But this charisma is not dependent on the leader alone, nor does it refer to an innovative and creative personality.

As time went on Mussolini became a thorough cynic as far as the Italians were concerned. He seemed to forget Le Bon's warning (which he knew) that the leader must be at one with his followers. The leadership role became detached from its ideological and liturgical moorings. He was supreme and anything he did or said was law—whatever it was. The people were fools who had to be kept in their place. This was a general development in fascism. The leader's person was so central that it eventually supplanted the movement itself. Megalomania replaced national or community commitment. Hitler was transformed from a shrewd politician into a messiah who believed that he could do no wrong. He became a law unto himself, insisting that the people should consider themselves privileged to follow him in whatever he did. Mussolini, however, never lost his grasp on reality entirely. The more pragmatic background of Italian fascism may be partly responsible for this. The fact that Italy did have a king and that Mussolini never combined de facto and de jure supremacy should not be discounted either. He always had to be a diplomat at court. His growing sense of infallibility expressed itself in a growing cynicism about the people he governed.

However cynical, however captured by his own feeling of destiny, the leader must symbolize the dynamic of the movement. The stress on action already noted must be exemplified in the Duce; this was part of that charisma which enabled the leader to excel in everything. But this raised a serious problem. What was to become of this dynamic once the fascist state was securely established? We have mentioned already that restless fascist youth was protesting against fascism grown fat in power. This helped to direct the dynamic against the outside world; fascism began to assert the new nation's "rightful" place in the world. The fascist dynamic established the state against internal opposition and then expanded it against external opposition. Thus fascism was committed to creating international disorder. Not only its stress on action but also its philosophy of history made this a necessity.

History, the only reality, was in constant motion, progressing from lower to higher forms of political organization—from democracy to fascism. It was not static; after triumphing in one country it sought to make the ideal state dominant in the world. Men must move with history for history was the self-justifying wave of the future. This future belonged to fascist world domination just as it belonged to fascism within the nation. These ideas gave the leader who embodied this destiny a supreme confidence. History did not progress smoothly, however. The ideal state must struggle constantly with the regressive forces opposed to it. Victory was assured, but it came through struggle.

Mussolini wrote that the Fascist conceived of life as a duty, a struggle, and a conquest. Many historians have seen this concept of struggle as a reflection of Darwin's theory of the survival of the fittest. But this needs modification. Mussolini saw all life as a struggle. He equated this struggle with self-fulfillment to the point that, at times, it became a struggle for the sake of struggling—action for action's sake. Fascism's struggle was not for the survival of the fittest; history had already decided that fascism was the wave of the future. Its triumph within the nation had proved this; thenceforth the struggle was merely a matter of self-fulfillment, of a search for an inevitable victory.

The ethical norms of society were no longer related to intrinsic standards or to eternal verities. Instead, duty to the fascist state and to its leader became the criterion of moral behavior. Where ethics had once been linked to Christian ideas, however vaguely defined, now they were linked to the fascist ideology of struggle and history. Not to use force against the enemies of the regime, not to smash their windows, not to destroy them—these were evils. The sensitive novelist Franz Werfel neatly characterized it: "Not the murderer but the murdered person is guilty."

Fascism was not the only system that interposed an ideology between the individual and his ethical and moral standards. Even in some of the democracies that opposed totalitarianism in the twentieth century, the concept of intrinsically good and bad actions was no longer related to values outside human determination. Loyalty oaths, declarations revealing one's political inclinations became widespread. A western democracy even demanded that specialists in chicken diseases bring their ideological orientation in line with that of the government. This development and its implications were well stated in a recent Soviet textbook on communist morality; communist ethics reject all attempts to regard the personal life of a Communist as independent from his life in society and at work. All ethical norms thus tended to become publicly defined and it became mandatory for citizens to demonstrate adherence by declarations of allegiance to the dominant ideology. Though fascism was symptomatic of this development, it did not stand alone in this regard.

Fascist ideology demanded that these public ethics transform ethical values themselves. The Fascists quite consciously agitated against the bourgeoisie as they did against liberalism in general. When Fascists decried the bourgeoisie, however, they mostly meant the middle aged for they felt in tune with the young and dynamic. The emphasis was always upon youth as against the old, a dichotomy which was transferred to international relations as well. Here they talked about young as against old nations: those nations which they regarded as dynamic and those parliamentary democracies which they viewed as degenerate. Youth became an anti-bourgeois metaphor while, in reality, middle-class morality was accepted and praised. Fascism exalted the family, marriage, as well as an ordered and settled life style. Once more we can see in this acceptance of middle-class morality the taming of activism and that dynamic of youth which they praised in so many of their speeches.

How revolutionary was fascism? Socially it did not abolish hierarchy but brought new men, often of humble origin, to the top. Fascism was a stage in the modernization of the economy, for while private enterprise was preserved, efficiency was prized and, when necessary, state control was extended to sections of the economy. The Nazis as part of their five-year plan even nationalized much of the steel industry. Above all, fascism meant economic planning and flexibility. The ideology was not concerned with instituting a specific economic program and political needs always dominated. In the end this meant the possibility of planning, of experimenting with the monetary system (especially in Germany), and the emphasis on productivity under the auspices of the state.

Italian fascism, in particular, also fastened onto the disillusionment with the *risorgimento*—a feeling which had expressed itself in activism and in historical relativism. These older ideas became part of a new dynamic as they were mobilized for the struggle with foreign and domestic enemies. Fascism was committed to an internal order based upon complete dominance and an international disorder which would enable the dynamic to expand once the system had been established at home. In contrast to the communist utopia which could only be realized in the future, the fascist utopia commenced with its seizure of power. There could be no further changes in the state. This is an all-important ideological difference. Thus international expansionism was an integral part of fascist ideology while communism could be much more flexible. The Bolsheviks adopted communism in one country in the early Stalinist period; fascism could, by its very nature, never proclaim such a thing and mean it.

Fascism differed from country to country, although this discussion has centered mainly around Italian fascism which was the pacemaker. Mussolini was widely admired even in the democracies. Had he not produced order in his nation which the democracies seemed incapable of producing? From Winston Churchill (who expressed his admiration as late as 1938) to those who praised the Duce for making trains run on time, the wave of admiration accepted fascism as an alternative to ideologies which proclaimed a more thorough social and economic revolution. These men correctly perceived that fascism was mainly a revolution in ideology, that its real social reforms would be confined to such public works as draining marshes. The organic state did not require a revolution in the existing class structure.

Mussolini was imitated in practice as well as admired from a distance. Portugal (1928), Austria (1934), and Spain (1939) all became authoritarian nations. Their revolutions, however, had a different ideological base than did Mussolini's. The concept of the organic state with all its implications was central to their ideology. The leadership concept also played a dominant role. The difference was that the soul of the people did not express itself through the organic state and the "intuition" of the leader. The state religion of these nations was Catholicism. True, Italy also was Catholic, but its Catholicism was weakened as a political ideology by that anticlericalism which was a result of national unification. The Catholic political party which did come into existence had a strong social orientation. However, in these three nations the Church played an uninterrupted role in political life; there was no "papal question" that blocked national aspirations. As a result, Catholicism provided the dominant ingredient of the people's spirituality and in this manner it could be fused with nationalism. This is what was meant when the commentator on the Austrian constitution of 1934 said that "there can be no doubt about the purely Germanic character and Christian way of life of our overwhelmingly German and Catholic people."

The authoritarian state so defined had a strong corporate basis from the beginning, not through syndicalism but through Catholic social theory. This same commentator on the Austrian constitution explicitly mentioned *Quadragesimo Anno,* the encyclical of Pius XI which advocated self-government for each professional group—the transfer of public administration to autonomous, corporatist bodies. This idea was not new. In a previous chapter its penetration of Catholic social thought was analyzed. From this it followed that the lawmaking body should emerge principally from the occupational groups. Underlying this thought was the idea of the medieval guild in which everyone performed his duty in his occupation, where employer and laborer were bound together in a corporate structure. Mussolini had adopted a chamber of corporate organizations, but as with his clerical fascism, so-called corporative self-government was a sham.

The pope was delighted with the Austrian constitution of 1934 but in reality the corporatism which the Church advocated under the guise of reviving the medieval guilds was imposed and controlled by the government. There was to be no freely chosen corporative structure in Austria or in Portugal. Mussolini, whose corporatism was not of direct Catholic origin, also determined the action of his estates through a minister of corporations. Corporatism deliberately glossed over class tensions; general adherence to the principle of association served to solidify the opposition to that liberal and materialistic world which had atomized man.

However, there were differences between clerical fascism and Italian fascism. Clerical fascism advocated a different kind of morality which restrained the leadership. Traditional Catholicism would not allow a transformation of values; instead it reemphasized traditional Christian values. The dynamic was therefore curbed, or rather diverted into religious worship. No doubt this corresponded to the realities of the political situation. This theory of government was more at home in small and powerless states which, in any case, were not able to carry out successful external expansion. Not only was the dynamic crippled, but traditional morality was emphasized. The family was sanctified as the most important asset of the state and work became a religious duty—not, in this case, duty to a leader for the sake of national glorification but duty to one's religious convictions, which were also symbolized by the state. This concept of duty lacked any dynamic; its emphasis was on order and the stability of the state. The Catholic emphasis upon the family was illustrated in the Portuguese fascist constitution (1933), which in most respects was similar to Austria's constitution. In Portugal only the heads of families received the vote—a vote that could be cast, of course, for only one official political party.

Antonio Salazar (1889–1970) of Portugal was especially influential in the 1930s. Nations in crisis, like France, were drawn to his example, and books explaining the phenomenon were legion. Salazar came to power without a struggle (1928) while Chancellor Dollfuss in Austria had to suppress the workers in order to inaugurate his regime (1934). The Portuguese dictator explained his philosophy of government in a way that appealed to many plagued by the chaotic conditions of the postwar world. The crisis of our day was not a crisis of liberty, but of authority. Political parties based upon the citizen can have no meaning, for man in isolation is an abstraction when he should be a part of a community whose goal is the common good and whose legitimacy derives from God. Government must not be dependent upon a majority or even a minority; instead the government is power ruling according to divine right. Therefore governments should function independently of parliaments and elections. This authority, however, was conceived of in moral, Christian terms. Salazar acknowledged the "mystery and power of the infinite demanded by Christian consciences." He meant, of course, an organic state founded on Catholic premises. Yet, in the same speech, he hoped that the Church would refrain from political action within the state and promised that the state would not interfere with the Church.

Salazar maintained that there was religious freedom in Portugal, and Austria certainly possessed this freedom. This was misleading, for the Catholic faith was the explicit basis of the governmental structure and morality. The Church directed the educational system and indeed most of the intellectual life. What Salazar meant was that the Church should not be concerned with the actual administration of the nation, that here the dictator must be supreme. The Church did, however, provide the ideological foundation upon which he based his power. As long as his power was not menaced religious freedom could be allowed, though in the nations concerned this hardly constituted an issue. There were few Protestants in Austria and hardly any in Portugal. In the latter nation a small number of Jews were readmitted, while Austria, which had a large Jewish population in Vienna, became overtly anti-Semitic.

This clerical fascism stressed authority, sought a connection with a historic, Catholic past, and lacked the dynamic of Mussolini. The leader was not the embodiment of a dynamic destiny, a new messiah, but rather an exemplification of the Catholic Christian morality upon which the state was built. But even here there was some variety. While Vichy France, under Marshall Pétain, followed the general pattern of clerical fascism, Monsignor Tiso in Slovakia (1939–44) combined it with racism and collaborated reluctantly with the extermination of the Jews.

Fascism had introduced an alternative to parliamentary democracy in Europe; it had harnessed to its ideology many of the longings and ideas expressed in the nineteenth and twentieth century. In its Italian and clerical form, it seemed an acceptable alternative to many who yearned for order and purpose in life. In Germany, however, it took on a complexion which seemed extreme and frightening even to those who approved a Salazar or Mussolini. One historian exiled by Hitler could even proclaim that "Mussolini was different." How true was such an assertion?

# CHAPTER TWENTY-TWO

# *National Socialism and*
# *the Depersonalization*
# *of Man*

**N**ATIONAL SOCIALISM and fascism shared a common world view. Both rejected what they called the bourgeois system of values and substituted for it a belief in the organic state, as well as action and struggle. Hermann Rauschnigg, who was close to Hitler at one time, called the national socialist advance to power the "Revolution of Nihilism," and there was in German fascism something of the same emphasis upon action for action's sake that was seen in Italian fascism. Italian fascism based itself upon a view that history was the prime determinant of man's struggle; thus truth itself was relativized. Whatever had succeeded in history was a final reality, was a truth, and this success was due to the action of men of will. Hitler had a similar view of the importance of man's will, for this will, if sufficiently ruthless in the constant struggle, would transform man into a "heroic personality." Both shared also, and most importantly, the ideal of the organic state with which everyone must integrate himself for it expresses the soul of the people. With neither of these fascisms did this view of the state lead to an abrogation of the existing class structure or to social revolution.

The nihilistic element of national socialism did not stem from a pragmatic ideology, as in Italian fascism. Italian fascism rested upon a disillusionment with the ideas of the *risorgimento;* the background of German fascism was the revolt against positivism which had taken place at the turn of the century. Neoromanticism did not penetrate Italy to the extent it penetrated Germany. The "Revolution of Nihilism" in the North had from the very beginning an explicit ideological base unknown among the early *Fasci.*

This difference was to be of prime importance. Fascism everywhere shared a contempt for representative government, an urge for strong leadership and a realization that society must be reorganized along authoritarian lines. In Germany the ideology of national socialism gave these ideas a special complexion. A summary of this world view must necessarily review many things previously discussed: the concept of race, the new romanticism, the postwar nihilism, in short that intuitive view of the world which derived added strength from the war. National socialism was its climax; it put these things into practice. Yet, in the end, neoromanticism itself was transformed as nihilism triumphed over it. The apocalyptic vision of Heinrich Himmler and his SS, of a supranational state ruled by a race of Aryan supermen, was the final result of national socialist ideology. Indeed, the transformation of bourgeois values which fascism desired had a paradoxical result. On the one hand, those bourgeois values that had been stressed in the new romanticism, family life and rootedness, were retained; on the other hand, bourgeois values as a whole were rejected in the struggle for domination. The result was that Nazism had what seemed, at first glance, a split personality. For example, the Commandant of the Auschwitz concentration camp, who ranks as the greatest killer of all times, sent some two million people to the gas chambers. Yet he was a good family man, fond of nature and animals. But this seemingly fantastic moral contradiction was really part of the movement's ideology. Bourgeois respectability and genocide could be fused into one, for neoromanticism was accompanied by the "Revolution of Nihilism."

As did so many ideologies before and after the war, national socialism thought mankind lived in "extreme situations." Unlike existentialism, however, national socialism believed that humanity's extreme situation should be overcome—man in a void must find roots. Though life was a struggle, this struggle could be guided to a successful conclusion through the development of man's will. Like the nihilistic and the neoromantic ideology, national socialism rejected any intellectual approach to this struggle for existence; instead, the will had to be guided by "intuition." Thus does the intuitive view of the world so prevalent in the revolt against positivism appear once more.

This intuition enabled the individual to perceive the deep-seated will and aspirations of his race. Man was, at the same time, rooted in the race and guided in the struggle by its interests. Neoromanticism's ideal of rootedness and nature came to be dominated by racial thought. German neo-Romantics with their nature romanticism had no overt political program, yet they thought that the worship of the race would bring about their type of antibourgeois revolt. Nature romanticism could penetrate only the soul of the Aryan. Again, the phenomenon of racial ideas, which determined the struggle for survival in the thought of Houston Stewart Chamberlain and influenced the Austrian school of thought which considered the ancient Germanic past the sole repository of wisdom (and the only insurance against the loss of culture in the modern age), came to the fore. One is reminded here of Spengler's differentiation between culture and civilization: the importance of the soul as opposed to mere external progress. Culture was now infused with racial notions, and in the end this racist culture became the true reality, masked only by the superficialities of modern society.

Hans F. K. Guenther, the leading racial expert of the Third Reich, formulated these racial ideas in a classic manner: One could not rationally investigate the meaning, purpose, or worth of one's race—blood, race, and *Volk* were innate qualities which determined human capabilities as well as the progress of science. This was the ultimate reality. National socialist writers defined this as the "qualities of the soul." These qualities were described by one writer as the "peculiar laws of life concerning landscape, blood, and history which, when brought into a unity, make up the soul of a people." Reminiscent of neoromanticism, this view of reality emphasized the soul defined in terms of race. Its inherent appeal was, once more, a familiar one. It bestowed a rootedness upon members of industrial mass society by erecting an ideal way of life that was this society's very antithesis.

Nature, the Germanic landscape, was the essence of the race. Many leading Nazis were graduates of those postwar agricultural communes that were formed under the impulse of this mixture of romanticism and race. This was what Hitler meant when he said that "the Third Reich must be a nation of peasants or perish as the Reich of the Hohenstaufen perished." Such an ideal retained that same opposition to capitalist society exemplified by the change in the public spirit of Europe at the turn of the century. It opposed materialistic Marxism and that liberal capitalism which "atomized" the individual. The peasant ideal served as an expression of the mystique of blood and soil. As one national socialist writer put it: "Capitalism and peasant life are inexorably opposed to each other. Wherever Capitalism dominates the peasantry must wither away." Marxism saw its utopia in a state of the future which would be industrialized; fascism sought its ideal in a past which had not known the problems of the industrial age. Here was one basic difference between these two ideologies. Yet this national socialist ideal clashed with the reality. For under Hitler, Germany deliberately increased its industrial potential and the despised big cities grew ever larger.

External realities, however, were not important, for this ideology was concerned with the deeper truths behind the external world. An Aryan nation would neutralize the evils of industrialization. No longer would whole classes be dispossessed. Employer-worker relationships would be settled not on the basis of strikes but by a common interest in the race's struggle for fulfillment. Though Germany, unlike Italy, had no corporate framework in which to accomplish this, industrial relationships were still viewed in the same manner. Classes must remain, but they would be united in a higher purpose which bestowed upon all an equal status. Certainly the worker was not inferior to the employer; all were Aryans. Nevertheless he had to obey the owner. This usually resulted in longer working hours, for everyone, in his particular station of life, must do his duty for the race. The benefits of rootedness would thus penetrate industrial society and mitigate its nature. Despite this, a solid peasantry was regarded as the necessary root of the state, and Nazi legislation guaranteed that the Aryan peasant could never be evicted from his land.

The gap between the ideal and the real arose within the very concept of race itself. Aryans were supposed to have certain features and physical measurements. But many could not boast of this (including Adolf Hitler himself). As a result, men like Guenther utilized both Plato and modern sociology and constructed an "ideal type." Not everyone possessed all the Aryan characteristics but all Aryans possessed at least some of them and together they formed an ideal type. As part of an ideal, outward appearance did matter for it was the way you could tell an enemy from a friend. As this theory developed in the nineteenth century it effectively supported the ideology. The ideology became tangible, an important aspect for an ideology which demanded a commitment based upon intuition.

These racist considerations introduced an important element into the national socialist ethos, one that was not so prominent in other fascisms which lacked this type of ideological base. Hermann Rauschnigg formulated it well: ". . . instead of the individual or mass we have the type." Individualism, in any liberal sense, was impossible, for the common racial base determined one's place and one's life in society. The concept of the "mass" was rejected as an ideal, for race could enable the individual to realize his full potential. From the very beginning the National Socialists called for the abolition of the atomization of man in industrial society and sought to replace this atomization with a concept of man as a unit of race, of thought, and of feeling, a man who was therefore a complete personality. This man, unlike mass man, was not formed by environment—national socialism sharply rejected environmental theories— but by the life force inherent in his consciousness of race.

Since all men were classified into racial types, it was easy to stereotype those opposed to the Aryans. Because all of life's externals—society itself—masked the reality of race, men should be typed according to their one absolute characteristic, their racial composition. Given the Aryan ethos, this meant that inferior races like the Jews could not have true emotions, a true ethical orientation; indeed, they had to be types exemplifying everything evil. This last, combined with the concept of struggle, led naturally to a view of a world in constant war, a war of light against darkness in which there could be no neutrals and no quarter. Hitler himself summed this up when he wrote, "the differences between individual races, both externally and in their inner natures, can be enormous and, in fact, are so. The gulf between the lowest creature which can still be styled man and our highest races is greater than between the lowest type of man and the highest type of ape." It was a war of races and one's enemies, therefore, were not really human at all.

This reasoning is stressed because it explains the Nazi split personality mentioned at the beginning of the chapter. The Aryan way of life was that of the true and good, defined in terms of honesty, kindness, and concern for the family. The lower races opposed all this; moreover, they were "types" and could not be regarded as individuals in the liberal sense. What the Commandant of Auschwitz was murdering were types which lacked all individuality to him. Murder, in these circumstances, was depersonalized and completely remote from that Aryan life whose ethics coincided with those of the bourgeoisie. Italian fascism was never able to depersonalize its victims, but in Germany this was the rule. Mass extermination was made possible not only through bureaucratic efficiency but also because of such national socialist ideology. It was the complete personality waging war against people who could not be human in the Aryan sense (after all, they had no soul), who were inferior types. The necessity and morality of Nazi terror were codified in such arguments, and bureaucrats, who considered themselves ethical men, could sign extermination orders without qualms.

Many officials signed death orders who were not rabid National Socialists and who may not even have shared many of the propositions of the ideology. Here we see that interplay between consciously-formulated ideology and the mood of the times which is so important in cultural history. The new romanticism and racism had penetrated Germany so deeply as to constitute a mood and an atmosphere. Racial typology was therefore not a new thing but simply a heightening of a mood shared by many who could not have foreseen its ultimate consequences. The same was true for the longing for authority now crystallized into a specific leadership idea. Many bureaucrats signed mass extermination orders simply because the leader demanded it.

The concept of leadership drew all this into a unity and gave it a practical political direction. The elite of the party were "heroic personalities" whose will power forcefully expressed the direction prescribed by their racial soul. One of Adolf Hitler's most consistent criticisms of the German Republic was that it had substituted economic values for heroic values and equality for a necessary hierarchy of leadership. The concept of leadership was derived here as in Italian fascism from what Max Weber defined as "charisma"—the mystical quality which made a leader. The longing for this leadership was widespread in the twentieth century. Elitist theories propagated something very similar to this and neo-Romantics dreamed of a "great one, who woud be sent from above." The leader represented an alternative form of government to that of representative democracy which seemed futile to these men. The leader was envisaged as a democratic leader, a *primus inter pares,* rather than as one raised high above the people as a king or emperor. He was the center of the myths, symbols, and *mis-en-scène* discussed earlier. This leader was a prophetic leader; he grasped the future more clearly than other people. He was so intensely at one with the spirit of the race that he was able to reveal what had been hidden in the subconscious of every Aryan.

Because of this concept of leadership the relationship between the leader and his followers was intensely personal. It also dominated national socialist historical theory. History was a struggle of the racial soul to actualize itself and its potentials. This was connected with German idealism, with Hegel's world historical spirit. National socialism, however, regarded this German idealism as artificial because it was not based upon the roots of the *Volk.* History was not progress as such; neither was it a Darwinian struggle for the survival of the fittest. The race was fully formed at its very beginning. It was not a question of evolution but of smashing those obstacles that stood in the way of the race's final triumph. For this task the race had to be led by individuals who possessed qualities of leadership. "World history, like all events of historical significance, is the result of activity of single individuals, it is not the fruit of majority decisions." The leader thus became destiny incarnate at one with the racial soul and thus confident of his ability to lead the race to its triumph.

God had a place here, curiously enough. He became a kind of vague, universal source of life, but his only divine revelation was the call to destiny through the leader. God was closely tied to the fortunes of the race. As the leading ideologue of the party, Alfred Rosenberg, put it: "The God we honor would not exist if our soul and our blood did not exist." The religious attitudes of national socialism were confused, but in the main anti-Christian. Catholic and Protestant priests must be Aryans and thus adhere to the basic truth to which God was tied, that of race. Following the precedent of earlier racists, they sharply rejected the Old Testament because it was Jewish and thus a soulless legalism in contrast to the old Germanic legends and myths. Christ presented a more difficult problem. Some National Socialists abandoned Him completely in favor of the ancient Germanic gods and the cult of the Druids. Others, following earlier racists, proclaimed that Christ was in reality an Aryan; Galilee, they maintained, had never been Judaized. Most, however, simply transformed Christ into that ideal type so important in the Nazi mystique. Christ was blond, strong, and a typical charismatic leader; obviously he must have been of Aryan blood. Luther was His true prophet, the progenitor of truly German Christianity.

Their ambivalent attitude toward Christianity did not prevent National Socialists from exploiting, in their propaganda, the terminology of the religion they rejected. Goebbels constantly used phrases like "deliverance," "saviour," and "miracles." Familiar Christian words or expressions were transposed onto a different ideological base which made for a better understanding among the people.

A concept of culture sprang directly out of this ideology. "Culture is the essence of all racially-directed works of the soul and of the intellect of the people." The intellect, of course, originated in the soul. Culture differed from civilization which comprised merely the external habits of a people who had lost contact with their soul. Such was the foundation of what was called "practical work for culture in the Third Reich." *Gesinnungskultur,* culture defined as a way of thought, was the order of the day. The term was derived, not surprisingly, from Fichte. The three principal subjects taught in the schools were German history, German literature, and racial biology. National socialism, like Italian fascism, made few important cultural contributions outside its political style; moreover, for the same reasons Italian culture was barren: the new genres of art and literature were despised as "degenerate." Truth was "given" and art was only an elaboration upon it. Simplicity was stressed and all art which posed new problems was rejected. To cite Guenther once more: In the nineteenth century, because of the atomization of man, everything became a "problem"; the intellectualized, alienated man was praised and admired. But now man was no longer alienated, he had found his way back to the race; therefore the simple and rooted was better than the complex and problematic. Naturally this theory had a detrimental effect upon art, reducing it to the level of the picture postcards Hitler painted in his youth.

The romanticism implicit in the ideology fused with this kind of simplicity and rootedness. The historical novel revived and detective stories telling romanticized stories of the struggle of Aryans against Jews were recommended. This literature, with some exceptions, was highly moral, so as not to offend the Aryan ethos. It was filled with simple and honest peasants; rarely did sex intrude upon the story, and then in a most proper fashion. Novels centering on the sorry plight of Germans in alien lands were frequent and again they were somewhat like morality plays. The moral Aryans fought against the immoral people that surrounded them; the characters of these books always seemed to lead exemplary family lives. Literary history now tried to analyze literature according to racial factors. Nadler had anticipated these attempts when he classified German literature according to landscapes, assessing its nature through its fusion of race and the historical, natural environment. No great literature or literary history could emerge from this. It was a latter-day romanticism which emphasized bourgeois ethics, simplicity, rootedness, and emotion rather than the problems which faced man. Man's existential dilemma was, after all, solved.

The visual arts suffered a similar fate. The monumental architecture, which was a feature in Italian fascism, was used here as well. The style was classical. Since the eighteenth century in Germany the classics had stood for a healthy and beautiful world. Marx and Lassalle had written huge treatises on classical thought. It was not classical materialism, however, but classical artistic forms which exercised a special attraction for Germans. Racial thought accepted this preference. To many, the Aryans originated not only in the German forests but also in Greece. The Greeks of the creative period had been Aryans, but they degenerated through intermingling with inferior races. The Germans, therefore, were the true heirs of the Greek heritage. National socialist architecture's accent on simplicity and symmetry of style, the columns in Hitler's new Chancellery—all reflected this feeling. The sculptors Hitler admired and furthered were men whose works were both monumental and classical, who fused the classical ideal with the Aryan ideal type. Again, in sculpture no experimentation was allowed. All problems were now solved for all times.

National socialism's contribution to the visual arts was the same as that of the fascism to the south: the mass meeting with its dramatic symbolisms. The sacred flame, the lighted torches, the use of the masses as if they were a *corps de ballet,* and over all the brooding leader standing in isolation—all this symbolizing health and beauty. The mystical symbolisms of national socialism gave added meaning to these ceremonies. Everyone was supposed to be a participant in such mass displays; the spectator, too, had to feel that he was part of a mighty movement. Thus, the number of active participants about equalled the number of those who watched; this meant organizing the movements of huge masses of people. At the Nuremberg party meeting of 1934 a staggering total of 460,000 people actively participated in the rally.

Just as Mussolini rearranged sections of Rome so as to provide adequate settings for the monuments of an ancient and glorious Italian past, so Hitler replanned several German cities. His chief reason was to expedite mass meet-

ings and processions as well as for military considerations. If national socialism had survived, Berlin would have been replanned on as impressive a scale
as Napoleon III's rebuilding of Paris.

Fascist cultural accomplishments were thus restricted to elaborating a political liturgy and not to furthering individual creative endeavors. Indeed, its
ideology made such endeavors impossible. There was no outburst of creativity
as in Russia after the Soviet revolution. There was not even a residue of
creativeness, as there was under Stalin, when the musical achievements light-
ened an otherwise somber and barren cultural landscape. As a whole, nationalism was too tradition-oriented to allow even that. Past greatness and the roots
of the race alone were fit artistic themes and not the vision of some better
future.

National socialist ideology was not static; it developed. The principal
direction this development took was toward a certain kind of nihilism which
became a naked urge for power. The elements of this nihilism had always
been there. In its rise to power the party displayed a great deal of cynicism.
Most of its leaders knew that the "socialism" in the party title was a ruse to
get votes. One faction of the party, however, had believed in the "socialist"
part of the title. They wanted to combine the ideology with a socialist program, for this would establish a genuine equality among all Aryans and thus
solve the social problem. The dispute between this faction and the rest of the
party nearly wrecked the movement, but it was the Socialists who had to leave.
The class structure was left intact and was, in fact, an essential ingredient of
the world view. Of course, in the end, the party's nationalism proved equally
phony; eventually the racial element completely swamped even the nationalist
element. Hitler himself was no cynic, though a master politician. Yet he
always believed in the essential ideology, and it is likely that he knew he could
and should bide his time until his plans reached fruition. His political maneu-
vering, even the German-Soviet alliance, was a tactical decision which, in the
end, was meant not to hinder but to further the triumph of his racist ideology.
Yet by 1938 Alfred Rosenberg could write that "the sectarian triumphs over
the idea." He was correct.

The sectarian to whom Rosenberg referred was Heinrich Himmler
(1900–1945) and his SS activists who put a quest for power ahead of any
dogmatism. Thus they stripped the ideology of its supposed irrelevancies until
nothing remained except the "technique of absolute power." This was not,
however, an absolute return to the Free Corps mentality of Ernst Juenger. The
SS knew their quest for power would be successful. It had to be—they were
the elite within the Aryan people, the purest of the pure. Himmler attempted
to institute a criteria of selection through racial measurements and photo-
graphs. Moreover, Aryanism had to be established not only back to their

grandparents (the official definition), but for several generations. The SS elite had been selected by a similar process and they were educated in special elite schools romantically situated in old castles amid the German landscape.

The SS introduced an international element into the movement. They were joined, eventually, by the equally pure of other European countries. In consequence, they began to think of themselves as a supranational elite. The idea of race had always been preponderant; all else, even the state, were ephemeral expressions of a racial truth. Therefore it was not difficult to divorce Aryanism from nationalism; the nature of their relationship had always been one of alliance, their ideas were never inevitably linked together. In 1944 the office of racial politics ordered the term "German race" expunged from the vocabulary, for it had, by referring to a specific nation, a finite connotation to it, while the "Nordic race" was something universal. Here again was a rejection of environmentalism of any kind as well as a denial of a nationalist basis of the race. Symptomatically in that same year Himmler proclaimed that Hitler was the greatest Aryan leader, not just a leader of Germans. Near the war's end Hitler promised Himmler the area of Burgundy, now a part of France. There the SS would form a supranational Aryan state and dominate the world from this redoubt.

Race had triumphed over national allegiance. This supranationalism had always been present in national socialist thought. Race and not the boundaries of one state were stressed; all Aryans were part of a super race. To be sure, this made useful propaganda. Germany's boundaries had to be expanded to take in those enclaves of the super race still left in foreign countries. The claim was used in Germany's demand for the Sudetenland and for other regions bordering on the Reich. It went deeper than that, however. "Aryans of the world unite around the German heartland" may have once been the slogan. By the time Hitler promised Burgundy to the SS, however, even the idea of Germany as the heartland had been modified. The SS represented the development of the ideology toward doctrines of power and toward the creation of a race of supranational leaders. Whether it would actually have come about will never be known. The residue of this development was reflected in the statement of one young SS man after the war was lost:

> Youth [in the SS] has ceased to attach any values to the divergence of doctrines and ideas. For this youth the purpose of life is to live dangerously, and one's duty is to seize power; the means violence, the final goal an imperium which will embrace the entire globe.

The Burgundy project illustrated the unreality which eventually seized the movement. Just as Hitler came to believe that he was indeed infallible, just as he moved troops around which no longer existed, so both planning and ideology took ever less account of realities. The repudiation of the external as a habit of mind led to life in a dream world, a tendency that was accentuated as the war was lost. Yet this tendency was implicit in the very definition national socialism gave to reality. There were many stories told of the boy with perfect Aryan measurements and features who turned out to be a Jew, but this made as little difference now as Virchow's measurements of Berlin schoolchildren had made many decades before. What if there was no measurable difference between races? Science itself was the product of the race soul. The medical fads of the leadership relate directly to this. Quackery was superior to scientific medicine. Health fads such as Hitler's belief in the efficacy of porridge and mineral water also played a role. From this viewpoint, the movement degenerated into faddism. Perhaps the revived Druid cults and the marriage rite of mingling of blood belonged in this setting. Much of what seems unreal to us was part of that ritual element which was important to national socialism. The sacred flames and the Germanic festivals were a part of this and so were the initiation rites into the SS guards. National socialist ideology celebrated the revival of the Aryan after centuries of oppression and the victorious fight against the Jewish world conspiracy. They thought in terms of conspiracies and rituals. This gave an added attraction to the movement and, like all of this thought, provided simple explanations to the complex problems of the present.

The men and women who joined the movement and believed in its ideology were not criminals in any usual meaning of the word, for the question arises: Why did apparently normal and even intelligent people become believers? Sociological studies have shown that the SS men, even those of the Deathshead Division which operated the concentration camps, were not misfits. Nor were they, like so many of the originators of this ideology, frustrated or displaced intellectuals. Many of the men who, at the turn of the century, formulated this thought failed in their desire for academic careers. They thundered against intellectuals, professors who were people without a soul in contrast to the peasants on the land. But it is found that many SS had satisfactory careers before they joined. Ambition for advancement and status played a role and so did the all-pervasive German cultural atmosphere that has already been described as the revolt against positivism. These men, like the diverse thinkers previously discussed, were searching desperately for some truth. Having survived the holocaust of a senseless war, they wanted to face the postwar world with purpose and direction. For these men idealism, a purposeful world view, became of crucial importance. This may be as difficult to grasp in England and America as the tortured question of German youth after the Second World War: "What enthusiasm can I have now?"

The searchings of those intellectuals concerned with preserving freedom provoked no enthusiasm. Their ideas were too sophisticated, too much in the constant process of formation and re-formation. Marxism could fill the gap, and for countless people it did so. But national socialism was an ideology which had a total view of life which was opposed to Marxist materialism. In the German situation, particularly, the Marxist and national socialist ideologies confronted each other. National socialist ideology had a greater attraction for those born in the cultural atmosphere of the revolt against positivism; Nazism derived from a trend that had permeated much of the nation. Neoromanticism did not break with the past; it formed a continuity with it. One did not have to submerge oneself within a mass to gain status; one's status was secured for all time through a racial superiority within the existing class structure. Society was not to be overthrown in the name of racial change but was to be rebuilt upon its true and ancient foundations. It was small wonder that so many chose national socialism. Moreover, this thought shielded one from life's uncertainties. The leader would make everything come out all right.

Nor must national socalism as a refuge from the Marxist menace be underestimated. The Italian Liberal Albertini thought that Mussolini had saved Italy from socialism, and for many Germans Hitler had fulfilled the same function. National socialism was a bulwark against a world revolution which seemed, after the war, to be not only imminent but actualized in 1919. The middle classes remembered the revolutions in Munich and Berlin and had heard of the Soviet regime in Hungary. To them the destruction of order encouraged the spectre of communism, and this seemed to have been borne out in practice. As this class recoiled after 1848 into an accentuated nationalism, so now it fled to the waiting arms of national socialism. Anti-bolshevism was inscribed upon its banner and order was guaranteed. Not only would the social hierarchy be left intact, it would be reinforced by the party's own authoritarian predilections. These factors and the congenial cultural atmosphere go far in explaining the attraction of the movement. Once men and women had joined, the kind of morality described came into operation.

The case of Vidkun Quisling (1887–1945), the Norwegian Nazi, illustrates this attraction. He was undoubtedly a man of quick and brilliant intellect and had made his mark as the right-hand man of Fridjtof Nansen. He had helped Nansen in dealing with the problem of displaced persons after the First World War. He searched constantly for a philosophy of life, and this search, combined with a hate for the Soviets, drove him into national socialism. He thought he had found, in national socialism, the salvation of his nation. The appeal of an ideology which claimed continuity with the past can be illustrated through another and more famous Norwegian. Knut Hamsun was certainly one of the great writers of his generation. His novels dealt with the

Norwegian past—the toil of peasants on the land and the faith of the people. When Hitler came to power he was seventy-three years old and partly deaf, but it seemed to him that here was a man who had led his people back to the values he had been writing about, and the Nazi vocabulary of blood and soil encouraged this delusion. Hamsun was no racist. His support for Hitler was based on a most superficial understanding of the dictator's thought; yet he openly supported the Nazi party.

The case of Hamsun added another factor to the ingredients of national socialism. Hannah Arendt has called it the "revolt of the unpolitical." Like Hamsun, many Germans had an unpolitical orientation, a political naiveté upon which Hitler capitalized. This orientation was part of a belief that forms of government were unimportant, that it was the spirit which counted; it had contributed to the attacks on parliamentary government discussed at the beginning of the chapter on fascism. "Unpolitical" must be understood as applying to those men and women who thought political parties divisive, who were uninterested in democratic machinery because it did not have any relevancy to life. But such an attitude made for a naiveté in political matters which closed its eyes to the real consequences of fascist actions. Even those who tried to assassinate Hitler in 1944 shared these attitudes. Many of the conspiracy's leaders had once been Nazis. Goerdeler, for example, who was to be the new chancellor, had been Hitler's price commissioner.

These conspirators had become alarmed only when the implications of national socialism became more fully revealed in the first pogroms of 1938 and in the planning of war. They had accepted the milder formulations of the movement's program in 1933—then Jews were to be treated merely as aliens. When it came to formulating their own program they also wanted something "new," specifically an extraparliamentary form of government coupled to a rejection of Western bourgeois society. The various programs differed greatly, but the majority included some sort of a new spiritual impulse deriving from a nondenominational Christianity. The conspirators had not wanted to return to the German Republic and they certainly did not envisage something like the Federal Republic of today. Their fumblings typified the longing of their generation. They had at first endorsed Hitler's solution; then disillusioned and horrified at the Hitlerian reality, they rejected it but still wanted a society neither bourgeois nor parliamentarian. Though these men became martyrs, many others who were gradually disillusioned did not end by resisting but by resigning themselves to the situation.

The majority of those who collaborated with national socialism were Nazis only in a vague sort of way. They believed in Nazi ideology only because they thought it pointed the way to a better life; they thought little about what Hitler had written in *Mein Kampf*. Order would be restored, security assured, and the state of the nation would improve. All these things did, in fact, happen. They sailed along on the tide and when it became a storm they were caught. After all, Hitler did not begin to unfold his true program for the Aryan state until 1938, though from the beginning the signs were there for all to read. Most people, including the Jews, preferred to shut their eyes; the terrible things portended were unimaginable. But the horror came; for fascism all action and truth were relevant only to the ideology of the movement—what it demanded had to be done. In 1938 tiny groups began to conspire against the regime. Others, like the writer Ernst von Salomon, who wrote that "to do nothing is the only action," sat in their rooms while the police were arresting and beating Jews. Not everyone could become an exile or a martyr of his own free will; thus, their rarity in history.

These are some of the chief factors which made allegiance to the Nazi regime possible. That it was a kind of summation and a continuation of an older cultural atmosphere should be given the heaviest weight. It was possible for people to become enmeshed in the movement without thinking through the consequences of their action or inaction. What began as a matter of free choice between ideological and political alternatives ended up as the destruction of individuality. National socialism wanted to distinguish the Aryan from the masses, but in the end it pressed all its subjects into a common mold. An authoritarian ideology blotted out the slightest traces of individuality in any human endeavor. The more ruthlessly it was enforced, the more rigid was the mold in which the individual was placed.

The ideology came to be based upon a technique of terror. Nazis made full use of technology not as an end but as a means. Such uses ranged from the loudspeakers at street corners which broadcast the "gospel" to tapping telephone conversations. The whole population became enmeshed in the party's toils; the same was true of Italian fascism. Families spied on one another—a far cry from the kind of bourgeois family pictured in national socialist literature, but then these families were supposedly ideologically united. Leisure was organized for the cause as well. From grandmothers to young boys and girls, groups were formed to study and propagate the ideology. The population's leisure was ruthlessly appropriated. Duty in the labor corps for several months became compulsory for all young people. Not only was free labor provided for government projects but a moral value was placed on this work. A German youth engaged in healthy work outdoors, in nature, would be mystically bound tighter to the *Volk*. The official leisure time association, Strength Through Joy, took working people on trips to many parts of the world and became one of the most popular features of the regime, just as the *Dopolavoro* had been in Italy.

Life was organized by the party, and it was almost impossible to escape from this organization. The destruction of personal privacy is a concomitant of all twentieth-century totalitarianism. In fascism, whatever its type, the unity of the people meant not only an ideological integration but also a total organization. Herein lay part of the strength of the movement. Through membership in various groups, man got a spurious feeling of participation, of doing things to further the inevitable triumph of the cause. No longer was he atomized, "struggling in the deserts of individualism," as Romain Rolland put it. The German or the Italian felt cared for both at work and during his leisure time. Individualism was easily sacrificed for the sake of security and for the feeling, as one German professor put it, that life was worth living once again.

The destruction of individuality highlighted the defeat of liberalism in Europe. Individuality was reinterpreted in precisely the way many men in the previous century had changed its traditional meaning. Man's individuality was best realized if he was integrated into the cosmic and historical forces which dominated life. Both Hegel and Marx agreed here, and so did the neo-Romantics. The final results of the national socialist approach to man can be seen in the institution of the concentration camp. For here was the conscious construction of an instrument of depersonalization; here was a tool that would turn a man into the kind of person the ideology thought him to be. This process began with the arrest of the victim (always in the dead of night), and continued to the crowded cattle cars where there was an absence of food, and was augmented by the brutality of the guards even before the victim set foot in the camp. There the treatment became still more devilish. The inmates were never sure of life itself, which could be extinguished at the whim of any guard. They were kept in a constant state of overcrowding and near starvation.

But this was not all; their dignity as human beings was stripped from them in a still more systematic way. The SS who ruled the camps divided the inmates, giving some preferential treatment and the responsibility for operation of their block of cells. G. H. Adler in his analysis of the so-called model camp of Theresienstadt has related that the moral decline of the camp began with the institution of such a hierarchy. These men were the "elite" by the grace of the SS and they sought to survive by ingratiating themselves with their captors through harassing their fellow inmates. Hatreds grew up among the victims themselves and were exploited by the SS. Moreover, because of conditions within the camps, illegal traffic flourished in foodstuffs and the bare necessities of life. The SS knew of this and even encouraged it, for it meant a further breakdown in morality. Moreover, it provided a pretense for sudden punishments and deaths.

Adjustment to life in camp meant becoming immoral in order to survive. Only one's own person mattered and, apart from a disciplined communist minority, no solidarity ever developed among the prisoners. Adler put it well when he stated that the camps were designed to instill a moral nihilism in the inmates. This utter self-interest might be interpreted as a heightened sense of individuality but this was not actually the case, except in the crudest sense of the word. For all dignity, all consciousness of one's own personality, was systematically destroyed. Everyone was wholly dependent upon the SS, not only for food but for life itself. The nihilism involved was a sly and illegal assertion of instincts closer to animals than to human beings. The inmates, already broken by their horrible journey, were treated over long periods of time as depersonalized "goods," as statistics who were kept alive or killed according to their usefulness.

No doubt this treatment of prisoners of the regime could be duplicated by other societies. Imprisonment at Devil's Island must have had a similar effect on the Frenchmen sent there. But an all-important difference must be noted. This was mass terror, mass imprisonment, and mass extermination. It came about not because a crime had been committed but because those so treated were in the majority thought to be of an inferior race. It was the mass extermination of "types" which was involved, starting with a prison situation and reducing them to accepting the racial view of their personality.

Here modern totalitarianism revived slavery in its most extreme form. Indeed, Stanley M. Elkins has shown that many early American slaves had many of the same characteristics of these inmates of the modern concentration camp. They also exchanged their personality for an almost child-like dependence upon their masters. Jews were "given" to managers of factories which were working for the German state and, at times, to private individuals to use as they thought fit. Men like SS leader Heydrich, and later even his widow, held slaves of this kind. Indeed this slavery was sought after by the men and women in the camps for they could expect somewhat more humane treatment in such a position. For as slaves have discovered throughout the ages, the slave master needs their work and will therefore treat them with that modicum of humaneness needed to preserve their usefulness. What was true of the American slave master was true as well of the slave master under national socialism.

The revival of slavery thus accompanied the destruction of personality in the concentration camp. A human being was nothing more than a "mass" which one dealt with according to party regulations. The destruction of his personality was accompanied by the systematic destruction of his dignity and his moral sense. Such was the background of what is the most frightening phenomenon of this century. Multitudes of men digging their own graves and then, without resistance, lying down in them to be shot—all this under the supervision of a scanty SS guard. Their guns did not overawe these men and women; they docilely went to their deaths because they had been utterly robbed of their individuality, they had been systematically turned into obedient robots. Surely, here is the climax of that decline of liberty in our times which has been discussed so much in these pages. This is the ultimate price paid for viewing the individual as an integral part of larger, irrational cosmic forces.

Ideology was always the primary concern of national socialism. Reducing the Jews to the state just described fitted in with the concept of the Jew as cowardly and immoral, as the opponent who had to be destroyed. Away from the camp the SS lived respectable, bourgeois existences, kind to their children and their dogs. But the humans in the camps were below animals on the racial scale of values. In his memoirs the Commandant of Auschwitz could write with feeling about the flowering apple trees behind which lines of humans marched into the gas chambers. He could boast that he never touched a prisoner, and he was truly happy when the gas chamber was invented for now there was no personal contact with the dying at all. Rudolf Hess regarded his task as would an exterminator of insects. Here the danger of thinking about people in "types" is obvious. The men and women Hess sent to their death were for him "types," not humans.

As a consequence, among those like Hess, morality was something not intrinsic to all people but only to Aryans. The bourgeois morality which accompanied the rise of liberalism was integrated into a world view of struggle between Aryans and other inferior "types," particularly Jews. Ruthlessness against these was a necessity if the very morality which Aryans exemplified was to triumph.

Allegiances were defined in terms of an ideology. This had a more generalized result, the implications extending beyond national socialism itself as was mentioned in the last chapter. Treason had always been conceived of as an "overt act" or in terms of trafficking with the enemy. Despite the ideological conflict which was caused by the Dreyfus affair, the captain had been accused of a traditional act of treason, giving information to the Germans. With the advent of fascism this concept of treason changed in a significant manner. Treason was now defined as compliance or noncompliance with an ideology. Those who did not believe in national socialism were traitors though they may never have had any contact with a foreigner. In this manner, the whole concept of treason intruded into a realm which was purely subjective. Today's allegiance could be tomorrow's treason. This was one more way in which the terror worked upon those who were not an eternal enemy like the Jews. Treason so defined snarled the mind.

Yet this idea of treason did not remain the sole property of fascism. In the Soviet Union it came to dominate as well. Wherever a regime was based upon a set and "true" ideology, the new definition of treason was an essential part of its security. Loyalty to an ideology and not loyalty to the nation as a territorial unit was demanded. This was one more sign of the decline of the traditional definition of the nation which was discussed in the chapter on nationalism, for these ideologies were now thought valid beyond the boundaries of the state—they were universally "true." As was seen, the Aryan state lost its Germanic base. After the Second World War, and as a result of the cold war, such ideas began to penetrate even the democracies. One American judge condemned two traitors to death, citing among more concrete evidence, the "treason in their heart." But democracies have no one clearly-defined ideology, or at least have difficulties in arriving at one. From what is known of the European tragedy, these difficulties may well be their greatest advantage in the preservation of liberty as opposed to clearly defined and enforced "national purpose."

The changing concept of treason was a part of the depersonalization of man. National socialism represented, in the West, the climax of this trend because it believed in the primacy of ideology over all of life. It is certainly worth noting that an ideology which started out by ignoring outward reality on behalf of man's soul ended up by destroying man as an individual, indeed as a human being.

National socialism confronted Marxism in Germany as fascism confronted communism all over Europe. These dynamic systems of thought competed for men's minds just as they fought against each other in the streets. It is now communism to which the emphasis must shift in the next chapter.

# CHAPTER TWENTY-THREE

# *Marxism and the Intellectuals*

MARXISM in the West emerged strengthened from the First World War. Not only was a communist society being built in Russia, but in the years between 1918 and 1920 world revolution seemed to engulf Europe. During these years short-lived Soviet republics were established in Hungary, Poland, Saxony, Bavaria, and Berlin. There was never much liaison among these revolutionary centers, and nowhere did communism triumph without meeting continuous resistance from hostile forces. Eventually, all these regimes were overthrown. At the same time communist parties split off from larger socialist parties all over Europe. While the Socialists reaffirmed their allegiance to parliamentary procedures and to gradualism, the new communist parties looked toward the overthrow of existing society. The Russian revolution served as a constant example for them. Though the immediate chance for world revolution after the war had been lost, the grave social and economic problems of the 1920s encouraged a continual hope that such a chance would recur.

In spite of the defeat of communist revolutions in the West, the period between the wars saw an increase rather than a decline in the allegiance to Marxism. This increase was spurred on by both the vanishing certainties after the war and the rise of fascism. From the very beginning the Soviet Union fought fascism, engaging in a diplomatic campaign within the League of Nations to organize other European states against it. Moreover, the Spanish Civil War (1936–39) seemed to sharpen the issues. The legitimate Spanish government was attacked by a pro-fascist military junta. Both Italy and Germany openly supported Franco with men and material. The democracies went through the sham of "nonintervention" which, as everyone realized, benefited the Fascists in Spain. Only the Soviet Union came to the support of the legitimate Spanish government. Thus, through the force of events the appeal of communism in the West was strengthened.

Disillusionment with parliamentary democracy was heightened—the failure of democracies operating in a capitalistic economy to oppose fascism seemed proof of capitalism's collaboration with this totalitarian ideology. This, in turn, bore out for many a person the Marxist contention that fascism was an inevitable extension of capitalism. Just as Lenin had believed that capitalism in the age of imperialism would reach its apogee and begin its decline, so Marxist theoreticians now claimed that fascism was a last-ditch effort of capitalism to protect itself against the rising proletariat. John Strachey summed it up when he called the methods employed by fascism "the attempt to create a popular mass movement for the protection of monopoly capitalism." It has been seen in the last two chapters that this was certainly a naive and simplistic analysis of both Italian fascism and German national socialism, but in the face of such acts as the Spanish "nonintervention" it seemed to make a good deal of sense.

The result was that many of the best minds of the West saw fascism and communism as the only two real alternatives of their times. In any case, parliamentary democracy, under capitalism, would eventually turn fascist. This, as has been seen, underlay the despair of the old Julien Benda. The intellectual could no longer impartially damn both systems; he had to choose, even if this choice sacrificed liberty as he understood it. Similarly Romain Rolland felt that he had no choice but to side with communism against fascism. Though some, like Rolland, qualified their support with reservations about the necessity of preserving freedom, others brushed aside such scruples. Henri Barbusse (1873–1935), the most intellectual of the French Communists, felt there was an overriding need for "clarity" in the struggle. The goal of the coming revolution must be constantly kept in mind. In the cause of the revolution the intrusion of violence was just a "provisional detail"; the need for a flexible strategy was paramount. Barbusse, like so many others, believed that the Marxist revolution had to come sooner or later, for the dialectic of history was a scientifically proven process. Barbusse put it this way: ". . . there cannot be any serious errors of calculation in this geometry of social revolution, which is defined and formulated by the general principles of clarity (*clarté*)." France was dying, and in a Europe threatened by fascism there could be no other choice than the "truth." Rolland replied to Barbusse by stating that the intellectual, especially in times of revolution, had to uphold moral values and that the end could never justify the means. Barbusse's "either or" attitude toward communism was made on the basis of the Marxist dialectic. This was not, however, the only attraction of communism. Even if fascism had not existed communism would have had great appeal in the West. The issue in the 1920s was not only fascism but also human misery—the kind of discontent which drove people into nihilism, racism, and, eventually, fascism.

Many intellectuals felt that they could no longer isolate themselves from the masses, that the "human condition" required more attention than politicians seemed willing to give to it. Even before the war Croce's disgust with parliamentarianism had led to his brief acceptance of Marxism. Indeed, the same type of antiparliamentarianism analyzed in the chapter on fascism also played a role here. The fascist reorganization of society required the construction of a new and extraparliamentary form of government, and for communism it meant the same thing. A new and better society was to be born; Social Democrats were wrong in thinking this birth would come about through pressures from parliamentary majorities. After all, this was not the way the new society had come to Russia, nor the form it had taken there.

Communist literature proclaimed that this new society would give man back his natural dignity. The constant oppression of labor and the bloody wars of capitalism had stripped man of this dignity. In opposition to the rising tide of fascism, the Communists, especially the intellectuals, stressed this individualism. They viewed the coming classless society in terms of the restoration of individual dignity and rejected the individual's integration into state or race.

Such a stress, however, raised an important problem. If individualism was not to mean integration with higher and mystical powers, it did mean being an integral part of the struggling proletariat. Would this not mean, once more, subjecting human dignity to revolutionary strategy, to what Barbusse called the "social geometry of revolution"? In an authoritative textbook on communist morality (1956), A. Schischkin had this to say: "Communist ethic rejects all attempts to view the private life of a Communist as existing apart from his social tasks and his labor." Human dignity was not to be viewed in personalized, individualized terms.

The Marxist critic Christopher Caudwell (1907–38) will serve as an example of one interpretation of the geometry of revolution as it applied to individual creativity. The artist who stood above his milieu was a discredited bourgeois ideal. Caudwell based himself upon Marx's dictum that: "It is not the consciousness of men that determines their being, but, on the contrary, their social existence that determines their consciousness." Consciousness was a reflection of the social milieu in which man lived. Art, therefore, must be a social product. It was also to be a social activity, because only the recognition of revolutionary necessity could achieve social freedom.

Determined by material circumstances and by the necessity of working toward communism, art could not be an absolute. The problem of whether human creativity had to be subordinated to a purely relativistic and crude social realism arose from such analyses. Caudwell, like so many Marxists between the wars, endowed his theory with a material base much more single-minded in emphasis than that of Marx. Engels, for example, had placed a greater premium on the function of man's mind itself in the process of artistic creation. "In human history the laws [of the dialectic] assert themselves unconsciously in the form of external necessity in the midst of an endless series of seeming accidents." Georg Lukács, whose importance will be discussed, believed that ideas were created by man's mind through his genius. Once created, however, they had a dialectic of their own which meshed with the dialectic of history. Lukács eschewed the crude environmentalism of a unidimensional social realism. Caudwell did attempt to bestow upon poetry some degree of autonomy but not without closely linking it to the dialectic of history. In his *Illusion and Reality* (1938) he posited the origins of poetry in ancient tribal rituals. In the ancient harvest festivals collective work and folk poetry had formed a unity of feeling and action. The development of capitalism, with its consequent division of labor, smashed this unity, something which the poet, ever since, had sought to regain. Though poetry originated before the beginning of class warfare, it had to unite with the proletariat in order to recapture the vital source from which it had sprung. Capitalism had crippled poetry; only the proletariat could make it whole again.

Caudwell's definition of liberty must be understood not only for his explanation of the nature of artistic endeavor but for his whole concept of the relationship between individualism and society. Caudwell accused bourgeois intellectuals of deifying their liberty, when in reality it was "owned" by them like any of the products from which the majority of men (the workers) were excluded. Bourgeois liberty was a commodity—and one sold under false pretenses at that. "We attain freedom—that is the fulfillment of our will—by obedience to the laws of reality." These laws were not arrived at intuitively but scientifically; they were "the laws of motion of society." Liberty, like all else, could only function in accordance with these laws. Liberty was therefore the "consciousness of necessity," and because Marxism had grasped the laws of society it was a communist necessity which must determine liberty. Liberty was not an absolute; instead, it was dependent upon the dialectic, and only with the triumph of communist society would it emerge as a positive force.

Caudwell stressed the importance of material freedom as a precondition of intellectual freedom. From this point of view, the dictatorship of the proletariat—despite its censorship, in which he believed—would have more liberty than bourgeois society. For in this stage of development everyone could satisfy his material wants, nor would any man be asked to suppress his fellow man (except, of course, remnants of the bourgeoisie anxious to regain their monopoly). There are two elements in Caudwell's thought which must be emphasized, for they were common among many Marxists in this period. The first was an unshakable belief in science which held that Marxism was a social science as valid as those physical sciences Marx himself had called too mechanical. Only through science could external reality be known. This was positivism with a vengeance. The second element concerned the explicit materialistic base of this definition of liberty. Intellectuals would have to accept the suppression of intellectual freedom which was, in any case, trivial beside the truer freedom to be gained through the elimination of poverty. Obviously liberty was not a lofty aspiration; it was relative to the science of society and to the satisfaction of material wants.

More than Marx, and particularly Engels, these critics stressed the social basis of life, and their positivism came close to ignoring the power of ideas. At best they thought them pale reflections of social necessity. Caudwell himself acted out that "geometry of revolution" with which he identified himself. He was killed as a volunteer fighting for the Republicans in Spain.

The problem which faced intellectuals was clear: how to assert individual dignity in the struggle against fascism while integrating oneself with Marxist historical necessity. This was not merely a theoretical question but one which agitated all of European communism between the wars. It involved such problems as that of social realism in art as well as the exercise of private judgment in defiance of party control. The discussion of socialism against this background will reveal some important answers which, in turn, represent the contributions and the advances made by Marxist theory in the West.

Intellectuals attempted to liberate the Marxist heritage from the dogmatism and materialism which had become the program of the socialist parties. During the last decades of the nineteenth century many intellectuals sought to revitalize Marxism by turning to Immanuel Kant and attempting to infuse Marxism with ideals of man and truth derived from this source which Marx and Engels seemed to have neglected. The categorical imperative must apply to socialism: Man is an autonomous being within all of humanity; he must never be used as the means to an end; he can only be an end in himself. Such an emphasis meant that means and ends were closely related, and that therefore strategy, tactics, and the use of force were not permitted lest the cause of the revolution be contaminated. This "Kantian Marxism" did not deny the working of the historical dialectic, but as Kurt Eisner put it in a famous essay on "Marx and Kant" (1905), a humanist ethic stands above all concrete forms of society and provides the standards by which such forms must be judged.

The task of the intellectuals was to present such a socialist vision to the people who, once having grasped it, would realize the socialist society without resorting to an oppressive and anti-humanist dictatorship. Kurt Eisner became the leader of the revolution in Bavaria (1918), the only revolution ever started and directed by such left-wing intellectuals. This was a spontaneous revolution which began with a mass meeting, and Eisner, once in control, rejected forced nationalization and a dictatorship. But the abortive revolution was less important than the continuing impetus of a Kantian Marxism which attracted important writers and artists to its banner. Thus Ernst Toller condemned mass man in a play of the same name (*Masse-Mensch*, 1919) and exalted the individual: only through him can we arrive at a love for humanity. Clearly, such left-wing intellectuals could never really join any of the socialist parties and found themselves in even greater isolation. Not only in Germany, but in Italy as well do we find such socialist intellectuals between the wars. For example, Carlo Roselli emphasized eternal ideals of liberty and justice which must be a major part of attempts to abolish the capitalist structure. The liberal ideals of individual dignity and respect for all men must be separated from liberal economics and class structure.

Kantian Socialists saw themselves as preservers of the liberal ideal of freedom and the autonomy of man which had been so important in Kant's own philosophical system. For the most part those who attempted to introduce this Kantian socialism into the socialist parties were young Jews who in this way could transcend their origins and share in a common humanity. Here neither their Jewish nor their middle-class origins mattered for they exemplified a categorical imperative which existed potentially in every man and made him good. Such a socialism, which rejected all tactics and most discipline on behalf of the ideal, was rejected by socialist parties as heresy but it became a true alternative to young Jews who rejected both liberalism and Zionism.

However, such socialist idealism could also take on a Christian form, as in Ignazio Silone's novel *Bread and Wine* (1937). The anti-fascist hero, Spina, moving through the Italian peasant world, symbolizes a socialism which is the true Christianity. For Spina the struggle for liberty, the opposition to suppression in all its forms, leads to the belief that "he who thinks with his own head is a free man." Socialism is viewed as human dignity combined with Christian compassion. The dialectic and the class struggle have vanished.

The other great Marxist novel of the interwar years also belonged to this idealist category of Marxist thought, even though it contained no vision of Marxism as a new Christianity. André Malraux's *Man's Fate* (1933) placed a similar emphasis upon human dignity. His theme was not the fascism of Italy but instead the Chinese revolution of 1927. The hero, Kyo, was a communist revolutionary who had helped stage an uprising against the old regime on behalf of Chiang Kai-shek and the Kuomintang. Once they had triumphed, the Communists were, in turn, persecuted (and Kyo killed) by those they had helped to power. Kyo, like Spina, wanted to restore to the oppressed their lost dignity.

Kyo thought himself an integral part of the people—"He belonged with them: they had the same enemies." The people's daily tasks had to take on a new meaning, to become a faith. Man had to justify his fate by giving it a foundation in dignity which went beyond mere selfish interests. For the slave this foundation had been Christianity, for the citizen it had been the nation, but for the worker it was communism. There was a sense of the dialectic here, of historical progression. Compared to the more contemplative Spina, Malraux's hero was an activist. Marxism, for Kyo's father, was an inevitability which only strengthened his fatalism, a position roundly condemned in the novel. Communism engendered a will to fight in the worker, not a kind of opium-induced nirvana. The hero sank his whole being into the struggle. Thus, Malraux's novel was closer to social realism than Silone's.

Yet, here too, idealism came to the fore. The true revolution had a high moral purpose which it could not compromise. Thus the leadership should not betray the workers by assuming a temporizing attitude in the face of failure. Kyo opposed Vologin, the emissary from Moscow, who typified craftiness and strategy. For the man of the party, all actions were means to an end, however far that end lay in the future. For the young revolutionary death and failure were preferable to sullying the communist cause by sacrificing morality to tactics. Malraux, like Silone, approached Marxism from an idealist standpoint. He, too, saw justice, truth, beauty, and dignity as absolute values. The communist revolution did not create these values, they were eternal; one was a Communist because these values were embodied in the proletarian struggle. The movement must embody these ideals before, during, and after the revolutionary struggle.

It is surely no coincidence that the two greatest novels shared this attitude. It enabled both writers to portray their heroes as idealists and to bestow upon them individuality in their fight against both the party and capitalism.

Yet there was something static about such socialist idealism with its stress on eternal ethical values and the categorical imperative. However, there were other intellectuals who wanted to cleanse Marxism of positivism and determinism not through turning to Kant but through reviving the Hegelian heritage of Marxism. This meant an emphasis on movement and revolution through the dialectic with its battle of opposites, as well as stressing man's consciousness as against the iron laws of history. The collection of essays by George Lukács, *History and Class Consciousness* (1923), became the most important single document of the Hegelian renaissance in Marxism. Lukács, unlike the Kantian socialists, builds upon the class struggle—not as an inevitable and predetermined progression toward the victory of the proletariat, but as a struggle which depends upon the self-consciousness of the proletariat. This self-consciousness must be based on an understanding of history as the dialectical relationship between capitalism on the one hand and the proletariat on the other. Proper consciousness, then, means having knowledge of reality— human and social as well as historical—and with such knowledge men should pursue the class struggle actively. Thus the proletariat can unite consciousness and life dialectically as Hegel had done, life being the revolutionary attempt to change dehumanizing social and economic reality. Such unity Lukács called *Praxis;* it revolutionizes consciousness beyond the day-to-day reformist activities of the socialist parties and beyond communist organization and hierarchy. The Bolsheviks in Russia condemned Lukács's work as an idealistic deviation by intellectuals, and Lukács himself soon repudiated it. He believed that only through the proletariat could revolution come about and the Communist party was the one organization in touch with the proletariat and thus he felt the need to subordinate himself to the party lest he become isolated.

Nevertheless, the essential concepts of Lukács's famous book were retained, especially his influential criticism of culture. Indeed he was the most important socialist critic of art and literature of his times. Here he started once more with the concept of totality which he saw essential to the right kind of consciousness. Marxists must regain the total vision of man and society known in Shakespeare's or even Goethe's day. For, as Marx had said: ". . . knowledge of self and knowledge of the world cannot be separated." This knowledge gave an insight into the deeper connections of life and this insight was supplied by the Marxist dialectic—but not in any crude or schematic sense. An artist's true worth would be evidenced by the manner in which he linked man's character and his environment. The aesthetic quality of the work would depend upon the sensitivity and verisimilitude of this relationship. Here Lukács, like Marx, turned to Balzac who, through painting a kind of "higher abstraction," had concentrated upon the right proportion between character and background, creating a truer realism than had the naturalists. Mere reportage must never take the place of character analysis. Neither must this character analysis be abstracted from the milieu, and Lukács quoted with approval a sentence from G. K. Chesterton (of all people): "The inner light is the darkest kind of illumination."

The depiction of man both as an individual and an inextricable part of his environment seemed to beg the question, for this was having the best of two worlds. On the one hand, the character's total individuality must be revealed. Yet on the other, the intimate connections between character and environment must be illuminated. But Lukács did narrow the area within which this could be done. "Socialist realism takes as its fundamental task the formation and the growth of the new man." In the difficulties of his rise and in his struggles against society, the artist will find ample material illustrating both his individuality and his interaction within society. The "class enemy" must also be portrayed not as an abstract villain but through his false consciousness as a real person caught in the dilemma of the decline of his class. The villain, like the hero, must never be schematized; his dilemma as a living person must be understood. Moreover, action should take place within a specific historical context at a definite point in the dialectical process. It must not be universalized for then it might, once more, become abstracted. To solve the problem of individuality and aesthetics in Marxism one has to understand the human dilemma and the struggle for proper consciousness at a certain point in history. The writer must not only celebrate the triumph of the leader who, by his own will, overcomes the pressures of the old society, leading his people to victory; a writer has also to understand those who do not possess the dialectical tools to free themselves from bourgeois civilization.

The actors within such a drama must come alive through an internal development of character, through an analysis of individual morality and psychology. It must be clear, however, that even these aspects of individuality are a part of, and are conditioned by, the dialectical process. With Lukács, the great impersonal forces of history became human problems upon a human scale when the totality of individual struggle was revealed.

Lukács's guide was Engels's dictum that "every type is also an individual." Art could never be unidimensional propaganda, thus Lukács could state that contemporary Marxist realism was not art at all. To these critical formulations, Lukács added a concept of Lenin's, though in fact it had been implicit in Marx himself. In Lenin's condemnation of the "cult of the proletariat," the most important point had been that not all of bourgeois culture should be rejected out of hand. Marxism, he felt, must assimilate the most valuable achievements of the two-hundred-year development of bourgeois society. For most of that time span this society had been a progressive and revolutionary force. The rejection of its modern art forms was based upon the "reification" of bourgeois capitalist society (i.e., life becoming a "thing," an "object, like any goods"); but one could still learn from the age of bourgeois triumph, from the tremendous vision of a Shakespeare or even a Balzac—Royalist and Catholic though he was. Had not Marx and Engels themselves said that they were returning to the font of Greek philosophy?

Through emphasizing Kant or Hegel intellectuals wanted to transform

Marxism into a new humanism which recognized the importance of conscious human action and which linked mind and historical reality in *Praxis*. A third group of intellectuals must be mentioned, whose concern with Marxist theory and practice had a long-range effect upon academic circles. The *Institute für Sozialforschung* (Institute for Social Research) was founded in 1923, and as it was connected to the University of Frankfurt its ideas and theories came to be known as the Frankfurt School. The contributions of the school to Marxist theory began in 1930 when Max Horkheimer became the director, to be joined later by Theodor Adorno and the young Herbert Marcuse—perhaps the three most influential members of the Institute. They were instrumental in developing "Critical Theory," as their analysis of society is called.

"Critical Theory" was founded upon the Hegelian revival of Marxism which we have discussed and its emphasis upon *Praxis*. Conscious human activity interacted with the infrastructure of society, but it did so within the historical framework. Thus an economic base was crucial now, but it would not be so always; what would remain would be the effort to comprehend society as a totality. This emphasis led the Frankfurt School away from the centrality of the proletariat and class struggle. Society in its totality was for men like Horkheimer and Adorno expressed culturally rather than through class interests. From this point of view they saw mass culture as having perverted the consciousness of the proletariat and much of their theory was designed to come to grips with the evil of such cultural manifestations.

The emphasis upon individual consciousness and its relationship to a culture which was atomizing and oppressing man's true nature led the Frankfurt School to a logical conclusion: Psychoanalysis could be more fruitful as a tool of critical consciousness than the straitjacket of Marxist laws. Psychoanalysis became the mediating concept between individual and society. Though Marcuse attempted to connect Freud's death instinct with the elimination of the need for destruction in a socialist society, Adorno and Horkheimer became increasingly pessimistic about the possibility of social change. Freud showed that no real harmony was possible, that reason, upon which they had based much of their theory, was not strong enough to defeat the power of myth. The victory of National Socialism and the emigration of the institute to the United States (1940–48) led them ever more into pessimism and a denial of revolution. Their cultural criticism maintained the ideal of harmony of form and content against irrationalism (which they saw in mass culture with its mythical rhythms of jazz, etc.). Reason should have been the mediating force of society but it was not and psychological rather than sociological analysis meant an ever greater distance from a revision of Marxism.

What remained influential in critical theory was a concern with the dialectic and striving for a rational consciousness. Moreover, history played a cardinal role, for it showed that the economic forms of domination were now subordinated to a totality which lacked any proper mediation between consciousness and life defined as culture. The time was not ripe for overcoming the present and founding a new society.

The Frankfurt School departed further from Marxism than the other groups of intellectuals, though the concern with the "human essence" proved dangerous to any successful revolutionary practice which must contain discipline and strategy. These intellectuals were doubly isolated. First, they were outside any political party, coteries grouped around a journal. Second, they were Jewish to an overwhelming degree in the midst of a hostile Gentile environment. The theories we have discussed not only gave intellectuals a place within the workers' movement but could enable Jews to transcend their alienation and rejection, for they shared the "human essence" if not the working-class origins or occupations. The right kind of consciousness had nothing to do with one's origins; it was acquired through study and learning. Perhaps these renewals of Marxist theory were one of the chief Jewish contributions to modern times, and the most original, for these theories influenced the 1960s' student revolts in the United States and in all of Europe as well. They were an attempt to give Marxism a human face.

Yet, apart from such intellectuals, orthodox Marxism after 1918 contained at least two exceptions to the rule of a dreary and mechanical interpretation of proletarian struggle and victory: the proletarian school of painters in Mexico and the theatre of Bertolt Brecht (1898–1956), who had a monumental contempt for intellectuals, especially those of the Frankfurt School. Little need be said about the paintings of Diego de Rivera and José Orozco. They managed to combine social realism with those aesthetic criteria Lukács had desired. Oddly enough, he did not mention these artists as true social realists.

Bertolt Brecht evolved a completely new type of theatre by applying Marxist ideas to the drama. Brecht began with a facet in the relationship between the artist and the world yet to be stated in terms of Marxist theory. The "hero" must struggle to free himself from existing society so that he might lead the way to the future. The artist had, therefore, to stand outside present society and view it externally according to its place in the stream of the historical dialectic. For, said John Strachey, unless the writer or artist extricated himself from present-day society, he was himself infected by the decay of this society. For Brecht this meant that the spectator of a drama must not be allowed to empathize with the play's action; he must be a true "spectator," judging the life on the stage from the "outside." The spectator became an auditor who did not react to the individual characters in the play but judged the totality of the ideological picture presented.

For Brecht, the essence of social realism was its didactic function, not in the crude sense of unidimensional propaganda, but through allowing the audience to judge the whole play without becoming personally involved in any part of it. Thus his maxim "the worse the actors the better" and his slogans above the stage which drove home the ideological point. At all costs the audience must be kept from slipping out of reality into the dreamland of the imagination. Brecht called this the epic as opposed to the dramatic theatre. It stimulated the spectator's active criticism, forcing him to take a position toward the action upon the stage. People, said Brecht, must be gotten into the theatre "so that we can ask them to change the world as they would like to change it" —that is, in a Marxist direction. The historical forces of the dialectic could, in this way, occupy the foreground of the drama.

In this Brecht contrasts sharply with Lukács. For the latter, social realism contained an internal analysis of character and the morality and psychology of the individual himself. In Brecht, the characters were really unidimensional; the responsibility of choice rested with the members of the audience who were supposed to form judgments. Here was another attempted solution to the problem of Marxist individualism, but one applicable only to the theatre rather than to all creative intellectual endeavor.

Brecht always attempted to keep as close as possible to the Communist movement. Even so, he had to journey to Canossa to signify his obedience to the rulers of the East German Communist state. It was not without irony that in the years after the Second World War he worked upon a play based on the life of Galileo. Here was a man who under pressure of the Inquisition had recanted his "errors" which were in reality the truth, and he was treated by Brecht with sympathy and understanding. In the last scene, the transparency above the stage relates that, but for his recantation, Galileo might have ushered in the Enlightenment. On stage the great scientist is seated at a table with an officer of the Inquisition beside him, Galileo smacking his lips over a particularly luscious meal. There is no retribution as the curtain falls. Brecht posed a twentieth-century problem in a sixteenth-century guise, one which the party intellectuals felt in increasing measure.

To the dominant Marxist problem, that of individualism, another equally important problem was added: What was to be the relationship of the intellectual to the party? This was not merely a theoretical but a practical issue. Though the groups of intellectuals we have discussed stood apart, after the war many joined the party who were, in the last resort, unwilling to subject their individuality to party control. Reviewed at the beginning of the chapter were the reasons which impelled so many to become Communists. Some were unwilling to sacrifice high moral purpose to party directives. Other intellectuals, even if more orthodox, wanted to retain their privilege of freely evalu-

388

ating both Western communism and the Soviet Union. Fascist control of free speech had forced them to join communism because it seemed the only alternative to fascism. They were unwilling to submit to the kind of totalitarian discipline they were supposed to be fighting. Within the party they were faced by two types of Communists, neither of which had much sympathy for their sensibilities, the intellectual adventurer and the power politician.

The young Arthur Koestler (1905–1983) typified the former element. Communism was an adventure which gave a new meaning to Koestler's life rather than a firm ideological commitment. His was a restless mind always looking for new experiences and new adventures. The books which he wrote covering the communist phase of his life say little of importance about Marxism but a great deal about conspiracies and sexual license. Eventually Koestler became acutely aware of the conflict between Marxist doctrine and individual conscience. In his greatest work, *Darkness at Noon* (1941), such a conflict was central to the story. It was symptomatic, however, that Koestler eventually passed from communism to the nihilism of his *Thieves in the Night* (1946), which denied the validity of ideology or moral purpose in favor of the reality of force. Obviously, communism was too deterministic to capture his highly introspective and individualistic nature for long. In this sense his problem was that of the other intellectuals discussed.

Of more importance was the rise of the power politician in the Western communist parties for they emphasized revolutionary strategy and party loyalty at the expense of any ideological discussion. They willingly followed Moscow's lead in eliminating any independence of thought and speculation within the Western parties. Two Germans illustrate both the best and worst of this type of party functionary. Willy Muenzenberg was an organizer of genius who was able to manipulate men with an unparalleled skill. He was the originator of the "front groups"—artists, writers, and scientists whom he deluded into believing that they held the initiative while in reality he directed their activities. With a great deal of cynicism he masterminded, in this way, such well-meaning publications as the *Brown Book* against the Hitler terror. Ideas mattered little to him; the attainment of power was all important. By the 1930s Muenzenberg had become the most important Communist in the West. Stalin began to fear his power, and when the Germans occupied France he betrayed him to the Nazis and to a bloody death.

Muenzenberg's end shows the extent to which power rivalries dominated all communist relationships both internationally and within the national parties. It was in this atmosphere that our second example, Walter Ulbricht (1893–1973), got his chance. Ulbricht's career centered on his ambition to become the leading German Communist. In fulfilling this ambition all means were acceptable. His genius lay in correctly guessing the direction the power struggle was taking and thus behaving with complete loyalty toward those in power. His ideas were always a faithful reflection of those of the mighty. In Ulbricht, Stalin saw a convenient instrument and in Stalin, Ulbricht saw his ticket to power. He was correct and so was Stalin. By the 1930s Ulbricht had eliminated his rivals in the German party; Stalin helped him to finish the job when many German Communists fled to the Soviet Union after the advent of Hitler. After the Second World War Ulbricht became the ruler of communist Germany. The triumph of the party functionary and power politician was complete.

These events made the position of the intellectuals within the party increasingly difficult. Georg Lukács had to revise his works several times in order to avoid direct conflict with the winning side in the power struggle. This is what underlay the disillusionment of so many intellectuals for whom communism had become the "God that failed." It failed not so much in theory as in practice. Ever more rigid party control over thought and expression seemed to parallel what the hated Fascists were doing, a parallel exemplified for many by the Nazi-Soviet pact of 1939. Others, however, decided to wait it out, for they saw in the triumph of the Stalins and Ulbrichts a transitory stage in the history of communism. The determined fascist enemy could only be fought by maintaining a rigid discipline and leadership. Lenin himself had believed that the dictatorship of the proletariat was essential. Yet, as is known, Lenin's cultural formulations allowed for a far greater flexibility; he would not have been happy with the rigid cultural controls exercised by the latter-day politicians of the party. As a concomitant of this control a crude realism was in the ascendant. Even an opera by Shostakovich was condemned in the Soviet Union because "the people" could not understand it. In literature characters like "Fascists" or later "U.S. imperialists" were unidimensional, stereotypes of the sort Lukács had condemned.

As the "transitory stage" became prolonged an increasing number of intellectuals left the party. This exodus reached a peak with the crushing of the Hungarian National Communist government and the Hungarian uprising of 1956. What had started in the 1920s as the rather slow and difficult process of welding Western communist parties to Moscow had ended in the open victory of power politics and military might over ideology. The ideology which had seemed the only viable alternative to fascist totalitarianism had turned to ashes.

England differed from the Continent in the problem posed by Marxism and the intellectuals. The theories of the three groups of left-wing intellectuals we have discussed made hardly any impact while many intellectuals did join the small Communist party. But outside the party it was, above all, one man who represented the nonparty Marxist left. His international influence radiated through his books and his teaching at the London School of Economics and Political Science. Originally Harold Laski's (1893–1950) thought had revolved around the problem of political power. He had made important contributions to the theory of political pluralism—the idea that the power of the state must be limited by man's allegiance to institutions such as the Church or trade unions. Later, Laski came to feel that such groups were not of primary importance, but rather that the reality of political life could be seen in terms of the class structure and its relationship to the state. Laski concluded that Marx was correct when he viewed the state as merely an instrument of that class in society which controlled the means of production.

Economic power rather than political power came to be the key factor in Laski's analysis of the present ills of society. In books like his *Rise of European Liberalism* (1937) he connected liberal concepts of freedom with the growth and development of the capitalist system. Yet, to him that system seemed doomed in post–World War I society, and with it that unregulated competition of private interests which Liberals believed the basis of human freedom but which had led to a society based upon inequality. Society must change; it must deprive the businessman of his control of the means of production and bestow this upon all the people. Laski never believed that this would come about through revolution in England. In his earlier works he had harsh words for the doctrines of violent revolution and dictatorship of the proletariat. In the face of universal complacency about fascism, however, he began to doubt the effectiveness of the processes of parliamentary government. Given Laski's premises, one is not astonished that he focused on what he thought were the underlying forces of such governments.

Laski felt that rule through law and representative government would work only if "men feel that they have the great ends of life in common." The classes which were the victims of inequality did not, of course, share the ends of the dominant class. Thus revolution would become a possibility. But Laski could never reconcile himself to that possibility. Instead, he believed that reason and persuasion might yet build the new society without violence in England. Intellectuals must develop a new positive faith in the necessity of a moral society. In one tract he even likened the struggle of the Marxists to the struggles of the early Christians. For Laski, as for many of the intellectuals discussed, a Marxist society meant a moral society, a society brought into being by an application of human reason to contemporary events.

Though Laski praised the Soviet Union at a time when many other leftist intellectuals had ceased such praise, he never wanted to introduce the Soviet model into England. For the local Communist party he had nothing but the utmost contempt, and he steadfastly ignored Marxist politicians, power struggles, and changes in the party line. The crux of his message was that liberalism was dead, even in England; men would have to work toward that positive freedom which a society of equality insured. This work demanded of men both reason and moral purpose and the possible sacrifice of those freedoms which had been liberalism's glory, freedoms now vitiated by an unequal society. This sacrifice primarily involved economic freedoms and not those of the mind.

In France the issue in the 1920s was different from either England or Central Europe. The real faith of Communist militants was syndicalist and they dreamed of factories without bosses, society without exploiters, and a nation without a state. Leninism was gradually grafted onto the syndicalism. Yet France was largely a backwater of Marxist theory when compared to the German-speaking lands. Not until after the Occupation and the Resistance did Marxism truly get assimilated in France and raise much the same questions which had haunted Germany several decades earlier. Then theoreticians like Merleau-Ponty began to stress the dialectic and, with some hesitation, the unity of theory and practice not unlike that which Lukács had desired. But it was Jean-Paul Sartre during and after the war who moved from the shrug at the wall of death to what he regarded as a Marxist commitment. But that commitment included a humanistic impulse, to "reconquer man inside Marxism," through the dialectic to transcend man's present situation. Sartre began to advocate the union of philosophy and the proletariat: those who are most alienated from their own humanity. Sartre in his *Critique of Dialectical Reason* (1960) resumed the attempt made by Lukács in 1923 to stress a revolutionary humanism which would be practical even while rejecting determinism and scientism.

The attempts to humanize Marxism were similar in Western and Central Europe. Lukács, Sartre, Italians like Antonio Gramsci, and Harold Laski in England all sought the same goal: a revisionism which in the end made them outsiders within the structure of political parties. It was an isolation which drove some to pessimism, others to bitterness, and the aging Sartre into temporary Maoist euphoria.

After the First World War communism offered many intellectuals an appealing alternative to the fascist menace; it held forth the promise of a better society than that of a bourgeois civilization in decay. Yet there were several problems which had to be faced. How could a movement which stressed a return to human dignity believe in the necessity of a "social geometry" which posited the inevitability of revolution, and which, furthermore, demanded that all men integrate themselves with the dialectical workings of this necessity? This question involved the concept of social realism, and by raising it, a man like Lukács made an important contribution to the evolution of Marxist theory. But such contributions were vitiated by another problem, that of party discipline, and this problem was aggravated when the functionary and power politician gained control of the party machinery. The intellectual either left the party or subjugated himself to the party line. He could find a satisfactory refuge in the Marxist noncommunist left disorganized as it was or he was forced to work within the confines of social democracy.

Marxism had emerged strengthened from the First World War, and as a political movement it was to maintain and even increase this strength. As a cultural movement, however, it was in decline; it lost the best minds of the West, minds it had once attracted. It can be argued that since Lukács's work and that of the Frankfurt School in the 1920s and 1930s no new and fundamental contributions have been made to a Marxist theory. The questions which they believed should be raised by the Communist parties were never properly discussed or settled. A shallow realism and the cult of the proletariat were in full swing. Engels's admonition that man was an individual as well as a type was disregarded. Man was reduced to a type entirely determined by his position in the process of historical materialism. The bourgeoisie were bad and evil, workers were good. Marx and Engels struggled against such an over-simplification of their theories just as Lukács did—but they were defeated in the end. Men were typed by communism just as they were typed by fascist ideology—their life and death depended upon loyalty to or treason against an ideology. Under such conditions where could the intellectual find refuge? What alternatives were still open to him after the Second World War?

# CHAPTER TWENTY-FOUR

# *Confused Alternatives*

BEFORE 1939 many were sure that another world war would put an end to civilization. H. G. Wells's forecast of what would happen if Europe saw such a cataclysm seemed to bear out the most pessimistic conclusions of Oswald Spengler: The Continent would be reduced to barbarism and nothing worth living for would be left. Today this seems alarmist, but before the war such ideas frightened even those who wanted to resist totalitarianism and further disorganized their ranks. Yet Hitler and Mussolini tumbled from their thrones; Europe survived though partially destroyed and haunted by the ghosts of millions who would never return from battle. Though Europe survived as a civilization, many intellectuals were convinced that its cultural predominance was over. Books describing the "End of the European Age" were one of the first reactions to the postwar world. Political power had shifted to the United States and to Russia; all cultural activity would follow suit.

After Napoleon's fall many of the best minds of Europe had believed that a rebirth of liberty was at hand; the fall of twentieth-century Fascists did not immediately revive liberalism. European thought had become too estranged from this in the decades before the war. Instead, the reaction which came immediately after the Second World War was quite similar to that which set in after the First World War. Men's minds were saturated with thoughts of despair and insecurity. Ernst Juenger's nihilism had a widespread popularity among the postwar generation of the 1920s; that of his disciple Ernst von Salomon was equally popular with their descendants after the second holocaust. Salomon's point of view has already been discussed in connection with Juenger, and it was noted that, in Salomon's hands, the element of resignation received increasing emphasis. What do political ideologies matter— they are just slogans to dupe the people and the "only true action is to do nothing." No burning faith in a new democracy rising in Germany illuminated his pages. Ernst Juenger himself found his way back to a religious faith during the war. Once it was over, however, he wrote a phantasy, *Heliopolis* (1949), in which the hero escapes from the city into the cosmic spaces. In all of this one heard once more the old refrain that outward reality, including representative government, was a sham and an illusion.

Such ideas were not confined to Germany. Quite similar in content were Virgil Gheorghiu's *Twenty-Fifth Hour* (1949) and Curzio Malaparte's *Kaputt,* both best sellers. Gheorghiu added an element which can also be found in Salomon and which now assumed a renewed importance: the fear of technology. Totalitarianism had been vanquished, but a new totalitarianism was upon man which was just as complete as the old. Gheorghiu felt man would be reduced to technical slavery until he was rescued by the ultimate victory of the Orient over the Occident. Schopenhauer had already anticipated this for he, too, looked to the Orient and to Buddhism to provide a way out of the materialism of his age. Salomon believed that man had been reduced to a few lines on a questionnaire (*Frageboden*) that could be filed away. He made quite explicit the underlying basis of this fear—the depersonalization of man which the Fascists had begun would continue, not through Hitler but through the application of technology to the social sciences. Positivism had triumphed after all. This fear as well as the immensities of the war provided the ingredients for the nihilistic mood which set in after 1945.

To demonstrate the truth of this fear, writers turned to the United States. Two currents of thought came to be focused upon that nation. In the first place the old distinction between culture and civilization was revived, and second, the belief, within this framework, that a nation which had so successfully applied technology to social organization could only be a civilization, never a culture. Looking at the highly developed technological society on the other side of the ocean it seemed as if man had been truly depersonalized. Symptomatic of the popularity of this viewpoint was a book entitled *The Future Has Already Begun,* by Robert Jungk (1949), which went through nine editions in two years. Jungk described Americans as displacing their churches with skyscrapers and claimed that the president consulted a "thinking machine" for his political decisions. The United States was pictured as helpless before the technology which it had created. In essence, the book embroiders upon a theme as old as *The Golem* (1915). But now not only the Rabbi of Prague but a whole nation was held to be the victim of forces it had released but could not control. Whatever difference the war may have made, it did not sweep aside the fear that the human soul might be drowned in the complexities of the external world. Indeed, this has been a constant theme in these pages.

It is not surprising, therefore, that in France the existentialism of Sartre attained great popularity in the backwash of the war—not the Sartre, however, who later attempted to infuse his ideas with social meaning, but the Sartre who wrote *The Wall*, who held that man must act without hope. A generation of young writers, of whom Albert Camus (1913–1960) was the most famous, played variations upon this theme. Camus strongly emphasized the necessity of knowing evil in order to determine one's own fate, to make the existential decision. "There is no sun without shadow, and it is essential to know the night." Once man has known the night he knows himself to be the master of his days and his efforts will be unceasing. It is important to point out the greater possibilities in this French existentialism as contrasted to the nihilism already discussed. Camus, as did Sartre, for a time made common cause with the Communist party, although their uneasiness with this connection increased as their concern for the necessity of freedom in society heightened. Camus squarely recognized the importance of the external world, indeed to him it became the only important thing. Fate was a human matter which had to be settled among men.

French existentialism came to terms with reality, divesting itself of that despair so typical of nihilism. In the beginning, however, both viewed the world as irremediably lost and men as lost within it. Technology was blamed for much of the alienation of man from his society, yet this was not the only force contributing to his depersonalization.

Totalitarianism was defeated in the West. Yet for many it not only continued to exist in the East, but seemed to be marching toward victory. The Soviet Union had helped to win the common victory and now communism held sway in most of central Europe. To the nightmare of technology was added the nightmare of a new economic, social, and political totalitarianism. The great impact of George Orwell's *1984* was due to his skillful combination of both these nightmares. Man would be dehumanized through a totalitarianism which used the methods of technology to accomplish its end. By the time he came to write this book (1949), Orwell was a thoroughly disillusioned man. In his *Animal Farm* (1945) the issue lay between worthless men and pigs (who had his sympathy), in *1984* cynical politicians ruled over an inert

397

mass of men. Orwell felt the nightmare was really not a nightmare at all for the mass of men who were too stupid to understand what was happening to them. There was in Orwell the feeling that this would continue to be so; that it was inevitable. He lacked the kind of robust affirmation of the world which Camus possessed.

A much more profound analysis of the ills of the age was Ortego y Gasset's *The Revolt of the Masses.* Though written before the war (1930), its impact was made chiefly upon the postwar generation—it was then that the book gained most of its public. For Ortega Europe was between two stages of development. In the first stage, which had lasted until the end of the nineteenth century, liberalism had graced the age, "the noblest cry that had ever resounded in the planet"; the lineaments of the second stage could not be determined, they lay far off in the distant future. The present age was determined by the revolt of the masses, the coming to the fore of "mass man." Ortega did not use this term as a class expression but rather to describe the inertia of the mass of humans. More than mere inertia was involved, however, for mass man was irrational and violent; he did not reason but sought to impose his doctrines by force. Not only fascism and syndicalism were prime examples of this, but bolshevism as well.

Ortega termed this phenomenon a sort of primitivism. Modern mass man was a primitive whose nature had been scarcely touched by the golden age of civilization. He ruled today and therefore everything had become "scandalously provisional." Science and technology, themselves affected by this phenomenon, were ever more specialized and had lost their general principles. Technicians and scientists were subject to the same inertia as those surfeited by motor cars and aspirins. Primitivism destroyed values not only through its irrationality but by its creation of a science divorced from culture. Though bolshevism was a menace, so was the American concentration upon technology. Europe here was viewed also as a beleaguered fortress which was not merely about to lose its soul but had actually lost it already. There are parts of Ortega's analysis which ring true, for all through this book that irrational urge in the West which was contemporary to Ortega's primitivism has been traced, commencing with the change in the public spirit of Europe.

Ortega himself saw the future in terms of new liberal assertions within the framework of a united Europe that had left the nation state behind. The state was his enemy together with mass man; it prevented spontaneous historical action. His concept of unity was not that of the Christian West, but of a larger framework for man's actions based upon reason, intelligence, and individual freedom. Unlike Orwell and the other men discussed, Ortega thought the present nightmare only transitional; he was one of the few who reaffirmed liberal values on the basis of a historical analysis of culture. Still, it was mass man who dominated the contemporary age's dissolving values. In this, his most famous book, he sketched the resolution of the transitional conflicts of the present in only the very vaguest terms.

Ortega became part of the postwar atmosphere, though its major manifestations were a great deal cruder than his analysis. The books of Arthur Koestler, which have been discussed in a previous chapter, combined the negation of permanent values with nihilism and cruelty. Indeed, it is easy to see how these world views could lead to a cynicism and a cruelty toward one's fellow man. Emphasis on cruelty was not new. After the First World War there was a general exaltation of fighting, of brute force. Throughout this discussion a muted theme of cruelty has been in evidence. Racial concepts, with their idea of struggle and typology, resulted in concentration camps and mass extermination. But this is an extreme example. The love of the bizarre in romanticism and the penchant toward a reversal of values with the changing spirit of Europe also had a streak of cruelty. We have seen it exemplified in the humor of Wilhelm Busch. Nevertheless, after the Second World War this cruelty became accented, but vicariously, through a popular literature, certainly a part of the atmosphere that has been sketched.

Popular literature serves as an illustration of this cruelty—especially the renewed popularity of the detective story. Sherlock Holmes, as all know, was a gentleman who would never have taken pleasure in brutality. Such a detective story was, to be sure, an escape from reality into action but not into cruelty. George Orwell compared this type of literature with that detective novel popular in the 1940s, *No Orchids for Miss Blandish.* Cruelty and sexual perversion predominate in the story. Criminality was bad only because it did not pay. The police and the criminal were equally vicious; both were without any moral scruples. Yet this must not be overemphasized. When the American stories of Mickey Spillane reached Europe, the reaction was, at first, one of horror. Only gradually did they find a growing market. A case can be made that this literature catered to a growing sense of realism and that its popularity meant the end of the romantic impetus. This would, however, be far from the truth. It was stated that this realism was vicarious, induced by the belief in the reality of evil—indeed in its necessary predominance. The soul was drowned by totalitarianism and technology and the outlook was hopeless. Just like the hero of Sartre's *The Wall,* one might as well accept the inevitable and enjoy it. The pessimism of Thomas Mann's last great work, *Doctor Faustus* (1948), is based upon an analysis of politics and culture in twentieth-century Germany. Here artistic endeavor corresponds to political degeneration and, once again, the effort to detach artistic creativity from historical reality fails. The hero, Adrian Leverkühn, attempts to create pure musical form, a mathematical music: cold, precise and inhuman. But at the same time Leverkühn's double emphasizes a humanism which is helpless in the face of Nazi Germany. The alienation of man from himself and self-understanding are apparently resolved through the daemonic spirit which claims Leverkühn at the end. Thomas Mann once more moves within a neoromanticism which rejects the enlightenment, stresses the soul of a people (however daemonic) and is unable to synthesize art outside and inside history. Just as his first great novel, *The Buddenbrooks,* so does his last novel end with a vision of degeneration corresponding to the collapse of middle-class values which Mann forecast in 1906 and whose time seemed to have arrived in 1948.

Psychology in the postwar era increased its influence as an explanation and even acceptance of a "neurotic age" which led writers like Mann, who loved order, to despair. Men's minds were out of balance. This explained everything and, by explaining it, condoned it. The penchant of psychology to explain the world solely in terms of the mind now received full play. Cruelty and sexual perversion were natural outlets for frustrations induced by the suppression of the id by the ego. From this it followed that men were basically bad from the conventional standpoint. Psychology, which, as was seen, had already become a metaphysic, now provided a supposedly "scientific" explanation for evil which was generally accepted. Indeed, for some this became the true description of the "soul" of man—it was not technology or totalitarianism which was the enemy, but sexual frustration. Psychology was romanticized, sentimentalized, and here also the impulse toward the irrational persisted.

If one film is taken as an illustration this becomes still more apparent. *Forbidden Games* (1951) epitomized the atmosphere which has been sketched. In the French film two children play cemetery, treating death with the naturalness and morbid innocence of the very young. But such a film was an exception, not the rule. The vogue of Italian films after the war attempted a telling realism, dealing with the sufferings and problems of the common man. But this realism did not convey utter despair for it was always coupled with deeds of heroism by men and women who rose to the challenge of a moral cause. In Germany, at the same time, the film took such a turn toward a romanticism that it has been impossible to export it to the United States. Mother love, true sacrifice, and touching love stories against a Black Forest landscape provided its themes. Not only did the distinction between culture and civilization remain alive, but a renewed emphasis upon romanticism dominated this art form. In France as in Italy the realism consisted in cutting through the conventions of bourgeois morality rather than in attempting a different treatment of subject matter.

The appeal of the detective story derived in the last resort from its reversal of morality rather than from its realism, and this, too, was a part of nihilism and existentialism. If the outward world did not really make sense, why, then, should the morality to which it was dedicated? Such a view of morality was much more blatant and less subtle than the search for "sincerity" which made Gide admit his homosexuality. This was an open taunting of the bourgeoisie. But, once more, this was not new. After the First World War there was a similar phenomenon in the cabarets and cafes of European cities, and especially in Berlin. Now, however, it became more widespread and more extreme as the supposed security of the bourgeois age seemed to have vanished for all time. Attempts to disguise the female body were frowned upon; mentioning the unmentionable was good form in many circles. Dances like the cha-cha and jitterbug came to the aid of this rebellion against conventions with its ever greater excitement of the sexual appetites. To be sure, obscene literature was forbidden, but the difference between pornography and those detective stories mentioned above was slight.

The apparent quest for realism was merely an appetite for a transformation, not of society, but of personal morality. Even this was for the most part vicarious and seemed to have led merely to a somewhat greater frankness in the sexual realm. The basic middle-class morality, which was discussed in the chapter on liberalism, was further shaken but by no means abolished—it was still the norm of society. But there must not be a denigration of the longings which all that has been discussed represented—it was a search for a way out of a dilemma which was not new but a continuation of the whole impact of European thought. The artist Giorgio di Chirico (1888–1978) symbolized this continuity when he praised Nietzsche for having taught that life made no sense (1914). In his paintings he attempted to confront man with material objects divorced from human cognition: a nightmare confrontation between the human mind and a reality which becomes a metaphysical abstraction. In a similar manner postwar man confronted his world.

But this was not true of all people by any means. Some of the best minds were, once again, concerned with the problem of freedom. One of Chirico's fellow painters, Max Beckmann (1884–1950), was preoccupied with the fate of the individual, his essence and origins. Beckmann answered these questions by stressing the mystery of life, the unknown which was the only reality. Reality had to be penetrated as deeply as possible. But he rejected sentimentality, the mysticism of feeling; instead, he tried to imprison man's vitality within clear and straight lines, to make his paintings as simple as possible. In architecture especially, such a solution to the problem of individualism fired the imagination. For Le Corbusier technology had created chaos in the past, but now it could be used to construct, through clear and simple forms, outward expressions of creativity. A whole school of architects sought to infuse personal imagination into simple technical constructions. Possibly in architecture the postwar world found its most daring and original art form. But this solution to the human dilemma was, of course, a limited one and too symbolic for general appeal.

Architecture transformed European cities, but it had little influence on European thought. Instead, the concern for individualism through individual freedom became bound up with the Christian renaissance in the West. It grew in strength side by side with the pessimistic movements which have been discussed. It is not difficult to account for this renaissance. The very disorientation of society turned men back to spiritual roots, and these contrasted sharply with that totalitarian society based upon explicit non-Christian foundations. It was now argued that totalitarianism had come about precisely because men had abandoned Christianity. The postwar conflict between the West and the Communist world reinforced such an interpretation of events. Both Fascists and Communists were atheists and therefore the West must return to traditional Christian foundations.

This reasoning would have been less effective if certain Christian movements had not already exercised a continuing attraction from the past. Protestant existentialism and Catholic neo-Thomism had a tradition of intellectual appeal which has already been analyzed. They now revitalized the postwar Christian tradition. In Germany Ernst Juenger repudiated the doctrine of his youth and in his *Marble Cliffs* (1940) found his way back to Protestantism. In England, at the same time, C. E. M. Joad, a leading agnostic, confessed that the Nazis had turned his mind to religion.

Joad's reasons for conversion point out the essence of the Protestant revival. The problem of human evil occupied his mind. This evil was so widespread that it could not merely be seen as a by-product of unfavorable social or political circumstances; a different approach was needed. For Joad, Christianity provided the answer; it enabled man to face the reality of evil and then to transcend it. Not unnaturally, the Protestant renaissance was deeply concerned with the sinfulness of man and the evil which resulted from this. Existential in orientation, it asked man to confront his sinful nature, to understand it, and to have faith in God.

The influence of Karl Barth became even more important now than it had been before the war. The Church must not get entangled with the social gospel or with the state; it must serve a transcendent and unconditional God alone. At times Barth publicly wished for a renewed persecution of the Church so that it might purify itself and return to the reality of the man-God relationship. Such an ideology tended to view social improvement, indeed existing society, as secondary to a felt religious need. The Christian ideal of a society of love was a vision which could not be realized in the present or even in the determinable future. Christian existentialism, which held sinful man to be powerless before God and called upon him to submit to faith unconditionally, symbolized a despair with the world just as it had done after the First World War. But this despair was directed not toward nihilism but instead toward a revitalization of religion in terms of the individual. It was an attempt to make religion meaningful through the life of each person—and to make it relevant to his existential condition.

This acceptance of religion by faith meant the denial of religion as a historical phenomenon which had led to the Biblical criticism of men like Strauss in the previous century. Important theologians now saw both Christ and the Scriptures as symbols for the eternal confrontation of man and faith, for man's decision to make such a confrontation the central experience of his faith. Not only history but the idea of progress was irrelevant here. Progress brought with it not only good but also evil. The Christian ideal could never be reached though it could perhaps be approximated. For men like Paul Tillich (1886–1965) and Reinhold Niebuhr (1892–1971) human values and ideals were relative; they could never provide absolute standards. The trouble with the world was that men, ignoring the inherent evil within them, had exalted the human into a new idolatry. Clearly humanism, as some intellectuals like Stefan Zweig had understood it in the 1920s, was rejected now as it had been rejected then. Reason was not the measure of all things, it was not the ultimate reality. Since man was sinful, how could he provide valid ideals for himself?

Some Protestant Existentialists, however, attempted to make their religious concepts more immediately relevant to existing society. Reinhold Niebuhr, working in the United States, was important in this. The aim of religion was to strive for faith, the unquiet and disturbing immediacy of the encounter between God and man. Through this encounter men gained a vision of history and a perspective upon its workings which enabled them to grasp the necessary limitations of human activity. Once they had grasped this, men were better equipped to work for the best possible society on earth. No longer would human absolutes encourage man's belief that perfection was attainable in human society, that he was not a sinful creature before God. Neither life nor history could be understood solely on their own terms. The failures of civilization were due to the fact that men acted with a supposed freedom which they did not really possess, and therefore pride of power tempted them to go beyond human possibilities. The ideal of the Christian society must be the object of man's striving, but it was a goal that remained outside the finite character of the historical process.

John Herman Randall has called these Protestant theories "the very quintessence of romantic pessimism." They were rooted in irrationalism, rejecting rationalism as a valid substitute for faith. This Protestant renaissance differed from the nihilism discussed before, however. None of these theologians believed that nothing mattered or indeed that man was helpless in confronting the nightmare of the world. To be sure, society was bad, indeed hopeless, if compared with Christian perfection. The individual, however, could transcend history and human reality through a confrontation with God. In this manner he would understand the absurd as well as the evil and would thus be able to assert his individual freedom. Society would then be seen for what it was: a human creation with human limitations. The Christian could then work to improve it within the limits of the possible and not according to an ideal of total perfection which existed only outside of history.

Not all of these men applied their thought to society. Where they refused to do so the strictures of Randall might well be appropriate. Then this Protestantism did become an escape into a deeper reality, not of despair but of faith detached from life itself. One other Protestant approach to the postwar world sought to cope with it through a religious affirmation. This was concerned not only with the confrontation of the individual and God, but also with the relevance of Christianity to the totality of Western civilization. It attempted to make a positive connection between religion and the survival of that civilization. Once more such an ideology built upon an older tradition, for it sought to determine the pattern of a civilization's decline.

Considering the fears outlined above, this question of the relationship of religion and cultural survival was certainly a relevant one to ask. It had been asked after the First World War and Oswald Spengler had answered it in his pessimistic way. He excluded an emphasis upon Christianity as necessary for the "soul" of a civilization. Now, this question was answered quite differently. Christianity asserted itself as an optimistic rather than a pessimistic force, and, in this instance, the Christian renaissance did lead to conclusions far different from those arrived at after the First World War. At mid-century it was Arnold Toynbee (1889–1975) who provided the answer to the problem of the decline of civilizations, not Spengler. His popularity was as great as that of the earlier Spengler, but because he gave cause for hope instead of reinforcing feelings of despair and insecurity. Toynbee expressly refuted the deterministic concept that civilization was like any organism whose life span was determined by biological laws, just as he denied the idea that history was cyclical in nature.

For Toynbee, man was not a Sisyphus eternally rolling his stone to the summit of the same mountain and then helplessly watching it roll down again. Man was a creature endowed with a divine spark and not merely a statistic. Individualism was reasserted as a historical force. Man could build his own destiny; there was no reason why he must necessarily fall under the sway of technology or totalitarianism. Toynbee, however, did not view the individual as self-contained, guided solely by his own reason. He could only save himself by responding to the challenges of the times through a revitalized spiritual impulse. Central to his whole view of civilization was what he called man's "saving spiritual faculties." The Enlightenment's toleration was ephemeral because it was based not upon the Christian virtues of faith, hope, and charity, but upon disillusionment, apprehension, and cynicism. Christian virtues were the hope of Western civilization and if Western man would revitalize his spiritual faculties he would surmount the nightmare of his time and his civilization would survive.

It is worth noting that Toynbee characterized the rationalism of the Enlightenment as cynicism. There was no alternative to spiritual revival, and by that he meant Christianity in the West. His basic point was that Western civilization was a Christian civilization and that in this lay its salvation if only men could be brought to understand this and rise to its challenge. Toynbee rejected Spengler but he had one important concept in common with him: the distinction between culture and civilization. Civilization was doomed, for Toynbee as for Spengler, if it lost that spiritual impetus which made it a culture. The concept of the essential Christian nature of the West was, in this manner, bound up with a distinction which entered European thought with the romantic and the later, neoromantic viewpoint. These "spiritual faculties," the only salvation, lay beneath external reality; they were the only "genuine" force, defined in terms of Christianity, which could save man. For Toynbee, as for the Romantics, that force must break through into reality in order to become operative for the good of society. This breakthrough, however, would not come with the spiritualization of the power of the state, but instead through the Christian virtues of the individual.

Like other Protestant thinkers, Toynbee felt such a Christian's vision of the future would be in terms of the ideal Christian society. To the challenges of the present he would respond "with his eyes set on a shining light." This response depended on no one else but the Christian himself whom God can save through Christ, and in that salvation lay the hope of the continuance of Christian civilization. It is easy to see why Toynbee's ideas should have swept most of Europe. He offered hope for the future combined with a rejection of rationalism for the deeper spiritual impulses and all within the framework of individualism. This was bolstered by a monumental analysis of all known history, much more thorough and certainly more scholarly than that of Spengler. The appeal to historical truth went hand in hand with this concept of the Christian West.

Toynbee did not stand alone. Many men were increasingly concerned with analyzing the West as a repository of the Christian tradition in order to find an ideology for the times. Thomas Stearns Eliot (1888–1965) belongs here through his later prose works. The poet of "The Waste Land" found his way back to Christianity as had the author of the *Thunder of Steel*. A necessary relationship must exist between culture and religion and to Eliot this was a subtle but nonetheless tangible relationship which must inform any valid culture. Eliot did not deny the validity of other religions outside the West (no more than Toynbee), but Western culture itself must be a Christian culture. Moreover, this Christian culture gave unity to the West; "Christendom should be one." Eliot did not mean this in a catholic sense; he allowed for diversity of ideas and sects within the whole. Like John Stuart Mill, he believed that in an endless conflict of ideas the truth would emerge enlarged and clarified.

Nevertheless, Eliot posited an overall Christian consensus as essential to a true culture. Like Ortega, he believed that people were presently living in a "kind of doldrums" between opposing winds of doctrine. A choice had to be made between a pagan and stunted culture on the one hand, and a religious though imperfect culture on the other. Perfection cannot be reached on earth, but the Christian way of life was the answer to totalitarianism and materialism. Philosophies such as liberalism and democracy were not good enough— democracy without the spiritual impulse could be perverted into totalitarianism, while liberalism lacked any principle of unity. A common Christian way of life was therefore necessary, and education must provide an identity of belief and aspiration, the foundation of a common culture defined in Christian terms. Men must be educated to think in Christian categories if Western culture was not to decline into a pagan civilization.

Eliot believed that a Church was necessary and stressed the sacramental nature of the faith. His was an Anglican Christianity which believed that the Church, as the expression of the Christian way of life, had a function in the world and was not divorced from it as the Existentialists thought. Through it the West would once more recapture a cultural unity. Another reason for the popularity of this thought is touched upon here. The quest for the unity of the West was stimulated by two factors. The war was seen partially as a consequence of warring nation states; an end to future wars necessitated a Europe united around certain binding principles. Soviet penetration into Europe reinforced the need for unity in the now beleaguered fortress of the West. Christianity's binding principles could provide such unity. Thus the concept of a Christian West was colored by hope and affirmation, in a situation where a Spenglerian interpretation would have given up and delivered Europe, inevitably in decline, without resistance to the Soviet system.

The problems involved within this ideology are rather easy to state. There was no room for non-Christians in this definition of the West, and Toynbee saw in Judaism, for example, a mere historical fossil without spiritual impetus. This is reminiscent of the early Romantics who held that he who was not a Christian could have no real feelings. Moreover, Europe, conceived of as an ideological unity, served to divide it from the rest of the world. Most serious of all, the good society was postponed into the future, and a distant one at that. It was no coincidence that the postwar world marked a new interest in the apocalyptical ideas of the Middle Ages. The good society would come through a revived Christianity at the "end" of time, after a long period of incubation. As we saw, for some Protestants this was so far in the future that they believed human society could never be more than an approximation of the ultimate ideal; men would be better off if they realized this fact. For others, a revival of individual spiritual faculties must be brought about first and then civilization may begin an upward trend after the present, apparent decline.

Parallel with the Christian renaissance, the postwar world saw the growth of Christian political parties. Christian democracy had been suppressed by all the fascist regimes and it now rose with renewed strength. These parties were, as might be remembered, Catholic in origin. Apart from Italy, they sought to work through a generalized and vague Christian appeal, however. Yet these parties underwent a significant change. In the beginning, especially in Italy, the Christian Democrats had been reformers with a vision of Catholic social action before their eyes. In the postwar world the social component was increasingly displaced by conservatism. The Italian party split into two factions over this problem. Christian democracy became in Germany, Austria, and Italy the party which guaranteed property relationships by guaranteeing social stability. Moreover, these parties adopted a strictly liberal economic viewpoint. It can be said that the Christian parties became the conservative parties, a new conservatism (as they thought) resting upon Christian principles as a guarantee for stability.

Where they did attempt reform, the party was apt to split into factions. The older tradition of "Christian authoritarianism" asserted itself, opposing the tradition of Christian reform. Thus, in France, where other conservative interest groups existed in politics, the Christian Democrats (MRP) could not make any headway. In Germany, the party was successful in attracting Protestants, though the specifically Catholic nature of Christian democracy remained. For example, in Germany, wherever the party was supreme, the public school system was influenced by the Catholic or Protestant Church. In education, always a sensitive area for Catholics, separation between church and state was denied. These parties shared a view of Europe as a Christian whole; they accepted the ideals of a specifically Christian Western civilization. Such an urge for unity was interwoven with a historical vision of the Middle Ages when Europe was held to have been united both politically and religiously.

The resulting close relationship of church and state would have horrified a Christian Existentialist like Karl Barth who wanted to free religion from outward entanglements. Some who participated in the Christian renaissance tended to use Christianity as a political slogan of conservatism rather than as a call for the kind of cultural renewal which had occupied the minds of Arnold Toynbee or T. S. Eliot. The danger that such a political Christianity might discredit the Christian renaissance was great, and indeed everywhere by the 1960s this renaissance was over. A materialistic concern for political victories was difficult to reconcile with a spiritual renewal of Western civilization.

These political parties were not the only sign of a Christian Catholic renaissance in Europe; another tradition was also revived. Since the beginning of the century a group of intellectuals, especially in France, had combined Thomism with a devotion to freedom and democracy. Péguy was their inspiration and Jacques Maritain their chief spokesman both before and after the war. They also rejected the rationalism of the eighteenth century, not because it was rational but because it rejected the foundations of Catholic thought which was both divine and reasonable. We have already analyzed the ideology of this group of men. They offered the postwar world a secure and traditional concept of the universe, and at the same time an individual freedom through the Catholic concept of free will. This freedom was essential for society as it was for man himself. Individualism was integrated with cosmology on a divine basis. It has already been suggested in a previous chapter that this Catholic thought continued the liberal ideal of individual freedom into the mid-century at a time when it existed on a rational basis apart from the Social Democrats only in the minds of isolated intellectuals like Ortega y Gasset.

Christianity played a role at mid-century which it had not played in men's minds since the early Romantics and Conservatives of the previous century. It offered security amidst the dissolving certainties, an escape from the dilemmas which men like Orwell and Gheorghiu had posed. Nihilism and cynicism had never satisfied the longings of men in unsettled times; a more positive ideology was always required. Such longings were satisfied by the Christian renaissance.

But what of the left? Surely Marxism and social democracy emerged strengthened after the war. Social democracy emerged from the war only to be confronted with a serious dilemma. Communism had, during the fascist era, advocated a popular front. The deep fissure in Marxism was to be healed in the face of the fascist menace. As the Soviets penetrated into central Europe, pressures upon the social democratic parties became still greater and they were faced with a choice either to collaborate with communism or to remain separate and hostile. The German Social Democrats made that choice (1946) and broke with the Communists in the face of the division of Germany. The

French Socialists also rejected the popular front idea though they had been its pioneers before the war. In England the choice never arose at all because of the weakness of communism. But in Italy the Social Democrats split, the majority, under Pietro Nenni from 1947 until 1963, forming a popular front with the Communists against the Christian Democrats. This very choice which they made in repudiating the popular front propelled these parties into a moderate position, into thoroughgoing revisionism, which before this had never gained acceptance among all their members.

Economic prosperity further accelerated the movement of social democracy away from Marxist orthodoxies. Ideological flexibility became the rule, and soon even Marxist terminology was called into question. For Karl Marx, it might have seemed as if the *embourgeoisement* of the movement against which he had fought during his lifetime was now complete. However, parliamentary action for social reform remained a social democratic goal though disputes arose over how much nationalization of the means of production was needed to gain the ends of a more just society. In their ever more passionate attachment to representative government as opposed to any authoritarianism, Christian or lay, these parties became, in fact, the upholders of the liberal tradition in the postwar world. They based their viewpoint not, as did the Catholic intellectuals, upon the dictates of both divinity and reason, but upon the necessity of social reform and an approach to that reform which involved, to an increasing extent, a pragmatic analysis of society's concrete needs. Social Democrats accepted a Marxist analysis of history but directed its appeal away from that of class struggle to that of human reason.

Socialist parties were large and yet nowhere until the late 1960s did they obtain a continuing period in office. Once they had modified Marxism, their political appeal was, perhaps, too vague. They were in danger of becoming merely an alternative party which would carry out much the same policies as their opponents. In the realm of foreign policy they consistently fulfilled such expectations. England was an exception here. Labor did come to power after the war, and it did nationalize part of the economy. But since then it has been rent by bitter disputes over whether nationalization should be retained in the party's platform or whether it should be jettisoned.

With all their conflicts and dilemmas the Social Democrats did offer attachment to representative government and to liberal ideas of freedom on a nonreligious basis. That their philosophy and platform did not succeed for nearly two decades after the war may signal further decline of liberalism. However, at times, in both France and Italy the communist parties became the largest political parties, barely kept out of office by political manipulations and coalition governments. Obviously here was an ideology which was both positive and all-encompassing. Moreover, communism could promise sweeping reforms through the abolition of capitalism which no other party could advocate. For those workers and peasants who did not take part in the renewed European prosperity this proved attractive.

Indeed, if for some communism was primarily an ideology, there is ample evidence that many who supported it in France and Italy never thought of the movement in those terms. They wanted "land and bread" and Communists promised it—that was enough. Italian peasants went to church on Sundays and to communist rallies on Saturdays. No stringent prohibition of adherence to communism could succeed amongst Italian Catholics. No doubt the strong anticlerical tradition in Italy and France helped to produce such a phenomenon. Meanwhile intellectuals had an increasingly difficult time in the party. Already in the 1920s the party technician had triumphed over the intellectual; free thought was increasingly hampered by obligatory allegiance to the party line. That party line now definitely came from Moscow and reflected Joseph Stalin's ideas and attitudes. The purges of the 1930s had made Stalin's hold over European communism almost absolute, and the actual Russian presence in Europe after the war completed that process.

It is not surprising that most communist intellectuals found themselves out of step at one time or another. Those Marxist intellectuals who had any impact were not party members but men whose aims, so they thought, coincided with those of communism and who wanted to collaborate. Sartre was a good example of this in the mid-fifties. While the intellectuals were squeezed out of the party, the Marxist appeal among intellectuals continued, divorced from a communist organization which claimed to be the only custodian of the truth. In 1941 Edmund Wilson asked from the United States whether there was anything valid left of Marxism, and by that he meant valid for a serious ideological commitment. He felt the desire to be rid of class privilege based on birth and difference of income, the exploitation of some by others, and, finally, the vision of a cooperative society directed by the conscious, creative minds of its members were still viable ideas that commanded allegiance. At the same time he rejected as no longer valid the expropriation of the means of production by the state and the dictatorship of the proletariat.

Wilson, in short, accepted what had always been so appealing to Marxists of the heart, and in this he was typical of an impulse which continued outside the party's confines. He attributed the authoritarian features of the doctrine to the German background of Marx and Engels. As has been seen, such a contention cannot be sustained. In any case, by the 1940s the authoritarian aspects of the ideology had swamped that Marxism which he believed to be valid.

Little important literature or art came out of the Soviet Union and communist eastern Europe after the war or during the first decade after it. The creative Marxist intellectual found himself isolated from a communism which rejected him and from a socialism which had moved to the right. With the exception of England, where a part of the Labor party continued to favor basic Marxist presuppositions, Marxist intellectuals remained in their isolation.

The postwar Communist party took on a double aspect. On the one hand it was now a mass party with mass support, and on the other it was devoted to doctrinal rigidity. That rigidity was furthered by the developing cold war and the necessity of choosing sides. In such a situation it was not surprising that Moscow exercised ever more stringent controls. Rigid controls did not prevent some worthwhile literary and creative activity, especially in the Soviet Union. Music had always escaped the strict rigidity of dogmatic control, though even Shostakovitch was censored in the 1930s. There were, however, men like Sholokov whose cycle of novels about the Don Cossacks attained great literary merit. Yet, experimentation such as there had been in the new Soviet Union of the 1920s was lacking. The intellectual excitement of Soviet poetry and particularly films had made a deep impression upon the West then. This was no longer the case.

The end of the Stalin era for a moment relaxed this vigilance. The subsequent outburst of a long-suppressed creativity was startling indeed. In the Soviet Union Ilya Ehrenburg attempted once more to experiment with socialist realism, while Poland saw something of a renaissance of poetry and prose. Creativity of this sort was not necessarily anti-Marxist, for even Marxist intellectuals now got a new chance. Relaxation also demonstrated the still present current of romanticism and nationalism—the Hungarian revolution (1956) began with the reading of poetry by a student group. Nor is it insignificant that Georg Lukács, who has been singled out before as the most creative modern Marxist theoretician, joined the national communist government of Prime Minister Nagy. The rebellion was crushed by Russian troops and the period of doctrinal relaxation gradually liquidated.

It served to demonstrate, however, that Marxism as an intellectual rather than a power political movement still continued, if underground. It was to surface once more in the 1960s. At that time a new student generation, most of them born during the war, turned to Marxism in order to change a society whose structures they perceived as petrified and which seemed to disguise its desire to dominate others through a hypocritical allegiance to democracy. The motivation of this revolt was not so different from the earlier generational revolt which we have discussed in Chapter 13. Here also it followed long years of prosperity and security, though specific issues, in particular the Vietnam War, fueled the revolt. These students did not turn to Marxist orthodoxy, but instead to the critical theory already discussed in Chapter 23. Herbert Marcuse supplied the theory of this "new left" in his *One-Dimensional Man* (1964), in which individual consciousness was said to be the instrument needed to break open a closed universe and petrified structures. This consciousness must be based on the totality of human existence, best expressed through the aesthetic and artistic dimensions of the society in which people live. Marxism was used as a method of culture criticism, and this gave intellectuals pride of place as the vanguard of revolutionary action. German students, by and large, did not follow here. They possessed a native tradition to which they could refer: the soldiers' and workers' councils which had been part of the radical revolutions after the First World War.

The student revolt eventually became violent as it refused to make use of existing institutions and unsuccessfully faced the authorities in Berlin and Paris and on American campuses. This revolt of youth did not lead to any permanent change. It did not create Youth Movements or literary works of particular merit as had been the case with the earlier generational revolt. Nevertheless, in Germany several new causes in the 1970s revived a movement of protest by young men and women. Ecological issues seemed pressing, and so did the threat to human life from the use of atomic energy, then thought to solve the energy problem of most nations. The so-called German Greens were a heterogeneous alliance of ecologists, pacifists, feminists, and those who claimed allegiance to some kind of Marxism, from orthodoxy to critical theory. The Greens, unlike the new left, decided to work within existing institutions, and they successfully entered the federal and local German parliaments.

European fascism did not revive after the Second World War, but its bits and pieces were lying around, ready for use. Racism was still present in popular terminology and in popular attitudes. It seems, however, to have survived in Europe as a typology rather than as the coherent world view it once was. France can serve to illustrate this. There was, to be sure, no Dreyfus affair, but with colonial revolts against French dominance a bitterness entered French political life which was compounded by the weakness of the Fourth French Republic. In this situation anti-Semitism came to the fore once more, not as part of a coherent racial ideology but connected with an undirected longing for change.

The Poujadist Movement (1955–1958) was a revolt of small merchants and shopkeepers using traditional racist and anti-Semitic arguments against the Fourth Republic. It made a great deal of noise, but it lacked ideological cohesion. Racism tended for a time to lapse into traditional anti-Semitism., and the Jewish stereotype still had currency. This situation changed by the end of the 1960s when former colonial subjects emigrated to the mother country after independence. France acquired a sizable influx of Algerians and Britain a large black, Indian, and Pakistani population. These new populations revived racism in both countries, primarily directed against Blacks and those of color but sometimes encompassing the Jews as well. The United Front in Britain was much less effective than the FNP (*Front Nationale*) in France led by Jean Marie Le Pen in the 1980s. Though neither movement had any chance at power, or even of becoming a decisive political force, each demonstrated that racism, in spite of its association with mass murder in National Socialist Germany, was still present, to be used whenever the occasion warranted.

Racism and nationalism raise the problem of the continuing romantic impetus with which these movements were historically linked. Has this mood which makes up much of the theme of this book come to an end in the late twentieth century? The rejection of reason by many of the alternatives which the Second World War had created meant a continuation of this mood. Human beings attempted to penetrate beneath reality to find not only their roots but also their true selves. At times the true self was found in the pessimistic conclusions of secular existentialism or in a confrontation with God. What is important is that it was found outside society itself. Toynbee or Eliot, for example, wanted to preserve their culture by making it respond to the crises of mid-century through a spiritual reformation. Survival could be assured only if Christian principles guided the West. Yet the Christian renaissance among intellectuals was not destined to last. It was over by the 1960s. Once the immediate shock of the war had receded, secular ideologies moved to the fore once more attempting to explore the inner spirit of men and women. There was a trend amidst the vogue of psychology after the Second World War to regard all problems as problems of the mind. However, a new scientific interest in the working of groups existed as well, exemplified by the new departures of social psychology with its use of empirical evidence.

The interest in the nature of the group reflected political reality: movements like fascism, socialism, and communism, which were so strong after the First World War, were symptomatic of a new mass politics which operated much as Le Bon had forecast it would, through the use of symbols, of mass meetings and demonstrations—focused upon a leader— and which gave people a sense of participation. Parliamentary government with its political parties, debates, and rival interest groups could not compete here. It seemed to fragment society rather than providing the kind of cohesion which people demanded in times of crises. We saw earlier how, after the change in the public spirit of Europe, antiparliamentary politics triumphed in many nations in the years between the two wars.

*The Culture of Western Europe*

The Second World War seemed to have restored parliamentary politics in the West and to have put an end to the kind of mass politics which had dominated Europe in the interwar years. The essential trappings of mass politics continued to exist in communist eastern Europe: the importance of the leader, of symbols, mass meetings, and demonstrations. But it seems doubtful if those characteristics retained their effectiveness: now such politics were imposed from above and no longer addressed the felt needs of men and women in crisis, as had been the case between the two wars. The revival of the liberal outlook strengthened parliamentary government in the West. It provided a consensus among divergent political parties, from the Christian Democrats, through the so-called liberal parties, to the Social Democrats. All of these political parties, in varying degrees, supported free enterprise as well as political freedom and tended to substitute pragmatic considerations for ideological commitment.

Was such a return to liberalism accompanied by the kind of morality which, as we saw in Chapter 6, had tempered and restrained the liberal ideal of freedom? The gospel of work, of accomplishment, was certainly alive in the immediate postwar generation who had to rebuild their lives, and the notion of respectability continued to dominate social relations. The way of life of the middle classes, which by now dominated all of society, held firm. The moral pattern of respectability which had accompanied the "challenge of liberty" dominated communist Europe as well. After all, it had long ago conquered the working classes and here also it was thought essential to provide social coherence.

Yet with the passage of time this morality bent in the West, but not in the East, to accommodate the new lifestyles of younger generations. Greater tolerance prevailed towards those who had formerly been excluded from society for their eccentric behavior or their sexual preference. The women's rights movement revived once more, calling for equality between the sexes with much more success than the earlier movement at the beginning of our century. This greater tolerance, the extension of the boundaries of what was acceptable, was due in large measure to the success of the civil rights movement in the United States and its effect upon Europe. The prolonged but successful struggle for Black rights set off demands for more individual liberty on the part of middle-class youth. And yet, while this revolt broadened the range of acceptable change, respectability remained intact.

Here, once more, a theme raised in the introduction of the book is carried through the larger part of the twentieth century: every person must have an authority to which he or she can relate. Two world wars may have strengthened this need. As we have seen, many men and women continued to see this authority through what we have called a "romantic mood," but after the Second World War the emphasis upon liberalism and pragmatism in the West constituted a counterweight to attempts at translating this mood once again into effective politics. However, Europe after the Second World War experienced none of the grave social, economic, and political crises which had led to the dominance of totalitarian mass politics after the First World War. Yet the need for authority, the desire for a hidden but absolute truth, still presented a potential danger to the pluralism needed for the ever greater accommodation of individual identities by western society.

Nationalism had not died with the Second World War. But nationalism was not all of one cloth. The aggressive and cruel nationalism of the interwar years had triumphed over a patriotism which recognized the rights of all peoples to their national aspirations and which saw in nationalism but one step to the attainment of freedom for all mankind. For example, those who had fought for a united Germany in the age of Napoleon linked their national struggle to that of other peoples and to a vision of a new Germany which would grant the uttermost freedom to all its citizens. Nationalism as it evolved tended to become aggressive and chauvinist, opposed to the rights of human beings, seeing the nation as encompassing and directing all the hopes and aspirations of its subjects. After the Second World War, nationalism did seem to have repented its chauvinism and aggressiveness, its association with war. Now there was no longer any exaltation of battle—of war as the ultimate test of nationhood—but instead the attempted return to a more moderate concept of nationality which recognized the legitimacy of other nations and people to determine their own fate.

Where, for example, after the First World War war memorials praised the heroic fight, now some ruins of the Second World War were left standing as a reminder never to wage war again. While up to the Second World War a great number of youth had volunteered for war, believing in sacrificing their lives for their nation, most postwar youth would have found such a belief all but incomprehensible. The nation had lost some of its grip upon the peoples of western Europe: for the first time large-scale opposition to national wars became active and visible even during such wars. These wars were now those that supported one or the other faction in the Third World or—like the Algerian war in France—were colonial rearguard actions; ideals of freedom and self-determination which had been proclaimed during the Second World War could now be turned against one's own nation. European nations themselves denied any aggressive intent or territorial ambitions. Departments of war were now called ministries of defense in order to emphasize peaceful intent.

Nevertheless, more wars were fought by European nations after the Second World War than we can count in the much shorter span of the interwar years. National defense could be used as a pretext to stifle internal freedom just as much as the older preparations for war. Had modern aggressive nationalism merely masked itself behind the rhetoric of an older, peaceful nationalism? Certainly the new nationalism continued to find a home in much of popular literature which dealt with the heroism and the battles of the Second World War: here, too, we often find that cruelty which, as we have seen, the detective story projected. Moreover, national pride was still a considerable force, not just in the victorious nations but in defeated nations like Germany and Italy. But these currents of nationalism were now embedded in European-wide institutions like the common market and in alliances such as the North Atlantic Treaty Organization which transcended narrow national interests. No one could even imagine another European war, started and fueled by the rivalry among European states. The most bloody rivalry in modern history, that between Germany and France which had cost millions of human lives, was dead and gone as if it had never existed, difficult to imagine for a younger generation. While Europe itself was perhaps too weak to determine its own fate after the war and was dependent on either the Soviet Union or the United States, the end of Franco-German enmity must be counted among the greatest accomplishments of the postwar world.

The nationalism which has caused so much bloodshed still exists underneath the rhetoric of peace and defense. It still has the potential power to arouse men and women, to provide them with an authority, a hold in the speed of time, to satisfy their longing for a community which will end their loneliness and give them direction. Whether such nationalism once again breaks through into the open may well depend upon the strength of a renewed liberalism, parliamentary government, and the belief in the power of reason. But these alone are not enough. A balance must obviously be struck between emotional needs and rational approaches, but a search for this balance is a continuous quest whose final outcome cannot be predicted. Nevertheless, the same forces which sought to restrict the human vision in the past are still potentially present.

The word "potential" is important here, for historical continuities exist and especially with those ideas and movements which had met some of the needs of people in modern society in the past. Who would say that even after the Second World War and the Jewish holocaust racism is dead?

Just so, all the various systems of ideas contained in this book continue to exist as a potential ideological and political force.

To be aware of potential dangers does not necessarily lead to the belief that history will repeat itself. National Socialism and fascism were bound to their epoch, and the ideas of Karl Marx reflected a certain stage in the industrial revolution. But the fragments of our western cultural and ideological past which these and other movements used for their own purposes still lie ready to be formed into a different synthesis. The exceptions are racism and modern nationalism, static ideologies, as we have seen.

The future is still open, the rush of time is upon us. But just as there are continuities between the past and present, so there are guides to help us along the way. The cultural history we have analyzed can be one such guide, for the ideas which fill this book did serve to determine the perceptions of many people of their place in the modern world, and such perceptions are a guide to action. Culture as a state or habit of mind, to repeat the definition we gave in the first pages of this book, does give us a clearer understanding of how and with what results men and women confront the society in which they live.

# CHAPTER TWENTY-FIVE

# Culture and Civilization: One Historian's Conclusions

JN THE beginning of the introduction it was asserted that the very origins of the word "culture" determined its evolution in the nineteenth century, explaining the difference which Spengler had made between culture and civilization. Arnold Toynbee was to make a very similar distinction. Indeed it has become a commonplace to assert that a culture has a soul while a civilization is but the external condition of modern man. Europeans before and after the war have accused the United States, with its advanced technology, of being a civilization bereft of culture. More than mere self-assertion was involved here. A deep stream of cultural history was summarized in Spengler's famous phrase. What has been implicit in the previous discussions must now be made explicit: The romantic mood which underlay this distinction has not worked to the advantage of human freedom; rather it has helped thrust it into dire peril. The saying that reality must be transcended has a fine ring to it, but in practice this has meant an escape into totalitarian attitudes. The concept of a "secret" but determinable mechanism of history, the race or the *Volk*, led to the complete integration of the individual with whatever was identified as "genuine" or "true."

Is a materialistic positivism, then, the only other alternative, as the anti-Positivists seemed to have thought? After all, it could also lead to totalitarian attitudes. Moreover, the postwar fear of the victory of technology, of human engineering, has some truth to it. It lends itself to habits of mind which depersonalize man. More than technology is needed to create a civilization. Liberals thought that what was needed was the unity of reason and freedom. But liberalism's decline in this century involved a repudiation of this combination, a repudiation which gained strength with the passage of time. This ideal seemed too closely linked with the liberal concept of struggle, with an outmoded economic doctrine of laissez-faire. Nevertheless, concern with a freedom based solely on human reason was transmitted into these times by Social Democrats and by those intellectuals who refused to relinquish what they thought was their birthright.

In the liberal mind such freedom was closely linked to a concept of political democracy. Stressing representative institutions, Liberals saw society as a combination of interest groups whose conflicting ideas could best be resolved within such a framework. Political action, the reconciliation of conflicting interests, became the prime expression of individual man, as Tocqueville stated so eloquently.

Such political action was despised as a mere outward form of society by those who followed Spengler's concept of culture. That was one of the tragedies of this cultural development. How men govern themselves can be as important in determining their fate as any search for a reality beyond mere human institutions. Nevertheless, it is difficult to find a defense of representative government between the world wars. The age of mass politics and mass movements advocated a different definition of democracy. Political participation was defined through the acting out of a political liturgy in mass movements or in the streets, in finding security through the symbols and myths which constituted the drama of politics.

To be sure, after 1945 parliamentary government revived in the West and so did liberalism. Politics was again thought to be a special compartment of life whose impact on man must be limited. But then times were prosperous and the cold war stimulated the West to differentiate itself from communism, while at the same time the crimes of fascism shut off this alternative. A new bourgeois age seemed to have dawned after 1950, which might bear comparison with that which the First World War had concluded. Yet here also by the nineteen sixties a new generation rebelled, repeating the story of the *fin de siècle:* they called for a revival of politics which would embrace and renew man in the name of eternal human values. Discipline, tactics, strategy, and capitalism seemed to destroy human creativity. Such youth believed that man was good and that a bad liberal and bourgeois society had perverted him—a presupposition they shared with the neo-Kantian or Hegelian Socialists of earlier generations.

But all ideologies discussed in the book had to bend when they came into contact with reality. The voice of youth in the nineteen sixties was muted by the nineteen seventies as reality took over once more. The strength of liberalism and parliamentary government in western Europe has yet to be tested. The nineteen seventies open the first postwar decade of scarcity now that expansion has reached its limits. Moreover, terrorism by radical groups has proved effective in a highly urban and technological civilization. Can parliamentary government and liberalism survive this strain? It was not able to survive a similar crisis in the nineteen twenties.

The future is still open. The intellectuals and the youth of the last decade sometimes forgot that there can be no end to history, that the red dawn of the apocalypse has not yet succeeded in abolishing the rush of time. Men have tried to organize and to restrain the onrush of time through stressing rootedness and looking forward to an age when it would finally stop. But there is no end to history and no predetermination of how it will all work out. We might attempt to transcend history in order to preserve certain eternal values intact, but as we hope to have shown, historical reality can only be denied and ignored at our peril. There is always a rude awakening after the dream.

Perhaps all we can say is that, as Hegel believed, the present is always pregnant with the future, though in a world of scarcity the final synthesis of present and future may not lead to a heightened human self-consciousness and liberty. But, then, as Hegel himself has told us, happiness is not the end of history: the struggle continues and the end is not in sight.

# Index

Eisner, Kurt, 96, 382
Eliot, T. S. (Thomas Stearns), 350, 405–406, 408, 413
Elizabeth I (queen of England), 12, 66, 71
Elkins, Stanley M., 374
Ellesmere, Thomas Egerton, 66
Enfantin, Barthélemy Prosper, 169, 171
Engels, Friedrich, 156, 170, 176, 180, 181, 182, 183, 187–188, 191, 200, 211, 273, 380, 381, 385, 393, 410
Epicurus, 179

Feuerbach, Ludwig, 155–156, 157, 180, 181, 211
Fichte, Johann Gottlieb, 56–57, 58, 62, 82, 149, 150, 365
Fisher, Karl, 244, 245, 318
Fliess, Wilhelm, 269
Fourier, F.M. Charles, 91, 170
Francis Joseph (emperor of Austria), 287
Franco, Fancisco, 378
Frank, Leonhard, 305
Frantz, Constantin, 140, 141
Frazer, James, 188, 211, 273
Frederick II (the Great, king of Prussia), 61, 69, 311
Frederick William I (king of Prussia), 311
Frederick William II (king of Prussia), 61
Freeman, Edward August, 87
Freud, Sigmund, 23, 97, 184, 188, 220, 224, 267–274, 275, 276, 278, 279, 280, 300, 333, 386
Freytag, Gustav, 57, 58, 122
Friedell, Egon, 288, 289
Fritsch, Theodor, 95
Fromm, Erich, 271, 277, 278
Froude, Hurrell, 50, 73

Gagliani (travel agent), 132
Galileo, 388
Gall, Franz Joseph, 88, 268
Galton, Francis, 73, 93, 210
Gandhi, Mohandas K., 322
Garibaldi, Giuseppe, 113
Gasperi, Alcide de, 257
Gaugin, Paul, 221

Gentile, Giovanni, 148, 319, 348–349
Gentz, Friedrich von, 62
Geoffrey of Monmouth, 70
George, Henry, 197
George, Stefan, 220, 279, 298, 305, 306–307, 308, 309, 312, 314, 315
George III (king of England), 112
George V (king of England), 287
Gerlach, Ludwig von, 255
Gheorghiu, Virgil, 304, 396, 408
Gide, André, 190, 212, 220, 225, 227–228, 230, 231, 235, 238, 240, 243, 247, 260, 270, 279, 283, 305, 401
Gierke, Otto von, 123, 136
Gilbert, William, 227
Gioberti, Vincenzo, 78
Gissing, George, 14
Gladstone, William E., 131
Gluck, Christoph Willibald, 49
Gneist, Rudolf von, 123
Gobineau, Arthur de, 87, 89–90, 98, 242
Goebbels, Joseph, 365
Goerdeler, Karl Friedrich, 371
Goethe, Johann Wolfgang von, 14, 31, 34, 35, 40, 41, 42, 44, 58, 187, 230, 275, 325
Gramsci, Antonio, 190, 392
Gregory XVI (pope), 139
Grimm, Jacob and Wilhelm, 55, 269
Guenther, Hans F.K., 96, 361, 362, 365
Guesde, Jules, 194
Guizot, François, 75, 127, 128, 129, 130, 144–145
Gundolf, Friedrich, 307

Hacklaender, W. H., 12, 57
Haeckel, Ernst, 9, 207–208, 213, 220, 231
Hamsun, Knut, 370, 371
Hardie, J. Keir, 199
Harnack, Adolf, 265
Hauptmann, Gerhart, 213, 284
Haussmann, Georges Eugène, 285
Hegel, Georg Wilhelm Friedrich, 7, 20, 80, 83, 148–149, 150, 151, 152, 153, 154, 155, 156, 157, 158, 177,

# Index

# *Index*

LaVergne, TN USA
18 March 2010
176469LV00002B/1/A